# SHIRLEY WILLIAMS

# SHIRLEY
# WILLIAMS
## THE BIOGRAPHY

## MARK PEEL

Biteback Publishing

First published in Great Britain in 2013 by
Biteback Publishing Ltd
Westminster Tower
3 Albert Embankment
London SE1 7SP
Copyright © Mark Peel 2013

ISBN 978-1-84954-604-1

10 9 8 7 6 5 4 3 2 1

A CIP catalogue record for this book is available from the British Library.

Set in Adobe Caslon Pro and Perpetua Titling

Printed and bound in Great Britain by
CPI Group (UK) Ltd, Croydon CR0 4YY

# CONTENTS

# ACKNOWLEDGEMENTS

It was back in October 2000 that I first met Shirley Williams when interviewing her for my biography of Donald Soper. Before that meeting I had tentatively inquired whether she would be at all interested in my writing her biography and, much to my delight, she consented.

Over the course of the next decade she welcomed me into her home, answered my numerous questions and gave me access to all her papers. I am most grateful for all her efforts on my behalf and while I certainly don't expect her to agree with every word I have written I hope she feels my book is a fair account of her life and work.

I'm also very grateful to Shirley's daughter Rebecca and her late husband, Christopher Honey, for all their hospitality and help with this assignment.

Many people were kind enough to give up valuable time on my behalf in order to share their memories of Shirley Williams and I fully acknowledge the help of the following:

Lesley Abdela, Professor Graham Allison, Lord Alton, Lord Ashdown, Val Arnold-Forster, Gillian Ayres, Jennifer, Lady Balfour of Burleigh, Lord Balfour of Burleigh, Professor Alan Bishop, Mark Bostridge, Frank Bracewell, Shirley Bracewell, Carol Bracken, the late Sir John Burgh, Jim Caldwell, the late Lord Callaghan, John Campbell, Sir Menzies Campbell, John Cartwright, Professor Malcolm Chalmers, the late Ann Chesney, Michael Cockerell, Professor Ivor Crewe, Lord Dholakia, Owen Dudley Edwards, Andrew Duff, Kathy Eckroad, Father John Feighery, Julian Filochowski, Edward Flood, Lord Goodhart, Helen Green, Brian

Hall, Lord Hannay, the Right Reverend Lord Harries, Doreen Harris, Dru Haydon, Lord Healey, Lord Hennessy, Anthony Hill, Professor Stanley Hoffmann, Ben Hooberman, Enid Howard, Dr Anne Howat, Philip Hunter, Baroness Jay, Stephen Jones, Baroness Kennedy, Professor Anthony King, Hilda Lawrence, Richard C. Leone, Lord Lester, Frank Lindsay, Margot Lindsay, Lord Luce, Lord McGivan, Lord Maclennan, Lord McNally, Lucy Mann, Robert Mann, Professor David Marquand, Barbara Metcalfe, Peter Metcalfe, Baroness Neuberger, Lord Newby, Lord Owen, Samuel Passow, Lord Phillips of Sudbury, Lord Radice, the late Lord Rees-Mogg, Lord Rodgers of Quarry Bank, Rosemary Roughton, Helge Rubinstein, the late Hilary Rubinstein, Professor Michael Sandel, the late Patrick Shovelton, Lord Skidelsky, Jon Snow, Eileen Spencer, Professor John Spencer, Lord Steel, Edith Stokey, Lord Taverne, Baroness Thomas of Winchester, Mike Thomas, Lord Wallace of Saltaire, John Wilkins, David Wilkinson, Sir Ian Wrigglesworth, Dr Dorothy Zinberg.

Among the many libraries and archives which gave freely of their time I owe a special gratitude to Carl Spadoni, Renu Barrett, Kathy Garay and all the staff at the Vera Brittain–George Catlin Archive in the William Ready Division of Archives and Research Collections at McMaster University Library, Ontario. Working there was always most rewarding.

I would like to express my gratitude to the following archivists and librarians for all their help: Pauline Adams at Somerville College, Oxford; Howard Bailes at St Paul's Girls' School, Hammersmith; Colin Harris at the Bodleian Library, Oxford; Sandy Macmillen and Nigel Cochrane at the Albert Sloman Library, the University of Essex; Andrew Riley at Churchill College, Cambridge; Darren Treadwell at the Labour Museum of History, Manchester; and Jeff Walden, BBC Written Archives.

I am also indebted to the following institutions for giving me the opportunity to use material: Cambridge Library; Clacton Library; Colchester Library; Crosby Library; Edinburgh Central Library; Hertfordshire County Library; Local Studies Collection, Hull

History Centre; Liverpool Central Library; Special Collections and Archives, the University of Liverpool; the Library of the London School of Economics and Political Science; the Modern Records Centre at Warwick University; the National Archives, Kew; the National Library of Scotland; Nuffield College, Oxford; the Echo Library, Southampton; Special Collections, Leeds University Library; the State Library of Victoria, Melbourne.

I also owe a particular debt to Lord Rodgers of Quarry Bank for reading a substantial section of the book in draft and to Peter Metcalfe for reading all of it. They put me right on many points and made a number of extremely useful suggestions. Peter Metcalfe was also kind enough to give me access to a number of his papers and photographs.

Alan and Judith Bishop were the soul of hospitality on my many visits to Hamilton, Ontario, and I am indebted to them as I am to my agent, Andrew Lownie, for all his advice. Last, but by no means least, I would like to extend a special thanks to Iain Dale, Sam Carter and all the team at Biteback. They have been much pleasure to work with, not least Olivia Beattie, a great source of patience and good cheer.

# INTRODUCTION

With her engaging smile, seductive voice and somewhat flustered demeanour, Shirley Williams, Labour Cabinet minister and co-founder of the Social Democratic Party (SDP), has claimed a unique place in the national consciousness as one of its best-loved politicians. In a distinguished career spanning over sixty years she was for a long time touted as Britain's first female Prime Minister, then when that particular dream faded, she evolved briefly into the progressive alternative to Margaret Thatcher before her elevation to the House of Lords as a revered elder stateswoman. Now eighty-three years old, and over thirty years since leaving Cabinet, she can still fill a conference hall with ease and send the audience home with a song in its heart.

The daughter of a famous mother, Vera Brittain, Shirley's mind and personality were very much her own as she became a committed member of the Labour Party from her sixteenth birthday. After winning widespread acclaim for her spirited campaign in the safe Conservative seat of Harwich in February 1954, aged only twenty-three, her potential was finally recognised in October 1964 when she was elected MP for Hitchin as Labour returned to power after a thirteen-year exile. During those halcyon days when youth and modernisation were very much in fashion, Shirley, with her personable husband Bernard, one of the foremost philosophers of his day, seemed to be the perfect embodiment of this new era. An all-consuming public vocation combined with an apparent ability to find time to raise a family helped convince other women that they could do likewise. Her refusal to conform to expected standards of dress, appearance and punctuality might have shocked some, but it did nothing to diminish her appeal to a public attracted to her natural, unassuming style. On returning from an official trip to Hong Kong, she chose not to pull rank when her bags were subjected to a thorough search for contraband. Nor did she complain when, as a junior minister, she was booked into a dingy hotel in Brighton for the Labour Party conference, and years later, by which time a former Cabinet minister, she thought nothing of sharing a sleeping apartment on the Liverpool to London train with a complete stranger. The fact that she has continued to exemplify this plain living is all the more telling in light of the expenses scandal of 2009, which tainted so many of her parliamentary colleagues.

As a speaker she employed her angelic tongue with mesmerising effect to express enlightened sentiments with passionate sincerity. 'Shirley is someone', commented Marcia Falkender, Harold Wilson's long-serving secretary, 'who, in addition to her other undoubted gifts, is endowed with a quality that few male and even female politicians possess. It is an ability to project an idealized version of herself, a myth in which all those around her believe gladly and whole-heartedly.'[1] Her struggle on behalf of the underprivileged was unending, but although fiercely partisan in the heat of battle she was also a chivalrous warrior across the despatch box and well respected (indeed well liked) by many of her opponents.

In October 1971 she was one of sixty-nine Labour MPs who defied the party whip to vote for the Heath government's terms of entry to the European Economic Community (EEC). The following year she was put on the spot again when the party, contrary to her wishes, committed itself to a referendum over continued membership. The fact that she didn't join her fellow pro-Europeans in a mass exodus from the front bench but managed not to attract heavy censure intrigued her colleague Roy Hattersley, whose own refusal to resign won him few friends. 'For the first time, I realised that Shirley is surrounded by a beatific light that shields her from the harm and criticism which would be heaped on ordinary people,' he later wrote. 'It is an enviable attribute.'[2]

He later had cause to revisit that phenomenon after Shirley's traumatic defeat at the 1979 election, which left even grown men shedding a quiet tear on her behalf.

> During the Queen's Speech debate which followed the opening of the 1979 Parliament, I spoke immediately after Margaret Thatcher. The new prime minister interrupted me … with an unflattering comment about the recently defeated secretary of state for education. I mumbled a rebuke. The roar of approval from the benches behind me left no doubt that I was about to be carried towards the top of the shadow cabinet poll on the wings of Williams's reputation.[3]

As a campaigner Shirley utilised her indomitable energy to the full as she covered many a mile in search of elusive votes. Immediately at ease with strangers, she attracted large crowds of well-wishers keen to meet her, still more to confide in her. Those that registered a concern or grievance found a sympathetic ear and an intensely personal reply free of the usual platitudes. Her genuine friendliness and capacity to relate to all types, so rare in a politician, led people into thinking they knew her. Dick Newby, the former SDP general secretary, recalls her out canvassing with Roy Jenkins in an open-top lorry during the Warrington by-election of July 1981.

> As she passed a broken-down car, its grease-stained owner raised his head from beneath the bonnet and found himself within a few feet of Williams. 'Hello, Shirley,' he said, grinning broadly as if greeting a long-lost friend. No other contemporary politician could have evoked such a warm, familiar response from a complete stranger. For me, it captured, in an instant, the Williams magic.[4]

That magic has remained constant, but it isn't quite the whole picture. Apply the finishing touches and one has something more enigmatic. The publication of Shirley's autobiography in September 2009, which revealed some of the personal vulnerability behind the reassuring public façade, surprised many. In a brilliantly perceptive review in *The Spectator*, Matthew Parris called it 'sharper, franker, more self-critical, more vulnerable, and oddly more melancholy, for I think she thinks she's failed. Millions of us think we know her. We don't.'[5] It was a verdict similar to Polly Toynbee in *The Guardian*, who reckoned Shirley wasn't by nature given to self-revelation or introspection: 'mysteries remain, such as her barely explained Catholicism. You know her not much better, but you like her to the end.'[6]

For all her genuine warmth and ease among friends and strangers alike, Shirley Williams is more detached than meets the eye. 'Many people think they know me when they don't,' she recently observed. Her father described her writing as legible at first glance, apparently clear and simple, 'but when you look close it isn't. Rather like her fun character, only apparently extrovert.'[7] Inheriting her paternal grandmother's intense reserve, her enforced independence as a child in the USA, when separated from her parents for over three years, made her ever more protective of her freedom on her return. If her mother asked her tentatively where she was going when she saw her mounting a bicycle Shirley would simply reply, 'Out.' Later, when her parents moved to Whitehall Court, she greatly objected to the uniformed porters in the concierge recording incoming telephone calls and observing her comings and goings. Her friend Mark Bostridge, the co-biographer of her mother, describes her as a deeply private person who can get quite irritated if people pry too much into what she is doing. Even those responsible for organising her schedule can find she suddenly slips their leash with no one any the wiser as to her whereabouts.

This reserve became apparent to the journalist and writer Melanie Phillips in her study on women politicians. Despite Shirley's apparent insouciance about her image, she had managed to cultivate one that camouflaged part of her character. 'Interviews with her are rarely able to dwell on personal details of her own life, but are soon removed to the more abstract intellectual plane of her beliefs, principles and ideas.'[8]

It is the same if the conversation turns unduly personal. When pressed by one of her classes at Harvard to tell them more about her life she reluctantly assented, but only on the condition that it was out of class and even then she gave them few scraps to feed on. On being asked to contribute a chapter to the Festschrift of her second husband, Dick Neustadt, she declined, explaining that it was too personal, and when approached by her publishers to reveal more about herself in her autobiography, she went only so far in lifting the veil.

As a proud, resilient woman she was part of that generation who remained stoical in the face of misfortune so that even when her first marriage broke down or she suffered a political setback she never complained or sought self-pity. 'I have not cried and I am not that bothered,' she declared after losing her seat in 1979. 'I deeply believe that in politics you have to take the rough with the smooth. It does not help being too upset by these things.'⁹ Even in private she rarely traduces her colleagues or bemoans her lot. Her autobiography, aside from the odd barb at Tony Benn, David Owen and Tony Blair, is remarkably free of rancour, but while the benevolence which runs through every page is entirely genuine, her reticence masks a greater sensitivity than is sometimes realised. Her friend John Burgh, a former director general of the British Council, recalls how she was bitterly hurt by a couple of unwarranted personal attacks on her by *The Times*'s leading columnist Bernard Levin and couldn't understand how he, Burgh, could be so friendly with such a person. Her exit from the Labour Party, for all her distaste for its ideological extremism, could also be partially explained by the personal venom directed at her and her fellow moderates, especially by elements of the National Executive Committee (NEC), while her surprising refusal to support Roy Jenkins for the SDP leadership in 1982 was largely in reaction to a series of hostile briefings against her by some of his immediate circle. Perhaps most telling of all was her acrimonious battle with David Owen over the SDP's merger with the Liberals, which, though in essence a conflict of principle, was accentuated by her exasperation at his dismissive treatment of her and others over the previous years.

With her privileged background and charismatic personality, Shirley Williams could have enjoyed a carefree, comfortable lifestyle, but that was never her way. Family expectation, personal ambition and a desire to help others drew her into the fickle world of politics. As a free spirit who knew her own mind (she had already cast aside the patronage of Herbert Morrison, one of the leading ministers in the Attlee government), party loyalty for its own sake held little appeal. 'I would much rather choose something other than politics than be a serf to the party's dreary, unimaginative and not especially efficient machine,'[10] she intimated to her mother well before she was even elected. Once in Parliament she shunned its bars and restaurants, finding its male, public school culture no place for a young woman, and kept herself free from any faction. According to her former boyfriend Peter Parker, 'she has pursued her principles so singly it has led her to a lonely eminence'.[11]

As an able junior minister with the world at her feet, she hovered uneasily between conformity and dissent as the policies pursued by the 1964–70 Wilson government towards Rhodesia, Vietnam and immigration offended her liberal conscience. Twice she wrote out letters of resignation only to relent. Thereafter, Europe became the issue which detached her from the party mainstream, but while veering towards Roy Jenkins she never became part of his inner circle, his grandiose lifestyle directly at odds with her down-to-earth informality. When Jenkins left the government in 1976 to become president of the European Commission, she spurned the chance to inherit his crown as leader of Labour's centre-right. The politics of patronage, plots and positioning was never her scene. Ideas, principles and debate were what mattered. She would continue vigorously to oppose the left, but it would be very much on her own terms. For all Jenkins's attempts to enrol her in his putative new party throughout 1980 she resisted his overtures, only joining at the eleventh hour when all other options had failed. Thereafter she continued to hold her own counsel, turning down the opportunity to stand at the Warrington by-election in July 1981, despite the pleas of all and sundry, and to contest the SDP leadership when apparent favourite. This failure to seize the hour and the confession in her autobiography that she suffered from a lack of self-esteem mystified reviewers who saw in other instances a woman of powerful convictions and moral courage. It was but one of the many paradoxes of a person who revered her parents but felt uncomfortable living in their shadow; a firm believer in the sanctity of marriage who craved unfettered independence from her partner, a middle-class liberal who appealed to the tabloids; a rebel on the surface, a conformist at heart; an egalitarian who preferred the statelier ambience of the House of Lords to the intense partisanship of the Commons; a brilliant communicator in public, a less assured one in private, above all, a Labour loyalist who jumped ship to join a centrist party she had always derided.

Out of this maelstrom of paradox one quality stands out, and that is her essential niceness – a double-edged compliment in the political universe, for, as William Hague once brutally remarked, 'In politics, Mrs Williams, it isn't enough to be nice.'[12]

## Endnotes

1   Marcia Falkender, *Downing Street in Perspective*, Weidenfeld & Nicholson, 1983, p.252
2   Roy Hattersley, *Who Goes Home?*, Little, Brown, 1995, p.114
3   *Daily Telegraph*, 21 September 2009
4   *Dictionary of Liberal Biography*, ed. Duncan Brack et al., Politico's, 1998, p.381
5   *Spectator*, 16 September 2009
6   *Guardian*, 3 October 2009
7   George Catlin (GC) diary, 6 August 1966
8   Melanie Phillips, *The Divided House: Women at Westminster*, Sidgwick & Jackson, 1980, p.25
9   *Daily Telegraph*, 5 May 1979
10  SW to Vera Brittain (VB), 16 November 1958
11  Peter Parker, *For Starters: The Business of Life*, Pan Books, 1989, p.59
12  Oxford University debate quoted in David Walter, *The Oxford Union: Playground of Power*, Macdonald, 1984, p.199

# DESTINED FOR POLITICS

Shirley Vivian Brittain-Catlin was born in Chelsea on Sunday 27 July 1930. Her mother was the author Vera Brittain, later to win international eminence with her bestselling autobiography, *Testament of Youth*, and her father was Professor George Catlin, a distinguished political scientist.

Hailing from the villages bordering the Potteries in north Staffordshire as far back as the sixteenth century, the Brittains were of solid yeoman stock. What propelled them to a life of affluence was the acquisition of a papermaking business at Hanley in 1855 by Shirley's great-great-grandfather Thomas Brittain, a business-man of single-minded grit and sharp financial acumen. When he died in 1894, aged ninety-one, he left a fortune of over £130,000. His grandson, Arthur Brittain, born in 1864, the eldest of twelve children, lived in his shadow (Arthur's father died in 1885) and although responsible for developing new factories at Cheddleton, near Leek, when managing director, his ambitions were strictly limited. As a wealthy and debonair businessman of a certain standing, he set his sights on keeping his family to the manner born. In 1891 he had married Edith Bervon, the elegant daughter of John Inglis Bervon, a struggling musician who had been giving him singing lessons. She appears to have had certain reservations about the match, but her father's death the previous year had helped convince her, the third of his six children, to accept Arthur's hand as a means of escaping a life of penury. Following the wedding at Southport, the young couple settled in the more exclusive part of Newcastle-under-Lyme, before their move to the silk manufactur-ing town of Macclesfield in Cheshire. Here they lived in some style with their two children, Vera, born in 1893, and Edward, born in 1895.

Although more drawn to the artistic sensitivities of the Bervons (her mother was a gifted musician and stylish dresser), Vera, with her volatile temperament, couldn't escape some of the less wholesome features of her father's vast family. Aside from their tendency to fall out with each other, the Brittains were bedevilled by neuroticism and melancholia. Both Vera's father and his sister Edith committed suicide, the former in 1935 unable to come to terms with the loss of his only son. In his own fastidious manner Arthur Brittain was a kindly, gentle person capable of showering affection upon his children, but his petulant outbursts combined with his wife's ingrained fatalism helped account for Vera's own lifelong diffidence and tendency to fear the worst. Spending large tracts of her early years alone in the nursery with her brother Edward, she looked to literature to discover strong emotions, developing a remarkable facility for writing 'novels' herself.

In 1905, as part of their quest for greater social status, the Brittains moved to the fashionable spa town of Buxton in the Derbyshire Peak District. Here they lived the leisured life to the full, participating in the interminable round of tennis tournaments and musical soirées, a rather stultifying atmosphere that didn't appeal to someone of Vera's restless ambition, especially the patronising attitudes she encountered towards women. It was thus with some relief that she was sent away, aged fourteen, to St Monica's, an enlightened Surrey boarding school where her Aunt Florence was co-headmistress and where inspirational teachers fostered her literary talent and feminist convictions.

Leaving school with an enhanced determination to follow a life of independence, Vera spurned the social niceties of provincial Buxton and worked all hours to win an exhibition in English Literature to Somerville College, Oxford. It was an outstanding achievement but one that didn't fully register with her parents, steeped in values from a different era. The fact that an attractive girl with many an admirer in tow should place academic study above social advancement and marriage baffled them.

Vera duly went up to Oxford in October 1914 in the shadow of war, only to find that her priorities were soon to change. That year she had become close to Roland Leighton, a good friend of her brother's at Uppingham, a conventional Midlands public school, when he had come to stay. According to Vera's son John Catlin in his book *Family Quartet*, Roland combined in himself those attributes which appealed to Vera's sense of idealism and romanticism. For behind a virile appearance there lurked an acute sensitivity endowed with feminist sympathies and poetic insight.

Although the pair were rarely together, Roland exercised a growing hold over Vera's imagination, especially with the coming of war, a war in which he, Edward and their friend Victor Richardson eagerly enlisted in the prevailing spirit of King and Country. Slowly but surely their affection turned to something greater as he was posted to France and when he returned home for a brief period of leave in August 1915 they became unofficially engaged. As he departed for the front for the final time he bade her such a tender farewell that the memory of that last encounter on a crowded St Pancras platform lingered in her memory thereafter.

Roland's travails at the front had led to Vera abandoning her studies at the end of her first year for nursing to show solidarity with him and all those engaged in the war effort. It was while on leave from Camberwell hospital over Christmas 1915 that she received the devastating news of his death at the hands of a sniper's bullet, a tragedy that was to change her life forever. 'In the utter blackness of my soul I seem to be touching the very depths of that dull lampless anguish which we call despair,' she wrote in her diary. 'And I don't feel as if I shall ever rise again.'[1]

Her despair only deepened in 1917 when the war claimed the lives of Victor Richardson and Geoffrey Thurlow, a close friend of Edward to whom she had become greatly attached. From now on she invested all her emotions in Edward, the brother she had always revered, not least for his gallantry under fire which won him the Military Cross at the Somme.

In January 1918 he was sent to northern Italy to help stem a last-ditch Austrian offensive on the Asiago Plateau. Aware of the ferocity of the fighting in those parts, Vera rarely had Edward out of her thoughts as her anxieties about his safety grew. Those anxieties were amply vindicated when, on 18 June, she answered the dreaded knock on the front door of the family home to receive a terse telegram informing them of his death.

Crushed by this most crippling loss of all, Vera's grief and inner turmoil were complete. Having viewed the war at the outset in conventional idealistic terms, her subsequent experiences both at home and on the front line had stripped her of all previous delusions. 'For me, as for all the world,' she wrote in *Testament of Youth*, 'the War was a tragedy and a vast stupidity; a waste of youth and of time.'[2] 'I could have married Victor in memory of Roland, and Geoffrey in memory of Edward,' she was to reminisce years later, 'but the War took even the second-best; it left nothing. Only ambition held me to life.'[3]

Returning to Oxford in this fragile state, Vera increasingly came to rely on Winifred Holtby, a tall, golden-haired girl from Yorkshire, some four-and-a-half years her junior. Her outgoing warmth and irrepressible vitality made her a secure haven for Vera's stormier character, but what really brought them together were their mutual literary ambitions and highly developed social consciences. On leaving Oxford in 1921 they set up home together in London, and while serving their literary apprenticeships they worked avidly for the women's movement, the League of Nations Union and the Labour Party.

In 1923 Vera published her first novel, *The Dark Tide*, an indictment of sexism at Oxford, which caused something of a furore, especially at Somerville, her old college – yet equally it had its admirers, not least a certain George Catlin, who equated the feminist traits of the heroine with his own mother.

George Catlin's roots were Bedfordshire yeomanry. His father, the Rev. George Catlin, born in 1858, was a peppery Congregationalist minister who converted to the Anglican communion in middle age; his mother, Edith Kate Orton, the intelligent daughter of a carpenter from Leamington Spa in Warwickshire who was fifteen years her husband's junior. Their fractious marriage bedevilled his childhood as the fiercely independent outlook of his mother, not least her support for the suffragettes, antagonised his domineering father. Following a number of furious altercations she walked out on her family in 1915 and moved to London's East End, where she devoted herself to good causes. Her departure and her death from uraemia, aged only forty-four, in 1917, were an incalculable blow to the young George, especially since his father descended into depression and destitution.

Confronted with these most traumatic circumstances the young George increasingly had to assume responsibility for his father's emotional and financial state. Repeatedly rejected by the army because of ill health, he eked out a pittance of a living as a junior civil servant. Such were his straitened circumstances that he was forced to eat the bare minimum in order to take home enough food to his ailing father.

After a brief but glittering Oxford career, postponed 'til after the war, it was with some consternation that George narrowly failed to win a fellowship there, especially at All Souls. Whether this had anything to do with his tetchy relationship with his tutors or his recent conversion to Roman Catholicism is unclear, but his failure to gain full recognition for his accomplishments left him with bittersweet memories of Oxford. Desperate to earn his living, he accepted a lectureship in History at Sheffield University, and within a year was given leave of absence to take up a fellowship at Cornell University in New York State. It proved a shrewd move. Having established a great interest in political thought at Oxford, George helped set up the Political Science Department at Cornell and within a year he was offered a professorship. It was here that he began a year's weighty correspondence with Vera, two-and-a-half years his senior, following the publication of *The Dark Tide*. By the time they met a mutual curiosity had developed, and following the briefest of courtships, during which George's handsome features and romantic character proved irresistible, they became engaged in July 1924.

Vera had never regarded marriage as an end in itself and after her wartime experiences she doubted whether she would ever again be able to rekindle that romantic spark necessary for such a commitment. At the same time, recognising the futility of remaining single out of blind loyalty to the dead, and keen to have children, she felt able to enter an agreement with someone whose values seemingly reflected her own. Provided George understood the absolute priority she gave to her work over love and marriage she would be happy to oblige, conditions to which George, desperate to find stability in his life, reluctantly acceded. The fact that following a series of rows he intimated to Vera soon afterwards that she wasn't the woman he had fallen in love with punctured her confidence and led her to question his motives for marrying her. Such suspicions were to linger, which helps explain much of their underlying tension thereafter, so that amidst the genuine affection, there were the conflicting priorities and mutual recriminations of two highly vulnerable people in search of eminence.

After their marriage in June 1925, the Catlins headed for Ithaca, New York State, where George's academic career was progressing nicely. For Vera, the stay proved a crushing disappointment. After a year of boredom and unfufilment in a provincial backwater (and later in New York City) playing the part of a professor's wife, unrecognised for her own talents, she decided that America wasn't for her. Determined to pursue her literary ambitions she served notice on George that she was returning to London permanently, leaving him back at Cornell that September on a part-time appointment, unaccompanied and unhappy. In letter after letter he gave full vent to his misery, berating her for her selfishness and pleading with her to return to Cornell.

George's increasingly fraught state threw Vera into emotional turmoil, but despite mollifying him with a brief visit to the US the following spring she refused to countenance a permanent return. Her writing and the birth of their son John in December 1927 saw to that. Consequently, George in time began to compensate for her absence by turning his attention elsewhere, liaisons that did little for his wife's self-esteem. Returning home each June wasn't easy as he struggled to gain an equal footing in her affections compared to Winifred and, later, the children. According to John Catlin, the unconventional rules governing his parents' marriage told very much against his father, forcing him to compromise with his career in the US so that he could spend some time at home with his family. Inevitably all this widened the gulf between him and Vera, exacerbated by the central dilemma of her life: how to combine renown as a writer with her responsibilities as a wife and a mother. She later recalled the strenuous effort required to put her writing to one side to produce Shirley, especially as the excruciatingly painful circumstances of John's birth in December 1927 were hardly an inducement to have more children.

In April 1930 the Catlins moved to 19 Glebe Place, off the King's Road in Chelsea, a street much favoured by those of an artistic bent, and it was here, three months later, on 27 July, that Shirley was born. Though the birth was much less harrowing than John's, nevertheless, it took its toll on Vera, so that even with the help of a nurse she found looking after two energetic young children some undertaking, especially with George away for long periods. 'This year has been a very heavy burden to me,' she informed him in January 1931. 'I wish I could feel you thought the little girl was worth it; personally I think she will be – and to you, perhaps, more than to me.'⁴ Although comparing Shirley unfavourably with John, 'my masterpiece', whose looks she considered to be the replica of Edward's, she soon found much to rhapsodise about, not least her 'most heavenly' blue eyes, her golden curls and her affectionate nature. 'I think you will be charmed with her. Probably she will never be quite as heart-breakingly touching as John, but that's to her advantage – particularly later in the wider world, where life is always hard for the supersensitive.'⁵

Shirley's perpetual screaming when cutting teeth and her rage when failing to get what she wanted confirmed Vera in her earlier assessment that she was of feistier disposition than John, 'though she will be quite as intelligent, tremendously observant and assertive'. While Vera continued to harbour anxieties about John owing to his physical frailty and emotional vulnerability, the latter a reflection of her own character, she was much more upbeat about Shirley, suspecting that her charm and friendliness had much to do with her perfect health. Both in looks and character Vera considered Shirley to be George's child, even comparing her rages with those of his father. She assured him that if he were willing to exercise patience he would in time derive much warmth and kindness from her, such was her anxiety 'both to give and take all the affection possible'. Yet for all the leading influence Vera attributed to George over Shirley, her part shouldn't be underestimated.

A woman of iron self-discipline and ordered routine, Vera put every minute to good use in the pursuit of excellence. Impeccably turned out herself, she insisted on the highest standards of cleanliness and tidiness in her household, as well as ensuring that family arrangements were in good order. A stickler for honesty, it wasn't unknown for her to inform the Inland Revenue that she was paying too little tax, and when word reached her post-war that her household had been exceeding its legitimate rations she gave strict orders to her staff that any abuses should cease immediately. Her candour extended to her conversation and book reviews. She said what she thought, sometimes too caustically, without a view to the consequences, for popularity, however desirable, wasn't to be traded for the sake of integrity. At the same time the trouble she took with her core readership, especially young authors requesting help, was typical of an overriding benignity which manifested itself in so many ways. There was her care for her staff, her generosity to family and friends and her unsung work for a host of worthy causes.

Although desperately keen that her own children make the most of their talents, she chose to apply different standards from her own childhood, when self-expression had been frowned upon. Within reason she would give them their heads and encourage them to think and act for themselves, so that they could develop into self-confident individuals as much at ease in adult company as with their peers. Such trust, she reasoned, would hopefully induce a more creative and congenial atmosphere than the one she had experienced at home in Buxton. From these convictions Vera never wavered and years later she was able to derive a certain satisfaction from the writer Storm Jameson's observation that her greatest achievement had been the way she had prepared her children to cope with their wartime evacuation to the US without undue regret for her absence.

Glebe Place was a tall, unprepossessing late-Victorian house sparsely furnished aside from the top-floor attic overflowing with books. In common with that era, it was an orderly household, each meal at a set time with fairly predictable menus. It was also a highly disciplined one whereby Vera, having read the papers and answered her correspondence, repaired to her study every morning on the strict understanding that interruptions would be countenanced only in an emergency. The fact that she returned for another stint in the afternoon, and was often away lecturing, meant that the children, aside from Winifred, spent much time with their German governess, Fräulein Agnes Bleichenbach, a gentle soul they much liked and respected. Although her family estate and literary royalties left her well endowed, Vera, conscious of supporting a large household that included a housekeeper, butler, parlour maid, secretary and governess, avoided undue extravagance. Meat was never eaten more than three times a week, wine only appeared for a birthday and the children's pocket money was kept to a minimum. Indeed, for progressive parents, Vera and George were quite conventional in observing the social proprieties of the time. Conversation would be discouraged at breakfast while they read the newspapers, there was to be no sloping off after meals and a 6.30 p.m. bedtime was strictly enforced, although Shirley, emulating the young Vera, would read after lights out and recite endless stories to her brother.

'From the outset', Vera wrote in *Testament of Experience*, her second instalment of autobiography,

Shirley sustained the nursery adage which commends 'Sunday's child', for she put on weight steadily and was the easiest of infants to rear. Her affirmative attitude to life seemed to justify the instinct which had led us to name her after Charlotte Brontë's 'gallant little cavalier' … As she grew out of infancy she became a dynamo of energy; she never walked when she could run, and she climbed everything.[6]

Recognising her to be healthier and happier than her brother, Vera told George that John should be their priority. 'I rather feel we shall always owe him more than we do her,'[7] an opinion that found little favour with Shirley, who as a fiercely competitive, outward-going child proved more demanding of her love. She used to tax her mother by asking her a plethora of questions, such as whether she preferred bees to butterflies, persisting until she received a definite reply. Preoccupied with the closing stages of *Testament of Youth*, her first instalment of autobiography, during 1932, and aware there were limits to her time and attention, Vera decided to send Shirley, aged two, to the Chelsea Babies' Club, a progressive nursery school close by, figuring that being in John's company would be preferable to remaining at home alone.

Despite the conundrum of balancing these conflicting demands, Vera's ambition drove her on as she movingly recollected the litany of personal tragedies that had befallen her. The eloquence and originality of *Testament of Youth* made it an immediate bestseller on its publication in 1933, bringing her the fame and recognition she had always craved. It also made her a relatively wealthy woman in her own right and the keeper of the family purse, which, given her household's expensive overheads and her husband's meagre salary, assumed a certain significance since future comfort was dependent on her continual success. At the same time success didn't come without a cost, for her new-found fame exposed George's own predicament, much to his frustration.

Having presided over an influential national study into the workings and ramifications of Prohibition in the United States, the result of which brought about its immediate repeal, George published his doctoral thesis, *The Science and Method of Politics*, in 1927. Yet despite the high esteem in which he was held at Cornell and the undoubted fulfilment he derived from his work there, academia by itself wasn't enough to satisfy his ambitions. A committed socialist, albeit one of moderate tendencies, he longed to become an MP. The trouble was that the October 1931 general election was no time to be standing for the Labour Party given the recent failures of the MacDonald government to cope with the Great Depression and mass unemployment. With the party receiving a trouncing it was scarcely surprising that George should be defeated in the west London seat of Brentford & Chiswick.

It was of course much to George's misfortune that the Labour Party remained so adrift throughout the 1930s, but there were also more personal factors to account for his failure to get elected. There was his work at Cornell which prevented him from devoting the appropriate time and trouble to nursing a new constituency and, in addition to his deficiencies as a speaker, there was his shy, awkward personality which struggled to reach out to the wider electorate with their day-to-day concerns. Even his attempts to cultivate the rich and famous proved counterproductive, for his biggest flaw, according to Vera, was his penchant for pontifical monologues, delivered without consideration for the views of others. It was thus doubly unfortunate that he should sacrifice true renown in academia in search of a career in Parliament for which he wasn't suited. In 1935 George finally severed his connection with Cornell. It proved to be a fateful decision and one that he came to regret. Within months he was thrust into another general election, this time in an old-fashioned two-seat division in Sunderland, at a time when Labour was still recovering from its drubbing in 1931. Despite the warm response that Vera's speeches evoked on the stump (she was a much more adept campaigner than her husband), both George and his partner Leah Manning, the far-left educationalist, were defeated in an election that the National Government won comfortably.

Following this electoral setback George threw himself into a mission to help the victims of the Spanish Civil War, but his best-laid plans were frustrated by the obstructionism of the Spanish government. His failure to land a chair in Political Science at Cambridge merely added to his disenchantment. Only his continued success as a source of political thought afforded him some comfort at a time when Vera's career was in full bloom. By 1939 he was once again heading back across the Atlantic, this time to lecture at the American University in Washington and soon imploring his wife to come and live there, a plea she once again rejected.

Although Shirley departed quite happily for her first day at nursery school in September 1932, her extreme youth led to a rough baptism with her peers. 'She is very easily roused if anything or anybody annoys her,' commented her first report. 'On these occasions she is inclined to become very negative towards everybody and this continues for some considerable time.'[8] It took the rest of the year for her to find her feet and become fully accepted. By her second year the runes appeared much more favourable. Her growing sociability, her interesting observations on the other children's behaviour and her artistic creativity were all the subject of favourable comment. 'One forgets that it is only this term that Shirley has been working with the older group of children. She is well adjusted and happy. She is developing rapidly.'[9] The only cloud on the horizon was the upset caused by the absence of her parents from home. 'Has definite phases when she needs attention and approval of an adult. This seems often to correspond to the times when her mother is away' was the verdict of her report in March 1934.[10]

Shirley's demand for her mother's attention began to prey on Vera. When taxed about her maternal neglect at the time and later she was sensitive to the charge, especially since she had disapproved of the way her mother's generation had left their children to other people. She would later recall the heartbreak that the pain of separation from her children had caused her, never more so than during her three months in the US in 1934 when she would cry herself to sleep. Yet aside from ascribing her neglect to her perceived calling to make the world a better place ('I had gifts, even more standards, to pass on'), Vera claimed, quite justifiably, that her input into her children's upbringing was quite considerable. Not only did she take them for walks, enlightening them as to the different types of bird and flower, she also read to them after tea, and in John's case taught him the piano, before putting them to bed. When they were ill she looked after them, employing her nursing experiences to good effect.

If the children continued to harbour regrets that they didn't see more of their parents, they at least were fortunate in the range of surrogates to help ensure that both of them, especially Shirley, had happy childhoods. Entertainment in those early years often centred on Winifred Holtby, known to the children as Aunty Winifred. Tall, slim with golden hair, and invariably attired in a striking assortment of hats and dresses, she endeared herself to everyone by the radiance of her personality. 'For my brother and me,' Shirley later recounted, 'Winifred was the source of unending pleasure: stories, games, wild fantasies, exotic visitors … Our favourite game was "elephants". We would pile cushions high up on Winifred's back, and issue orders from our rickety howdah as she crawled carefully across the floor.'[11]

Such boisterous activity proved to be an exhausting business for a woman in brittle health, suffering from Bright's disease, although the unmitigated pleasure she derived from John and Shirley offered much in the way of consolation. During Vera's absence in the US in 1934 the children flourished under her watch, leading a more active social life than normal. There was still the occasional tantrum to keep Winifred up to the mark, but with a mixture of firmness and sympathy she coped admirably.

'I'm afraid your Shirley has a touch of genius,' she informed Vera after a particularly fraught day.

Three times today she flew into rages, hitting people, and screamed like a lost soul for nothing. I took her up to my room and reasoned with her … But I remember precisely the same rages in my youth. Horses used to drive me wild. I told Shirley so, and that tickled her. 'Aunty, are you sure it wasn't a donkey?' And that broke us both up. We had been very solemn and sanctimonious; but then we roared with laughter, rocking in each other's arms ... Whether it will cure her I don't know. But now she looks at me and whispers 'Donkeys' and goes off into fits of laughter. Adorable child![12]

In August 1935 Winifred provided her final service when she and Hilda Reid, a close friend of hers from Somerville, travelled to Wimereux in northern France to look after the children so that Vera could return home following the disappearance and death of her father, subsequently confirmed as suicide by drowning in the Thames.

'I went in to see them,' Winifred wrote to Vera on her arrival,

and darling Shirley was lying on her side; her clothes right off, her little brown legs all bare. She is gloriously brown. This morning they both came bounding into my room, Shirley ecstatic because I remembered to bring her pink bear ... I love the children ... They warm my heart and refresh my spirit, and who knows what sort of an academic busybody I might be without them![13]

Having enjoyed two weeks in the sun playing with the children on the beach and putting the finishing touches to her literary masterpiece *South Riding*, Winifred returned with them in good spirits, but once back her condition deteriorated fast. Within a month she was dead, much to the sorrow of both Vera, who was to write her biography, and the children. It was now that the unfailing benignity of Amy Burnett, the young cook, and her husband Charlie, the butler and general handyman, really came into their own.

Hailing from a large working-class family in Battersea, with parents afflicted by poverty and ill health, Amy was denied the grammar school education her intelligence warranted because her father couldn't afford the uniform. Able, industrious and sympathetic, she, along with her siblings, worked in the Catlin household pre-war, and soon her status was raised to general housekeeper in recognition of her growing indispensability. Not only did the Burnetts provide Shirley with additional food which eluded her upstairs, they also provided a whole human dimension of fun, games, gossip and affection. On top of this they took her to Battersea Park to learn tennis, accompanied her to the cinema and, as committed Roman Catholics, took her to church each Sunday. Their relationship was one of such mutual devotion that Shirley regarded the Burnetts as her proxy parents and their children as the closest of friends. Many years later, when Amy died, Shirley's wreath bore the poignant remark 'To my other mother'.

And of course there was George himself. Shirley's tendency to draw attention to herself chimed in well with her parents' stipulation that both children, contrary to Vera's own experience, should be accorded the same opportunities in their upbringing. 'My father gave me the single greatest gift with which a child can be endowed, self-confidence,' Shirley later recalled.[14] Given his own mother's suffragette sympathies and Vera's feminist convictions, it wasn't surprising that George should bring his daughter up to feel the full equal of her brother. Whether it was allowing her to climb his bookshelves to the ceiling, introducing her to important people and their ideas, or encouraging her to follow her own instincts, Shirley was taught never to think of herself as inferior to men.

Believing like James Mill, the father of J. S. Mill, that even infants could grasp complicated ideas, George would read extracts from the *Summa Theologica* of St Thomas Aquinas to her when she was only four or five, carefully explaining the meaning behind the texts. He also talked to her about history, the classics and philosophy and introduced her to Dante, Milton and Dickens. His influence on her was mainly an intellectual–political one, coupled with a fierce ambition for her future eminence. Yet equally his charm and sociability, along with his boundless optimism, all left their mark as Shirley developed the lighter touches that eluded her mother. Not that she lacked gravity. Even at the tender age of seven she appeared to grasp the general significance of her mother's mission to the US, for when

George was bemoaning an unusual paucity of correspondence from Vera, Shirley leapt to her defence. 'Mummy is very busy in America. You must not expect her to write too many letters. She wants some quiet to work. You must not expect too much of Mummy.'

'The babe is too, too bright. Dangerously so,' George informed Vera with glowing pride.[5] So entranced was he by her precocious wit and intelligence that she could do no wrong in his eyes, making him the most reluctant of disciplinarians and easy prey to her strong-willed temperament. Even when admonished by her mother, Shirley was rarely fazed, such as the occasion when she and John ran away from Vera in the street and vanished for some time. Having sent them to bed in disgrace on their eventual return, Vera later went up to see them and while finding John very subdued, Shirley was irrepressible as she bounced around on her bed.

The children, as Vera was constantly reminding George, were very different: Shirley the swashbuckling extrovert imbued with an aggressive morality, John the quieter, less confident type more at home in his own company. Unlike his sister, who always needed entertaining, Vera found that she could leave John to his own devices outside her study as she worked. Brought up to be critically observant he, in time, held values very different from the rest of his family that found expression in his painting and musical composition, but during those formative years of the 1930s he proved to be a stalwart ally of Shirley when circumstances brought them together.

Protective towards his younger sister, John showed a kindness and a tolerance that were the ideal foil for her more boisterous personality. He later recalled that she could be quite a handful with her intellectual jousting and irascibility, but from the moment he helped teach her to walk, he enjoyed looking after her and accommodating her wishes. Whenever Vera felt compelled to reprimand Shirley during those early years John would stand before her with glowering eyes and say angrily, 'I don't like you.'

Happy in each other's company, they spent many an hour playing together, be it in the home, the garden or on the beach when on holiday. One of their favourite games was dressing up, another was building serried ranks of soldiers in preparation for battle between their respective armies, a game which offended Vera's pacifist convictions.

Because of their close relationship, John's departure to The Downs, a Quaker boarding school near Malvern, in September 1938, left a huge void in both of their lives since he much preferred the company of his sister to the boys he met there, while Shirley roamed the house like a lost soul without him. The fact that going to the US in June 1940 meant being reunited with one another made their evacuation much more palatable than it might otherwise have been.

Because of George's gregarious nature Glebe Place and, later, 2 Cheyne Walk, Chelsea, the elegant six-storey Georgian terrace house to which the Catlins moved in 1937, often played host to leading lights within the progressive firmament. Such occasions offered much in the way of curiosity for the children. When dressed in their nightclothes, they would peer through the banisters at the various dignitaries arriving such as the writers H. G. Wells and Rebecca West and the actress Sybil Thorndike. It was Shirley's privilege to serve lemonade to George Lansbury, sometime leader of the Labour Party, and bounce on the knee of Jawaharlal Nehru when the future Prime Minister of India came to tea to meet fellow socialists sympathetic to the cause of Indian independence. John Catlin later recalled how, having sat and listened in respectful silence to the views of their guests, Shirley and he would discuss the points raised in conversation. Such experiences gave them a remarkable fund of knowledge for their age and, in Shirley's case, a facility for mixing with illustrious types in all walks of life.

Ever since Shirley had been pushed round the streets of Brentford & Chiswick in 1931, aged one, as her father unavailingly sought election to Parliament, politics had been in the blood, and the historic events of the 1930s provided plenty of material for discussion. 'What I did understand,' Shirley later remarked, 'was that no one would pay me any attention unless I engaged in political conversation too. "You're only interested in Hitler, not me," I informed them at the age of five … That politics was the most exciting of all the exciting things in the world I never doubted.'[16]

Shirley's precociousness at home gave her a head start when she enrolled at Mrs Spencer's Academy, a small preparatory school in Kensington, aged five. Proudly informing her mother that she was the only person in her class who could read, she was in many ways the model pupil, especially in English and History, where her interest and aptitude were most evident. With her literary heritage it perhaps wasn't surprising that she became entranced by the world of poetry and plays, as she recited long tracts of the former and acted out scenes from Shakespeare, something at which she excelled, not least because of her photographic memory.

On paper her well-honed critical faculties and prodigious vocabulary made her a highly gifted, if occasionally careless, essayist whose literary gems won her much praise from her teachers. 'She has a most unusual gift for expressing herself,' wrote her English teacher. 'Her stories show a vivid imagination, a sense of the dramatic and of form, and a mastery of words.'[17]

In History these same skills, allied to a profound empathy with the past, were readily evident. 'I think Shirley listens attentively to the stories of Primitive Man, and enjoys tales of Greek heroes, but she often remarks, "I don't call that a very exciting adventure,"' stated one report.[18] Another referred to her excellent memory and trenchant opinions on the people she was studying.

With her competence in other subjects, especially geography, her promise as a pianist and her intrepidity in the swimming pool (even her cricket improved), there seemed little about which to quibble. And yet despite her all-round accomplishments Shirley didn't feel entirely comfortable in this genteel milieu of smart uniforms and straw boaters. 'I'd like to go where there aren't so many nice children,' she told her mother, and soon she was to have her wish.[19]

A year or so earlier George had come up with the idea of sending both children to the local elementary school for a term. Not only would the money saved pay for a family holiday to Germany, which in the event didn't materialise, but the opportunity to mix with children from all types of backgrounds would broaden their horizons. His initiative was welcomed by John and Shirley, but nothing further came of it until September 1938, by which time the deteriorating international situation decreed that John be evacuated to a school in the country. For Shirley, though, the opportunity still existed.

The year 1936 had been a pivotal one in Vera's life. Ever since 1921 she had placed her hopes for a new world order on the League of Nations, but its failure to quell Japanese aggression in Manchuria in 1931 and Mussolini's conquest of Abyssinia in 1936 called into question its effectiveness in maintaining collective security. That March she and George had been in Germany, where they had listened to Hitler in grim fascination as he deployed his sinister manipulative powers over his countrymen. Later in June she attended a mass meeting of the newly formed Peace Pledge Union (PPU) at Dorchester under the auspices of a charismatic Anglican priest, Dick Sheppard, whose experiences as a padre in the First World War had converted him to Christian pacifism. Such was the intoxicating effect of that Dorchester meeting and Sheppard's magnetic personality that over the course of the next few months Vera exchanged the cause of collective security for fully fledged Christian pacifism, and in 1937 became a sponsor of PPU. This now became the guiding passion of her life, not least during the Second World War, when her principled opposition to war and the destructive bombing on Germany came at great personal cost.

From the time of Hitler's annexation of Austria in March 1938, George was beginning to toy with the possibility of sending the children to the US, where he felt they would be much safer in the event of a German invasion of Britain. Vera, recalling the pain their previous separations had caused her, was far from enamoured with the idea and constantly told him so. She did, however, agree to the four of them going to the US in September 1938 as the crisis between Germany and Czechoslovakia escalated. By the time they arrived in New York, the tension had been defused by the Munich Agreement, which ceded the Sudetenland to Germany, enabling them to make a quick return.

While Vera continued to fret about the future and John returned to The Downs, Shirley became properly acquainted with Christ Church Elementary School, Chelsea. Here, in Dickensian surroundings, thirty children sat supervised by a teacher on a high wooden stool with a cane across her lap. As the only middle-class child in the school, Shirley found the wretched condition of her fellow pupils deeply disconcerting. Some were so poor that one family in her class had to take it in turns to come to school because they were forced to share boots, while for many the sweets they received from the London County Council each Christmas were their only presents. Conscious that her privileged position would make her a target for assault in the playground, she invented a Cockney accent and ensured that she returned home from school via the basement entrance, leaving her classmates to assume that she was the cook's daughter.

The tactics seemed to work. The headmaster was delighted with her and Vera reported that Shirley had adapted completely to the company of other children, despite her competitive instincts in the classroom. When issued with one piece of paper for an essay, she was far from impressed: 'One piece of paper is no use to me,' she said. 'These girls write so slowly. I want more.'[20] Particularly satisfying was the progress she made in arithmetic, where the standard of teaching, according to Vera, was better than in many private schools, and in English, where she gained full marks.

By the time these words were written Shirley was destined for her third school in less than a year as Hitler caused further palpitations by unleashing ferocious propaganda attacks on the British and stepping up his persecution of the Jews. Vera remained unconvinced about the need to evacuate the children to the US, but was concerned enough about their safety to want them out of London. That January she looked around Oldfeld, a Quaker boarding school run along progressive lines situated outside the Dorset town of Swanage, with stunning views of both the downs and the sea. She warmed to the headmaster and his wife and a week later she formally enrolled Shirley for the summer term.

Back in the middle of February 1939, Shirley had been diagnosed with tonsillitis and the decision was taken to have her tonsils out. The operation, costing twenty guineas, was duly performed in early April and Sister told Vera that Shirley had been 'astonishingly good'. Within hours she was reading voraciously and recovering rapidly, aside from her disquiet about the looming impact of war. On 15 March, Hitler had invaded Czechoslovakia and three weeks later Mussolini invaded Albania. These naked acts of aggrandisement marked a sea-change of mood in Britain, with patience towards the dictators fast diminishing. Against a background of planes roaring overhead, hurried ARP preparations and excited chatter of the nurses, all of which unnerved Shirley, Vera decided to remove her from London to the quieter sanctuary of Bournemouth. It was while staying there in a hotel that she appeared in her mother's bedroom one night shivering with fear, having endured nightmares of a headless body being deposited on her bed from air raids. The following evening was little better; thereafter her anxieties eased. Her father recorded how he once found her patching together a broken toy chest and when he advised her that she couldn't do it without glue, she replied, 'I can do it. The Fuhrer can do it, or thinks he can, and so can I.'[21] In unseasonably good weather she played contentedly on the beach with John and then, when the new term beckoned, she was the very model of self-possession as she bade farewell to her family at the station. 'Shirley went to school; looked a darling in her navy and white uniform,' commented Vera. 'She joined the carriage of London girls at Bournemouth. Complete sang-froid and no tears ... It was we who walked home feeling forlorn!'[22]

After a number of perfunctory letters from Shirley over the course of the next few weeks, Vera was heartened by a reassuring one she received from the headmaster's wife at the end of May. 'Shirley is thoroughly at home and seems to be enjoying life to the full. She certainly lives at high speed, but is not apparently at all over-tired. She is doing well in work and games, and rides with great spirit.'[23]

'Excellent beginning in every sense. Good start at riding' was the headmaster's brief but encouraging report at the end of the term.[24] His upbeat assessment wasn't quite the whole story, however, as Shirley's own autobiography makes clear.

As befitted a Quaker establishment the headmaster and his staff were able and caring, as well as offering a decent standard of teaching. Yet away from official gaze a culture of bullying resided. Shirley later recounted how she was one of the ringleaders in the dormitory as she and her friends tormented the more vulnerable types with horrendous questions about themselves and their families in an attempt to make them cry. It was an aberration in her conduct that was quickly consigned to the past.

At the end of her first term Shirley didn't return to London but remained close to the south coast as a result of an exciting discovery the previous holiday. It had long been one of Vera's ambitions to own a secluded country retreat where she could concentrate on her writing, but such plans had been thwarted because of George's dislike of the countryside. Now, with safety ever more at a premium, she renewed her mission and while holidaying in Bournemouth that April she came across a former groom's cottage in the hamlet of Allum Green in the New Forest. Although the cottage itself was fairly dilapidated, she immediately fell for it and purchased it out of the proceeds of *Testament of Youth*. With the Burnetts on hand to help decorate her new home, she spent those first few months there completing *Testament of Friendship*, her memoir of Winifred Holtby. Later she was joined by the children, who explored the wonders of the forest, unaware of the events unfolding across the Channel.

On Friday 1 September Hitler invaded Poland, sparking off a final bout of frantic diplomatic activity as Neville Chamberlain, the British Prime Minister, strove in vain to avoid the war he always dreaded. Two days later, on a beautiful warm Sunday morning, Shirley was summoned from the garden to the small upstairs study. There, in the company of her mother, John and the Burnetts, she heard the Prime Minister's melancholic voice on the wireless informing the country that, following the expiry of the British and French ultimatum to Hitler to remove his troops from Poland, they were now at war with Germany. Sitting between her two children it suddenly dawned on Vera that, despite all her efforts, her hopes of avoiding another war had collapsed in ruins, and as she faced up to the reckoning she dissolved into tears. While Charlie Burnett slipped out to get her a handkerchief, Shirley hugged her mother and all but licked her face like a puppy. 'Poor Mummie! Don't cry, Mummie!' she whispered. 'It'll be all right in the end, really it will!'[25]

Too young to understand her mother's severe reservations about war, Shirley saw it in terms of 'heroism, adventure, excitement' as she and her schoolmates back at Oldfeld listened to air-raid sirens and occasionally watched the odd air duel from the slit trenches carved in the green downs.

With Paris falling to the Germans on 14 June 1940 and a German invasion of Britain now a near inevitability, the question of the children's future returned to preoccupy their parents. Having seen Hitler in the flesh, they were under no illusions as to what a Nazi invasion would entail, presentiments amply borne out after the war when both their names were found included in the Gestapo's black list. Neither could expect to survive since both had been prominent in their attacks on Nazism. George was now heavily involved in working for the British cause in the US and Vera could easily join him there, but as a leading member of PPU she felt compelled to stay. Reluctantly she conceded to George's wish that the children should go to America, especially since they had many a trusted friend there who would look after them. One such person was Ruth Colby, one of Vera's most ardent admirers from the time of their first encounter in 1934 when Vera was touring the US, and when she was back there in early 1940, she stayed with the Colbys at their home in St Paul, Minnesota. There, amidst much heartfelt discussion about the children's future, Ruth had offered to have them and now, come June, she was as good as her word.

As Britain's position became ever more perilous, a government scheme to send children overseas gained momentum once the US and dominions came forward with offers of help. On 20 June the Children's Overseas Reception Board was formally established under Geoffrey Shakespeare, a distant cousin of Vera's, along with her friend Thelma Cazalet, a Conservative MP who also happened to be a feminist. Uncertain as to what to do with John and Shirley, Vera sought counsel from Cazalet. Her advice was unequivocal; they should send them to the US at once under their own auspices as the government scheme only catered for a proportion of the children. The next day George spent hours enduring the lengthy queues that descended on the Passport Office and American embassy to get the necessary documentary forms in order before contacting Thomas Cook to apply for passes on a Canadian Pacific liner. Vera then cabled her close friend George Brett, the president of Macmillan Company, her American publishers, and asked him to keep the immigration authorities satisfied by guaranteeing the well-being of the children so that there was no question of them becoming public charges. He and his Macmillan colleague, Jim Putnam, readily complied.

And yet the doubts persisted. George called 23 June 'a hell of a day with V driving me up the hill and down again over the children's evacuation to USA'.[26] He felt that on balance they should go and go soon, but Vera, fearful of them being torpedoed, was less than convinced. Yet amidst the heartbreak Vera's intellectual clarity reasserted itself and, accepting the premise that not only would the children be safer in the US but that she or George would be over there periodically, she bowed to the inevitable. Arrangements for a quick despatch continued and once news of their berths on a Canadian liner departing from Liverpool had been confirmed by Cook's, these were duly implemented.

On 25 June, John and Shirley returned separately from their respective schools to London. At first Shirley looked pale and miserable, reluctant about going to the US, but perked up as soon as she saw John and proceeded to regale her parents about her two successive nights in the air-raid shelters. That night, having packed their trunks, Vera lingered when drying Shirley and brushing John's hair, contemplating what the future held for them. 'How I sympathize with her', George confided to his diary, 'when she says the children were just getting nice and interesting and now this is such a shame.'[27]

The next morning they boarded the crowded boat train to Liverpool. Among the many agitated parents on board was Jan Struther, the author of the bestselling wartime classic *Mrs Miniver* and acquaintance of Vera, who was accompanying her two young children to the US, where she would be reunited with her lover. She asked Vera whether she was going too and looked crestfallen when Vera replied she wasn't; she was only seeing them off. 'I looked at John and Shirley,' Vera later recalled in *Testament of Experience*, 'and felt sick at heart. In that inexorably speeding compartment, familiar words seemed to hang in the air between Jan Struther and myself. "Lord, let this cup pass from me!"'[28]

Once they arrived in Liverpool they were ushered into a large covered shed to wait interminably for the immigration officials, much to the distress of the younger children, many of whom began to cry. As the only children with re-entry permits to the US, John and Shirley were given priority treatment through immigration. Then, having bidden a fond but composed farewell to their parents on the windswept quayside, the two of them boarded the gangway of the *Duchess of Atholl* without as much as a backward glance, full of excitement for their journey into the unknown.

### Endnotes

1 *Chronicle of Friendship: Vera Brittain's War Diary 1913–1917*, ed. Alan Bishop with Terry Smart, Gollancz, 1981; Fontana, 1982, p.341
2 Vera Brittain, *Testament of Youth*, Victor Gollancz, 1933, p.290
3 VB to GC, 14 September 1952
4 VB to GC, 17 January 1931
5 VB to GC, 20 March 1931
6 Vera Brittain, *Testament of Experience*, Gollancz, 1957, p.62
7 VB to GC, 8 March 1932
8 School report, Chelsea Babies' Club, December 1932
9 School report, Chelsea Babies' Club, December 1933
10 School report, Chelsea Babies' Club, March 1934
11 Shirley Williams, *Climbing the Bookshelves*, Virago, 2009, p.22
12 Winifred Holtby to VB, 19 September 1934

13  Winifred Holtby to VB, Quoted in Vera Brittain, *Testament of Friendship*, Macmillan, 1940; Virago, 1980, p.404
14  *Climbing the Bookshelves*, p.3
15  GC to VB, 7 December 1937
16  *Climbing the Bookshelves*, p.18
17  School report, Mrs Spencer's Academy, July 1938
18  School report, Mrs Spencer's Academy, December 1935
19  Quoted in VB's letter to GC, 8 July 1938
20  GC diary, 26 April 1939
21  GC diary, 26 April 1939
22  VB diary, 27 April 1939
23  Vera Hickson to VB, 26 May 1939
24  School report, Oldfeld, July 1939
25  Quoted in Vera Brittain, *England's Hour: An Autobiography, 1939–41*, Macmillan, 1941; Futura, 1981, p.11
26  GC diary, 23 June 1940
27  Ibid., 25 June 1940
28  *Testament of Experience*, p.257

# 2

## AMERICAN ODYSSEY

Before John and Shirley could savour the security of the US, they had to cross the submarine-infested waters of the north Atlantic, where the German predators of the deep lay in wait for Allied or neutral shipping. Such a fate befell many a vessel, including the evacuee ship *Arandora Star*, which set sail five days after the *Duchess of Atholl*, and the *City of Benares*, destroyed that September with the loss of seventy children, putting paid to the evacuation scheme.

Too young to be fully alive to the potential perils of such a voyage, Shirley couldn't but detect the collective sense of relief among the older passengers once the liner reached the sanctuary of the New World as they glided up the waters of the mighty St Lawrence.

On disembarking at Montreal, John and Shirley were met by Margaret Mackenzie, a friend of the Colbys, and taken under her wing for the night. The next afternoon she put them on the train to Toronto, en route to the twin cities of St Paul and Minneapolis in Minnesota. As their journey continued the next morning in brilliant sunshine across the plains of the American Midwest, Shirley discovered a whole new vista of unending space opening up.

> Here were the huge skies, the cornfields running to the horizon, the massed evergreens of the forests. Working with so large a canvas, God had created a landscape of bold colours and massive shapes ... Never had I experienced so strong a feeling of freedom and independence as on that train. Everything seemed possible.[1]

At 7.15 that evening, the two of them arrived at St Paul to begin their new life in the US. 'My heart sank when I saw them get off the train: they seemed mere babies!' Ruth Colby wrote to Vera, but after a sound night's sleep they quickly responded to the warm embrace of her family, displaying no signs of homesickness.[2]

Ruth Colby was a pillar of the Midwest in a state which was overwhelmingly white, prosperous and clean-living, the legacy of its Scandinavian-Lutheran heritage, and also liberal in its politics, reflected in the formation of the Minnesota Farmer–Labor Party in 1918 and the success it attained during the inter-war period.

It was perhaps Ruth's agricultural upbringing that prompted her to follow such an unorthodox vocation for a Minnesota housewife, for besides being a patron of various causes and charities, she was also State chairman of the Women's International League for Peace and Freedom. It was through this institution that she had come into contact with Vera when she had hosted her on her visit to the States in 1934, and the iconic status she accorded her bode well for John and Shirley's time under her care. Aside from providing a loving home and catering to their everyday needs, Ruth was meticulous in escorting them to the local entertainment and playing host to their friends. She was well supported in her new responsibilities by her husband, Woodard, a highly respected paediatrician, and teenage son Gage, a handsome naval ensign training in medicine, who happily adopted Shirley as the younger sister he had never had.

In accordance with his services background as a naval commander in the First World War, Woodard Colby was a more formal figure than his wife, a man of few words, old-fashioned courtesies and impeccable standards. Yet although the children were expected to be polite and punctual and observe the proprieties of the household (he was always Dr Colby whereas she liked to be addressed as Rue), he hid his light under a bushel. For under a gruff exterior lay the most compassionate of men, devoted to the children and their welfare, qualities which in turn won him their respect and affection.

The Colby home in St Paul, the older and less commercial of the twin cities, was a white timber-built house three storeys high, complete with a sizeable garden. Used to forming their own entertainment the children spent much time reading, playing the piano, and, in Shirley's case, tending to animals, especially her beautiful black Siamese kitten, Figaro, on whom she doted. Indeed, so content were they with their lot during those first few weeks that time passed by at a gallop. The only cloud looming on the horizon concerned the plans for Shirley's education.

Back in 1937 Vera had befriended on a visit to Texas Miss Ela Hockaday, who ran a boarding school for 'well-bred' children. Warming to her emphasis on sophisticated chic, which she felt would modify the traditional gaucherie of the English schoolgirl, Vera was all set to send Shirley there at some later stage in her education. Now, with fate decreeing her presence in America, she seemed destined for Texas that September while John remained in St Paul.

The plans met with fierce resistance from Shirley. Not only had her time at Oldfeld turned her against the concept of boarding, it would mean separating herself from John, who remained her great companion and protector. Her stance won firm backing from Ruth, whose immediate and intense affection for Shirley was matched by her dislike of boarding, especially the ethos of the Hockaday school. She conveyed her reservations to Vera, who acknowledged the reluctance of the children to be separated, but felt that there was a danger of them becoming too dependent on each other. It was to no avail. Up against the concerted opposition of Shirley, Ruth and George Brett, and with distance against her, she felt compelled to back down. 'Shirley is relaxed for the first time since she came, and to tell you how happy she is about staying with John and us would sound like boasting,' Ruth crowed to Vera.[3]

A week after these words were written, George Catlin, now back in the US with Foreign Office support to try and secure American cruisers for the British war effort, travelled to St Paul for a family reunion. 'You need not worry for a moment about the children,' he reassured his wife. 'They are frightfully well, frightfully happy and not detectably worrying in the least. There is complete adaption of individual to environment. Both are obviously pleased with their schools.'[4] Amidst the obvious pleasure on all sides with the reunion, George was concerned about the deterioration of Shirley's manners, a trend which Vera had first detected at Oldfeld, and the complete ascendancy she had exerted over Ruth. 'She was domineering, unruly and aggressive,' he reported, and could do with the discipline of a boarding school to eradicate her self-centredness.[5] He wasn't, however, prepared to raise the issue of Miss Hockaday, especially since Shirley had settled so quickly at Summit School, her new junior high school in St Paul. Although the youngest in sixth grade by five months, she soon became something of a talismanic figure with her peers, admired for her running and her stories of war back home. Soon the invitations were flooding in and barely a weekend went by without some form of social engagement.

Summit School, one of the leading fee-paying girls' schools in the state, differed from its English counterparts with its absence of uniform, its informal atmosphere and a curriculum more geared to personal development than to academic rigour. As soon as she arrived, Shirley was examined by a psychologist who declared she was suffering badly from shock and that no one was to mention the war in her presence. Some time later, when her class was invited to talk on their most interesting experience, Shirley spoke with animation about the bombs that had fallen on Swanage. Although the Colbys deliberately refrained from discussing the war at home, and only listened to the news after the children had gone to bed, Ruth found her generally more interested in the presidential election between Franklin Roosevelt, a statesman she much admired, and his Republican challenger, Wendell Willkie, for whom her father had briefly worked as an adviser on foreign affairs, an election that Roosevelt won comfortably.

Sharing an acute interest in politics, Ruth talked with her at length on the subject and took her to meetings of the Farmer–Labor Party, which, besides encouraging her internationalist ideals, cemented their already burgeoning relationship. 'Shirley is going to be a person who can do almost anything she wants to do,' she informed Vera.

She is so bright and warm hearted and so determined to be a boy in this Man's World that I find her tremendously interesting, lovable and amusing. Sometimes in our intimate conversations, however, she displays astonishing evidence of staunch feminism. 'A woman would never do such a thing,' she will exclaim over some masculine folly. And again, 'We women can do some things – lots of things – better than men, can't we, Rue?'[6]

Given her aptitude for making friends, Shirley casually announced at dinner one evening that, having gained the post of class secretary for that semester, she had persuaded the girls to consider electing her president for the forthcoming one. To help her realise her ambition she and Ruth organised a Christmas lunch party and bobsleigh ride. In response to Vera's reservations about her unruly behaviour, Ruth admitted that Shirley could be overbearing towards John, especially in argument, and that her manners left something to be desired, but attributed much of this to the unfortunate legacy of Oldfeld. 'I pray that my method of reasoning everything out with her will win her away from her notion that it is smart to be naughty.'[7] Revelling in the company of the children, she told Vera that they weren't a burden but a joy.

The responsibility, though, of tending to other people's children was always present, especially during the dark days of December 1940 as George, having finished his secondment at Kansas City University, was travelling home on board the *Western Prince*. Torpedoed by a German submarine in mid-ocean, he and his fellow passengers were subjected to a nine-hour ordeal on the open seas in lifeboats before they were rescued by the crew of a small freighter and taken to Gourock on the Clyde estuary.

The news of their father's rescue provided John and Shirley with a timely boost for the festive season, which, with its complement of skiing, skating and children's lunch parties, was one of pure joy, so very different from the drabness back home.

The new semester began with Shirley's successful election to the class presidency, an election which meant flouting the convention of anyone holding major office for two successive semesters. 'It is the first goal for our little politician,' Ruth informed Vera, 'and I think she would have considered her year at Summit a total loss if she had failed.'[8] Believing her capacity for friendship extraordinary in such a young child, Ruth reckoned that Shirley had become more thoughtful and better mannered, although her patience could be sorely tried when asked the same old questions by well-meaning people, such as whether she liked America. Her form mistress, the popular Eliphal Nichols, while critical of her carelessness, was much impressed by her performance, which saw her top of the class in every subject except arithmetic. 'Shirley has made us all love her. She is a joy in the classroom. Her eager interest, cooperation, her intelligent comments and questions, and her unfailing good temper and fine sense of humour are a great satisfaction to me every day of the week.'[9] According to Miss Nichols, Shirley was her favourite and she made little effort to conceal the fact, a position the rest of the class readily accepted, such was their affection for Shirley. When Ruth said goodbye to Miss Nichols at the end of the school year, Miss Nichols told her that Shirley was one of her chief reasons for wanting to return the following year. Shirley's stock remained high at Sherwood Forest girls' summer camp, located on the beautiful Deer Lake in the pine forests of northern-central Minnesota. Not only did she participate in the full gamut of activities on offer – riding, swimming and canoeing – but her charm and vitality, according to the staff, won the unstinting admiration of all. Employing her acting potential to the full, she won the second prize in the costume party as a sailor representing the spirit of the Royal Navy, and brought the house down with her Cockney accent. In addition to the communal revelry and singing around the camp fire, there were also her more reflective moments, as these patriotic sentiments demonstrate.

> O England, my England
> So brave and so true.
> My heart, as in exile

Is aching for you.
Is this your last battle?
No it cannot be.
For Britons are still living,
Still brave and still free.[10]

Shirley's endeavours continued to astound Ruth. 'Certainly she has the greatest degree of physical stamina and muscular resilience matched by mental activity that we have ever seen in an eleven-year-old. She will be a power in the world one day if she sets her heart on it.'[11]

By the time these words were written Shirley had departed for Connecticut on the east coast for a month's stay with Jim Putnam and his wife Marion (Mannie), a talented sculptress. It had been arranged that she would accompany her brother, but in an act of teenage defiance John had at the last moment refused to go, electing to stay at Stillwater, an artistic community college run by a great friend of Ruth's. There he enjoyed the company of students considerably older than himself and fell deeply in love with a girl from Duke University, North Carolina. Cosseted in this environment in a way that he wasn't at St Paul Academy with its militaristic tradition, or with Ruth Colby, whose earnest idealism he didn't share, he decided to abscond when it was time for him to leave. His recalcitrance won him a reprieve of another three weeks there, Ruth recognising that his passion for painting was genuine, but besides upsetting the Putnams and Bretts, who were due to host him thereafter, it caused his parents much embarrassment when acquainted with the saga.

John's absence in no way detracted from Shirley's holiday with the Putnams at Rowayton, Long Island. She arrived by plane, none the worse for travelling alone, and immediately took to her hosts, especially the delightfully sympathetic Mannie and her charming son Christopher, whose enormous stature belied his tender years. Together they preoccupied themselves at the local amusement arcade and on the beach. 'Shirley dives in for shells like a little

fish', Mannie wrote to Vera. 'I think her adaptability is remarkable.'[12] From the outset she was accepted as one of the family and so
enchanted was she by the hospitality afforded her that the day of her
departure to the Bretts was a bittersweet occasion. In floods of tears
she clung to Mannie, begging her not to send her, such was her
intense dislike of Isabel Brett. When Mannie finally persuaded her to
go she sat motionless in the car beside Isabel in total silence until
they reached the Bretts' house. Her mood didn't improve on arrival
when she discovered that she had been banished to the guesthouse
with the servants, much as she liked them, not least because they
reminded her of the Burnetts. In general she felt patronised by a
woman who felt uncomfortable in the presence of children. Her
views matched those of her mother who thought Isabel cold and
snobbish, although she recognised that her own special friendship
with Isabel's husband hadn't helped. It was because of this that she
had looked to house the children elsewhere in the US despite the
Bretts' offer to give them a permanent home.

Shirley also had qualms about George Brett, whose robust
personality and right-wing Republican views made him hard
for her to relate to. The feeling wasn't mutual. He enjoyed taking
her swimming, and their walks through the rolling Connecticut
hills with four dogs did much to raise her spirits, so much so that
Isabel remained totally oblivious to her true feelings. Like the
Putnams, the Bretts were totally enchanted by her, George calling her a 'perfect peach', and in a move of considerable temerity
he contacted the Colbys to see whether they could wean her away
from Minnesota to New York where they would find her a suitable
school. His attempted coup upset Ruth, who strongly believed that
Shirley should at least be consulted about her future, not least the
idea of boarding in the east, which in her eyes was a retrograde step.
She confessed to feeling heartbroken at the thought of losing her,
but felt honour-bound to let Shirley have the final say.

Stung by Ruth's animated reaction, Brett quickly climbed down,
recognising her prior claim. 'It would be difficult for Mrs Brett and
myself even to suggest that she stay in the East now that we know

you want her,' he conceded. 'I warn you, though, Ruth Colby, the longer you have her the longer you are going to miss her when she returns to her mother. She is indeed a darling.'[13]

Ruth was overjoyed and relieved in equal measure. A week later she met this tanned figure walking sturdily off the plane amidst the adults, dressed in striped sweatshirt and cotton dungarees. Having hardly had time to draw breath Shirley blurted out, 'Do you know what? Isabel Brett tried to bribe me to stay. She told me she would buy me a dog and maybe a horse – only I knew she wouldn't because she is stingy...'

'What did you say?' inquired Ruth.

'I said, St Paul is my American home. Summit is my school, and I am going home to Rue.'

'That was that,' Ruth told Vera. 'I am ashamed of myself to feel so thoroughly pleased, so completely recompensed.'[14]

Back at Summit, Shirley had little difficulty adapting to the senior school with its six-mile round trip by bicycle and its longer hours. For while never working at full capacity, she continued to progress nicely, gaining honours in English, social sciences and algebra. The only blot on her escutcheon was her performance in home economics, where indolence in class led to enforced sessions after school to finish her sewing. She attributed her lack of proficiency here to Vera's indifference to the subject, a claim her mother acknowledged. Vera did, however, urge her to learn what she could as she recalled its uses during her wartime experiences nursing, cooking and darning socks.

That summer Shirley again went to camp at Sherwood Forest, Ruth's presence on her birthday a real tonic. Revelling once more in the range of activity on offer, she made great progress with her swimming and gave further glimpses of her charisma by entertaining the other girls at night with her mystery stories, as well as dominating the cast in play rehearsals. 'Shirley has been so nice these past few weeks,' commented Kay Shepherd, the leader of the camp, to Ruth. 'Really, she is the most interesting little girl I have ever encountered. Her fiery imagination plus that amazing vocabulary spices up any situation,'[15] a view endorsed many years later by Evelyn Storberg, one of the other girls present. She recalled Shirley's endearing personality and impish sense of fun, complete with her very colourful language, especially the night she and her fellow campers were trying to ward off some bats in their cabin.

Shirley's success in the US stood in growing contrast to John. His first year at St Paul Academy had been a productive one with encouraging academic results and a headmaster whom he much respected. Inheriting his mother's solitary temperament he seemed in need of few friends and, encouraged by the Colbys, he found ample fulfilment in his painting, the highlight of which had been his time at Stillwater. The fact that he became obsessed with his girlfriend seemed to be to the detriment of his work since he admitted to losing interest thereafter, with a consequent decline in his grades and the end of any hopes of a scholarship to Harvard. The teachers did try to engage with him, but he rarely responded, finding much to criticise in both them and his fellow pupils, whom he found boringly superficial. The fact that he loathed sport and rejected invitations as consistently as Shirley accepted hers meant that his popularity dwindled as rapidly as hers mounted. On these grounds Ruth thought a change of scene desirable. The decision to move schools, made without consultation, greatly troubled Vera and George when they heard about it, especially since his head-master spoke highly of John. The mystery only deepened when they discovered that he had been sent to a military academy some seventy miles away, given Ruth's objection to boarding and the increased cost incurred because of wartime inflation. They conveyed their concern to George Brett, who undertook to get to the bottom of the mystery. Weeks later, towards the end of John's first term at Pillsbury Academy, Brett explained all: how John's frustration with St Paul had been taken out on Shirley and Ruth, suggesting that Ruth's motive for sending him away had something to do with restoring peace at home. When he came to write his memoirs, John admitted that the regime at Pillsbury wasn't quite as harsh as had been depicted and that he came to appreciate his three years in the

US as an opportunity to enhance his self-development. That this time of comparative freedom had also brought out his innate rebelliousness and wilful single-mindedness, especially in his fraught relationship with Ruth, he also readily conceded.

John's predicament preoccupied Vera at a time when she was suffering much in pursuit of her principles. Amidst the mayhem of the Blitz which had led to the closure of Cheyne Walk and a peripatetic existence for a number of months, she heard that her application for an American visa had been rejected. No official explanation was given, but her pacifist activities, especially her fortnightly 'Letters to Peace Lovers' were deemed troublesome by the authorities. Undaunted by severed friendships, abusive letters and the undermining of her literary reputation, she continued to plough her lonely furrow, strengthened by her burgeoning Christian convictions. She published a couple of pacifist tracts and besides campaigning tirelessly for food relief in both Nazi-occupied and neutral Europe, spoke out forcefully against the Allied bombing of German cities.

With George initially away for much of the time and unable to see John and Shirley, Vera was inevitably lonely. Yet, whatever her tribulations, her letters to her children were affectionately upbeat, complimenting them on their accomplishments, enthusing about their pleasures and sympathising with their concerns. When referring to the war and the misery it unleashed she didn't hide her sentiments but couched them in sober, balanced tones, replete with shafts of idealism about the future.

It isn't surprising that she sought the children's return at the earliest opportunity, especially given the escalating cost of their school fees. Her growing anxiety on this score prompted generous words of reassurance from Brett, who told her that Ruth and he would continue to cover all costs and that if once the war was over she had the means to repay some of it, then she could do so at her leisure.

At the same time, with the Atlantic something of a death trap, both he and Jim Putnam advised Vera against anything premature, so that her hopes of 1942 being the year of reunion were dashed.

Informed by Thomas Cook that the chances of a passage were much greater if the children travelled separately, she and George made John their priority because of his indifferent record at school.

The lingering uncertainty about her departure doesn't appear to have affected Shirley. She continued to be in clover, hosting for a second year a blissful Easter house party dedicated to riding and cycling, and attending summer camp, all signs of a less fraught transition to adolescence than that of her brother.

Back in 1940 when she and John had arrived in the US, she was very much the younger sister, prone to the preoccupations and foibles of any normal ten-year-old. Thereafter for the next three years in the outdoor culture of Minnesota she played the part of the tomboy to perfection, even eschewing the honour of accompanying the captain of the junior football team to the First Formal, the prestigious school ball to which every aspiring girl sought an invitation. Yet aside from her carefree existence Shirley's intellectual horizons were developing fast as she absorbed the local newspapers and discussed current issues with Ruth. All of a sudden her letters home assumed a new profundity. 'Please don't think that we in any way object to your returning plan,' she assured her mother after Vera raised the matter diffidently. 'We certainly do remember that England is our country and we are just as fond of a torn, shabby England as a rich prosperous "posh" one. Its people, and its spirit, in good times or bad, remain the same. Continue with your plans. We'll agree.'[16] 'Actually little Shirley is far more aware of people – other people – than John,' commented Ruth to Vera. 'To John the war is a damned nuisance, to Shirley it is a terrible thing happening to people.'[17]

Despite signs of this growing maturity, her parents took some convincing. 'I wrote five novels before the age of eleven,' Vera reminded Ruth. 'A little less popularity and a little more concentration would do our young woman no harm.'[18] Their concerns remained throughout 1942 despite the continuing satisfying tenor of her reports. 'Shirley, as you know, is a year younger than the other girls in her class,' Sarah Converse, the headmistress, informed Ruth that November, 'but is fully able to do the work. In fact, she is an extremely interesting student. I have her once a week in current history: she is exceptionally well informed and her vocabulary is broad and interesting for a child of her age. I think she has unusual possibilities.'[19]

For all the honeyed words her report didn't greatly impress Vera. 'Perhaps it might do her good to let her know that her mother at the same age was three years younger than her class-mates and managed somehow or other to be near the top of the form!' she informed the headmistress.[20] She told Shirley to spend less time socialising and more time practising her writing.

> I am sure I was a horrid child, and certainly I was never anything like as popular as you seem to be. But one can overdo popularity, which is pleasant but not essential (whereas consistent practising of your gift of art is essential from the earliest ages if you are ever going to do anything in the world) … So don't spend too much time on your school friends, charming as I am sure all of them are. Heaven forbid that at eighteen you should have become a cocktail-party-girl surrounded by young men and women but with not an achievement to your own name.[21]

Her words in turn prompted a spirited response from Shirley.

> Mummy, I'm surprised that you should feel that developing one's talent is more important than friendliness. I don't go to late parties and balls at all. I am limited to scattered lunches and overnight times. That you who tried and is trying to make the countries friends with each other should value brain above friendliness – that surprises me. Convicts are awfully clever usually, but have few friends. To quote Ruth, 'Talent is useless unless supported by something else.' … I have a lot of ambition, but I don't want particularly to be an opportunist! After all, even you had not accomplished too much at 18.[22]

With ironic timing Vera's next missive, written before Shirley's broadside reached her, bore a very different stamp.

My sweetheart, I can't think of you as a child any longer – you look almost a young woman, and such a pretty one! – I am very pleased that you are so fond of animals, because I am sure that people who grow up loving animals will never want to be cruel to humans, and there is so much cruelty about just now, especially to children, that every person who grows up kind is worth a dozen of the others. One day you will carry on lots of the things I have tried to do, and do them better.[23]

Although her schooling hadn't pushed her to new heights Shirley's time in the US had been a formative one. She had arrived with John as a mere child and left a young woman in some ways well advanced for her years. The vast open spaces had fuelled her adventurous instincts, and the New World emphasis on open informality and incorrigible optimism blended with her own sunny temperament.

'America became my other country, an aspiration if not a motherland,' Shirley wrote in her autobiography.

It was, in that simple and heroic time, a country undivided by class, united by the war effort, a country of flourishing and vibrant communities with a shared sense of its exceptional destiny … Many evenings, I lay on the floor in the dark listening on the gramophone to Dvorak's *New World* symphony, inundated by the sound and the images it evoked. I had found, I thought, the country where, in the words of Wordsworth I once learned by heart, 'Bliss was it in that dawn to be alive / But to be young was very heaven.'[24]

Endnotes

1   *Climbing the Bookshelves*, p.33
2   Ruth Colby to VB, 7 July 1940
3   Ruth Colby to VB, 3 September 1940
4   GC to VB, 23 September 1940
5   GC to VB, 4 October 1940
6   Ruth Colby to VB, 10 October 1940
7   Ruth Colby to VB, 21 November 1940
8   Ruth Colby to VB, 13 January 1941
9   Eliphal Nichols to Ruth Colby, 24 February 1941

10 SW poem, July 1941
11 Ruth Colby to VB, 7 August 1941
12 Mannie Putnam to VB, 23 August 1941
13 George Brett to Ruth Colby, 3 September 1941
14 Ruth Colby to VB, 10 September 1941
15 Kay Shepherd to Ruth Colby, 16 August 1942
16 SW to VB, 8 February 1942
17 Ruth Colby to VB, 2 February 1942
18 VB to Ruth Colby, 4 November 1942
19 Sarah Converse to Ruth Colby, 4 November 1942
20 VB to Sarah Converse, 9 December 1942
21 VB to SW, 13 January 1943
22 SW to VB, 14 February 1943
23 VB to SW, 17 February 1943
24 *Climbing the Bookshelves*, p.44

# 3

## TURBULENT YOUTH

Even more than her journey out, Shirley's trip home on the *Serpo Pinto* in September 1943 was quite an adventure, as the ship ran into the worst cyclone the captain could recall in twenty-five years. These were dog days, but Shirley drew strength from the friendship of the only other unaccompanied child of her age, Rosemary Roughton, an ebullient doctor's daughter from Cambridge. On arrival in Portugal they made the best of their time at the Palace Hotel, Estoril, near Lisbon, where they were interned while they awaited transport home.

Eventually, after nearly a month's wait and a torrid ride back in a RAF plane, Shirley's three-and-a-half-year odyssey ended at a damp air force base near Bristol on the morning of 17 October. There she was met by George, who confessed to being near tears on seeing his darling daughter, 'very hale and beautiful'. He escorted her back home and noted her joy as she dashed to her nursery cupboard to find her old toys.

While this was all happening, Vera was lecturing in Nottingham, unaware of the surprise that awaited her. As she staggered in the front door that evening, tired, wet and hungry, George, having ushered Shirley behind the curtain, shouted to her from the first floor room.

'Come up here! I've got something to show you!'

'In a minute,' she replied. 'Just let me get my wet coat off.'

'Don't wait. Come up at once!' he insisted.[1]

Vera obliged and opened the upstairs door to see him standing alone, smiling in a large empty room. Suddenly the window curtain was swept aside and out danced Shirley in scarlet sweatshirt and plaid skirt to embrace her mother. 'For the moment,' Vera informed Ruth, 'I couldn't believe my eyes and thought I was seeing things from fatigue; then I realised that it was indeed she – my own little darling.'[2]

Immediately struck by how pretty Shirley had become, so different from the red-faced little creature who had departed three years earlier, Vera compared her delicate features and clear blue eyes and skin to those of a fairy.

It took little time for Shirley to be reacquainted with the reality of war, beginning with an air raid on the evening of her return, and the next fourteen nights saw many a quick retreat into their shelter as bomb splinters fell in the garden. She impressed her mother with her poise during this ordeal, but it wasn't the ideal backdrop to life at her new school.

Founded in 1904, St Paul's Girls' School, Hammersmith, was one of the premier girls' schools in the country, renowned for its academic credentials, dedicated teaching and musical pedigree. Presiding over this turbulent period in its history was the formidable figure of Ethel Strudwick, an unflinching disciplinarian, and an ageing Common Room whose values belonged to a bygone era.

Beginning there halfway through the Christmas term in the Lower Fifth, Shirley had much to prove after three years of academic coasting in America. 'Shirley has intelligence,' commented her form mistress, 'but to make full use of her opportunities she must be much more methodical.'[3]

As she began to make up lost ground the next term, especially in Latin, English and History, her studies were once again interrupted by the war. Intensive German air raids on London in mid-February played havoc with her homework as she was obliged to keep really late hours. With Amy Burnett unhappy about keeping her young daughter in London, Vera was forced to close Cheyne Walk yet again and with accommodation in town at a premium the Catlins had to settle for a one-bedroom flat, which meant no room for Shirley. With her safety paramount (the school itself was damaged by bombing) and the Roughtons willing to have her, she headed to their home in Cambridge in late February. St Paul's were sorry to see her go and hoped her departure would be merely temporary. 'We have enjoyed having her very much,' Ethel Strudwick wrote to Vera, 'and she seems to have settled down with much ease and pleasantness.'[4]

Before she left, Shirley accompanied her parents to a party given by Sir John Mactaggart, a wealthy donor to the Labour Party, and his wife, at their opulent home in Park Lane, with Herbert Morrison, the Home Secretary, among the guests. All of a sudden a fierce raid brought pandemonium to proceedings, necessitating a move down from the penthouse flat to a safer apartment on the third floor. It was here that Shirley found herself in the company of the Home Secretary. For the next two hours, until the all-clear was given, she engaged him in animated conversation, giving him the benefit of her advice on a range of subjects. Fortunately, Morrison was much taken by her precocious intelligence, calling her a remarkable child. Two weeks later he invited her to lunch at the Home Office. Once she had been reassured by her mother that she wasn't receiving preferential treatment, Shirley accepted and over a lunch of sausages and mash she told him that she didn't judge people by their class but by their intelligence; why, incidentally, did he go around in such a 'posh' car? Once again warming to her company, Morrison told his secretary that he trusted he hadn't spoilt her, but she did so attract him. It was the beginning of an innocent friendship for Morrison, who muddied his reputation as a wily political fixer by acting as a generous patron of aspiring female politicians.

Shirley's lunch with Morrison gave her a welcome respite from the Roughton household, where she had found the general commotion disconcerting, especially the lack of privacy to read. The staple diet of bread and jam and potatoes also had her longing for Amy Burnett's cooking. Yet, for all that, Rosemary's mother Alice, an overworked GP, was kindness itself, and finding Shirley 'a joy in the house' as well as a suitable friend for Rosemary, suggested to Vera that Shirley stay on for the summer to participate in the tuition she was organising for her daughter and several other girls. Vera gladly accepted and for three months Shirley was tutored in maths, modern languages and English, the latter by the disabled literary critic John Hayward.

Shirley's other main preoccupations were riding and looking after her new puppy, a black and white mongrel collie called Treve. In compliance with her long-held wish, Vera had bought her a fox terrier puppy for Christmas, but ten days later she bowed to veterinary advice and had it put down after it contracted a rare skin disease. Her decision left Shirley distraught. Vera did make amends, however, by giving her Treve as a replacement, and although something of a liability to the Roughtons because of his tendency to eat food reserved for the adults, he became her constant companion.

After the February raids had brought a temporary halt to Shirley's education at St Paul's, Vera had once again seen boarding school as the solution. In March she visited Frensham Heights, a progressive school in Surrey, and liked what she saw, but her initiative dismayed Shirley, who begged her to discount the idea. She wanted to return to St Paul's and even suggested living with her grandmother to facilitate this, a suggestion which Vera raised with Edith Brittain before dismissing it as too impractical.

With London remaining vulnerable to bombing, Vera didn't give up on Frensham Heights. She delicately broached the subject with Shirley in correspondence and on receiving no reply she asked Alice Roughton to try to rid Shirley of her assumption that she had previously been sent away for her mother's convenience – although Vera's pre-war confession to George of sheer elation now that both children were finally boarding somewhat undermined this. The fact that Ruth Colby had been so dismissive of boarding had only accentuated Shirley's belief that her parents should never have sent her away.

I hate the idea of any boarding school. It somehow puts you above people who aren't so lucky in money as you, and I would hate to be a snob. Besides, I loathe the product of all the boarding schools I've seen, a horrid racquet carrying female, with an ugly straw hat, mustard coloured stockings, and a mind dressed up in snobbery. Ugh! I also hate the mock religiousness and goodness of the repulsive places. Somehow people turned against you when you go to boarding school – and I always prefer identifying myself with poor people rather than the smug bourgeoisie.[5]

Under no illusions as to her daughter's phobia about boarding, and fearful of the lasting damage it could do to their relationship, Vera gave way. Hoping to find a reputable day school within the vicinity of the New Forest, close to her cottage, she wrote to Ida Hillman, a pacifist friend of hers in Bournemouth, to see whether she could recommend anywhere in town and a family with whom Shirley could lodge during the week. Hillman wrote back offering to have her and recommended Talbot Heath, a grammar school for girls.

The headmistress agreed to take her and Vera made arrangements for Shirley to live with the Hillmans during the week, returning to the cottage at the weekend. 'School is going quite well for me down here. Almost all the girls are very polite and pleasant and I'm sure you would approve of it if you saw it,' Shirley informed her grandmother after a few weeks. 'The teachers are mostly good and quite strict. There's quite a bit of homework, but not really much.'[6] One of her favourite teachers was Dorothy Rowe, a contemporary of Vera's at Somerville. Shirley joined her PEN club and excelled at it. 'Shirley shows a keen interest in her work and has made good progress,' commented her form mistress at the end of her first term. 'At the beginning she found it difficult to co-operate but now she is much more helpful and should prove a valuable member of the form.'[7] She concluded by urging her to take a greater pride in her personal appearance, a familiar refrain over the course of the next few decades and one upon which her landlady quickly alighted.

Ida Hillman was an intelligent, domineering woman unhappy with her lot in life, being married to an ice-cream maker turned sausage maker and living in Boscombe, the less affluent part of Bournemouth. She took out her frustrations on Shirley, finding fault with every foible, real or imaginary. Soon the atmosphere had degenerated to the extent that Shirley, dreading the hectoring nature of her landlady, took refuge in her room and lived for the weekend. Recognising a clash of strong-willed temperaments, Hillman admitted to Vera that their relationship had been decidedly fraught. The greatest bones of contention, she reported, had been Shirley's table manners and her tendency to strew the house with her belongings.

The next time Hillman put pen to paper it was with some indignation following a long midnight vigil at Bournemouth station awaiting Shirley's non-arrival from London. Berating Vera for her daughter's uncaring and thoughtless behaviour and her failure to make her more responsible, she intimated how Shirley had caused much needless anxiety during her stay. She had tried to discipline her and point out her insensitivity to others, but apparently the seed had not fallen on very fertile soil. Hillman admitted that she was rather fastidious, but her contention that Vera's repeated absences made it all the more imperative for others to instil in Shirley the values of good communal living drew a rather pained response. 'I don't think you really meant to suggest that I had never made any effort to make Shirley responsible and reliant, though it is what you actually said!' Vera went on to explain that her daughter's untidiness, absentmindedness and reserve about her plans were in the blood, asseverating that she was the living replica of her paternal grandmother. Having described the circumstances that destroyed that particular marriage, she continued, 'If I were to nag and catechise Shirley I should similarly wreck my relationship with her and probably with George, who remembering his mother whom he adored, would bitterly resent it. It is better to risk her being inconsiderate – though I admit that this is sometimes hard on others!'

She ended with a barbed reference to Hillman's niggardly manner. 'When I don't catechise her she usually tells me everything voluntarily; and she is much better when alone at taking care of herself than her apparent harem-scarumness would lead you to suppose.'[8]

For Vera, the return of the children had been a rare light in the darkness as she continued to speak out against the immorality of war. Outraged by the indiscriminate Allied bombing of German civilians and the tone of triumphalist reporting, she vowed to fully expose the horror of the suffering and destruction involved. Her bitter tract *Seed of Chaos: What Mass Bombing Really Means*, published in 1944, attracted little comment in Britain, but in the US, where extracts were printed in a pacifist magazine, it aroused the nation to fury, with the more intemperate critics accusing her of being a Nazi lackey. Given these ferocious assaults on her reputation and the major disruption to home life caused by the renewed intensity of enemy raids on London, Vera's nerves were badly frayed – not the best condition to deal with two feisty teenagers.

This was evident during the harsh winter of 1944–45 when life at Allum Green became unduly fractious as the children engaged each other in an interminable war of words. Brought up to think and express himself freely, John soon found that his mother's devotion gave him a great sense of power over her. This he increasingly used to devastating effect as he grew into a young man. Feeling neglected as a child while Vera concentrated on her writing, and unsympathetic to the causes she espoused, he also felt the burden of parental expectation weigh heavily on his shoulders as he struggled to give full rein to his potential. In the Midwest the strong seeds of unfettered independence and rebellious instincts which he inherited from his mother had been given every opportunity to germinate, although not in a way that gratified the eye of the beholder. In retrospect, Vera felt that the relative comfort of Minnesota had done her son no favours because it permitted him to think only for himself whereas back home he would have more likely imbibed the communal ethos bred by the sufferings of war. Unhappy about leaving the US, John, despite two relatively productive years at Harrow, soon found himself floundering. For, as he later admitted, his compulsive urge to break free from his parents and their values was complicated by the uncertainty of what to believe instead. The fact that he lacked a strong sense of vocation served only to deepen his inhibitions, thereby blighting his relationship with his family. 'I suppose we were the wrong people to have children,' Vera confessed to her husband. 'The only thing now is to share and thus to halve the disciplining we both detest!'[9] With Shirley this had been something her mother had long been dreading even when pining for her during the war, since previous experience had revealed her to be a domineering character 'with a deep core of rigid prejudice which is very difficult to move'. Vera had confided to Ruth Colby,

> At whatever age I get her back, I am sure I shall have a struggle because I feel she will resent both the re-exercise of my authority and the circumstance of returning to a more melancholic and much less comfortable country … like her grandfather she feels herself somewhat entitled to have things to go right for her.[10]

Now in the full flush of adolescence, her self-confidence immeasurably strengthened by her American adventures, Shirley's casual lifestyle and combative demeanour placed her at loggerheads with her highly disciplined mother. 'Her vehement inhibitions are one of my greatest difficulties,' Vera complained after Shirley repeatedly refused to wash her hair. 'She won't take education from us.'[11]

It wasn't all bad news. Shirley was a source of great comfort to her mother after John's black moods and even when tempestuous herself she never said cruel things. What's more, Vera informed George, she, unlike John, really worried about other people and what she could do for them. Although reckoned to be a law unto herself at Talbot Heath, her teachers credited her with a steady improvement over the course of the year and regretted her return to St Paul's. 'Shirley's lively interest in all her work is stimulating and she will attain a really high standard if she can work more neatly,' noted her final report. 'She will develop greater powers of leadership when she gives more thought to the details which go to make a successful whole.'[12]

Shirley was also politically active as war gave way to peace in Europe and a general election loomed. Used to political rallies in the US, she attended a Liberal Party meeting and quizzed its candidate in

Bournemouth about his views on nationalisation. 'Surely this young woman hasn't a vote?' he replied. With Churchill expected to benefit from his victorious war leadership, few anticipated anything other than a Conservative victory, but the party's lukewarm response to the Beveridge Report advocating a programme of universal welfare did it no favours. As the results began to emerge it soon became clear that it had suffered a massive defeat. Once the result was certain the Catlins travelled to Labour's headquarters at Transport House, where Shirley congratulated a jubilant Herbert Morrison, before going on to County Hall to listen to many of the newly elected Labour MPs in London greet the dawn of a new world.

In September Shirley returned to St Paul's, her independent spirit to be sorely tried by a hidebound conformity which outlawed even the most innocent of liaisons with the opposite sex. The one concession to progressivism was the lack of a uniform, an unusual occurrence for a public school, except for a beige 'sack' for games and a curious bowler hat. According to Jennifer Manasseh, a fellow pupil later to become her sister-in-law, Shirley with her healthy tanned face, American denims and trainers, stood out against a background of war-weary faces, brown lisle stockings and sensible shoes. She also recalled another act of individuality. Because of a shortage of books in that austere age it was then the custom for girls at the end of the summer term to purchase books from the year above. Unlike everyone else, Shirley amazed Jennifer by giving hers away free. 'Her generosity of spirit and frequent scrapes and escapades endeared her to all except the teachers.'[13] On one occasion during assembly, with the High Mistress and staff all gathered on the vast stage looking out towards the girls, Shirley caused mayhem by climbing up the long curtain across the front of the big assembly hall and making outlandish gestures behind their backs. As her antics sent the girls into convulsions of laughter the increasingly irate High Mistress remained oblivious as to the source of the distraction from the serious business of the daily homily.

Such misbehaviour often landed Shirley in trouble with the authorities and in a battle of wills with the High Mistress. Miss

Strudwick regarded crying as a sign of remorse after the miscreant had been subjected to a verbal lashing, but Shirley, despite undergoing the full treatment, refused to buckle.

Teaming up with a mischievous group of friends such as Gillian Ayres, later a celebrated abstract artist, and the twins Helen and Margaret Meyer, Shirley was a natural leader, openly intent, according to Gillian, on becoming the first woman Prime Minister. In class she used to be a source of distraction by sending torn-off notes to her friends in her spidery handwriting, complete with drawings and jokes about the teachers. At lunchtime they used to goad the prefects, whose task it was to ensure that all the girls went outside, by repeatedly climbing the wall bars in the gym on to the balcony above, before passing through an adjoining door into the school and walking down the stairs past their bemused superiors. On one particular occasion Helen Meyer (later Green) had reason to be particularly grateful to Shirley for her support. A keen artist, she had been awarded the Senior Art Prize by outside adjudicators, only for the school to overrule their decision in favour of another girl on the grounds that her reputation didn't merit such recognition. So incensed was Shirley by this miscarriage of justice that she made it her business to complain to the authorities, and to good effect as they agreed to make Helen joint winner.

The girls' friendship flourished out of school. They would relax at weekends playing tennis, visiting galleries and getting away with a lot. Gillian remembers Shirley as lively, curious and very nice. 'There was nothing about her to dislike.' On Sunday afternoons the two of them would traipse through the bombed-out streets of the East End to teach art at a children's club owned by the school. It was a tough baptism in community service as the local children were nothing if not rough. They called both of them Blondie, but Shirley and Gillian gave as good as they got in return.

Their enterprise showed in other ways. During the spring of 1947 Shirley organised for the four of them to go on a walking trip to discover the source of the Thames, staying in youth hostels along the way. Later that summer they went cycling in Cornwall, Treve as ever in Shirley's basket, where they swam naked off Land's End and camped in a farmer's barn to escape the relentless rain. As teenagers in a more conformist era, they were given a remarkable degree of freedom by their parents, but there were limits to their indulgence. Helen Meyer recollects the time Shirley rang her up and asked her round to help wash Treve. As Helen was carrying the tin bath down the stairs she tripped and fell, sending water gushing down the stairs. Before she had finished mopping it up a rattled Vera appeared and proceeded to bawl at her for her carelessness. The Colonial Secretary was coming to dinner that evening.

Shirley's eighteen-month absence from St Paul's caused few impediments to her academic progress. This was borne out by her excellent results in her School Certificate, which enabled her to matriculate with six distinctions. Although annoyed by her failure to get a distinction in English Language, she derived consolation from achieving the second best set of results in her year and was the only person to get a distinction in English Literature. Ethel Strudwick wrote to congratulate her and a delighted Vera surmised that Shirley must have worked much harder at school than she appeared to have done at home.

Back at school, a number of the so-called 'brains' in her class were less than chuffed that Shirley had stolen their thunder, while the staff, sensing a potential scholar in their midst, began to take her seriously – attention that she treated with wry detachment. It didn't alter her determination to go the London School of Economics (LSE). She did, however, readily respond to the intellectual ambience of the sixth form and found fulfilment in teachers passionate about their subjects, such as Rosamond Jenkinson, an authority on Chaucer, and Margaret Higginson, a great lover of poetry. In History she greatly enjoyed the classes of Miss Patrick, a peppery Irishwoman, especially her lectures on German Unification, although not the occasion she ridiculed her in front of the class. Presenting her with a hairbrush, Miss Patrick told Shirley to use it. 'It may help your appearance.'

Others spoke in similar vein. 'She must try to realise her responsibilities as one of the senior members of the school and to cure her habit of unpunctuality,' commented her form mistress at the end of her first term in the Lower Sixth when she had reported late on nine occasions.[14] Six months later she wrote that 'Shirley has ability but must not despise the humbler qualities of tidiness and punctuality'.[15]

Shirley's adolescent idiosyncrasies about dress and appearance continued to tax her mother, but the principal cause of dissension appeared to lie deeper. For all her robust independence, she, like her brother, resented the absence of a settled family life and undivided attention once her parents resumed their travels post-war. What's more, she wasn't slow to convey her thoughts. Vera wrote to George in October 1946,

> While you were in Italy, Poppy [her family nickname] inflicted on me several of the usual conversations ... about being 'left to nurses' and the importance of mothers bringing up their children themselves. I wonder if she will ever fully realise that the main question regarding herself was not by whom she was to be brought up, but whether she was to exist at all.[16]

A few months later Vera was beating a similar drum.

> Being alone in the house with Poppy is no sinecure; she wants so much undivided attention, and is resentful if she does not get it. Last night she kept me up till 2 a.m. holding forth in the usual domineering voice on the usual themes – the wickedness of being 'rich', the virtue of being poor, mediocre and obscure; and our failure as parents to provide her with 'home life'– by which she admitted she meant all the members of the family sitting round the fire knitting, talking, and listening to the wireless, instead of getting on with their work. Sometimes I think she genuinely would have preferred Amy as her mother rather than myself. I find such a reversal to type (and to reaction) both depressing and irritating.[17]

Such sentiments were rarely those of George Catlin, possibly because his frequent absences shielded him from the worst of

Shirley's domestic deficiencies, or, more likely, because when present he chose to retreat from the sound of gunfire. Temperamentally closer to his daughter than to either Vera or John, George was her main political and spiritual mentor. When in residence he would take her to church on Sundays and afterwards discuss the lengthy sermons of the formidable parish priest, Mgr Alfonso de Zulueta. Given the choice of religious denomination by her parents, Shirley followed the lead of her father and embraced the tenets of the Roman Catholic Church, much attracted by its internationalism and commitment to social justice. 'Keep to the Socialism of the Right and the Catholicism of the Left', George advised her. 'And be completely sincere in each without veering about to please all men' – advice she has closely followed throughout her life.[18]

While the war had been a gruelling experience for Vera, it had been a frustrating one for George, with little gainful employment coming his way once he returned from the US in 1940. Although no pacifist himself, he was tainted by his wife's activities as he narrowly lost out on a couple of nominations for safe Labour seats. Convinced that there would be no election before the autumn, he set off to San Francisco in April 1945 to report on the conference establishing the United Nations, only to hear of a summer election once he had arrived. For a man desperate to enter Parliament it came as a bitter blow to miss out on the most favourable opportunity yet for a Labour candidate, and such was his consternation that for the next two years he suffered from chronic insomnia. What's more, it once again placed his marriage under strain as he attributed his misfortune to his wife's pacifism. (The two spent as much time apart as they had pre-war.) Although he continued to crave political recognition, George increasingly began to channel his latent ambitions through Shirley, who, he felt, possessed that element of steel in her character which he lacked, to go alongside her intelligence and charm. After he took her with him to the Labour conference at Bournemouth in May 1946 he was unstinting in his praise. He informed Vera that she had left golden impressions with ministers and their wives which would stand her in excellent stead.

When Vera relayed her reservations about Shirley's constant carping he told her to stop worrying. She took her far too seriously. 'I suspect she was merely getting Socialist rhetoric off her chest.' He conceded that she could be inconsiderate and rather too gauche when parading her own views, but reckoned that she was less selfish than most girls. 'I am very pleased with her. The core is very sound indeed,' a view to which he adhered as her stock continued to rise.[19]

Ever since she had become a Labour Party member aged sixteen, Shirley had belonged to the Chelsea Labour Party, a curious mixture of eccentric middle-class idealists and working-class pragmatists. Keen to be the youngest MP, an ambition fully supported by her parents, there were no limits to her dedication, not only in distributing leaflets and attending branch meetings, but also on one occasion queuing for three hours outside Parliament to listen to Ernest Bevin, the Foreign Secretary.

That Easter (1947) she and Vera had been guests at Frating, a 360-acre cooperative farm near Colchester founded in 1943 to cater for conscientious objectors. The invitation had come from the farm manager, Joe Watson, a blast furnaceman from Consett, County Durham, who had migrated south when work had dried up during the Depression. Through the community movement Watson had become acquainted with Vera, one of its patrons. They became good friends and Shirley in turn became entranced by this ex-boxer and Christian socialist, finding that she had much to learn from him. Despite the wintry conditions, she was in her element, shutting up hens, feeding cows and cutting frozen cabbages in the moonlight. She also made a great impression on her fellow workers, one of whom told Vera that he thought her one of the best and most exceptional people that he had met.

As a former Somerville graduate, Vera's desire that her daughter follow in her footsteps was natural enough. She had taken every opportunity to promote this citadel of learning while accepting that Shirley's interest in the LSE, a bastion of left-wing progressivism, was genuine enough.

Vera's regret was only compounded when sent the LSE entrance papers, since she thought them very taxing. She informed George,

> The only point I am trying to make is that she can't count, for certain, on getting into the LSE, and it therefore seems a pity not to try for Somerville. The serious pity would be to miss both. And one has to remember about Somerville that she has the inestimable priority, for these days, of having been registered since she was four; they also want her, whereas the LSE is indifferent.[20]

While Vera remained in Devon, where she was busy writing, George discussed Shirley's future with her, aware that St Paul's felt her too young to sit the Somerville entrance exam. Aside from the fact that she would be flouting school policy by taking the exam a year early without the benefit of having sat the Higher School Certificate, they felt she lacked the care and commitment to do full justice to her potential. Their reservations had little impact as she was firmly resolved to leave school at the end of the following term. The most to which she consented was an attempt at the Somerville entrance exam that year as a dry run for the LSE. In the event of her unexpected success at the entrance exam, her plans to apply for the LSE were consigned to history.

Once apprised of the decision, Vera wrote to Janet Vaughan, the principal of Somerville, and a former contemporary of hers there, to explain the rationale behind Shirley taking the entrance exam while still only seventeen. 'She has always been extremely interested in politics and hopes to enter the House of Commons at an early age. This is not a wild ambition, two Cabinet Ministers are keenly encouraging her…'[21] Having regaled Dr Vaughan with her political activities, Vera told her that Shirley's change of heart about Somerville was partly in deference to her own belief that Oxford would give her vehement and articulate personality a profound quality that she wouldn't get at the LSE.

Shirley performed well enough in the entrance exam to be summoned to Somerville for interview. Suspecting that she was there courtesy of her mother's lobbying on her behalf, she made clear her disapproval of such preferential treatment, but once Dr Vaughan had disabused her of these misconceptions she made a great impression as they discussed politics. Returning home afterwards, she casually mentioned to Vera, 'I think I've got a Schol.' Genuine modesty aside, her greatest pleasure, according to George, was proving the sceptics wrong, since not one of her teachers had given her a ghost of a chance. When they discovered she had become the youngest ever pupil from St Paul's to win a scholarship to Somerville, their reaction was distinctly lukewarm. 'Shirley is apt to annoy people by inconsiderateness in little matters,' wrote Miss Patrick, her form mistress, in her final report, 'but a combination of real ability and intellectual modesty should take her a long way. I am sorry to lose her, and we wish her every success.'[22]

Keen to gain more practical experience of the outside world before going up to Oxford, Shirley decided to return to Frating for a six-month stint and started there in January 1948 as second cowman to a herd of Ayrshire dairy cows. Although the hours were long and conditions arduous, especially when suffering from an excruciatingly painful cut to her leg, the result of an accident with a machine, she found much to enthuse her. Aside from her friendship with the Watsons, Shirley became particularly close to Trevor and Enid Howard, engaging in many a theological discussion with the former, a pacifist who later became an Anglican priest.

At the request of Joe Watson, the Labour agent for Harwich, Shirley helped campaign for the candidate, Morris Janis, but because of her Frating commitments she wasn't able to accompany her father to the Labour conference in Scarborough, much to his indignation. He called the decision quite crazy, especially since her 'playing at farming with a quite unrepresentative group' was 'a waste of time', views that weren't shared by Vera.[23] She reminded him that Shirley was now a registered farm worker and surmised that Herbert Morrison and others would be more impressed by her absence due to regulated land work than by her mere presence.

That May, Shirley was invited along with Tom Deacon, the

secretary of the London Labour League of Youth, to represent the League at the first post-war conference of the German *Jungsozialisten*, the youth wing of the Socialist Party (SDP). They were the first British delegates to attend any youth conference in an official capacity since 1939.

After flying to Frankfurt, the two were driven by a young German driver in a British Control Commission car across a barren landscape of derelict cities reduced to rubble. Their 250-mile journey took nine hours, as the lights of their car failed in a Bavarian village. Arriving in Hof, their destination in the American zone, after midnight, they were deposited at a hostel for American GIs, some of whom had girlfriends who were still teenagers.

The conference of 1,000 German and foreign delegates was opened by Kurt Schumacher, the leader of the SDP, who talked about his hopes for a new socialist Germany. Later, and without warning, Shirley was asked to make an impromptu speech. She rose to the challenge superbly, bringing her audience to its feet with her vision of a new world order. Her words also enthused Tom Deacon, three years her senior. He was unstinting in his praise of her back at Transport House.

Shirley's triumph in Germany was a timely boost for Vera, then grappling with the painful last phase of her mother's life after she had suffered a cerebral thrombosis that April. The time and effort involved in looking after her rekindled in Shirley all her previous resentment about her grandmother. The two of them, while capable of bouts of affection, had never been close, reflecting the generation gap and a difference in values. From earliest times John had always been Edith Brittain's favourite, and now as Shirley grew up into a determined young woman, her grandmother was disconcerted by her tendency to arrive late, dress casually and speak her mind. On one occasion when summoned by Edith to try on a dress made by her crusty housekeeper, Miss Keiley, she simply failed to appear, as George, no admirer of his mother-in-law, gleefully informed Vera.

When apprised of the serious nature of her grandmother's illness, Shirley was chiefly sorry for Vera, knowing how much she, Vera, had done for her mother, especially since the death of her husband in 1935. In response to an appeal from Amy Burnett, she came up from Frating to help out over the weekend of 20 June and a week later she was present during the final stages as her grandmother slowly lost consciousness.

For all their differences in character and the numerous demands her mother had placed upon her, Vera greatly missed her and much appreciated the solace Shirley brought her over the course of the next few weeks. 'Yes, that small girl, I agree is something like pure gold in all the fundamentals,' she wrote to George, 'and for this reason should, I think, receive more consideration than she gets in the small things as well as the great. While you and John are always wanting this room or not she clamours for nothing...'[24]

Having decided to leave Frating earlier than planned to escape the infatuation of a young suitor, Neave Catchpole, son of Vera's good friend Corder, who had proposed to her, Shirley arranged a farming job elsewhere. After a bleak week weeding carrots on Romney Marsh in Kent, she took the night train to Newcastle upon Tyne for further work experience. Receiving little joy from the local Labour Exchange and three farms in Consett, she cycled to Whitley Bay, ten miles from Newcastle, to seek hotel work. Striking lucky with the first one she approached, Shirley signed on at the Cliffe Hotel as a housemaid for 18 shillings a week. It proved an exacting assignment, for not only were the hours long and the food basic, the accommodation, with its cold water and bed, which she shared with another girl, was most spartan. She liked her fellow workers, all teenagers, 'a grand lot of lasses, very friendly and kind', yet for all the mingling their outlook was very different from her own. Most talked solely about canny lads, their recreation amounting to picking up older holidaymakers on the local promenade in pairs. As a free spirit herself, Shirley found it hard to comprehend how most girls were utterly incapable of doing anything alone; more important, she worried about the way they were likely to live such barren lives. 'This is an experience of dreariness and drabness and of the utter boredom to which our lack of Christianity and the principle of profit before people has condemned so many millions of human beings,' she informed her father.

> It is impossible to read and to create in any sphere, and the spirit finds little inspiration in dishes.
>
> I often think that we intellectuals, who so often become leaders sociologically, do not realise our own responsibilities. You and Mummy preach tolerance and considerable freedom in marriage and outside it. Maybe you are right, and such tolerance is desirable, but eventually most people will follow the lead that has been given, without understanding your distinctions or appreciating your reasons. So now here, among ordinary folk, all kinds of aberrations occur, with results which are desperately destructive, no one seeing anything very wrong in going out with a married man, but his wife is devoured and embittered with jealousy.[25]

Shirley returned home to find her father had wangled her a weekly column on a new Indian newspaper, *The Nation*, and some work experience. As a result of his prominent position in the *Nouvelles Equipes Internationales* (NEI), the leading voluntary organisation working for closer European integration, George arranged for her to accompany him to its three-day conference at The Hague in September as a secretary. There she won many new admirers, not least the deputy Speaker of the French Assembly, her only faux pas being to oversleep on the final morning, thereby keeping the departing taxi waiting, much to the displeasure of the Duchess of Atholl, the leader of the British delegation.

Her final assignment that summer gave her the chance to shine on the public stage when responding to a public summons following a complaint from a neighbour about the aggressive demeanour of her dog, Treve, especially his habit of nipping the wheels of children's tricycles. The magistrate advised Shirley that if she felt she had a legitimate case to answer, it would be in her interest to appear herself rather than have an older person appear on her behalf. It was advice that she was more than happy to accept. ('Please see that

both the dog and Poppy's hair are washed before they go to court,'
Vera badgered George.)[26] In a powerful bit of theatre with everyone
staring directly at her, the eighteen-year-old defendant remained
the model of self-possession as she not only gave evidence in a clear,
confident manner but was clinically incisive in her cross-examina-
tion of the plaintiff and the policeman. She called Charlie Burnett
in defence and was about to call her neighbour when the magistrate
suddenly dismissed the case much to everyone's pleasure, not least
the dog's as he waited outside the courthouse with George. The
next day Shirley left for Oxford.

**Endnotes**
1   Quoted in *Testament of Experience*, p.322
2   VB to Ruth Colby, 20 October 1943
3   School report, St Paul's, December 1943
4   Ethel Strudwick to VB, 25 February 1944
5   SW to VB, 27 June 1944
6   SW to Edith Brittain, 12 November 1944
7   School report, Talbot Heath, December 1944
8   VB to Ida Hillman, 29 May 1945
9   VB to GC, 3 January 1945
10  VB to Ruth Colby, 6 January 1941
11  VB to GC, 4 January 1945
12  School report, Talbot Heath, July 1945
13  Jennifer Manasseh (Balfour), 'Testament of Kinship: A Memoir of Vera Brittain',
    October 1995 (private collection)
14  School report, St Paul's, December 1946
15  School report, St Paul's, July 1947
16  VB to GC, 4 October 1946
17  VB to GC, 12 March 1947
18  GC to SW, 2 February 1948
19  GC to VB, 14 June 1946
20  VB to GC, 7 June 1947
21  VB to Janet Vaughan, 21 November 1947
22  School report, St Paul's, December 1947
23  GC to VB, 16 May 1948
24  VB to GC, 27 June 1948
25  SW to GC, undated but probably August 1948
26  VB to GC, 30 September 1948

# 4

## 'THE RED QUEEN'

'Like no sight on earth the first glimpse of the towers from the London train moves me to tears' – Vera's depiction of Oxford as she recalled the central part that it had played in her life and especially its association with those whom she loved most.[1] Not surprisingly, for ambitious parents with high hopes for their children, she and George were keen that their children should follow in their footsteps and receive an educational experience so rich that it would serve as an effective bridgehead for future prominence.

Owing to the special circumstances arising out of the war whereby ex-servicemen in their mid-twenties, many of them from modest backgrounds, constituted the majority of the undergraduate population, this was an exhilarating time to be at Oxford. For, in contrast to the idle decadence of the Brideshead era of the 1920s, this was a generation in a hurry, keen to seize the myriad of opportunities that the university had to offer and leave their mark on the future.

Somerville, founded in 1879, was the oldest and most pioneering of the five women's colleges. Industrious, non-denominational and progressive, its emphasis on intellectual attainment and public service had bred an impressive range of luminaries among its alumni: writers such as Vera, Winifred Holtby and Rose Macaulay and the novelist Dorothy L. Sayers. More recently, two aspiring politicians, Indira Gandhi and Margaret Thatcher, had passed through its doors, and now under the inspirational leadership of Janet Vaughan, a leading haematologist, this commitment to a broad education remained very much intact.

Appointed principal of Somerville in 1945, Dr Vaughan gave her all to the college in addition to continuing her research and raising a young family. Although devoted to all her charges, and much loved in return, she held a special affection for Shirley. From that very first interview they discovered a mutual interest in public service and left-wing politics. When her hectic extracurricular life began to cause havoc with her work Shirley was fortunate to find an understanding principal inclined to show clemency. For much as she liked her undergraduates to get Firsts, Dr Vaughan recognised that it ranked as a lower priority than producing good citizens. Her foresight was to be well rewarded as Shirley lived up to expectation. When, as an elderly woman, Vaughan forsook the loyalties of her lifetime and left Labour to join the SDP it was overwhelmingly out of affection for her former student.

Although life in Somerville conformed to post-war austerity with tasteless food and frozen rooms, the atmosphere in women's colleges had become more liberating compared to the restrictions of the 1920s, with greater opportunity to be in the company of men. It so happened that the 1948 vintage in Somerville contained a particularly interesting mix from a wide range of backgrounds, a number of whom became lifelong friends of Shirley. Leading the field was Val Mitchison, the beautiful, unconventional daughter of the Scottish novelist Naomi Mitchison, an associate of Vera's, whose home at Carradale on the Kintyre peninsula became a favourite haunt over the years. There was also Phyllis Cook, a policeman's daughter from Birmingham, Helge Kitzinger, the daughter of Jewish refugees from Germany, and Ann Chesney, an accomplished debater and chairman of the University Liberal Club. Her recollections of Shirley are of a bright, bubbly person who would mix with everyone provided they were interesting, one of those fortunate people who operated on three parties per day and four hours' sleep per night. 'Yet alongside the easygoing charm, she was in essence very serious-minded with a quaint sort of innocence about her.'

Outside college there was the same breadth of friendships: Hilary Rubinstein, son of Vera's much-loved solicitor Harold and later to marry Helge Kitzinger; Bill Rodgers, a Labour Club stalwart and future Cabinet minister; William Rees-Mogg, the future editor of *The Times*; and Tony Richardson, later a renowned film director. Above all, there were John and Eileen Spencer, highly principled Quakers whose tiny flat in Wellington Square proved a welcome retreat from the hurly-burly of university life. It was there that Shirley met a former officer in the Scots Guards called Robert Runcie. He was the proud holder of the Military Cross, contemplating holy orders, and as he wrestled with his future destiny he engaged in many a theological discussion with her. By the end of her first term he had seen the light. Having taken a First in Greats, Runcie entered theological college, the first step along the road that was to lead to his appointment as Archbishop of Canterbury in 1980.

'Life is heaven and heaven is wonderful' was Shirley's initial verdict of Oxford as she found herself inundated with invitations to tea (then the social highlight as few undergraduates could afford lavish dinners) and drinks in the Union.[2] Drawing on her wide circle of contacts she soon cut a magnetic figure among the university elite, her many admirers captivated by her vitality and charm. When Tony Richardson confessed to being half in love with her, he spoke for many. Primrose Minney, later a journalist with the *Essex Chronicle*, recalled a familiar figure on the Oxford landscape because she was always in the limelight. 'She addressed meetings, wrote articles and acted. And she was everywhere. At every party and first night.'[3] Similarly as she strode briskly down the High Street or rode around on her antiquated bike, she would be accosted by many people, some simply to greet her, others in search of a consoling word as they regaled her with their latest problem. According to Robin Day, the renowned political interviewer, she was the most celebrated female undergraduate of her time, while to Robert Robinson, the well-known broadcaster, she had a great flair for friendship that led everyone to believe that they were her best friend. It was an atmosphere in which Shirley thrived and a talent she deployed to good effect. 'Even then she had this genius for making people do things for her – a sort of sophisticated equivalent of carrying her books home from school,' said one former suitor. 'If you loved Shirley, you were somehow put to work. Little things, mostly, and all done by kindness; she took it for granted that you would comply and you did.'[4] Yet keeping her many admirers happy with her presence was no easy task and inevitably there was consternation when she failed to respond to some invitation or stood someone up at the last minute, but any ruffled feathers were soothed with a fulsome apology, a powerful weapon in her armoury that has enabled her to wriggle out of many a tight corner down the years.

Having gained permission to switch disciplines from History to Politics, Philosophy and Economics, Shirley found that her work, comprising two essays a week (men only had one), invariably took second place to her crowded extracurricular activity. Inevitably an early port of call was the Oxford Labour Club, the largest political club in the university, its ranks swollen by the likes of Denis Healey, Tony Crosland and Roy Jenkins in the years immediately before the war. It so happened that many of the leading lights of Shirley's vintage were reared in the same stable, their intellectual pedigree and social democratic ideals providing a distinctive presence in progressive circles over the coming decades. Numbered among such luminaries was the future bishop Stanley Booth-Clibborn, the journalists Ivan Yates and Michael Shanks, and MPs Bill Rodgers, Dick Taverne, Brian Magee, Shirley Summerskill and Bruce Douglas Mann, all of whom except Summerskill later gravitated from Labour to the SDP.

Part of the kudos of Oxford's political clubs stemmed from their ability to attract leading politicians and public figures. It so happened that Vera, a frequent speaker over the years at the Labour Club, was due to address it during Shirley's first term as part of a programme which included Emanuel Shinwell, Barbara Castle and Douglas Jay. 'If I may say so, I think you would find my daughter Shirley Vivian Brittain Catlin a useful member of the club (she might be useful in finding distinguished speakers for the club),' Vera informed Will Camp, the secretary, weeks before Shirley's arrival. 'Please don't let her know that I have commended her in this way! But she really is a rather unusual girl.'[5] Her letter proved a real fillip to Camp, who told Vera that they needed some talented and industrious female members since at present they had only two. As a handsome and intelligent 23-year-old who had seen service in Palestine, and later gained renown both as a novelist and a public relations specialist, Camp had a certain cachet. When Shirley's inquiries about joining the Labour Club took her to his room in Oriel he impressed her as he read her extracts from his latest novel, *Tell it Not in Gath*. Soon they were good friends, as Vera noted on her visit to Oxford in November. 'He and Poppy seem to have fallen considerably for each other,' she told George. 'She remarked "Will was nervous because he looks on you as a possible future mother-in-law."'[6] Prior to Vera's talk, Shirley felt much agitated over lunch and during it chewed her programme, fearing that her mother would let her down in front of her new friends, but in the event she need not have worried. Vera's aptitude as a platform-speaker once again served her well and her talk generated such interest that the questions were still flowing when the chairman brought proceedings to a halt. Later, in a letter thanking Vera, Camp described Shirley as 'superlatively brilliant' and commented that 'everyone seems to be in love with her'.[7] His views were echoed by Janet Vaughan, who told Vera that Shirley was likely to get engaged long before finishing at Oxford and with Vera's blessing suggested that she, Janet, advise her strongly to resist marriage, much less going down, before she was twenty-one. What Shirley made of such advice isn't recorded, but for all the attention of Camp her affections had fallen on the chairman of the Labour Club, Peter Parker, whom she first set eyes on at the club's first meeting of the term. It so happened that the meeting involving the War Minister, Emanuel Shinwell, was a particularly tempestuous one and Shirley later recalled how Parker seemed to be revelling in the occasion.

From the moment I saw him presiding over the Shinwell meeting, I was bewitched; it was truly a *coup de foudre*, something I would earlier have denied was possible. I tried to think of ways to meet him, without becoming obsequious. We did meet again, when he was judging auditions for parts in Experimental Theatre Club plays and I was one of those participating.[8]

The son of an engineer, Peter Parker was brought up in France and China. On his family's return to England, he was educated at Bedford School, excelling in all sports as well as displaying a flair for oriental languages and acting. Leaving school in 1942, he joined the army and was promoted to Major in the Intelligence Corps by the age of twenty-two, but this success was more than offset by the loss of both of his brothers in the war. Their early deaths drove him to fulfil their dreams as well as his own. Demobilised in 1947, Parker headed for Oxford, becoming president of the Lincoln Junior Common Room and captain of its rugby XV, besides playing a leading role in university drama, politics and poetry. In November 1948 he was featured as the 'Isis Idol', the weekly profile of a leading figure in the university. Having paid tribute to his magnetic character and his many accomplishments, it concluded by calling him 'a considerable man ... liable to end up a great one'.[9]

'In every way he had been a star,' wrote Bill Rodgers. 'He was a man of effervescent and restless charm, with an instant capacity to make you feel that no-one in the world mattered to him more than you. In this he had much in common with Shirley, and he matched her in his energy.'[10] When they came across each other in theatrical and political circles a strong mutual attraction soon developed. Parker later recounted, 'She had a beauty, a radiant energy in her: shining blond hair ... and she had a speed and concentration of thought and expression that made her enchanting company and a fine public speaker ... I fell for this self-propelled, enchanting, tough-minded, husky-voiced politician.'[11]

With their mutual talent for debating, politics and the theatre, they quickly became Oxford's most glittering couple. He taught her to dance and invited her to stay in Bedford, while she nursed him with devotion when he tore his cartilage 'We reflect each other's moods fairly faithfully,' Shirley informed her mother. 'Did Daddy tell you how the Rector of Lincoln eulogised the guy when he asked him whether he'd heard about Peter … Dad is beginning to think this is a bit more possible than he thought. He'd better. It is.'[12]

This was bad news for George because he never cared for Peter, believing him to be too egocentric for his daughter and concerned that an early marriage might derail her political prospects. ('I should never forgive myself if she married the wrong man because I had not taken the trouble to introduce her to the right one,' he had confided to Vera before Shirley went up to Oxford.)[13] He wasn't amused either to hear Vera say 'It's Roland's voice', recalling her lost love of the First World War, when Peter rang Shirley at home. Vera, on the other hand, empathised with his loss of two brothers during the war and on acquaintance became ever more attached to him. Her partiality won support from John, who was reading Psychology at New College. He told her that he rated him as highly as anyone that he had met at Oxford.

From the outset Shirley had taken it upon herself to start a campaign to get women elected to the Oxford Union, the private debating society founded in 1823 and renowned the world over as a reputable training ground for aspiring politicians. She received staunch support from Michael Summerskill, chairman of the Labour Club, and son of the Labour minister Dr Edith Summerskill, as together they aired their views in *Isis*.

> This is a University where there is much lip-service to freedom of thought, speech and opportunity. It is scarcely consistent with this that one section of Oxford's population be debarred, by its sex alone, from the activities of Oxford's most famous society – debarred, in effect, not just from a private club but from full participation in University life.[14]

Their polemic induced a fierce reaction. 'Miss Catlin's demand for a change in the rules of a society of which she is not a member savours of the impertinent,' complained one reader.[15]

'It was to be my first, and not my last, encounter with what today would be called institutional sexism,' Shirley recalled, although in truth the elaborate formality of the Union wasn't to her taste.[16] After participating in one of its debates many years later in 1980, she wrote disparagingly of 'childish upper-class undergraduates in evening dress. What a hopelessly ... elite place Oxford is.'[17] More her scene was the women's debating society that she and Ann Chesney founded. She also spoke with William Rees-Mogg at the Newman Society, the university's oldest Roman Catholic institution, and helped launch the Somerville–Lincoln discussion group on topical affairs.

Inheriting from her mother a mastery of words, Shirley was a natural performer on a platform and on the stage. In addition to her empathy with an audience and eager flow of language, she had as her greatest asset a beautiful husky voice. Leaning upon the expertise of the actress Sybil Thorndike, a family friend, she learnt to project it so, like any accomplished actress, she could reach the back of a large hall without having to raise it. This in turn helped her to evoke atmosphere, combining lucidity and logic with a burning sincerity that appealed to people's better instincts. According to Margaret Higginson, her English teacher at St Paul's, she had a flair for winning the attention of the most difficult of audiences. 'She is the only speaker I have ever known to capture the interest of an audience of East End club girls and maintain it for an hour, a feat which from long experience I should have considered impossible had I not seen it done!'[18] Although Shirley held strong views, Higginson admired her respect for the views of others and her refusal to resort to personal invective or superficial judgement.

By her final term at school she had become chairman of Debates and already a speaker for the Labour Party. The way was thus clear for her to let loose her eloquence on Oxford. According to Dick Taverne, sometime chairman of the Labour Club, her voice and extraordinary gift for persuasiveness in argument combined with her charismatic personality left an immediate mark. He felt she would have been a natural president of the Union had her gender permitted it. Instead she gravitated towards the theatre.

Shirley's foray into Oxford theatre coincided with its golden age, such was the profusion of talent on display: Kenneth Tynan, Robert Robinson, Tony Richardson, Ronald Eyre, Peter Dews, Jack May, William Gaskill and John Schlesinger all launched their various careers at the university. Theatre life was dominated by the well-established Oxford Union Dramatic Society (OUDS), which for two decades had flourished under the benign leadership of Neville Coghill, a distinguished English don much idolised by his charges. In addition to OUDS there was the Experimental Theatre Club (ETC), founded in 1936 to produce modern, unconventional plays and revues, giving those of lesser experience the opportunity to shine.

It was into this sophisticated world that Shirley stepped very soon after her arrival, appearing in such plays as *Tom Thumb, Sing Out the Night* and scenes from Dryden's *Marriage A-La-Mode* directed by William Gaskill.

During her second year she transferred from the ETC to OUDS and featured in Pembroke College's *A Phoenix Too Frequent*. The critics were won over. 'There remains Miss Shirley Catlin and the memory of her Dynamene gives both the play and production the bewitching benefit of any doubt we may have had,' commented David William, later an eminent director, in *Isis*.[19] Her acting caused some ructions with her father, who felt that the theatre was an unwelcome distraction from higher things.

Shirley reproached him,

This disapproval really annoys me a bit. I fail to see why I shouldn't try out what talents I have in the sunny air of Oxford when I shall never have another chance. To become eaten up by single-track ambition at 19 seems to me a little unpleasant, to put it mildly ... After two years of Oxford I venture into five days of acting (after God knows five terms of politics and two of *Isis*) and get told that Oxford isn't a theatrical playground. Damn it![20]

This wasn't the end of her thespian activity. That May she appeared as Abstinence in *The Castle of Perseverance*, alongside Jack May,

Robert Robinson and John Schlesinger. She also auditioned for a production of *King Lear* which was to tour the US that summer and was pleasantly surprised to be cast in the leading role of Cordelia, becoming alongside Josée Richard the first Oxford women to participate in a tour of this type.

The company, calling themselves the Oxford Players but consisting mainly of OUDS members and sponsored by the society, were touring as guests of the American National Theatre Association. Before they departed they performed in Oxford and at the Fortune Theatre off Drury Lane in the West End under the direction of Tony Richardson, who in the event was unable to accompany his cast to America. He was replaced by David William.

The cast of *Lear* was a strong one with Peter Parker as the King, Ronald Eyre as the Fool, Peter Dews as Gloucester and smaller roles for Robert Robinson and John Schlesinger. According to Roger Lancelyn Green, the well-known children's writer and Oxford academic, attending a pre-tour rehearsal, Parker's Lear exhibited a towering majesty from the moment he came on stage, while Shirley's Cordelia was the most authentic he had ever seen, 'attractive, sympathetic, but possessed with the family temper'.[21]

The America to which Shirley returned was much more troubled and fractious than the confident place in which she had grown up during the war. The anti-Communist backlash engendered by post-war Soviet aggression had been lent some substance by the subversive activities of a few government employees. On top of this came the outbreak of the Korean War the next year following the invasion of South Korea by Communist North Korea.

With the US embroiled in one of its most pernicious witch-hunts, led by Joseph McCarthy, the unscrupulous Republican senator from Wisconsin, it was an inopportune time to be visiting. The twenty-strong troupe arrived to a surly reception in New York after thirty-two hours of travelling to begin their demanding schedule of nine states, fifteen venues and twenty-two performances in six weeks of oppressive heat. With money tight, this was very much culture on the cheap as they covered great distances in their battered convertible and station wagon to distant outposts of the Shakespearian universe. Their first port of call was Valparaiso, Indiana, a small university town which conformed to the Midwest model of white frame houses, neatly kept lawns and shady sidewalks. Shirley found that its audience of 200 at the Lutheran College lacked sophistication but they were sympathetic, as were their more intelligent counterparts at Ann Arbor. Less appealing to her were their counterparts at the University of Illinois in Purdue, the 'most incredible crowd of hicks and clots who seem to find much of this play very funny'.[22] Overall, she found American audiences to be less sophisticated than Oxford ones, especially in the way they identified with a particular character, so that Cordelia attracted an enthusiastic following in a way that Goneril or Regan didn't.

Away from the applause, Shirley was profoundly perturbed by the gung-ho mentality of her hosts towards the Korean War, where US troops constituted the bulk of the UN force sent to defend the pro-Western South Korea. 'America, Oh America has let me down this time. The same kindness, the same energy, but the incredible unthinkingness, lack of imagination, unbelievable overconfidence and almost complete stupidity.' Decrying the country's narrow provincialism, she reported that even those sympathetic to the Labour Party seemed intent on war, supremely confident in their sense of predestined victory. 'And my heart sickens in me. I no longer feel that I will not avoid my own *Testament of Youth*.'[23]

From Chicago, an exciting city, the troupe travelled to Oxford, Ohio, and then to Boston, before heading back down the east coast. Amidst the receptions and broadcasts, one of which featured Shirley comparing the political situation in Britain to that of the US, she and Josée Richard assumed responsibility for washing the players' costumes from the young wardrobe mistress, who had collapsed in the wake of a doomed love affair. These additional responsibilities at the end of a long drive of anything up to 500 miles in a jolting old wagon caused her to flag. What kept her going was the adrenalin of performing to appreciative audiences and the consistently favourable reviews that *Lear* received, with Peter being compared to the best on Broadway.

With New York in the grip of tension the troupe discovered that its departure would be subject to interminable delays as its plane had been commandeered for the airlifts in Korea. With finances running low, the majority had to make do with cheap, uncomfortable accommodation, but fortunately for Shirley, Peter whisked her off to friends of his in Connecticut for a lingering farewell prior to his taking up a year's industrial fellowship at Cornell and Harvard.

Shirley's success in the US was a fitting finale to her thespian career, as her final year was dedicated entirely to politics and academia. She had arrived at Oxford a model social democrat fully supportive of the Attlee government and its mission to change Britain. Much of this was down to the influence of her parents with their sympathy for the underdog, allied to the progressive ethos of the Farmer–Labor Party in Minnesota.

Yet for all the political grounding that she received at home, Shirley had a mind of her own, so that while sympathetic to her mother's pacifism and feminism she was neither a pacifist nor an active feminist herself. She also adopted a more uncompromising line on private education, inherited wealth (Vera was constantly having to dissuade her from disinheriting herself) and the eradication of poverty. What primarily drove her crusade against the latter was her exposure to some of life's darker corners, unusual for a child of her class. There was her exceptional closeness to the Burnett family from which she gained a poignant insight into the hazards of working-class life; there were also her two terms at Christ Church Elementary, her five months as a farm labourer and her brief stint as a waitress in Whitley Bay. All this was in contrast to the open informality of Minnesota where class prejudice seemed minimal and opportunities much greater. By the time she went to Oxford, Shirley was well able to make friends who transcended religion, nation and class, a characteristic that has remained a feature of her life.

From her first day she became absorbed in the Labour Club, contributing to its magazine, the *Clarion*, before her appointment as its editor. Keen to expand the club's membership, she was bitterly disappointed to have missed being elected club secretary by four votes, not least because a number of her friends 'forgot' to vote, so sure were they that she would win.

In the summer of 1949 she and Val Mitchison embarked on a two-month tour of Europe as they headed for Klagenfurt in Carinthia for an International Camp of Socialist Students, hitch-hiking through West Germany on the way. The camp was at a picturesque spot close to a lake, but the atmosphere failed to match the splendour of the location. The heavy-handed Teutonic organisation, the loud-speakers blaring out rasping music and the ideological brainwashing weren't conducive to genuine socialist camaraderie, although they met up with George Thomson, later a leading Labour Europhile, and his personable wife Grace. What they did appreciate was the generosity of the local British Army officers stationed in Austria under the occupation, not least their friends Michael Summerskill and David Lane, the latter later High Commissioner in Trinidad and Tobago and Ambassador to the Holy See. They gave the girls pints of wine in Austrian Bierkellers and supplied them with dinars for their trip into Yugoslavia.

There they found a country in liege to its charismatic leader, Tito, whose portrait was omnipresent. They stayed in the one hotel in Bled, which was pleasant, but with food strictly limited and money tight they were forced to live on a meagre diet of black bread, strawberry jam and sardines smuggled in from Austria.

In February 1950 the Labour government sought re-election and Shirley, despite her multifarious commitments at Oxford, rallied to the cause. Having given a good account of herself in a Union-organised debate against the Conservatives, she was part of a Labour Club contingent which canvassed in Devon and Cornwall. Her efforts, which included addressing several large rallies, weren't enough to get her friend Pat Duffy elected in Tiverton. As she and Ann Chesney listened to the results throughout the night with Robin Day in St Edmund Hall, Shirley was disappointed by Labour's overall performance. Its achievement in creating the universal welfare state had been a formidable one, but the cost in terms of higher taxes and regulation had alienated many. With the Conservatives a much more credible force than they had been in 1945, Labour's vast majority had all but evaporated. Governing in future would be a fraught business.

As the Labour Club began to lose some of its post-war lustre, Shirley, the secretary for the Trinity term, was prevailed upon to stand as chairman for the Michaelmas one. Her opponent was, she wrote, 'a hell of a nice guy called Ivan Yates, ex-Treasurer and present Canvassing Officer – dry, humorous and ironic. I don't mind too much who wins, I think he'd be good. At least half my motive is breaking the old tradition of no woman Chairman', as she thought it high time the Labour Club elected a woman to that post.[24] Proposed by Dick Taverne, she duly won by sixty-one votes to forty-seven, a victory which placated her feminine sensitivities. 'But dear me the work this vac. I wonder if and whether I'll ever get a degree.'[25]

Shirley's term as chairman was a busy one, with Hugh Dalton, Edith Summerskill, Emanuel Shinwell, Dick Crossman, Victor Gollancz of the Left Book Club and Jim Callaghan heading the list of speakers. Callaghan always recalled being met off the train by this dynamic young woman with sparkling blue eyes, while Shirley thought him very handsome and approachable as she made toast for him on her gas fire in her room in Somerville. It was the beginning of an enduring friendship. Helping her to run the Labour Club in his capacity as treasurer was her friend Bill Rodgers, a shrewd northerner from Liverpool whose blunt, uncompromising outlook was rather different from her own, a fact that rather coloured their relationship over a lifetime together in politics. Although in awe of her stellar qualities, most notably her friendliness, her mental agility and her prowess as a speaker, Rodgers also noted her intense ambition and 'a vague element of sometimes straying from the whole truth which she would probably justify as a desire not to hurt anybody'. Displaying her great persuasive powers, she would get him to take unpopular decisions on her behalf, something he fell prey to thereafter, 'but too little was ever at stake for a serious row'.[26] He also thought that there were inconsistencies in her convictions – between her Roman Catholicism and her intellectual integrity, between her comfortable prosperous background and a desire to be 'one of the people'. He recalled the occasion she was reluctant to tell him she was flying to Rome when he was hitch-hiking. 'She has had few crises in her life I imagine. But one day she will have to face such issues. Perhaps it is only natural that she should want to postpone that day, and in any case she is still quite young.'[27]

Throughout her first two years the sheer range and depth of her extracurricular life had often been at the expense of her work so that essays were often rattled off in the small hours to meet some looming deadline. Already during her second year there had been mutterings about withdrawing her scholarship, and by the time that Shirley returned from the US the backlog was so great that she worked with real intensity during the rest of the vacation. It was enough to unnerve her mother. She wrote to Margaret Hall, Shirley's glamorous economics tutor and a person she held in high esteem, to seek help. Freely confessing to having little influence over Shirley's habits, Vera asked Hall whether she could try and persuade her to go to bed really early say one night in three. 'She is terribly handicapped by her popularity,' she continued, 'and very much at the mercy of her friends. There are about 300 of them, both boys and girls; each thinks that he or she is the only one, and persuades Shirley that it is her moral duty to spend just one day in each year with him or her!'[28] In reply, Hall expressed concern at her haggard appearance. 'All through last year, as a matter of fact, she gave the impression in tutorials of having had far too little sleep.' She had mentioned this to her and had tried to persuade her that real enjoyment and success would only come if she felt fresh,

> but it is awfully difficult to do anything about it … She is a perfectly delightful person and able and I have only been afraid that she would be so disappointed (and it would be so unsuitable)

if she got a third or lower. I hope I have not seemed to be too
brutal in pointing this out to her.[29]

The situation was deemed so serious that there was once again talk
of her scholarship of £30 per year being withdrawn, and it needed
Hall's intercession on her behalf before the college authorities to
save her that embarrassment. Not that that proved a great consolation to Shirley in the short term as she continued to grapple with
the backlog, especially in philosophy, 'this cold mechanical little
subject'. Gradually, however, the wheels began to turn and within
weeks of her final year the improvement was self-evident. 'I'm
beginning to entertain hopes of a good degree', she intimated to
Vera, 'but this hangs on a thread.'[30]

That Christmas Shirley accompanied her father to Rome to
celebrate the final festivities of the Holy Year. They stayed at the
Grand Hotel and had a wonderful time, having perfect seats at St
Peter's for the Christmas Midnight Mass. On their final day, after
visiting the Sistine Chapel, they had a special audience with Pope
Pius XII, who asked Shirley, dressed in a veil, about Oxford.

Back in Oxford, she continued to struggle with the amount of
work, especially philosophy, but was now working at full throttle
'and that's all I can do'. Her good intentions continued throughout
the rest of her time, although she thought it 'quite absurd to be
doing Schools [final examinations at Oxford] when the world may
only hold together for another year or two'.[31] 'I don't do anything
else but work ... Bar accidents I will get a second, I think, but not
more' was her verdict in May. 'It isn't that easy to work since none of
my particular friends seem to give a damn for their results.'[32] In her
efforts to overcome her problems with philosophy she enlisted the
help of her Balliol friends Bernard Williams and Tom Sebestyen,
the latter the son of Jewish refugees from Hungary. Their tutorials
proved enlightening and helped her to gain a creditable Second.
Even better than this was her success in winning a Smith-Mundt
Scholarship to study Economics and American Trade Unions at
Columbia University, New York, and a Fulbright Travel Scholarship.

She was due to begin that September, but managed to persuade the American embassy to postpone her study to January so that she could participate in the forthcoming general election.

For all the turgidity of Shirley's final two terms, not helped by the absence of Peter, Oxford had been everything that Vera had promised it would be. It had thrown up many opportunities, given her countless friends and enhanced her reputation in many different fields. In turn she had so beguiled and adorned it with her presence that prophecies of future greatness became something of a Greek chorus. 'I can't see exactly where she will fit in in the Labour Movement,' Bill Rodgers confided to his diary, 'and I doubt whether her success will be as quick and remarkable as it has been here ... But she is a rare character and I can't believe that she will fail to make her mark.'[33]

**Endnotes**

1   VB to GC, 20 March 1952
2   SW to VB, undated but sometime in October 1948
3   *Essex Chronicle*, 19 December 1952
4   *Guardian*, 4 November 1978
5   VB to Will Camp, 28 August 1948
6   VB to GC, 6 November 1948
7   Will Camp to VB, 9 November 1948
8   *Climbing the Bookshelves*, p.82
9   *Isis*, 17 November 1948
10  Bill Rodgers, *Fourth Among Equals*, Politico's, 2000, p.177
11  *For Starters*, p.58
12  SW to VB, June 1949
13  GC to VB, 24 July 1948
14  *Isis*, 16 February 1949
15  *Isis*, 23 February 1949
16  *Climbing the Bookshelves*, p.83
17  SW diary, 3 June 1980, SW Papers (private collection)
18  Margaret Higginson, reference for SW, December 1951
19  *Isis*, 8 February 1950
20  SW to GC, undated but probably February 1950
21  Cited in Humphrey Carpenter, *OUDS: A Centenary of the Oxford University Dramatic Society*, Oxford University Press, 1985, p.168
22  SW to VB, 2 August 1950
23  SW to VB, 12 August 1950
24  SW to VB, undated but likely early June 1950
25  SW to VB, undated but likely early June 1950
26  Bill Rodgers, *Fourth Among Equals*, p.32

27  Bill Rodgers diary, 12 June 1951
28  VB to Margaret Hall, 6 October 1950
29  Margaret Hall to VB, 7 October 1950
30  SW to VB, 7 November 1950
31  SW to VB, 5 February 1951
32  SW to VB, 1 May 1951
33  Bill Rodgers diary, 12 June 1951

# 5

# THE YOUNG CAMPAIGNER

On 17 July 1951 Shirley returned home from Oxford, telling her father that coming down marked the end of her childhood. Days later she lunched with Herbert Morrison, who asked her whether she would be his private secretary. When she declined, explaining that she didn't want to become anyone's private secretary, he said, 'Ah my dear, you always hold me at arm's length.'[1] After a successful twenty-first birthday party for fifty of her friends she left for a La Jeunesse de NEI conference in Luxembourg to discuss the unity of Europe, only to find that such a concept was still very problematic for Catholic intellectuals on the Continent. Nevertheless, her colleagues proved open-minded to new ideas as they strove to find a peaceful alternative to Communism. She returned buoyed by the experience, not least the evenings spent in nightclubs, dancing with one and all. After a brief holiday in Ireland with Vera, she repaired to Scotland with the new man in her life.

Roger Bannister, a Unitarian from modest roots in Harrow, had gone up to Oxford in 1946 to read Medicine, the first member of his family to go to university. Earnest, upright and relentlessly focused, the commitment he showed to his studies was matched by his phenomenal prowess as an athlete, which, in time, saw him become the first person ever to run the mile in less than four minutes. Accompanying his singular personality was a genuine modesty and charm, 'the epitome of the understated hero', as the historian Peter Hennessy has called him.[2] 'Probably the secret of his popularity and his ability to get the best out of people,' opined *Isis*, 'is his sincere interest in them.'[3]

When Roger met Shirley that June he was wrestling with the

consequences of an unofficial engagement to an American girl, while Shirley was facing up to a possible life without Peter as his year at Cornell drew to its close. Although there were those like Norman Painting who felt that the basic chemistry between them had been wrong on the OUDS tour the previous year – he recalled sharing one nocturnal heart-to-heart confessional with Shirley about the travails in their respective relationships – there is no doubt that Shirley, whatever her reservations about Peter's roving eye, continued to be devoted to him. She told her parents that she was 'as happy as a lark' with him in the US, where playing opposite him had been a true partnership of equals since neither had tried to outdo the other in the accolades that came their way. Returning home without him wasn't easy and she waited in anticipation for his news. At first the letters were frequent, but then began to dry up, reigniting fears that she could lose him. 'Peter juggles with too many things, too many people to be nice to,' she mused. 'Charm is his bank account on which he draws perpetual cheques. And one resents it and sees through it.'[4] Her anxiety deepened over Christmas when Vera thought her unusually tired and depressed, and for good reason, because Peter's life had indeed taken an unexpected twist. Gillian (Jill) Rowe-Dutton, a glamorous medical student at St Anne's, ex-fiancée of Kenneth Tynan's and Shirley's rival for Peter's affection at Oxford, had called him out of the blue in the late autumn to say that she was on an obstetrics research fellowship at a New York hospital. Despite the distance between New York and Cornell, they spent much time together and soon realised that they were fated for each other.

While awaiting developments on the other side of the Atlantic, Shirley had accompanied Roger to the Amateur Athletics Association dance that June, the evening after he had triumphed in the mile race. With him wilting under the unremitting publicity that his success on the track had prompted and her grateful for his support in Peter's absence, they sought solace in each other's company in the empty expanses of the Scottish Highlands. Sharing a mutual interest in mountaineering and the great outdoors they hiked in the

Trossachs before staying with the Mitchisons at Carradale. There, in that enchanting setting, they climbed and swam and Roger would run along the long white sands. He returned thoroughly refreshed and increasingly attached to Shirley. She in turn wrote to Peter to inform him about Roger although adamant that he, Peter, was still foremost in her affections. In his reply, Peter told her that although he was very fond of her he didn't love her. (Later, in his memoirs, he wrote, 'We loved each other happily and a bit desperately, as if in our hearts we knew we would run out of time and lose one another in our rush of ambitions. Which is what happened really.')[5] His words had a deafening sense of finality about them, for when Shirley rang up his home the following month to find out when he was due home from the US, she discovered that not only was he back already but also engaged to Jill, with the wedding due to take place that December. The news came as a shattering blow and although she reacted to it with dignified fortitude the pain lingered. Writing to a friend from the US, she admitted that Peter 'still lives in the shadows of my room and echoes somewhere in my heart though I try not to listen',[6] while two years later her father wrote that 'Poppy never recovered from the Peter Parker tragedy'.[7]

Shirley's loss coincided with the decision of the Prime Minister to hold a further election as Labour attempted to break out of the stranglehold of its minuscule majority, which had made governing an increasing difficult business. With the party still reeling from the ramifications of the Korean War and the resignation of Aneurin Bevan over prescription charges for dental care and spectacles, the circumstances hardly seemed propitious for a pro-government swing. Yet with its core vote remaining rock solid in support, a close battle once again loomed.

The distress over Peter caused Shirley a temporary loss of interest in politics. Her indifference concerned Vera enough to ask George to contact Transport House to secure her a number of speaking engagements for the election. She need not have worried. On 5 October Shirley was asked to become the Labour agent in Chelsea, the youngest in the country, and for the next three weeks she worked eighteen hours a day for Fred Tonge, a genial Paddington booking clerk, in his battle against the Conservative, Commander Alan Noble. With the Conservatives enjoying a small swing in their favour that eventually enabled them to return to government with an overall majority of seventeen, there was never going to be a major upset in Chelsea, but Shirley's selfless efforts in pursuit of a hopeless cause didn't go unnoticed. 'Your warm and lively personality made a deep impression on all who came into contact with you,' wrote Jack Briskman, the secretary of the local party. 'We also appreciate your act of extreme generosity in donating to the Party a substantial part of your salary.'[8]

The election over, Shirley tried to get work in a factory, but with nothing immediately forthcoming, and with little opportunity to see her Oxford friends, Roger aside, she wondered whether the pursuit of a glittering career had come at too high a price. Eventually she found employment as an operative at a tin-printing works in Chiswick.

On 22 January 1952 she set off for the US. Accompanied by her parents and the Burnetts, she boarded the train at Waterloo utterly deflated, the most depressed her father had ever seen her, as there was no sign of Roger. He had been unavoidably delayed on his suburban train and despite sprinting through the station on to the platform, scattering people in all directions as he went, he arrived just as her train was vanishing around the bend. There was more heartbreak at Southampton when Vera, dejected about the thought of losing Shirley for a year, bade her a tearful farewell. Their relationship, somewhat fraught in adolescence, had blossomed once Shirley had gone to Oxford and shown her mother the affection Vera always craved.

One reason why I love you so much is that, as an adult, you largely share my adult convictions; the belief that what matters most is to leave behind a slightly better world for the weak and the oppressed – the victims of war, cruelty, of exploitation and racial intolerance. But with these convictions you combine, dear child, far more gaiety and social charm that I have ever had ...

But even in the adventures don't forget that your life is meant for use and not to be thrown pointlessly away. So take reasonable care of yourself my love![9]

Though embarrassed as a Socialist to be travelling cabin class rather than tourist class, Shirley was at least able to compensate for a generally dull voyage by eating well and experiencing genial company. She was met by Ruth Burdick, an associate of George's at Cornell, in a snowstorm and taken to Zelma Brandt's, Ruth Colby's literary agent, where she stayed until term began. Not short of contacts, she was able to re-establish links with Mannie Putnam, who introduced her to a wide circle of her friends, but none of this could compensate for the company of a girlfriend that she could trust and a man she could love. Above all, in the 'asphalt jungle' of New York she longed for the sound of wind in branches, and the smell of grass after rain 'as makes me sick for England'.

Founded in 1754 as a private university, Columbia was New York's oldest institution of higher learning and one of the eight Ivy League universities, although its compact urban campus in north-west Manhattan was far removed from the neo-classical elegance and cloistered tranquillity of Harvard or Princeton. Having established itself as the US's leading research university with a reputation for brilliant teaching, Columbia had become a mecca for students and scholars the world over.

International House, situated in the district of Morningside Heights with its vistas overlooking the Hudson River, was a self-contained residential centre catering mainly for overseas students attending educational institutions in New York. Unlike many students who stuck to their own nationality, Shirley mixed with all types. One who became a close friend was Guido Declerq, a Catholic intellectual from a small Flemish village in Belgium; another was Leontyne Price, the neophyte African-American soprano from Mississippi en route to operatic greatness, who treated her to Gershwin's *Porgy and Bess* as they sang arias to each other in the showers.

As with her visit in 1950, this was an inauspicious time for Shirley to be visiting the US, as the McCarthyite purge against anyone deemed to be ideologically suspect continued apace. It was into this climate of suspicion and mistrust that she stumbled in one of her very first seminars when she confronted Marvin Lee, an ex-Korean soldier with fervent left-wing sympathies, in front of the rest of her startled classmates. Her reference to his Marxist views didn't impress the tutor, who later told her in no uncertain terms to be more guarded in her comments since in that combustible atmosphere people's careers were at stake.

Shirley's faux pas didn't impede her progress. Her professor liked her first paper and within a few weeks had invited her to the faculty seminar on labor, one of the recognisable advisory bodies to the government on the subject. She was the first ever student to contribute to it, and later a member as opposed to a visitor. At the end of the spring seminar she was awarded a B+ for her work on Trade Unions as Political Structures and an A- on Economic Research. She also found doors opening to her elsewhere as her status at union conferences was construed as that of a Labour Party delegate, helped by a letter of introduction from Herbert Morrison, rather than a student. At a Labor Education Association conference at Philadelphia in March she was introduced by the chairman as a rising star in English politics, an accolade which earned her a free lunch. In Washington, 'relentlessly beautiful after New York', she conducted a host of trade union interviews and was offered a couple of jobs, but she declined, partly because she disliked the harshness and brutality of American political life.

In Cleveland, Ohio, 'a raw, dirty industrial town', her words at the Autoworkers Conference were rousing enough to win her further invitations to speak and she appreciated the genuine warmth of her hosts when out socialising in the city's bars, especially their lack of condescension towards a young female companion. After spending Easter at Harvard, 'a solid looking university, not as lovely and gracious as Princeton', visiting her old Oxford friend Rodney Donald, then studying at its business school, Shirley returned to Columbia.

New York she considered a big disappointment; the wealth of the Catholic Church in America offended her and 'the sheer effort of remembering to be polite to so many people over here is exhausting without really profound love for anyone'.[10] She skipped part of a class to support a strike of university cafeteria workers in their quest for higher wages, much to the delight of her tutor, who commended her on her return. She also found that International House, while lacking the intellectual dynamism of Oxford, had become more fulfilling, not least a concert there comprising the music and language of all tongues which 'gave her again the feeling of one world and one humanity'. She joined a newly formed dramatic society and an Asian-European political group composed of people involved in politics in their respective countries. After the final House Sunday supper of the semester and a midnight ride on the bumper cars at New Jersey's funfair, she repaired to a bar for a discussion on God, man and each other with a brilliant Hindu and an American Jew of sterling integrity. 'The combination is electric and satisfying.'[11]

At the end of May Shirley decided to visit Cornell University out of curiosity, especially given its links with her family and Peter. She kept her visit to herself, but no sooner had she arrived than a car drew up beside her and a voice cried out, 'Shirley Catlin, I'm darned.' It turned out to be a young couple she had known at Oxford who were now attached to Cornell. They immediately took her under their wing and provided her with a memorable weekend that included a party in her honour and consecutive nights of late-night dancing with the same partner. His name was Wally Wohlking, a tall, gentle merchant seaman turned academic teaching Industrial and Labour Relations at Cornell. Although unwilling to be drawn into anything too serious, Shirley had won yet another ardent admirer because hardly had she returned to New York than he turned up for a week's walking and swimming. Doubtlessly he would have stayed longer had she not committed herself to a summer of travel. Her companions for the first part were Rodney Donald and Guido Declerq. Between them they raised the money to buy a small, elderly Mercury car and headed off south.

After the squalor of the 'somewhat miserable' Mid-Deep South, they revelled in the gaiety and grace of New Orleans 'in its gentle green decay'. They stayed in the Vieux Carré, with its lazy ironwork balconies, listening to Dixie jazz bands before branching out west through Houston and the parched wastes of Central Texas and El Paso. Then it was on via the open spaces of New Mexico, Nevada and California to the magnificent metropolis of San Francisco, its spectacular harbour nestling in the hills adjoining the mighty Pacific.

Going their separate ways from there, Shirley now devoted much of her time to her research project on American trade unions. She headed up the rocky Pacific coast through the redwoods of north California and the pines of Oregon to the capital, Portland. After unavailing efforts in Seattle to meet up with Dave Beck, the noto-riously pungent boss of the Teamsters union, the most powerful single union in the US, she made for St Paul, Minnesota, her first visit since she had left nine years earlier. Staying with Woodard Colby, now separated from Ruth, who was living in New York, she was warmly embraced by old friends. Most of them were now married to successful businessmen and those that weren't were growing impatient aged twenty-three. As she sampled once again the leisurely calm of that distant part of the US and featured in a flattering profile in the *Minneapolis Star*, Shirley nevertheless came to see the limits of this provincial lifestyle. 'Much as I loved it here (and still in a way do) I am glad I left when I left,' she wrote to Vera. 'Many of my friends here say they have never known a moment's unhappiness, but I would rather my life had the unhappiness and the greater richness that goes with it – to crack the mould is vital.'[12]

From Minnesota, Shirley took a 400-mile detour to Kansas City in Missouri to meet up with her father, who was lecturing there at the university. He thought she looked very well and more attractive than he had ever seen her. He told her that the struggle for seats for the next election was now on and she should make an early return, advice she found quite troubling. Then it was on to Chicago, which that year was hosting the Democratic Party convention. Unlike today, when they merely stage a coronation for the winner in the electoral state primaries, conventions then really did act as king-makers, none more so than in 1952. Their choice of Adlai Stevenson, the Governor of Illinois, met with Shirley's approval as she had warmed to his languid charm and upstanding integrity, although she wondered 'whether the man can withstand the pressures'. 'The convention was frantic, fantastic, fatiguing,' she enthused.[13] Thanks to her friendship with the political director of the Congress of Industrial Organizations (CIO) she was able to get into several union caucus rooms to see American politics played out in the raw.

From Chicago she went to an American Federation of Labour (AFL) summer school in Madison, Wisconsin, where she discovered the warmth and idealism of the union delegations, alongside the prejudice and plain stupidity. 'Cynicism is so much more of a curse than naiveté,' she told Vera. 'I was well liked there, but it cost me a lot of emotional effort. I find I have to be careful not to alienate myself from such people by excessive intellectual sophistication. I now believe that this is the key to Daddy's lack of political success.'[14] Her analysis tallied with Vera's. George's undoing, she felt, was his belief that celebrities mattered more than the humble. 'If one tries to take a God's view of people one gets some disquieting results. Who enters first into the Kingdom of Heaven – Charlie [Burnett] or Herbert Morrison?'[15]

A week later Shirley was the toast of the Iowa State CIO convention at Fort Dodge not only for her talk on British trade unionism but also for her solo rendition of 'Tipperary' at a beer party organised by the slaughterhouse workers. More socialising was in evidence when she returned to Cornell. Buoyed by the presence of her friend Madeleine Zimmermann, they went riding, swam in one of the campus's turbulent gorges and attended several parties. 'How pleasant it is to find a girl of one's own age I can talk to intellectually, rather a rarity over here.'[16]

September was given over to further union researches in Louisville, Kentucky, and a CIO summer school in St Louis,

Missouri. At the latter she had her eyes opened when attending a meeting of 'spicy' tough hill people who believed in picketing with a shotgun, claiming that shooting a strike-breaker was no worse than shooting a dog.

> The United States sometimes seems like a country of extraordinary brutality after England. People haven't time to be polite, and violence is reflected in conversation and politics and the casual attitude towards crime.
>
> But it also seems like a country where spontaneous friendliness is as common as hedgerow flowers, where most people, however unequal, are treated as equal and where everyone feels there is still much growing to do.[17]

While Shirley toured America, she continued to be aware of developments at home. There had always been the assumption that she was destined for politics and Parliament, an assumption assiduously cultivated by her father. Her mother, impressed by the quality of her writing as a young girl in the US, hoped that she would become 'one of the really distinguished political journalists among English women'. She continued to entertain such aspirations during Shirley's final year at Oxford after her 'brilliant *Isis* articles', reasoning that such a career would blend more easily with marriage and motherhood than teaching, which appeared one of the possible alternatives. 'There is also the advantage that if you stand for Parliament you have the backing of your newspaper.'[18] Prior to her departure to the US, Joe Watson had raised the possibility of Shirley becoming the Labour candidate for Harwich and although work commitments had precluded her from visiting the constituency for an extensive period, a speech she had given at Holland-on-Sea gave notice of her potential.

Watson accentuated his efforts following the resignation of Morris Janis as Labour candidate for Harwich on winning the party's nomination for the Bedford division. In July he informed Vera that he was putting Shirley forward as a possible candidate at the constituency meeting in September. He then wrote to her to explain his tactics.

> Until then I am canvassing for you as much as I dare. Of course not only are you the most outstanding candidate on the list, I really believe you could pull it off. And to my dismay, do you know the most important popular item in your favour? I dropped a hint that you have the ambition to be the first woman Prime Minister and the poor old dears visualise fame for Harwich in consequence.[19]

At the constituency meeting Watson duly secured Shirley the nomination but because she couldn't be formally adopted in her absence, he allowed himself to be nominated on the clear understanding that he would retire in her favour once she returned.

Throughout Shirley's time in the US she had kept up a regular correspondence with Roger and although she was resigned to 'gracefully withdrawing' once he was reunited with his American girlfriend, such a separation was understandably painful to contemplate, especially since he continued to shower affection upon her. 'Oxford, that dream of branches and bright gold meadows enriches our intellectual life and infinitely complicates our emotional life,' she told her father.[20] Her sentiments were exacerbated by her return to Minnesota in July when many of her old friends treated her as someone who had lost out on matrimony. Despite the fact that she wasn't ready to settle down, still less to have children (she admitted that her experiences of staying with many young families had left her feeling utterly cold about them) a nagging feeling persisted that undue procrastination could cause her to miss the boat. 'But I sometimes wonder how many civilised exits I will make and whether there will ever be an entrance.'[21]

Her musings drew a spirited response from Vera.

> To be regarded as having 'lost out' on matrimony at 22 – my hat! It reminds me of the wailing of the Buxton ladies when I announced

my intention of going to Somerville. 'Oh, Mrs Brittain, how can you let your daughter go to Oxford! Don't you want her to ever get married.' I hope you are impervious to all such nonsense.[22]

She accepted that marriage to Roger, 'an admirable young man', was now unlikely, but agreed with George's observation that he would probably have been a martinet of a husband. Although very fond of Roger, George had always pinned his hopes on Robert Bruce (Balfour), the heir to a Scottish peerage, hopes quickly dashed by Vera, who told him that their daughter's egalitarian principles wouldn't stomach the prospect of inheriting a title.

While Shirley maintained her low-level attachment to Wally and fended off both a Princeton teacher's proposal of marriage and 'a slightly hopeful Texan who introduced me to his mother, always a danger-sign',[23] another twist was added to the tale. It so happened that her Oxford friend Bernard Williams was spending a year in Canada on National Service, flying planes for the RAF in preparation for combat in Korea, and when Shirley was invited to take a friend to the home of Mo Walton, Mannie Putnam's mother, in Westport, Connecticut, to exchange ideas ('the more rebellious the better'), she chose him. It proved an inspired choice, for the handsome Bernard was invigorating company as he and Shirley walked in the sunlit woods of that enchanting fall. He also captivated his hostess, an accomplished pianist and a major sponsor of the composer Béla Bartók, with his rich fund of musical knowledge and languid charm. 'This is the most wonderful man,' Mo kept telling Shirley. 'You have to marry him.' Shortly afterwards, Bernard turned up in New York for a fortnight's leave and there they lived it up, going to several plays, the opera and a memorable performance of *Guys and Dolls*. Describing him as 'quite brilliant – a charming, gentle and very cultured person', Shirley told her mother that 'despite him imagining all kinds of future', she was 'very fond of him, but as usual no more'.[24]

On the return voyage on the RMS *Mauretania* she was the life and soul of the tourist class as she danced every night 'til 2 a.m. She arrived looking very chic in a smartly cut wool dress and pearls, bearing expensive gifts for family and friends with money earned from her speaking commitments. Immediately she was happily reunited with Roger, who spent much time in her company thereafter. 'I suspect it is he who will eventually be your son-in-law,' Vera told George in a revision of her earlier assessment as she welcomed Shirley and her friends to their new flat in Whitehall Court.[25] The change in atmosphere was immediately evident. 'Like you, she treats me as a sort of glorified secretary plus housekeeper, leaving me to answer her telephone messages and send them, and clear up teacups or glasses after herself and some young man, while she dashes off with said young man, returning at 3 a.m!'[26] While recognising that Shirley's ways weren't her ways, Vera found it quite fun and a pleasant change from being alone. 'My name is probably mud in Whitehall Court as so many boys turn up in the small hours either going or coming, but I don't care. Poppy is utterly trustworthy.'[27]

With the selection meeting in Harwich fast pending, Joe Watson was very keen for Shirley to appear almost immediately and so within days of her arrival she addressed the monthly meeting of the Manningtree Labour Party on 'Trade Unionism in the USA'. No sooner had she finished speaking than she was bombarded with questions for two hours and in a *tour de force* proved more than equal to the challenge. Two weeks later in Clacton, despite some anti-female and anti-Catholic sentiment, the executive endorsed her by the overwhelming majority of sixty to five. 'Shirley Catlin is a girl who has done most of the things other girls only dream about,' commented Primrose Minney in the *Essex Chronicle*. 'That is because she is very talented and is not afraid to try her hand at anything,'[28] a quality she later demonstrated at a local Labour Brains Trust when thick fog had delayed the arrival of the principal guests. 'In the short time she was speaking Miss Catlin impressed as a first-class orator, who should prove to be a lively new personality on the political platform,' reported the *Essex County Standard*.[29]

While she was establishing her political credentials in Harwich, Shirley was also trying to gain suitable employment. Although the

BBC had shown an interest in her when she applied for a job there in the summer of 1951, it had no vacancy at that time. She applied to be the editorial assistant to the TUC, the youth officer to the UN, and at both the *News Chronicle* and *Daily Mirror*. The job at the TUC came to nothing and the UN considered her too young and inexperienced, but was sufficiently impressed to consider her for a secondary position as secretary for Education in World Citizenship just when the *Mirror* was making encouraging noises. Ever since her appearance as an 'Isis Idol', the *Mirror*'s proprietor, Cecil King, had followed her career with interest and had employed her fellow Idol, Val Mitchison, as a junior royal reporter. Keen to have someone of Shirley's talent on his staff, he offered her the enticing prospect of becoming a junior news reporter for £14 per week. The offer placed her in something of a quandary as she knew that the UN job was likely to be hers if she wanted it. She recognised that it offered the better working conditions as well as the opportunity to keep abreast of political developments and to travel for at least two months per year. She also disliked the thought of the *Mirror* and had received an unflattering account of its staff from Val Mitchison. On the other hand, it paid double, gave her journalistic experience and 'the right politics albeit the wrong approach'. When she sought the advice of Arthur Creech Jones, the Colonial Secretary in the Attlee government, he told her to accept the *Mirror* every time, as did the editor of the *News Chronicle*, Robin Cruikshank. She did, much to the UN's regret – and that of her father, who correctly predicted that Shirley would 'loathe the *Mirror* before long'.

The *Daily Mirror* under Cecil King was then in its heyday with a circulation of 5 million, making it the nation's most popular news-paper. Abrasive, populist, working-class and pro-Labour, although not slavishly so, it nevertheless took its politics seriously and boasted a gifted team of writers with a real flair for investigative journal-ism. They didn't, however, take kindly to a couple of Oxford female graduates in the office and Shirley soon discovered that she was out of kilter with its macho drinking culture and profligate expenses claims. 'The poor child is hating the *Mirror* job,' Vera informed

George after her first couple of weeks.[30] Warned by Cruikshank that it would be tough, Shirley didn't quite appreciate how tough, as she worked long hours and endured the scorn of a features editor brusquely dismissive of any article he deemed not up to standard.

As a news reporter, much of Shirley's time was consumed with mundane features about new ideas in lamp designs, the etiquette of being a good secretary and the demise of square-dancing, as well as social trivia such as 'The Deb of the Year'. She also covered the celebrations in Stoke Newington, east London, on Coronation Day and, days later, managed a front-page splash when reporting on the Duke of Edinburgh playing polo at Cowdray Park, Midhurst, after he had been denounced by Church of Scotland ministers for playing on a Sunday. Acting on a tip-off she found him lifting a tankard at the presentations afterwards and inquiring cheekily, 'Am I allowed to drink champagne on Sunday?'

Most of the time she found the work distinctly unrewarding, given the long hours involved and the intrusion into people's privacy. In October 1953, barely eight months after she had started, Shirley left the paper by mutual consent, with a good reference but uncertain as to where to turn next. She tried *The Observer*, but David Astor, its editor, irked her by suggesting that as she was obviously only interested in marriage, he didn't see why he should help, sentiments he later admitted were spurious.

The experience of the *Mirror* had left Shirley deeply depressed, especially when college contemporaries had found useful work, and caused her parents much concern. Vera wrote to Victor Gollancz and Arthur Creech Jones to see whether they could give her 'the kind of parental guidance she won't accept from us'. Creech Jones certainly did and managed to dissuade her from becoming a class-room teacher, believing, like Vera, that her talents could be put to better use. He did, however, in his capacity as vice-president of the Workers' Educational Association, encourage her interest in adult education, advice that she was to act upon in a part-time capacity. There also appear to have been informal soundings with Herbert Morrison, for George's diary on 7 November reported Morrison's willingness to find her a safe parliamentary seat and help her become a junior whip provided she adhered to his political line and gave him an occasional smile. None of this made Shirley amenable as her links with him became more tenuous.

She explored other avenues of employment, but with nothing concrete on offer she reverted once again to journalism and her salvation came from Peter Galliner, the head of the Foreign Department at the *Financial Times*, a conservative-leaning paper, still very much a male preserve, not least for Oxbridge graduates. One such employee was William Rees-Mogg, who ironically had struck gold as a result of Shirley's profile of him in *Isis* when she let slip the fact that he read the *Financial Times* every day, information that its editor happened to pick up.

Although intrigued about employing a woman and a socialist, Galliner had to convince the paper's chairman, Lord Drogheda, a charming man but no feminist. It said much for Galliner's persuasive powers that he was able to win Drogheda round, helped by Shirley's undoubted pedigree and the fact that because she was a woman he could afford to pay much less, although her salary of £700 per year was still quite a hefty sum for those days.

The Foreign Department, founded in 1951 and very much Galliner's creation, generated much financial advertising by its syndicated articles for foreign newspapers about global economic and financial trends. With few colleagues to cope with the growing demand for *Financial Times* material, Shirley had her work cut out reading the foreign news and distributing weekly reports to the papers with whom it had syndicalism arrangements, but according to Rees-Mogg, she was an accomplished journalist well able to cope with the anomaly of being a woman in a man's world.

Before Shirley began her stint at the *Financial Times*, politics intervened. She was staying in Paris over the Christmas–New Year period when Vera was alerted to the news that Sir Stanley Holmes, the MP for Harwich since 1935, had accepted a peerage and a by-election was in the offing. With some difficulty she managed to locate Shirley and get her back for the Special Meeting of the local party on 2 January. There she was formally adopted for what would be a tough baptism in the public domain, especially since the Churchill government was beginning to savour better times economically. Labour, in contrast, remained directionless and divided, not least over foreign policy, where the left-wing Bevanites were much less sympathetic to the nuclear deterrent than the bulk of the party. The writ was issued on 19 January, which allowed for a three-week campaign in conditions totally alien to electioneering as the country was ravaged by bitter east winds of near gale force and engulfed in deep snow.

In addition to a cluster of small villages, the Harwich division was based around the three coastal towns of Harwich itself, a decaying ancient port, Clacton-on-Sea, a popular holiday destination and Frinton-on-Sea, a more genteel version of Clacton. Apart from brief Liberal interludes it was a predominantly Conservative seat, although Sir Stanley Holmes had followed in his predecessor's footsteps by calling himself a National Liberal, that section of the Liberal Party which supported the National Coalition Government of the 1930s. Shirley's opponent, Julian Ridsdale, a well-connected Sussex fruit farmer and former intelligence officer, fought under the banner of a Liberal-Conservative, bringing a withering response from Shirley. No self-respecting MP would accept that title, she said, as the two of them went head to head over nationalisation, industrial unrest and the economy.

Combating the arctic conditions, which inevitably affected audiences, especially in the rural areas, Shirley, with Joe Watson to rely on as her agent, ran a highly energetic campaign, addressing more than seventy meetings and capturing the imagination of the locality. 'She keeps in fine spirits,' reported Watson's wife, Doris, to Vera, 'despite the really terrible weather and my unavailing efforts to warm this great cold house. I try to get her to bed at reasonable times and up without much success – but she does not seem to be taking any hurt whatsoever.'[31] Despite her age – at twenty-two, the youngest ever female candidate – and refusal to stoop to personal attacks, she was no shrinking violet, rising above the media's

patronising description of her as 'cute little Shirley Catlin' dressed
in long socks and woolly scarves. According to Bill Law of the
*East Essex Gazette*, she particularly shone in front of the true blue
National Farmers Union, helped by her experiences of working
on the land at Frating. They liked the way that she went straight
to the core of the question, particularly the old chestnut about land
nationalisation thrown up by one old character. 'The answer was so
bold and direct that he forgot his supplementary.'[32]

Although the Conservatives had traditionally prided themselves
as the party of the countryside, Shirley, sensing that they were
vulnerable on agriculture, chose to make it an electoral issue for the
first time since the war. At her meetings she quoted various reservations about the new arrangements which had emanated from
resolutions of the recent annual meeting of the National Farmers
Union, a body, she rightly pointed out, which had no affinity
with the Labour Party. These reservations centred on the damage
inflicted on British agriculture by a policy of free trade, unrestricted
imports and overproduction. Condemning the drift from the land
since 1951, Labour, she said, would counter this by bringing modern
facilities to farm cottages and nationalising neglected land, from
which the government would sell the leasehold to tenant farmers, making enough finance available to restore the land to good
order. Yet for all her eloquence and the wretched living conditions
of many agricultural labourers and their families, she found that
deference to their employers and landlords precluded many of them
from giving her their vote.

Boosted throughout by leading members of the shadow Cabinet
and the sturdy efforts of her London friends led by Bernard
Williams, she was joined by her parents for the campaign's closing
stages. On the Tuesday before polling, George spoke in tandem with
Edith Summerskill in Harwich before 'Poppy appeared late, spoke
brilliantly and answered questions very well'.[33] The next day he was
in action again, this time in Brightlingsea with Arthur Greenwood,
the prelude to a packed eve-of-poll meeting in the Cooperative
Hall, Harwich, where the tough-looking dockers cheered Shirley

to the echo, especially her confident assertion that Labour could win. On polling day itself, a heavy fog descended in the afternoon, deterring a number of Harwich's council tenants from going out to vote, but Vera was buoyed by a local agent's prediction that Shirley would cut the Tory majority to 3,000. At the count George noted 'the balanced mixture of anxiety and nonchalance' in his daughter's face as she awaited the result. Eventually, at 3.20 a.m., in front of fifty hardened people on the freezing Clacton Town Hall steps, it was announced that on a 59 per cent turn-out the Conservatives had held the seat with a 5,997 majority. Shirley gave a charming concessionary speech wishing her opponent good luck until the next election, but once inside the hall she appeared rather crestfallen by the result, which, as Bernard admitted to Vera, had fallen short of expectation. She later cheered up after she had analysed the figures and discovered that her performance compared favourably with the two other Labour by-election results on the same evening. The *Ipswich Evening Star* observed the small swing to the Conservatives in Harwich despite Labour's 'highly promising young candidate in Shirley Catlin'[34] and Bill Law told Vera that Shirley had made a powerful impression on the area, 'managing in some way of her own to project the whole woman'.[35]

That September Shirley, on her re-adoption as Labour's candidate for Harwich, recognised the immense effort required to convert it to socialism. 'This is a part of the world in which people on the whole accept new faces, new thoughts and new ideas rather slowly,' she said, 'but having accepted them remain loyal. It is tragic that they should remain loyal to a dog whose day is done.'[36] And in that spirit of loyalty, Shirley brushed off a couple of attempts to entice her elsewhere. The first approach came from the neighbouring constituency of Maldon, a Labour marginal held between 1942 and 1955 by the maverick left-winger Tom Driberg, claiming that she had a better chance of winning there than in Harwich. This was obviously true, but having committed herself to Harwich, she wasn't rising to its bait or that of Wycombe, a Tory marginal.

On 7 April 1955 Churchill finally retired and his heir apparent,

Anthony Eden, immediately called for a fresh mandate. With the economy booming and the opposition still in a fractious mode, it was no time to be fighting a seat such as Harwich for Labour. In a campaign that lacked passion, Shirley talked about the need to give ailing towns a blood transfusion by bringing in light industry, and later made headlines by expressing the wish to see Clacton become a socialist Blackpool. Although she was again well served by her army of volunteers and by her own standing, it was difficult to buck national trends as the Conservatives substantially increased their majority. George noted a poster attached to a car saying 'Vote for Ridsdale, the kingdom of Bevan is Nye' and the ticket collector at Clacton told Vera that Shirley had a very affable personality, but that he would be voting Tory as he didn't want to see Bevan as Prime Minister. In addition to fear of the left, Ridsdale had proved a popular MP and, helped by the presence of a Liberal candidate on this occasion, who won votes mainly from Labour, the Conservatives, on a much higher turn-out than in the by-election, were able to increase their majority to 9,464. The Liberal, Wolf Askt, an eighteen-stone widower, lost his deposit, but caused a mild flutter at the count by remarking that if Bernard didn't marry Shirley, he would continue to propose to her.

And aside from her political baptism there were more personal matters for Shirley to attend to. For all her potential suitors, love and all that it entailed was proving something of a dilemma for an ambitious girl anxious to balance the conflicting ideals of personal independence, family commitment and professional fulfilment. 'I suppose ever since Peter I have been hunting quite impossible ideals which even Peter really didn't satisfy,' Shirley informed Vera back in October 1952,[37] while eighteen months later she admitted to George that she didn't want young men to be in love with her, but, equally, was piqued when they weren't. For several months after her return she saw plenty of Roger, so much so that Vera told George the following March that they were 'practically engaged'. This might have been wishful thinking on her mother's part, Shirley later recollected, since Vera was very fond of Roger, but while insistent that their relationship evolved into one of close personal friendship as their differing priorities became ever more apparent, George's diary of 1 June 1953 does note 'Shirley unhappy about Roger Bannister'.

With Roger now off the scene and Shirley turning down repeated marriage proposals from other hopefuls – Vera counted some twelve overall – attention focused primarily on Bernard, who ever since his return home the previous February had pressed his suit. At first she was slow to respond, but with her two flatmates, Helge Kitzinger and Madeleine Zimmermann, all in favour of the match, she gradually succumbed and by December 1954 they were engaged.

Bernard Arthur Owen Williams was born in September 1929 at Southend-on-Sea in Essex, the only child of a talented architect. Always top of his class at Chigwell School, a minor public school in Essex, he won a London County Council scholarship to Oxford in 1947, but relinquished it on getting one from Balliol. While reading *Literae Humaniores* he became a magnet for PPE undergraduates, who shunned tutorials in order to listen to his philosophical discourses in the Junior Common Room. After graduating with congratulatory honours he was elected a Fellow of All Souls, aged twenty-three, the youngest don in Oxford, before becoming a Fellow in Philosophy at New College, dazzling his colleagues with his quicksilver intelligence and razor-sharp wit. Yet for all his glamour (according to Vera, it was rare for an Oxford don to be tall, slim and handsome) and accomplishments, he wasn't an overbearing type, full of swaggering self-importance. Rather, he was sensitive and modest, as well as being devoted to Shirley and her career, qualities which Vera was quick to detect.

Darling Poppy,

I am glad you have chosen and I think that you have made the right choice. Of all the men you might have married Bernard obviously has far and away the best mind, and he is also, I believe, the only one who is capable of putting you before himself. (Indeed, you may even have to defend him against his own readiness to give way to you.) He will not fail you nor frustrate you, and there are very few men of whom, in relation to their wives, it is possible to say that. The election proves his capacity for sustained and disinterested loyalty in small, tedious and exacting ways.[38]

A party for 100 was held at Whitehall Court to celebrate, and Shirley told Vera that she wanted a large, exciting wedding, a request which her mother was only too happy to oblige. Typically Shirley spent much of the day before writing an article on French exports, and on the morning of the wedding, Saturday 2 July 1955, was on the phone fixing up her adult education classes for the autumn.

That afternoon, in gloriously sunny weather and almost thirty years to the day since Vera and George's own wedding in the same church, 300 guests gathered in St James's, Spanish Place to witness Father de Zulueta perform the nuptial rites.

Dressed in a white and gold hand-woven sari wedding gown which Vera had bought in India and a long tulle veil, Shirley, with Helge Kitzinger and Madeleine Zimmermann in attendance, looked radiantly happy as she came up the aisle on George's arm 'like a golden angel from a medieval picture'. Her arrival at the altar seemed to relax Bernard, who lost all sense of nerves, and together they made their vows with clarity and commitment.

Afterwards, at a sparkling reception in Hutchinson House's magnificent ballroom, the joy of the married couple was evident as they mingled easily with their guests. In speeches of rare quality ('worthy of Oxford at its best', pronounced Vera) Arthur Creech Jones, on behalf of the bride, recalled that one of his first memories of Shirley as a child was shouting down a Labour candidate she disapproved of, while George Engle, the best man, in paying tribute to Bernard's brilliance as a don, compared him to Socrates, eliciting a witty response from the groom. The proceedings concluded with a rousing send-off as Shirley, as ever hatless, waved happily to one and all. Later in the evening when Vera and George travelled to Heathrow by taxi to see off the happy couple on their honeymoon, Vera was greatly touched to be given an affectionate kiss from

Bernard. 'Such a spontaneous gesture from such a shy young man. He has much of his father's charm.'[39]

After a blissful honeymoon in the Aegean, Shirley and Bernard began married life in a ground-floor flat in the unfashionable surroundings of Clarendon Road, Notting Hill, which meant enduring the twice-weekly inconvenience of being woken prematurely by the clanging sounds of community dustbins being emptied. Keen to find something rather better they turned down Vera's offer of a flat in her house in favour of sharing a house with Hilary and Helge Rubinstein. Realising that big Victorian houses designed for large families and domestic help, of the type in which Shirley had grown up, were much cheaper than modern ones, they struck lucky with the first such house they looked at in Phillimore Place in Kensington. The only problem was the price, at £6,800, which raised doubts in Shirley's mind as to its financial viability (she was the highest earner of the four of them), but she caved in to the entreaties of the others. She borrowed £2,200 from her mother, became joint owner with Helge and they moved in October 1956. It was a decision they never regretted, for not only did they appreciate the additional space but also the superior location, with Bernard in particular delighted to have exchanged the slum noises of Notting Hill for the gentility of Kensington.

With three floors at their disposal, the Rubinsteins occupied the ground floor, the Williamses the first and the top-floor flat, which they let out to deserving cases, many of them from overseas. As the Williamses' guests flowed into the Rubinsteins' quarters, Helge couldn't help observing that 'It wasn't so much an open house, it was more like the Suez Canal.'[40] Yet she never complained, symptomatic of the harmonious relationship that existed between the two families. Sharing the same front entrance, they looked after each other's children and acted as joint hosts to their overlapping circle of friends. 'Friends predicted that the arrangement couldn't last,' Hilary Rubinstein later recalled. 'It says a great deal about the Williamses' generosity and tolerance that the two families instead enjoyed a halcyon relationship.'[41]

Marriage brought no let-up in their work. While Bernard continued to flourish at Oxford, Shirley, in addition to the *Financial Times*, was preoccupied with adult education classes and her political activities.

Having cut her teeth in Harwich and won golden plaudits from the party elders the challenge of finding something more winnable was now her priority. It proved to be a frustrating business even for an able young woman in sympathy with the general tenor of the party under its new leader, Hugh Gaitskell, a person she much admired. For all its commitment to equality in principle, the position of women within the Labour movement had always ranked a very poor second to men, especially in the unforgiving world of the trade unions, where physical strength and a robust camaraderie seemed to predominate. They used their majorities on local constituency committees to select one of their own, especially in a safe seat. Given that most of Labour's safe seats were in Scotland, Wales and the north of England, the chances of a southern, middle-class intellectual like Shirley winning through were all the more remote.

Having spurned the opportunity of fighting several Conservative seats Shirley was persuaded by Leah Manning to try her luck in Epping, a Tory marginal she held for Labour between 1945 and 1950. She did and gave a good account of herself, but lost out by one vote to Donald Ford of the Cooperative Movement. 'I don't blame them, but it was a little saddening' was her philosophical reaction to the tactics employed against her by the local association, which included questions ascertaining her views on birth control, in clear breach of local rules which deterred any candidate being asked about their religious beliefs.[42]

Other seats such as Oxford, Cambridge and Chelmsford were dangled before her, but she failed to respond. Even Southampton Test, a Tory marginal, occasioned nothing more than a perfunctory interest. On the way to the final interview she spent her time on the train talking to a female employee of a women's magazine rather than writing her speech. Up against five other candidates, all men, she was selected by the overwhelming majority of twenty-eight to four, despite the offer of one of her rivals to contribute a large sum towards his electoral expenses. Any doubts she had about accepting were assuaged by the advice of George Blackshaw, Labour's national agent and a good friend of her father. He encouraged her to take it, especially since it had a large Catholic vote and an excellent local organisation confident of winning back the seat.

It so happened that her adoption in Southampton coincided with the climax of the Suez crisis, when British and French armed forces invaded Egypt to reoccupy the Suez Canal, nationalised earlier that year by its fiercely anti-imperial leader, Gamal Abdel Nasser. The decision fuelled vitriolic protest back home, where the Labour opposition under Gaitskell accused Eden of criminal folly. On Saturday 3 November, while bitter scenes were being played out in an emergency sitting in the Commons, Shirley, Bernard and Vera waited outside to boo Eden when he emerged. 'What a one-track mind child it is,' Vera informed George, 'she talked, breathed and ate the crisis.'[43] The next day they all attended the mass Labour demonstration in Trafalgar Square, the biggest of its kind Vera had ever seen, and the day after that, Shirley addressed a rowdy 'Law not War' meeting in Ipswich Cooperative Hall.

With the US leading bitter international opposition to the British and French landings, submission wasn't long in coming. Eden's reckless action had cost the country dear and brought about his own demise, for within weeks he had given way to Harold Macmillan and was never to hold office again.

Shirley was getting restless. At the end of 1956 the *Financial Times* had raised her salary by £250, but she hankered after further responsibility, especially the opportunity to write editorials, a request denied her by her editor, who refused to contemplate a woman in such an elevated position. By now a regular speaker at Treasury School conferences, her talks were considered so authoritative she was offered a post at the Treasury as head of Women Information Services explaining economics to women's organisations. The job sounded interesting enough, but Shirley felt bound to decline because an active political career such as hers would breach the traditional neutrality of the civil service.

In January 1958 University College in Ghana had invited Bernard to teach philosophy for two terms, beginning that September. With a generous salary of £1,000 and free travel and accommodation, the opportunity was too good to miss, although with an election pending Shirley would have to return early. It also brought to an end her links with the *Financial Times*, much to the regret of Lord Drogheda, who told her that she would be greatly missed. 'You set a model for everyone by your industry, your cheerfulness, your long-suffering: and Coleman Street will not be the same without your happy smile.'[44]

Arriving in Ghana in September, they found a prosperous country on the back of its thriving cocoa trade and a proud, self-conscious people basking in their new-found independence under their char-ismatic ruler Kwame Nkrumah, whose personal ascendancy Shirley compared with that of Franklin Roosevelt during the early days of the New Deal.

University College, founded in 1947, was situated on a hill at Legon, seven miles outside the capital, Accra, its red-roof halls in oblongs around a central court divided from each other by roads and lawns. Further out were the bungalows of senior staff, over-whelmingly Europeans, complete with gardens of bright flowering shrubs and lizards. It was here that Shirley and Bernard were housed in a ground-floor flat complete with wooden furniture and domestic help.

In a country where everything started early, Bernard was soon being put through his paces, lecturing three times per week at 8 a.m. and more during the evening, in addition to copious amounts of tutoring and marking. Thanks to some favourable remarks from the Labour academic Barbara Wootton when she had visited the university the previous term, Shirley soon became a tutor in Economics with Fellows rights. Her teaching programme consisted of a class on economic theory, a specialist course for higher execu-tive civil servants and a seminar on international trade for seven third-year students. On top of this, she taught an extramural class on economics for sixty-six students of the People's Educational Association in Accra and another on international affairs for eighteen leading citizens comprising bright young men in white shirts and shorts, and shy young women in bright patterned kente cloths. The venue, a local school in the village of Mampong, twenty miles to the north in the bush, caused considerable disruption because of hooting lorries, bleating goats and chattering children. An additional hazard was the inadequacy of the big pressure lamp which came on at 6 p.m. after sunset, so that studying in the gloaming was no easy matter.

Despite the effort involved in preparing her lectures from scratch, Shirley greatly enjoyed her teaching and the focus on Third World affairs. She developed an easy rapport with her students, finding them to be polite and dignified, and won their respect for her ability to detect plagiarism in their essays. She also cultivated good relations with local traders. 'The ordinary people go in for a lot of haggling, but are always prepared to come down if they're overcharging and usually rather charmingly laugh their heads off at being found out.'[45] She discovered the children to be happy and humorous, the villagers friendly and helpful, so that she felt safer there than on the streets of London or New York. 'These are not fanatical people, and not violent people; they are dignified, gay, unbitter, and still seem to react to our race-conscious excesses more in sorrow than in anger.'[46]

And yet for all its ebullience Ghana remained in many ways a country in thrall to its antiquated customs such as polygamy, tribal rights and the spirits. One evening when Shirley and Bernard were paddling with friends they encountered two African fishermen who demanded money. Given their threatening tone they went back to their car and drove a little further down the coast, close to where friends of theirs were sitting in the moonlight. Once again they were accosted by the same pair and having seized a bottle of beer from them, one of the fishermen ran off into the sea until the water came up to his chest. He then held his arms above his head and made a swooping gesture towards the sea, pouring drink into it, before turning on his heels and running away. 'The belief in magic is certainly still strong,' Shirley observed, 'most villages have their fetish priest, and certainly hills or fountains are associated with jujus, and must not be approached ... The educated Africans are very scornful about all this "bush religion" as one put it to us. But there it is, and it still holds sway.'[47]

On 11 January 1959, after Christmas with Nigerian friends in Lagos, Shirley returned to Britain to prepare for the election, leaving Bernard to complete the spring term without her. Ever since winning the Labour nomination for Southampton she had remained cautious about her prospects, especially once the Conservatives began to recover under Macmillan's astute leadership. 'It will be a near-miracle if Labour wins the election, and a real miracle if I can win Southampton,' she intimated to her parents.

> I am not really sure that this country can change or wants to. It is as if Macmillan, in some brilliant way, has tucked Britain up in a cosy world of cars and refrigerators and lulled it to sleep to the music of Elgar, and now no one wants to wake up and go into the challenging and terrible world of today...

She missed the space and gaiety of Africa and the bubbling vitality of its people, while being concerned about its future.

> I feel as if no-one knows Africa is on the brink of an explosion, and no one will change his Anglo-Saxon white arrogance, and no one will wake up to see that if one gives a race no hope, it eventually turns to violence. The time in Central and East Africa is terribly late.[48]

She wrote to the editor of *Woman's Hour* and the head of the BBC's women's programmes to offer them a talk about her African experiences. The BBC was interested and invited her to participate in a well-established programme called *The Brains Trust*. She arrived for the recording in a pallid condition, having eaten something untoward at Tony Benn's the night before, leading the producer to suspect that she had a hangover. She recovered enough to hold her own on the programme and enthralled all those who saw it, especially compared to the formidable figure of Margery Perham, an Oxford academic and ardent supporter of African independence. It proved to be a pivotal moment in her career in broadcasting, as she became a regular participant on both radio and television thereafter, her beautiful rich voice and natural empathy with an audience making her a producer's dream.

*The Brains Trust* had been a welcome diversion from a tedious six weeks campaigning in Southampton, staying with a Labour councillor in his frozen home and pouring oil on troubled waters as petty feuding engulfed the local party. Her burden was lightened by an Easter reunion with Bernard in Rome looking at churches before returning to Oxford and settling in a pleasant light flat. She was glad that being a don's wife wasn't forever. 'It's such an appendage sort of thing to do, a kind of unnecessary ornament on the substance of the University which is so much dedicated to itself.'[49]

In April she and Bernard attended a protest rally in the Royal Albert Hall in support of Nyasaland independence, at which some racist hecklers tried to break up proceedings. The cue for the descent into chaos came when one of the hecklers, sitting in the row behind Shirley and Bernard, threw a thunderflash at an inoffensive West Indian. Then, as tempers flared, they both became embroiled in the melee that followed. As Shirley persisted in punching a large man in the stomach, she looked round to see Bernard flying backwards over a row of chairs having suffered a crack on the nose. He returned to the fray only to be knocked back a second time, and then as he geared himself up for a third attempt, the stewards regained control. Describing the whole affair as 'rather exciting', Shirley was amused to hear Bernard's assailant mutter as he was being led gently away, 'What disgusting brutality.'

Despite the highest ever Labour membership in Southampton Test, a willing team of party workers and an encouraging swing in the 1957 local council elections, Shirley remained sceptical about becoming its next MP. Nothing which had occurred throughout 1959 had given her cause to revise that prediction. For aside from a booming economy fuelled by a blatant electioneering budget, Macmillan's image as a world statesman had been boosted not only by a trip to Moscow, but also by a successful visit from President Eisenhower on the eve of the campaign. Labour, in contrast, while more united than at any time for a decade, had struggled to present an alternative vision that appealed to a younger, more affluent generation keen to cash in on the consumer revolution.

On 9 September, the day after Parliament was dissolved, Shirley detected a strong cynicism towards both parties among the professional middle class and predicted a Tory victory, albeit by a smaller majority. 'I am least buoyed up personally by the perfectly genuine thought that I don't mind what happens as far as I am concerned.'[50] 'The Test division is reasonably open,' opined *The Times*,

> and if anyone can lower the Conservative majority of 3,842 it is Mrs Shirley Williams, Labour, the first woman to contest a seat in Southampton, who is a journalist and economist.
>
> Mrs Williams is slightly assisted by certain movements in population since 1955 and perhaps by the absence of a Liberal, and is ready to expound the complexities of the aircraft industry and international shipbuilding without turning a hair.[51]

'... she combines a tireless social life with a passionate interest in Africa, Economics and the Common Market,' declared *The Observer*. 'She is one of the few politicians who are both dedicated and self-critical, with a first-class brain.'[52]

Up against John Howard, a Surrey chartered accountant, Shirley threw herself into the campaign with her usual gusto, riding on the pillion of her agent's motorbike or being escorted to meetings by Bernard in his green sports car. A consummate campaigner, she genuinely enjoyed meeting people, listening intently to what they had to say and replying in straightforward language devoid of political clichés. At more formal meetings her natural fluency proved equally effective as with minimum preparation her speeches radiated authority on almost any subject and left her audience feeling upbeat.

Endeavouring to expose the darker side of Conservatism, she contrasted its central message of prosperity for all with the struggle faced by the left-out millions. It was to help these people that Labour was asking the more fortunate to pay more tax. She promised to resign should her party fail to make good its manifesto commitment to increase the weekly pension by an additional 10 shillings.

Although behind in the polls, Labour quickly found its feet with its polished broadcasts and Gaitskell's assured leadership, so much so that some even began to dream of victory despite their leader's gaffe of appearing to promise an increase in pensions without any accompanying increase in tax. Commentators judged it the defining moment of the campaign, but its significance has almost certainly been exaggerated. In the end the years of plenty proved too irresistible for many floating voters, especially those living in the south, and the Conservatives' majority nearly doubled to 100. Southampton Test was one of the first constituencies to declare and the crowd gathered by the Municipal Buildings learnt that, despite Shirley increasing her vote by nearly 1,000, her Conservative opponent had comfortably hung on. 'Parliament loses one of its most colourful young women, Shirley Williams,' commented Robert McKenzie, the psephologist and broadcaster, minutes after she was cheered by her supporters for her concession speech. To them, she had been an inspirational figure, with H. T. Willcocks, the veteran local agent, rating her one of the finest candidates he had ever had the pleasure of working with in a campaign.

When Shirley returned to London and visited her parents that weekend Vera remarked that she had never seen her look so tired. She took defeat philosophically, but deep down it hurt. 'Poppy is clearly pretty depressed with every prospect of the Party being out of power for the next four years or so,' George confided to his diary. 'Vera says it reminds her of the little girl, as she then was, who retired to her room in distress when her little dog was so ill that he had to be put to sleep.'[53] Yet this was no time for sackcloth and ashes. There was work to be done and Shirley was determined that the party should quickly learn lessons in order to remain a viable force for the future.

**Endnotes**

1   GC diary, 26 July 1951
2   Peter Hennessy, *Having It So Good*, Penguin Books, 2007, p.275
3   *Isis*, 16 February 1949
4   3 November 1951, SW Papers (private collection)
5   Peter Parker, *For Starters*, p.74
6   SW to Phyllis Cook, 17 February 1952, SW Papers (private collection)
7   GC diary, 22 October 1953
8   Jack Briskman to SW, 24 November 1951, SW Papers (private collection)
9   VB to SW, 23 January 1952
10  SW to GC, 6 April 1952
11  SW to VB, 10 May 1952
12  SW to VB, 15 July 1952
13  SW to VB, 27 July 1952
14  SW to VB, 3 August 1952
15  VB to SW, 9 August 1952
16  SW to VB, 25 August 1952
17  *West London Free Press*, 1 November 1952
18  VB to SW, 6 November 1950
19  Joe Watson to SW, 27 September 1952
20  SW to GC, 27 April 1952
21  SW to VB, 22 August 1952
22  VB to SW, 25 August 1952
23  SW to VB, 17 October 1952
24  SW to VB, 17 October 1952
25  VB to GC, 30 November 1952
26  VB to GC, 28 December 1952
27  VB to GC, 29 December 1952
28  *Essex Chronicle*, 19 December 1952
29  *Essex County Standard*, 16 January 1953
30  VB to GC, 17 February 1953
31  Doris Watson to VB, 17 February 1953
32  Bill Law to VB, 15 February 1954
33  VB diary, 9 February 1954
34  *Ipswich Evening Star*, 15 February 1954
35  Bill Law to VB, 15 February 1954

36 *Harwich and Dovercourt Standard*, 1 October 1954
37 SW to VB, 17 October 1952
38 VB to SW, 19 December 1954
39 VB to GC, 18 July 1955
40 *Sunday Times Magazine*, 5 April 1981
41 *The Times*, 26 June 2003
42 SW to VB and GC, 6 February 1957
43 VB to GC, 4 November 1956
44 Lord Drogheda to SW, 1 September 1958
45 SW to VB and GC, 6 October 1958
46 SW to VB and GC, 17 November 1958
47 SW to VB and GC, 17 November 1958
48 SW to VB and GC, 12 January 1959
49 SW to VB and GC, 4 May 1959
50 SW to VB and GC, 9 September 1959
51 *The Times*, 24 September 1959
52 *Observer*, 4 October 1959
53 GC diary, 15 October 1959

# 6

# INTO PARLIAMENT

After defeat, the inquests, all the more painful because of the gravity of that defeat. Not only had the Conservatives increased their majority for the fourth successive election, the first time that this had occurred since Britain had become a mass democracy, it was Labour's worst result since 1935. The fact that Labour performed particularly badly in the West Midlands and the south among floating voters and the young raised real concerns about its continuing viability in this more materialistic age. Amidst the many post-mortems carried out by all sections of the party, those closest to the leadership were adamant that far-reaching change was imperative. Tony Crosland had pointed the way in his seminal *The Future of Socialism* in 1956 by stressing the priority of the mixed economy and improved public services over nationalisation and planning in the struggle for equality. Now, three years later, beginning with a meeting of the Gaitskell circle on the Sunday after the election, questions were raised about revising the Labour constitution, severing the link with the trade unions and even changing the name of the party.

The next day Shirley appeared on BBC's *Panorama* to provide a young candidate's perspective on the painful choices facing Labour. She echoed the earlier conviction of a leading Gaitskellite, Roy Jenkins, about the need to ditch outdated dogma, comments which caused a stir on the left. The next week in an article in the *Sunday Times* entitled 'Labour and Radical?', she gave substance to these views. Unless the party was able to transform itself it would never appeal to enough of the growing new middle class of wage-earning families with television sets, washing machines and cars.

Accepting that bureaucracy, industrial disputes and nationalisation had damaged Labour's credibility, she didn't advocate a break with the trade unions, but warned against the baleful effects of unofficial strikes, demarcation disputes and the role of the shop steward. The need for elected officers in the trade unions was long overdue.

Having dealt with Labour's own legacy of conservatism, she then questioned whether it could transform itself into a radical party which continually questioned established and conformist ways of thought. 'It must work to extend the frontiers of individual freedom even when individual freedom is inconvenient or unpopular.'[1] Participation in making these decisions must be extended to a much wider proportion of its citizens.

Others were less guarded in their determination to break away from the shibboleths of the past and with Gaitskell insistent that the revisionist case be aired in public, the backlash wasn't long in coming. Bevanite hostility, driven by ideological purity and personal animosity, was only to be expected after the great feuds of the previous decade. More damaging was the attitude of the trade unions, who, for all their focus on the practical matters of day-to-day living, clung to Clause IV (nationalisation) as a symbolic longing for the better world they craved. By the time the party met at Blackpool on Saturday 28 November for an abbreviated post-election conference, the mood had distinctly darkened, so that any hopes Gaitskell had of persuading his party to embrace major constitutional change appeared doomed. Seemingly aware of this growing resistance, he merely talked about downgrading Clause IV as opposed to abandoning it, but even this modification precipitated passionate declamations from the left. In its bitter salvos against the leadership the left overplayed its hand and the next day saw a number of moderates coming out in staunch defence of Gaitskell. Denis Healey lambasted the culture of opposition for its own sake whereby loud cheers in the conference hall failed to translate into votes in the ballot box. The party had to close the gap between the activist and the voter in order to get elected.

Healey's argument was taken up by Shirley. 'One thing that

should be on all our consciences today is that five million Africans in Central Africa are moving to slavery because we lost the last election.'

Claiming that there was a great deal that they could do about it she urged the trade unions to be the first and not the last to point out the inefficiencies in industries yet to be nationalised. She asked the NEC to use the economic surplus for socialist purposes. Above all, it should take a stand on the impoverishment of public services. 'Does it really make sense that when someone has an accident in a 1959 car he should have to be admitted to an 1850 hospital to be cured?'

Calling on the NEC to help women consumers and develop an attractive youth policy, Shirley told her audience in no uncertain terms that if they didn't put their rancorous bickering behind them they not only wouldn't win another election, but would also go the way of some socialist parties in the West.

She ended with a rousing call for unity punctuated by frequent bursts of applause.

Let me say just one other thing. We have in Mr Bevan and Mr Gaitskell two leaders who can take this Party to victory. Do not let us set them against each other or draw satisfaction from the blood they take from each other, but realise that the only person to get satisfaction from this is Mr Macmillan. It is not just saving ourselves, saving the Labour Party. In ten years' time the Soviet Union is probably going to have more power in the world than the United States. Unless we can show a policy to the people holding on to democracy by the skin of their fingers, a policy which offers them socialism with democracy (and I stress democracy because not many people have been doing that), then it is not only Britain but it is the whole world that will go down in chaos.[2]

The speech was a sensation. Tony Benn called it brilliant, Edith Summerskill ranked it the speech of the conference and among the many delegates who complimented Vera and George on Shirley's performance on the train back to London were Bevan, Gaitskell and George Brown. In contrast Gaitskell left Blackpool with his authority badly eroded, his attempt to modify Clause IV in ruins.

The dissension over nationalisation was nothing compared to the rumpus which developed over the party's defence policy. Ever since its inception in 1958 in response to the proposed development of the British independent deterrent, the Campaign for Nuclear Disarmament (CND) had rapidly expanded and with the conversion of a number of the larger unions towards the unilateralist line, most notably the Transport and General Workers Union (TGWU) under Frank Cousins, the pro-American Gaitskell faced a potentially lethal opposition at the 1960 party conference. After a passionate debate he narrowly lost the vote on unilateral disarmament, but his defiant resolve to 'fight and fight and fight again' to overturn the decision enhanced his status both within the party and the country. Shirley, as an enthusiastic supporter of Gaitskell, wished him well although she refrained from joining the Campaign for Democratic Socialism (CDS), the body formed by Bill Rodgers within the Labour Party and trade unions to ensure that multilateralism triumphed, which indeed it did at Conference the next year.

Where she played a more active role was in the debate over Europe, an issue about which Gaitskell was much more lukewarm than the vast majority of his closest followers. In May 1961 she was a signatory to the Common Market Campaign launched by Lord Gladwyn, a former ambassador to the UN, and Roy Jenkins to endorse Britain's entry into Europe, and that September she became president of the newly formed Labour European Committee.

Her appointment took place amidst growing concern about the position of West Germany within the Western alliance. Such influence, Shirley told the conference, would only grow if Britain stayed out of Europe, since it would leave West Germany leading a European bloc as powerful economically as the Soviet Union. 'We must get this absolutely straight: West Germany is economically dominant unless this country goes in. That is why I feel that this country has an obligation to go in and help to lead the third great bloc, as it will be, in the world.'³

Her speech enthused *The Guardian*, but her stance placed her at odds with the anti-European mood within her party, so that even the pragmatic Gaitskell, wounded by past battles, adopted a much more strident tone at Conference the following year. Playing to national sentiment, he denigrated the European idea and talked in emotive terms about 'the end of a thousand years of history'. He concluded with a glowing tribute to the Commonwealth and derided the government's assurances that Britain's entry into Europe wouldn't damage her interests.

While Gaitskell's diatribe brought the majority of the conference to its feet and went a long way towards reuniting the party, thereby helping to consolidate his leadership, it left pro-Europeans such as Shirley bitterly disappointed as she contemplated the rocky road ahead. ('Such strange chauvinist bedfellows,' she told George.)⁴ Not only had the European cause received a major setback, but also the position of the social-democratic right within the party, given the fissures which began to open up.

Throughout Labour's feuding Shirley had remained slightly detached from the fray thanks to her new responsibilities at the Fabian Society.

The Fabian Society, founded in 1884 by such intellectual giants as Sidney and Beatrice Webb and George Bernard Shaw, had a proud history in developing progressive ideas. Yet despite the efforts of Bill Rodgers, its outgoing general secretary, to revitalise it, the 1950s in general were a fallow decade, its influence over the Labour Party minimal. As its most recently co-opted member, courtesy of Rodgers, Shirley had been charged with the responsibility of recruiting younger members and establishing an under-thirty committee which would enjoy considerable autonomy, an objective brought to fruition the following year with the establishment of the Young Fabians. Much of this was down to the efforts of Dick Leonard, the assistant secretary, and when Rodgers announced his resignation in early 1960, it was he who went head to head with

Shirley for the vacancy. Thanks to Rodgers's support, Shirley was duly appointed, a decision which greatly disappointed Leonard, but in a spirit of magnanimity he informed her that there was no one else whom he would rather see appointed. Others felt the same way. Gaitskell told her that they could not have made a better choice and the *Manchester Guardian* called her the most important woman in the movement since Beatrice Webb:

> After all the superlatives one should not perhaps be surprised ... to find a woman with a good deal of charm and no stridency, whose forward-looking views are completely unaggressive. The overwhelming impression she gives is one of intellectual honesty, a very contemporary woman whose simple courtesy is hardly of this age...[5]

Shirley aimed not only to increase its membership but also to develop new ideas on a broad range of topics. Leading through personal example with her talks to local societies, lecturing at summer schools and frequent appearances on radio, her efforts soon brought results. Membership began to grow, research groups mushroomed and the Young Fabians flourished despite their continuing elitist image. Michael Cockerell, the leading BBC documentary maker, then on the executive of the Young Fabians, has recollections of Shirley going round the table and asking everyone where they came from. When Cockerell said that he was from Oxford, she replied, 'Oh Oxford, not another one.'

The proliferation of pamphlets attracted favourable reviews in the press. 'Under the direction of Mrs Shirley Williams the Society seems well set to recapture its old glories and become once more the power-house of ideas,' opined the *Sunday Times* towards the end of her first year in charge.[6]

Keen to tackle subjects 'too hot for the Labour Party to handle' such as the problems with the trade unions and the public schools, Shirley brought politicians, scientists and experts together who encompassed a broad spectrum of opinion. Aside from inviting

Michael Shanks, a former colleague on the *Financial Times*, to conduct an ambitious survey of the nationalised industries, she herself was responsible for a study into the relationship between Labour governments and private industry. She also commissioned a major study into the welfare state by Professor Richard Titmuss of the LSE and wrote much of an influential pamphlet called 'The Administrators', calling for the modernisation of the civil service.

As Shirley revitalised the Fabian Society, she faced a dilemma of balancing her political ambitions with her personal life. Neither proved entirely straightforward and the evidence suggests that she was more ambivalent about standing for Parliament than were her parents on her behalf, although this may have been partly a veneer to cope with further rejections following three failed attempts previously. Whatever the reason, it all points to a certain equivocation in her personality that rather dogged her career.

Back in October 1958 she had suffered a miscarriage in Ghana, 'a mixed misfortune since if I had had the baby, it would have been in May and consequently no election'.[7] The following August, while on holiday in Belgium, she endured a similar ordeal and spent ten days in a nursing home after an operation. Now, with the election out of the way and Labour still in the wilderness, her priority seemed more geared towards starting a family than becoming an MP, a development that concerned Vera enough to write a long missive on the matter.

I don't want to butt into your correspondence with G about standing for Parlt again, but feel I should be remiss if I didn't say how much, this time, I agree with his point of view … Nothing gives a woman so much potential power as being an MP, because nothing else apart from being in the Royal Family carries so much publicity. Today publicity is power, and this is only deplorable if you use power in the wrong way … You have this opportunity or will sooner or later, and I don't want to see you throw it away … your gifts as a potential Parliamentarian are unique (James Griffiths, whom we saw at the Marquands last week, said this).

Not only have you the intelligence and the good health and an ideal appearance (when you look after it!) for the job, but your ability as a speaker is more than out of the common. I always feel at ease on platforms myself and if I have any charm at all it is on platforms that it comes out, but I know well that your ease and your charm on platforms is ten times greater than mine. These things are power, and one shouldn't let all the power remain in the hands of the ungodly.

I know that Parliament means endless and boring persistence and much frustration, and it is hard to combine with family life, but if Edith and Margaret Thatcher can do it, so can you...[8]

When Shirley again became pregnant in September 1960, Vera wasn't exactly euphoric about the news. 'I think she is quite pleased though both she and I would rather see her in Parliament!' she intimated to a friend, in words that seemed to rather misrepresent her daughter.[9] Weeks earlier Shirley had told George she reckoned that the Conservatives would be in power for ten years and that in these circumstances she found the thought of being an MP too frustrating. On 20 May 1961, after spending the previous night at the cinema, she gave birth at 10.55 a.m. to Rebecca Clare, who weighed in at 7 lb 9 oz. They were in hospital for a week and then within a month a buoyant mother was back at work, with Rebecca in her carrycot nestling under her desk in the offices of the Fabian Society. After they holidayed in Wales, she informed Vera that Rebecca was coming on well, but fretted about her chances of survival during a particularly turbulent period in the Cold War. 'It is, as you say, terrible to see these little headless things growing up in such a world – and one can only pray that they may have the chance to grow up, which seems at least questionable.'[10]

Starting a family kept Shirley's parliamentary ambitions in check, a fact which continued to cause George some anxiety. Back in June at a party at the Indian High Commission, he noted Clem Attlee nodding approval when Sybil Thorndike had remarked that Shirley must become an MP. He thought it scandalous that the party hadn't found her a safe seat and, acting on some advice from Edith Summerskill, now the MP for Warrington, urged her to make herself known in Lancashire, where her Catholicism could well be an asset. 'No one doubts your ability. But glamour fades and achievements are forgotten unless one fights every election.'[11]

George's desperation to see Shirley in Parliament was related to his own failure to get there and his determination that she shouldn't suffer a similar fate. Although unsuccessful with Faversham, a Kentish marginal held by the Conservatives, because she was a woman, Shirley was courted by Wallsend, a safe shipbuilding seat on Tyneside with a strong Catholic vote. The regional organiser, D. F. Algar, thought it worth a try as it was a weak field, but she affected no interest. Aside from claiming no links with the constituency, she pleaded family commitments. 'For personal reasons, it looks as if I will probably have to give the next election a miss anyway. My daughter is only eight months old, and it seems a very bad policy to have only one child.'[12] She did, however, express some interest in the Conservative marginal of Doncaster, an area she knew well through her friendship with Pat Duffy, a native of those parts, and where she had many friends willing her to stand. In July 1962 her nomination was endorsed unanimously by the General Management Committee (GMC) and the secretary-agent wrote to her to say that she was the favourite, especially since any influence he wielded would be placed at her disposal. It was to no avail because she decided to withdraw once she discovered that she was pregnant again. That wasn't all. In August George heard that she was contemplating resigning as secretary of the Fabian Society. 'I am at a loss to understand her plans,' he wrote in his diary, 'it seems as if she is inclined to be a "good wife".'[13] Days later he wrote to her to advise her to persevere with her political career and 'not to wrap her talents in a napkin'. He was on the verge of writing to her again when he heard that she had suffered another miscarriage. He confessed to some hesitation as to whether to send it, 'but since she is still flying off to Fabian Society meetings ... I decided to do so'.[14]

Shirley's domestic circumstances appear to explain why she had placed her parliamentary ambitions to one side, although Vera's letter to her friend Faith Moulson of 9 October suggests this wasn't the entire reason.

> Shirley is not a parliamentary candidate at the moment as the Fabian Society and the baby take up much of her time but they are not so much the real problem as the fact that she does not see eye to eye with the Labour Party high command on the question of the Common Market.[15]

Barely had these words been written when a vacancy occurred in the Labour-held marginal of the Colne Valley in Yorkshire following the death of the incumbent Glenvil Hall. Florence Price, a pillar of the local party, wrote to her CDS colleague Bill Rodgers asking for recommendations. Rodgers suggested Ian Winterbottom, MP for Nottingham Central between 1950 and 1955, and Shirley, convinced that she would be a first-rate candidate. Shirley did express an interest, only for Price to inform her that she would be using her influence on behalf of Winterbottom – not that it counted for anything, as he lost out to Pat Duffy.

While the family debate about Shirley's future was raging, a grave crisis suddenly erupted over the state of Gaitskell's health. Having spent a few days in hospital before Christmas he was readmitted early in the New Year and was diagnosed with lupus erythematosus, a very rare immunological disease, exacerbated by a severe viral infection. His condition rapidly deteriorated and he died on 18 January. The sense of shock throughout the country was profound, not least to Shirley, who had prayed hard that he would live. 'He must have been worn out by the years of strain and endless work,' she told her father, 'and it is an irony almost on the scale of a Greek tragedy that he should have been cheated of the Prime Ministership he had every reason to expect, and had, in fact, been growing into – none of us can really plan what we will become...'[16] On further reflection she conceded that Gaitskell had often lacked imagination and flexibility. 'But that he developed in the end into a great man, I don't doubt.'[17] Looking ahead to his potential successors she felt no one stood close to him in comparison. George Brown, the standard-bearer of the right, was deemed too much of an emotional bully, while Harold Wilson, the favourite, failed to inspire trust.

Gaitskell's illness seems to have caused Shirley more heart-searching about her future intentions, for days before his death she had written to Sara Barker, Labour's national agent, to inform her that she now felt able to put her name forward for consideration as a candidate. Barker responded cautiously, careful not to raise her hopes too high for the next election.

Her assessment appears to have convinced Shirley that her time hadn't yet come. 'I think I can say without exaggeration that through research work, television, articles and plain talk, I have much more influence on policy than the average MP in that bear garden,' she assured her parents. 'I may indeed stand; but I have no illusions at all about the splendours of parliamentary life. I see far too much of it. Two months before he died – no less than that – Hugh asked me to stand. I think I would have done. Now I am not so sure.'[18]

Her words caused them some dismay, but their protestations were in vain, for when they next raised the subject she seemed even more downbeat in her reply.

> An election looks possible in May, in which it is highly unlikely that I will stand or be asked to do so. If I don't it will be, however, my own main responsibility. That's all there is left to say, and I do ask you to consider the subject closed for the time being.[19]

At the end of March she and Rebecca left for a three-month sabbatical to the US to join Bernard, who had been on secondment to Princeton since January, but also to carry out an intense programme of lecturing in her own right. She was also a guest at the annual Americans for Democratic Action convention in Washington, meeting many high-ranking people including Arthur Schlesinger Jr, the eminent historian and special adviser to President Kennedy. 'The mood was one of disillusion with the Administration,' she reported, 'partly on civil rights and domestic affairs, partly on foreign policy ... Kennedy talks but doesn't deliver ... One gets the impression that most articulate Negroes are tired of being patient.'[20]

In May they undertook an exhausting tour to Chicago ('violence and yet more violence'), Syracuse ('horridly ugly little town'), Boston, where Bernard went to Harvard, and Toronto, where Shirley launched an Ontario Fabian Society. Her visit was marred by her fourth miscarriage and an uncomfortable four-day stay in a hospital in Quebec which took its toll.

They finished off with a visit to the desegregated South, acutely conscious of the 'desperate' civil rights business. 'Whether Kennedy can get his bill through is now crucial. There will be marches on the Capitol if he doesn't, and there may well be riots in Northern as well as Southern towns ... one can almost feel the excitement in the streets.'[21]

From the US it was on to Jamaica for a holiday, while events began to stir back home. The Labour candidate for the Hitchin Division, Vivian Ramsbottom, suddenly resigned because of his wife's serious illness, leaving a vacancy in a seat crucial to Labour's re-election prospects and one, contrary to what Shirley wrote in her autobiography, that it expected to win. On 12 June Jim Raisin, the Labour Party's northern Home Counties regional adviser, rang George to ascertain whether Shirley would be willing to be a candidate and appear before the forthcoming selection committee. The call caught George completely unawares because with Shirley incommunicado he wasn't sure of her exact whereabouts. Thankfully, the agent knew him and was prepared to accept his undertaking that she would accept unless they had word to the contrary. 'Hitchin has fallen vacant; will be won; and when it is (as will be) distributed, is safe,' George cabled Shirley when he discovered her location. 'I sense that there will be a feeling of disappointment if you do not accept. But this you have to do without delay by cable.'[22]

'She will upbraid me,' he wrote in his diary, 'but it is easier to pull out than to get in.'[23]

'This is an excellent prospect,' Raisin advised Shirley, drawing attention to the substantial increase in Labour's vote there since the last election. 'Apart, therefore, from current political trends, we really do expect this to be won … I expect there will be some good nominations but you would have a very good chance of selection.'[24]

The Hitchin division, consisting of five towns and thirty-six villages and serving an electorate of 88,000, was the fifth largest in the country. It was also one of the most culturally diverse. While Hitchin, Baldock and Royston, traditional market towns, and the surrounding villages conformed to the profile of many south of England divisions, Letchworth and Stevenage were very different; the former the first garden city, with its ethos of progressive high-mindedness, the latter the first of the new towns created under the 1946 Act to cope with London's burgeoning population. With its emphasis on new high-tech industries such as aerospace, its young classless families and well-planned city centre of glass and chromium, Stevenage was a world away from the grouse moor privilege of Harold Macmillan's England or the abject desperation of 1930s Jarrow. Politically, Hitchin had traditionally been Conservative territory, its one Labour MP coming on the back of the 1945 landslide, and the incumbent, Martin Maddan, was well respected for his feisty independence on behalf of the locality, but was now considered vulnerable as troubles continued to mount for the Macmillan government.

After the Conservatives' third successive victory in 1959 some Labour figures wondered whether they could ever win again, but within eighteen months the political landscape had changed quite drastically. A faltering economy formed the backdrop to a faltering government, culminating in the ignominious resignation of John Profumo, the Secretary of War, in June 1963, following his lie to the Commons about his affair with Christine Keeler. The affair seemed to bear out all too clearly Macmillan's increasingly tenuous grip at the helm, an old man out of touch with the times. Labour's new leader, Harold Wilson, in contrast with his meritocratic background, seemed the very essence of youthful dynamism as the party united behind a mantra of modernisation.

Encouraged by Bernard to stand for a division which he thought tailor-made for her, Shirley was one of six candidates approved by the Hitchin Labour Party's GMC on 19 July. A week later, after they had all spoken for fifteen minutes and answered questions from the eighty members present, the voting began. In a straight fight between Shirley and Bob Price, a local headmaster and chairman of the Hitchin Urban Council, she won by thirty-nine votes to twenty. While Price was most gracious in defeat, she expressed confidence about gaining Hitchin, but told George that if Labour didn't win next time it was finished.

As Shirley nursed her constituency in the run-up to the election (she resigned as general secretary of the Fabian Society in March 1964), she concentrated her main efforts on Stevenage and Letchworth, where over half the electorate lived. The big question confronting the former was the government's plans to double the size of Stevenage. Having digested all the arguments and consulted with local councillors she came out against further expansion, but stood by Labour's official policy that no decision would be taken until a public inquiry had been held. Her stance placed her at variance with Maddan, who opposed all extension, and the Liberal candidate, Elma Dangerfield, who supported it on the grounds that it guaranteed continued full employment.

As the candidates suspended hostilities throughout August, the return of full employment saw a significant recovery in the polls for the Conservatives, so that when Sir Alec Douglas-Home, the Prime Minister, announced the date of the election as 15 October, the Labour lead had almost disappeared. Before official campaigning commenced, Harold Wilson addressed a 700-strong 'Women of Britain meeting' in Stevenage. He was introduced by Shirley, who thought it appropriate that he should have come to the first of the new towns created by the Attlee government. It was bursting with energy and ideas, but was overburdened by overcrowded classes, insufficient teachers and lack of post-school training. It was a line she reiterated at her adoption meeting when she accused the Conservatives of wasting the talents of young people and presiding over a nineteenth-century social system.

This is a Party so lost in admiration for itself, that it hardly has time to turn round and see what it has done to Britain ... Let us send these people back to their grouse moors, their owner-occupied houses and to their public school system, and we will get on with the job.[25]

Up against a highly regarded incumbent who attacked Labour over comprehensive education, and a charismatic Liberal, Elma Dangerfield, who was winning converts in the villages by highlighting local issues, Shirley was taking nothing for granted. Touring all corners of the division, she spoke at 100 meetings, providing a separate election slip for each of the five main towns, and flourished at the hustings. 'Mrs Williams reels off the language of scientific man, talking computers and electronics fluently with the most technical of them,' reported *The Times*.[26] 'Everyone enjoyed working for her,' recalled Helen Grant, a stalwart of the Letchworth Labour Party and Shirley's hostess throughout the campaign. 'She never let us get too serious – a very remarkable gift.'[27]

With the main parties neck and neck during the first week of the campaign the 3.4 per cent swing Shirley needed in Hitchin seemed some way off, but the polls turned inexorably Labour's way thereafter, especially after the publication of dire balance of payment figures for September. In contrast to Wilson's adeptness as a campaigner, Douglas-Home's authority visibly waned as he struggled on the hustings. Days later he was subject to constant barracking in Stevenage town centre as he berated Labour's anti-nuclear policy, the prelude to a bruising encounter at the Birmingham Bull Ring when he couldn't be heard amidst the tumult. (Locally, the Conservative agent complimented Shirley for opposing heckling by her supporters at some of her opponent's meetings.)

After weeks of autumnal sunshine, polling day was the wettest for weeks, especially in the south-east, but this did nothing to detract from the high turn-out and the sense of anticipation that engulfed the constituency. Inside Hitchin Town Hall, as the count neared its completion, Bernard sauntered to the front of the stage to peer into the boxes of counted papers that hadn't yet been put on the racks. With a smile he returned and said quietly, 'They're nearly all yours, darling,' and gave her a victory kiss. Shortly before midnight the candidates appeared before the boisterous crowd chanting 'We want Shirley' that had assembled on the steps of the town hall to await the result. Three times the returning officer had to call for silence so that he could finish his declaration. When he announced that Shirley had won by 34,034 to 30,649 votes, a majority of 3,385 over Maddan, this was the signal for her supporters to surge towards her as she thanked her campaign team and paid a gracious tribute to her predecessor for all his work on behalf of the constituency.

Shirley's victory on the back of a 5.7 per cent swing helped Labour to the narrowest of victories, as it returned to government with an overall majority of four. She was one of six new women in the Commons – all Labour – and the second youngest woman out of the twenty-nine elected overall (the highest number, incidentally, 'til 1987). 'Shirley Williams is the gay and brilliant daughter of a left-wing couple,' commented *The Observer* that weekend, 'and is married to a professor of philosophy. She has stood four times for Parliament in the last 10 years and it is a disgrace to voters that she did not get in before.'[28] Other papers paid her similar compliments and, weeks later, the *Daily Mail* in an article entitled 'Could she be Britain's first woman premier?' interviewed Vera about her daughter's prospects. She said that Shirley becoming an MP was a dream come true and didn't rule out the possibility of her one day becoming Prime Minister. She certainly had 'the right brains, education and temperament for that office'.[29] It was a lot to live up to.

Endnotes
1   *Sunday Times*, 18 October 1959
2   Labour Party Conference Annual Report, Transport House, 1959, p.144
3   Labour Party Conference Annual Report, Transport House, 1961, p.219
4   GC diary, 3 October 1962
5   *Manchester Guardian*, 18 April 1960
6   *Sunday Times*, 15 January 1961
7   SW to GC, 30 October 1958
8   VB to SW, 27 December 1959
9   VB to Patricia Battey, 12 December 1960

10 SW to VB, 11 September 1961
11 GC to SW, 20 October 1961, SW Papers (private collection)
12 SW to D. F. Algar, 2 February 1962, SW Papers (private collection)
13 GC diary, 16 August 1962
14 GC diary, 2 September 1962
15 VB to Faith Moulson, 9 October 1962
16 SW to VB and GC, 20 January 1963
17 SW to VB and GC, 24 January 1963
18 SW to VB and GC, 20 January 1963
19 SW to VB and GC, 2 February 1963
20 SW to VB and GC, 7 May 1963
21 SW to VB and GC, 20 June 1963
22 GC to SW, 12 June 1963, SW Papers (private collection)
23 GC diary, 12 June 1963
24 Jim Raisin to SW, 12 June 1963, SW Papers (private collection)
25 *Hitchin Pictorial*, 24 September 1964
26 *The Times*, 12 October 1964
27 Helen Grant to VB, 20 October 1964
28 *Observer*, 18 October 1964
29 *Daily Mail*, 4 November 1964

# 7

# INTO GOVERNMENT

Labour's return to power in 1964 after thirteen years in exile was an occasion of great euphoria not only for party activists but also for all those committed to change in a Britain that remained steeped in its past.

Determined to make a difference from the very beginning, Wilson exuded an aura of purpose as he launched an ambitious programme for the new parliament, and his infectious optimism helped enthuse the Parliamentary Labour Party (PLP), keeping it relatively united in a way that seemed near impossible after the divisions of the Gaitskell era. It wasn't only the government with Jim Callaghan, Denis Healey and, later, Roy Jenkins to the fore, that comprised fresh blood. The 1964 intake of Labour MPs, containing a rich crop of talent, stood comparison with most vintages. With their pro-European ideals and ethos of enlightened tolerance it wasn't surprising that Shirley should have been drawn to many of them and she spent some time with the likes of Brian Walden, Roy Hattersley, David Ennals and Christopher Rowland, formulating ideas and exchanging gossip. Hattersley relates in his memoirs how for a few months in 1964–65 new Labour MPs were very much in vogue, especially with an early television current affairs programme called *Tonight*, and how he and Shirley were among a group of four who competed vigorously to appear on it.

And yet for all Shirley's exhilaration at being an MP and serving her constituents there was a less wholesome side to Parliament which remained with her thereafter. As one of only twenty-nine women MPs, four of whom had been educated at St Paul's (and ironically, given its elitist character, all Labour MPs), it was still very much the quintessential male club with archaic rules and customs. Aside from the exclusive atmosphere of the Smoking Room, where women were made to feel distinctly unwelcome, she found that there was something anachronistic about all-night sittings, the barrack room camaraderie and the raw tribalism of the party battle, not least the need to call on the sick to vote on a matter of some importance, given the government's minuscule majority at that time.

> After watching the sad little procession of sick Members, the stretchers and the beds made up in Ministers' rooms for those unable even to walk, one feels that the private game has gone on too long and has been ludicrously savage.
>
> At its least edifying the House of Commons is like a minor boys' public school.

She thought this particularly applicable to the 'great occasions' when backbenchers duly bayed and shouted. 'In the end, however, the great occasions may reveal something about men, but they reveal virtually nothing about the issues.'[1]

From the moment Shirley entered Parliament she became Private Parliamentary Secretary (PPS) to Kenneth Robinson, the Minister of Health. A PPS was traditionally a position of unpaid service to a minister, but the enlightened Robinson, a most dedicated and honourable public servant fully committed to female equality, turned it into something more elevating. He took her to departmental meetings, sought her opinions and discussed policy with her. Yet although keen to raise her profile and impress her superiors, Shirley was no blind careerist. She opposed the government's robust policy of immigration controls and berated it for undue lenience towards the white minority government of Ian Smith in Rhodesia as it sought independence from Britain without offering any constitutional guarantees of black majority rule.

As negotiations between Wilson and Smith meandered on aimlessly throughout most of 1965, Shirley was one of thirty-three backbenchers at Conference who called for a new Rhodesia and every form of economic sanction, and a military one if necessary, if Smith made a unilateral declaration of independence (UDI). Their cause wasn't helped by a major blunder by Wilson when he ruled out military force during a visit to Rhodesia in October, thus handing the initiative to Smith in this war of wills. After his account of his trip to the Commons, David Ennals, PPS to Barbara Castle, moved for an Adjournment of the House, a device for securing an immediate debate on a matter of great public importance. The Speaker refused to accept it, but word reached Ted Short, the Chief Whip, that Ennals was going to hold a meeting with Shirley to draw up a motion advocating a Royal Commission. Short sent Ennals to see Wilson, who read him the riot act, and gave Shirley a copy of PPS rules, which forbade them to sign any motion unless they had cleared it first of all with their minister or the Chief Whip. This intra-party spat left little impact on the wider scene. No longer fearing a military invasion, Smith now felt impelled to announce UDI on 11 November – much to the indignation of Britain and the rest of the world. Parliament passed the Southern Rhodesia Act reasserting its authority over its errant colony and legalising economic sanctions. 'Rhodesia will be the absolute talisman or touchstone of international politics in the next few years,' Shirley told the Letchworth Young Liberals. 'I think this will be the deciding case as to whether blacks and whites will be able to live together in multi-racial societies.'[2]

When the matter was debated in Parliament she criticised the Conservatives for being more sympathetic to the Smith government now that they were in opposition. No one who thought seriously about the situation in Rhodesia could believe for a moment that the rest of Africa would permit the illegal regime to survive.

With the opposition saddled with another uninspiring leader in Ted Heath and divided over Rhodesia, Wilson's own mastery domestically looked all the more telling. Following a significant swing to Labour at the Hull North by-election at the end of January 1966, he sought a dissolution at the beginning of March to secure a proper mandate. With the election fixed for 31 March, few doubted that Labour would be returned with a healthy majority, but in Hitchin Shirley was nothing if not cautious, especially since Elma Dangerfield, the Liberal candidate at the previous election, was now working for the new Conservative one, John Stokes, a management consultant with reactionary views. What's more, with no Liberal standing this time, the fear was that the 9,500 Liberals who had voted for Dangerfield might follow her lead into the Conservative camp.

Shirley need not have worried, for, aside from national trends, her local popularity counted greatly in her favour. Making much of the government's economic record in reducing the national debt and giving greater help to the public services, she contrasted seventeen months of Labour dynamism with thirteen years of Tory neglect. At a hastily arranged town hall debate, her dismissive treatment of John Stokes impressed Vera, who marvelled at how tough her daughter could be. With Hitchin swinging Labour's way like the rest of the country it soon became clear that the absence of a Liberal candidate played to Shirley's advantage as she captured most of that lost vote. With her majority swelling to 9,750, better than she ever expected, she once again gave her rapturous supporters much to celebrate as Stokes left the count looking very subdued.

Labour's emphatic victory, an overall majority of ninety-seven, gave Wilson the opportunity to inject fresh talent into his government at lower level and Shirley, along with Ennals, Peter Shore, Edmund Dell and Dick Taverne, was one of the 1964 class to be promoted. She was the last of the junior ministers to be told and arrived at Downing Street breathless, having run through the rain from the Treasury because she couldn't be found when Wilson wanted to see her. Her new position of Parliamentary Secretary to the Minister of Labour came courtesy of a personal request from the minister, Ray Gunter, and won the approbation of the press. The *Mirror* paid tribute to her debating prowess, *The Sun* thought she was probably the most gifted of all the women MPs, and *The Guardian* opined she had merited her chance to show her ability.

The Ministry of Labour was among the least glamorous of departments in Whitehall and described by Gunter, a right-wing trade unionist, as 'a bed of nails'. Aside from its pursuit of worthy objectives such as promoting industrial health and safety, its main *raison d'être* was pouring oil on the increasingly troubled waters of industrial relations. Yet despite the permanent air of crisis that seemed to engulf the department, the atmosphere among its employees was remarkably relaxed, so that Shirley found herself among friends. While only there for nine months she soon became acquainted with the full gamut of its responsibilities at a time when the ministry was becoming increasingly responsible for the government's unpopular prices-and-incomes policy.

Unwilling to consider devaluation as a remedy for the £800 million balance of payments deficit it inherited – Wilson recalled the humiliating devaluation of 1949 – the government was obliged to fall back on some form of incomes policy. In March 1965 a voluntary pay norm linked to national economic growth was instituted, but with earnings rising too rapidly throughout the rest of the year, a Bill imposing statutory wage control was in its embryonic stages when the 1966 election was called.

Doubts about sterling, deemed to be overvalued and vulnerable to speculators, remained dormant in the weeks leading up to the election, and, according to Wilson's biographer, Ben Pimlott, it needed only one jolt to cause disaster. The catalyst for trouble came from the National Union of Seamen who wanted a reduction in hours from fifty-six to forty-six per week, the equivalent of a 17 per cent rise in pay. The Seamen with its left-wing leadership didn't rank high in the Labour pantheon of trade unions and, desperate to avoid wage inflation careering out of control, the government backed the employers. The union retaliated by launching an immediate strike, causing massive disruption in the docks and inflicting maximum damage on the economy. While Wilson set up a state of emergency and an independent court of inquiry under Lord Pearson, Shirley faced something of a conundrum. Recognising the dangerous nature of the seamen's job, she accepted that their pay fared badly compared with many other industries and merited redress. Her sympathy waned, however, as the strike's calamitous effect upon sterling became ever greater and the union refused to accept the Pearson compromise, which gave it much of what it wanted.

On 28 June Gunter, under considerable physical strain, suffered a minor heart attack and was despatched to Wilson's home on the Scilly Isles to recuperate. His absence meant a tough baptism for Shirley as the only other minister in the department, but she appeared quite unabashed about attending Cabinet to report on the strike and answering for all departmental business in the Commons.

On 1 July the seamen's strike was eventually settled, but the seven-week dispute had exposed all too clearly the fragility of the economy. The selling of sterling continued apace, not helped by the resignation of the left-wing trade unionist Frank Cousins from the Cabinet in protest at the publication of the Prices and Incomes Bill, which imposed a six-month wage freeze followed by another six months of further restraint. With George Brown, the Secretary of State for Economic Affairs, reluctant to lead in committee, it fell to his junior minister, Bill Rodgers, and Shirley to bear the gruelling responsibility of guiding the Bill through. With the opposition unhappy about the timetable and Labour rebels such as Cousins fighting it clause by clause, especially the new Part Four, which gave the Department of Economic Affairs complete power over prices and wages, thirty-five hours were spent in committee, including two all-night sittings, in order to help get the Bill into law before the recess. At the second sitting, from Thursday 10.30 a.m. to Friday 11.21 a.m., with one three-hour break, there were heated exchanges, most notably when Cousins – now an ex-minister and a member of the select committee – walked out to register his protest over the Bill. Eventually, thanks to the sensitive leadership of the committee's chairman, Harold Lever, its marathon passage was completed, much to Brown's delight as he grabbed Shirley for an impromptu dance of celebration.

In January 1967 Shirley was appointed Minister of State at the Department of Education. Her departure was much regretted by the Ministry of Labour and by the trade unions, whose initial wariness of dealing with a middle-class woman had soon evaporated as they found her more receptive than Gunter. At the same time her promotion delighted her parents ('Give me a joyful heart, O Lord', George wrote in his diary) and the educational Establishment.[3]

Shirley's new responsibilities brought her face to face with an issue about which she felt passionate – the need for a fairer education system. Like almost all affluent left-wing parents of that era, Vera and George had never hesitated in educating their children privately, apart from Shirley's brief spell at a state primary, but those six months, as previously mentioned, appeared to have assumed a crucial significance. (She always mentioned this school in her personal particulars and rarely St Paul's despite spending much longer at the latter.)

Aside from her disapproval of the social divisions emanating from private education, Shirley, while never denying the excellence of much of the teaching she received at St Paul's, chafed under the rigidities of its arcane rules and petty hierarchies. The undue emphasis placed upon social deportment and cultural conformity seemed all the more contrived after the classless informality of the US, where anything seemed possible. One of Shirley's great virtues was her genuine ability to mix with all types, and the poverty of aspiration she encountered among so many of the downtrodden, especially women, she attributed to a selective educational system that condemned the overwhelming majority to failure. She wasn't alone in her analysis.

The 1944 Education Act went some way towards enhancing educational opportunity by raising the school leaving age to fourteen (soon to be extended to fifteen), but its tripartite system of schooling failed to stand the test of time. At their best the grammar schools offered an outstanding education and a ladder of opportunity to many from modest backgrounds such as Harold Wilson, Roy Jenkins, Ted Heath and Margaret Thatcher, but they were very much the exception rather than the rule. Most children fell foul of the eleven-plus, an exam that favoured those from the middle class, and were consigned to the less prestigious secondary modern. The consequent dearth of vocational expertise and untapped talent highlighted the need for an educational system that was more socially inclusive and attuned to the needs of industry. While the impetus for comprehensives emanated from the London County Council and parts of Wales, there was also support from the suburbs, where an increasing number of middle-class children had lost out at eleven. By the time the Conservatives left office in 1964, some 200 comprehensives had been established and many more were in their embryonic stage.

Once again Shirley was fortunate in her minister, although a very different type from both Robinson and Gunter. Aside from being one of the party's leading intellectuals and keeper of the Gaitskellite flame, Tony Crosland, with his glamorous appearance and scintillating conversation, could be riveting company. His *Future of Socialism* was seen as the classic revisionist text on social democracy and his presence was much sought in Fabian circles when Shirley was its secretary. Although uninterested in female and racial equality ('Here comes Williams with her bleeding heart for Africa' was a familiar Crosland jibe), his willingness to absorb fresh ideas, his abhorrence of class prejudice and passion for a fairer educational system made him the perfect mentor. He was happy to give her her head, but advised her to 'Go for two or three key issues and leave the rest, with instructions, to civil servants', advice she found it hard to adhere to as she became immersed in superfluous detail. Her unmethodical approach frustrated Crosland, who told her that she was quite a good minister but she couldn't see the wood for the trees.

With educational policy still overwhelmingly the preserve of the local authorities, there were strict limits to what any government could do, but with many opting to go comprehensive, Crosland merely went with the flow by issuing Circular 10/65, drawn up by Michael Stewart, his predecessor, requesting every local authority to submit a plan. While the vast majority complied, some reluctantly, others, like Surrey, resisted, so in order to bring opponents into line Crosland took advantage of Labour's increased majority by making capital expenditure for schools dependent on their local authority's commitment to 10/65.

In August 1967 Crosland was switched to the Department of Trade and replaced by Patrick Gordon Walker, who for all his academic credentials never seemed at ease in his new portfolio. Shirley compared his perpetual anxiety about every pending engagement and discussion to the White Rabbit in *Alice in Wonderland*. She liked him and found him more engaging than his melancholy appearance suggested, but much less formidably clever than Crosland. His vulnerability was soon evident when he allowed himself to be badgered by the newly appointed Minister of State, Alice Bacon, a former teacher, into removing Shirley from the schools portfolio to that of higher education. Although she deeply regretted being ousted from the comprehensive campaign, she found the conversation of university academics and scientists more stimulating than that of the teachers. An early highlight was the meeting of twenty-eight educational ministers from both Eastern and Western European countries in Vienna to discuss 'Access to Higher Education'. Held in the splendour of the Hofburg Palace, Shirley, who danced a rather eccentric polka with the Danish minister at the Burgomaster's Ball, described this rare encounter between the two systems as an uplifting experience, not least the relative absence of propaganda. She gave a robust account of the British higher educational system commending the very high staff–student ratio, the low wastage rate and the general grant which provided access to all, but conceded that the low percentage of women students at 26 per cent needed improving. 'We came off surprisingly well,' she told her parents, 'with a proportion of students from working-class homes twice as high as the next most progressive Western country, and ranked at very nearly the same level as Eastern Europe. I was the only woman minister of course, which also helped us to look rather broadminded!'[4]

Shirley's work at Education took place against an unstable political background as Britain's industrial malaise caused a further run on sterling. When the government bowed to the inevitable and devalued the pound by 14 per cent in November 1967, Callaghan felt compelled to resign as Chancellor, leaving his successor, Roy Jenkins, to pick up the pieces. His two years of 'hard slog' meant painful cuts in government expenditure, including education, and the postponement of the raising of the school leaving age to sixteen led to the resignation of the mercurial Lord Longford.

It also embroiled Shirley in a tiff with Dick Crossman, the Lord President of the Council and Leader of the House of Commons, and a man she never entirely trusted. On 13 February 1968, the night before an opposition vote of censure on the education cuts, Shirley rang Crossman to say that she wanted to see him. Crossman was engaged at the time and asked her to ring him early the next morning. She didn't, but her secretary later rang him to say that Shirley was off to open an institute of education in Birmingham. When Crossman discovered from John Silkin, the Chief Whip, that, despite her late-morning engagement, she wasn't planning to be back for the evening vote he was furious, and so was Wilson when Crossman regaled him with the facts.

After protracted negotiations between Silkin, Shirley and Crossman, Shirley agreed to be in the latter's office by 8 p.m.

Crossman recorded in his diary,

She came in looking very disturbed, but before she could make a speech I said, 'You ought to be here for the big censure debate.' 'This debate has nothing to do with me,' she said. 'I deal with universities.' Of course there is an impossible relationship between Shirley on the one hand and Gordon Walker and Alice Bacon on the other. I don't blame her for finding Patrick pretty miserable and Alice Bacon's voice unbearable but I do blame her for the kind of disloyalty which makes her absent herself during a vote of censure. She's trying to avoid responsibility for the education cut of which she doesn't approve.[5]

Crossman's accusation that Shirley had tried to pair herself[6] for the censure debate in order to disassociate herself from the government's policy was a serious one. Determined to set the record straight, she sent Wilson a long letter laying out the facts. She explained that she had a long-standing engagement at the Birmingham Guild of Students' debating society, coupled with a morning engagement to open the new institute of education. On 7 February, before the publication of the following week's parliamentary business, her private secretary had written to the pairing whip informing him that she had a ministerial engagement on 14 February and asked for a pair. The subsequent publication of parliamentary business led to her cancelling her visit to the Guild of Students, but, after consulting Gordon Walker's private secretary, not the morning one.

> While I was in Birmingham, I received a message from the Chief Whip ordering me to return immediately. Mystified, I rang and explained that I was returning anyway on the 6.15 p.m. train, that this had been agreed, and that I could not walk out on a ceremony involving the presence of representatives of many local authorities and colleges of education throughout the West Midlands without considerable damage to the Government's standing. He was very fair, and agreed I might stay for this purpose, returning immediately afterwards.
>
> When I got back to the House that night shortly after 8 p.m. I went to see the Lord President about another urgent matter. He then mentioned to me the interpretation of my conduct set out at the beginning of this letter. This, of course, explained why the Chief Whip had ordered me to return.
>
> Apart from the fact that my request for a pair predated my knowledge of the debate or its subject, and was withdrawn when my office realized what was on, I find it appalling that such interpretations could be placed on my behaviour without an explanation being sought by colleagues with whom I believed I was on friendly terms. I give you my word that if I found a Government policy unacceptable I would resign; trying to sneak out in the way implied would be absolutely contemptible. I hope,

therefore, that you will feel you now have the true facts of the matter, as I have tried to put them before you.[7]

The year 1968 will long live in the memory as the year when youthful idealism and individual libertarianism of a post-war generation erupted in anger across Western Europe and the US. As traditional institutions and values were openly derided the Vietnam War became the banner around which a conglomeration of minority causes gathered.

Although Britain was less affected by the tumult than France and the US, her university campuses seethed with unrest. As the higher education minister, Shirley wasn't immune to this raging passion. At Southampton University, en route to the Senior Common Room, she encountered placard-waving students blocking her car, shouting, 'Gordon Walker out', as they demonstrated for higher grants. In an act of raw courage she marched straight up to them and entered into a twenty-minute dialogue in what looked like an open-air seminar. Having listened to their grievances she calmly explained that there were limits to how far the government could go in increasing social expenditure faster than gross national product (GNP), especially when students fared better than many other groups. Weeks later, in a debate on universities in the Commons, Shirley expressed her support for responsible student consultation and maximum autonomy for student unions, but cautioned against any destruction of the system which enabled the questioning to take place. 'We cannot, on the one side, condone violence from the Left Wing because we have sympathy for it and, on the other, be unwilling to condone violence from the extreme Right Wing because we lack sympathy for them.'[8]

The student disorders helped claim the scalp of Gordon Walker, who had never really settled at Education. 'There appears to have been some rather ill-concealed pleasure at Patrick's departure in the Department,' she informed George.[9] His successor, Ted Short, she respected as a man of austere integrity and decisiveness, as befitted a former state school headmaster, if not always the most effective of communicators. As tempers began to subside she helped him draw up an Education Act that gave students full representation on university courts and academic boards and provided autonomy for student unions, but drew the line at giving them any say over assessment or exams. The Act also required polytechnics and further education colleges to have governing bodies which, Shirley ensured, contained adequate representation of staff and students.

Growing economic retrenchment had helped revise opinion about the future of British universities. At a seminar at the LSE in January 1969, Shirley outlined some of the hard choices they could face over the course of the next decade or so. One was to increase the qualifications of entry into higher education in order to reduce numbers; another was to find ways of reducing costs.

These thoughts were further amplified in the Commons that July when replying to a call from the shadow Education Minister, Sir Edward Boyle, for the government to provide better value for money in higher education. She felt that the most plausible route to reducing costs without impairing quality lay in the restructuring of the academic year. The proposal, which had emanated from the Committee of Vice-Chancellors and Principals, was for three fifteen-week terms in which students would only attend two out of three rather than the then arrangement of three ten-week terms. 'The danger is that more would at last begin to mean worse,' commented *The Teacher*, the journal of the National Union of Teachers. 'The rapid expansion of British universities in the last decade has largely confounded the Jeremiahs who said quality would fall when the student turnover was stepped up. But the shift system outlined by Mrs Williams would almost certainly compromise the peculiar excellence of the British academic tradition.'[10]

On 25 September she met the University Grants Committee and Committee of Vice-Chancellors and Principals, the former under Kenneth Berrill, at University College, London. At issue was the means by which the higher educational system would cope with the projected growth in the number of students throughout the 1970s (636,000 projected for 1976 and 780,000 for 1980), some 40 per cent more than Lord Robbins, the great advocate of university expansion, had anticipated. Having laid out the facts Shirley stressed the need for increased efficiency, and pressed the universities to reform, be it shorter courses, a less generous staff–student ratio or the introduction of student loans.

The recommendations, later known as the thirteen points, were much discussed within the world of higher education and overwhelmingly rejected in the name of university autonomy and academic excellence. As they made their opposition known, Shirley bluntly told them that if they didn't adopt this kind of restructuring they would eventually find themselves short of funds, a prediction that came all too true during the 1980s.

In October, as negotiations continued behind closed doors, Shirley was moved from Education to be Minister of State at the Home Office as part of a major government reshuffle, Wilson's eighth, at middle-ranking level. According to Crossman, who had wanted her as his Minister of State at the Department of Social Security earlier in the year, her removal was 'a nauseating disrespect for departmental work ... She has been an outstanding Education Minister and she ought to be allowed to run her course.'[11]

'Mrs Williams's departure will be regretted by the many people in further and higher education who have come into contact with her refreshing personality and highly articulate intelligence,' noted the *Times Educational Supplement*,[12] although its diarist did suggest that 'the sheer volume of activity she generated did not help the smooth flow of departmental business'.[13] Civil servants discussing her style with A. H. Halsey, the sociologist and adviser to Tony Crosland, claimed that she behaved more like an executive officer than a minister of the Crown.

If Wilson had thought that Shirley's membership of the government would muzzle her he was soon proved to be mistaken, as she continued to push collective responsibility to the limits.

When Kenya had won its independence in 1963 the then Colonial

Secretary, Duncan Sandys, had promised an absolute right of entry to the 185,000 Asians there who held British passports should the Kenyatta government discriminate against them, something it duly did. When 13,000 landed during the first two months of 1968 and with many more poised to come, senior Conservatives including Enoch Powell, the shadow Defence Secretary, began to call for the revoking of the right of the Asians to enter. Their call didn't go unheeded, for whatever the moral obligation to honour the promise, the political climate was hardly conducive to a further influx of immigrants. Consequently Jim Callaghan, the new Home Secretary, rushed a Bill through Parliament at the end of February restricting the entry of Kenyan Asians to Britain to 1,500 a year, and their families. Liberal-minded members on both sides of the House were offended by the Bill's restrictive practices, with thirty-five Labour MPs rebelling, and *The Guardian*, appalled that anyone with a British passport should be turned away, called for the resignation of some ministers. Whether that editorial in any way pricked Shirley's conscience is unclear, but on that same day she wrote Wilson a long letter of resignation. Having outlined her unease about the education cuts, she told him that the Immigration Act placed her in an impossible position. She recognised that the strain on public services in certain parts of the country made unrestricted entry impossible, but she couldn't defend the idea of two levels of British citizenship, nor the breaking of commitments entered into by a British government and embodied in a law of such recent date.

She was dissuaded from resignation by Mark Bonham Carter, the chairman of the Race Relations Board, perhaps because of Callaghan's belated concession that Britain would accept those Kenyan Asians with British citizenship expelled from Kenya and with nowhere else to go, but the row didn't abate. Hitchin Labour Party quizzed her about the restrictions on immigration and she told the local paper that no one could be proud of the fact that the government had decided to limit the right of British citizens of Asian origin coming into the country. They couldn't afford for these people to be stateless.

The festering question of race once again exploded into view that April when Enoch Powell's 'rivers of blood' speech warned in chilling terms of racial conflagration should immigration be left unchecked. At a Labour Party meeting in Bath, Shirley warned that Britain must avoid the type of racial problems then afflicting the US in the aftermath of the assassination of the civil rights leader Martin Luther King. She admitted that repatriation of immigrants was possible, but if they were compelled to return 'we would cease to be a civilised country – indeed we would be no better than Nazi Germany in its attitude towards its Jewish citizens'.[14]

During the autumn of 1968 Shirley was once again preoccupied by the crisis in Rhodesia. Following the failure of the HMS *Tiger* talks in December 1966 and the ineffectiveness of sanctions, relations with the errant colony remained mired in deadlock as Wilson sought to find a way through the maze. It said much for his sense of optimism that, despite Cabinet presentiments to the contrary, he felt confident that he could broker a deal. To help things along, he abandoned his insistence that there should be no independence before majority rule, although his new list of six principles necessary for independence ultimately pointed to that destination. When he and Smith met on board HMS *Fearless* in October 1968, the latter effectively stalled on the former's proposals, causing more dismay within Labour ranks. As George Thomson, the Commonwealth Secretary, was sent to Rhodesia for further discussions Shirley wrote to Wilson to tell him of her grave doubts about the proposals.

The effects of a settlement on *Fearless* lines, or worse, on the United Nations and the Commonwealth will be serious. Equally bad, in my view, are the possible effects on the Labour Party and on attitude in this country. We might find ourselves aligned against the developing world, and the developing members of the Cw and Canada, and on the same side as South Africa. I do appreciate how difficult the dilemma is, but the price of a settlement (unless Smith concedes more than he has so far) seems likely to be too high, anyway for me.[15]

In his reply, Wilson asked her to accept his determination that there would be no settlement outside the six principles to which the government and party as a whole had subscribed. He believed that the proposals would represent an honourable settlement of a tragic problem and would open the way for the real economic and political advancement of the African population of Rhodesia.

On the eve of Thomson's visit Shirley remained unconvinced, as did other young MPs such as David Ennals, Reg Prentice and Gwyneth Dunwoody. The question of her resignation again surfaced and her constituency agent, while calling it pure speculation, didn't categorically deny it. In the end the failure of Thomson's visit, prompted once again by the refusal of the Smith government to concede black majority rule, preserved the unity of Wilson's Cabinet but at some cost to the future development of Rhodesia.

Shirley's frayed relationship with the government also extended to the field of private morality, where even the convention of a free vote didn't entirely prevent trouble. As a liberal broadly in the Jenkins mould, Shirley might have been expected to have been a committed follower of the more permissive ethos which gained currency during the 1960s. Yet to the bewilderment of many of her closest friends whose principles were firmly etched in an enlightened humanitarianism, Shirley's Roman Catholicism often pulled her in the opposite direction, most notably in her opposition to the 1967 Abortion Act and over divorce. Although a Bill allowing for easier divorce ran out of time in the 1967–68 session of Parliament, the government agreed it would be reintroduced in the next session. Its decision caused complications because of the introduction of the Labour backbencher Edward Bishop's Matrimonial Property Bill, which, in bidding to complement the Divorce Reform Bill, sought fairer financial provision for wives who might have been divorced against their will.

While most advocates of divorce reform were sympathetic to Bishop's Bill, the Law Officers thought it unworkable and as the matter was under consideration by the Law Commission, the government decided to oppose the Bill at second reading, with a three-line whip for ministers and a two-line whip for backbenchers. The decision, reaffirmed the day before the debate at Cabinet, and handled insensitively by the Chief Whip, John Silkin, prompted a dramatic revolt by Labour MPs at a meeting of the PLP. In a defiant speech Shirley referred to the promises already given by some ministers to vote for the Bill. The Chief Whip's summons had put her into 'considerable conflict with her conscience'. Just before she spoke, Wilson and the Lord Chancellor left the meeting, to be joined by the Chief Whip. After hurried consultations they returned a few minutes later to announce a free vote in an attempt to find a negotiated solution. The following day *The Guardian's* Ian Aitken reported on the speculation among MPs that Wilson's volte-face was down to 'the intervention of Mrs Williams, who is not only an extremely attractive feminist but a Minister, too'.[16]

After Bishop's Bill passed its second reading, Wilson, unhappy about his government's maladroit handling of the affair, wrote to Shirley in high dudgeon.

> Had I known about your intervention I would certainly have referred to it. It would have been to say what now must be said that it is quite contrary to Government practice for Ministers, whether at Party Meeting or anywhere else, to disassociate themselves from Government policy, which on this occasion was made fully clear by the Lord Chancellor…
>
> I recognise, of course, the difficulties which all Ministers face, not only in relation to Government measures, on which you have had occasion to write to me more than once, but on the particularly tricky problems caused by many Private Members' Bills. But in neither case is it possible to disassociate oneself from one's collective responsibility and to continue to remain a member of the Government.[17]

In her reply Shirley accepted that she merited criticism, but claimed that she wouldn't have spoken at the party meeting if the Bill hadn't been a Private Member's Bill that presented issues of conscience to her. She professed ignorance of the government's opposition to Bishop's Bill until she received the whip, while recognising that the minutes of the legislative committee would have informed her of this fact.

Although Bishop's Bill passed comfortably he agreed to withdraw it in return for a promise that legislation would follow in the next session based on the Law Commission's findings over matrimonial financial relief, and that the Divorce Bill wouldn't be implemented until such legislation had been introduced. The success over better financial protection for divorced spouses stiffened opposition to the Divorce Bill (Shirley was one of two ministers to oppose it), so that the government, while theoretically neutral, felt compelled to intervene to secure it as much time as it needed and impose a three-line whip to get it through report stage.

Shirley's transfer to the Home Office was in part a typical Wilson ploy to use her Catholicism to good effect in a department heavily embroiled in the politics of Northern Ireland. Aside from her disappointment to be leaving Education in the middle of crucial negotiations with the universities about their future, a move to the Home Office gave her little cause for satisfaction. The government's immigration policy continued to upset her and now that her responsibility for that policy would become much more personal she once again toyed with resignation. Clearly she was soon to have second thoughts, because she never sent her letter.

The Home Office was one of the great departments of state, with a miscellany of different responsibilities from immigration and the criminal law to prisons and Northern Ireland. It was to be Shirley's lot to have responsibility for prisons, parole and pornography, as well as the non-military side of Northern Ireland. She also secured an early triumph in the Commons over the abolition of capital punishment.

In 1965 capital punishment had been suspended for five years, and with the Murder Act due to expire in July 1970, the government decreed in 1969 that the matter should be settled once and for all. This meant that by pressing for outright abolition it would be turning its back on its previous argument that the final decision should rest on the murder statistics of the intervening five years.

Following the government's announcement the shadow Home Secretary, Quintin Hogg, moved a Commons motion censuring it for trying to force a decision before the relevant statistics for 1969 were available. Such peremptory behaviour, he argued, would increase the likelihood of backbench pressure to restore capital punishment during the next parliament.

His words were abruptly dismissed by Shirley. In one of her more trenchant Commons performances she insisted that there was no constitutional issue at stake. The wording of the 1965 Act didn't compel the House to wait for a five-year period. The figures in any case wouldn't be available until after the Act expired and what, in any case, did the House expect to learn from them? She reminded it how much time it had devoted to the matter over the years and declared that it risked creating the dangerous anomaly of the Abolitionist Act lapsing before it had calmly debated what to put in its place. 'I trust that we shall tomorrow take a decision; a final decision; on this matter and, speaking for myself, I hope that that decision will be to remove once and for all the shadow of the gallows from this humane land.'[18] According to Hugh Noyes in *The Times*, Shirley performed an able demolition job on the Tory case, and the next day the permanent abolition of capital punishment was approved by a hefty majority.

None of this gave cause for complacency in the battle to maintain law and order. With the prison capacity then increasing at over 1,000 per month to 37,000 in March 1970 due to the growth in crime, the whole system of penal institutions had come under severe strain, with chronic overcrowding leading to serious outbursts of disorder. Confronted with this situation and with the knowledge from her own visits to these archaic establishments, Shirley was acutely aware that more prisons with better facilities were needed, not least for washing and hygiene, but they were expensive and took time to complete so temporary measures were often necessary.

The crisis in the prisons made for a sombre mood at the Prison Officers' Association conference in May 1970. When it was her turn to respond Shirley offered delegates little cause for comfort either in an immediate easing of the staff shortage or in a curb on the rising prison population. She said that while attempts were being made to improve accommodation at existing prisons and implement refurbishments at others, this would only account for a small proportion of the 12,000 prisoners then sleeping three to a cell.

The state of the prisons, along with the high rates of re-offending, convinced her that fresh solutions were needed to cope with offenders, especially those who were problematic rather than dangerous. Parole, she told the annual conference of Probation Officers, was the way forward, as the early signs of this recent innovation had been encouraging, and should be accompanied by more non-custodial sentences.

Shirley's arrival at the Home Office came in the wake of the historic decision to send British troops to Northern Ireland as Catholic civil rights protests gave rise to violent retaliation from the Protestant community. While Callaghan took prime responsibility for security, she continued to work closely with all sides to allocate generous quantities of government aid to the province. Ulster, she told George, required an American 'new deal' type scheme to cure it of its lingering high unemployment. Perhaps her most telling experience was the onslaught she faced from Ian Paisley, the uncompromising Unionist leader, regarding Catholic plots at the Home Office, to which she didn't respond. ('In Ulster, personal attacks are never ignored; it may teach him a little English cool.')[19] Not surprisingly she preferred her previous portfolio at Education because it was intellectually more stimulating. 'This job demands, of course, very political skills. Jim has them in abundance. The longer I work with him, the more I admire his sheer political ability – though not, on the whole, his policies. Too conservative for me.'[20]

After several years of unremitting gloom 1970 brought an upsurge in the government's fortunes. With the balance of payments improving fast, the large Tory lead of the previous autumn had all but disappeared and Jenkins's well-received Budget fuelled talk of an early election. Labour's encouraging performance in the Scottish local elections (then held days before the English ones) enhanced that prospect. 'If it goes on next Saturday in England too, that incredible little Yorkshireman will have got his sums exactly right,' Shirley wrote to George. 'So we might have a June election before the Test matches with those damned Springboks and the long hot summer starts.'[21]

The English elections, following the lead from Scotland, boded well for the government and confirmed Wilson in his hunch that June indeed was the right month to go to the country. In Hitchin, now the fourth largest constituency in the country with an electorate of nearly 110,000 (a rise of 19,000 since the previous election), the Liberals this time fielded a candidate, while the Conservative candidate was Richard Luce, the Director of the National Innovation Centre. The latter recalled Shirley as a formidable opponent endowed with sensible views and great charm. When they had joined forces the previous year at the mass meeting to oppose Nuthampstead as the site for London's third airport, she, as the sitting MP, had raised no objection to him, her opposite number, being placed alongside her on the platform. When he challenged her to a public debate during the campaign she, to his surprise, agreed. The result was a spirited exchange at the Free Trade Hall, Letchworth. All three candidates agreed on many ethical issues, although major differences emerged over housing policy and international aid. During the campaign Shirley received a major boost not only from a glowing endorsement from Wilson on a visit to Stevenage, but even more from a flattering editorial in *The Times* under the heading 'Does Labour Care?' Questioning its image as the compassionate party, it saw little difference between the parties and their status and ambitions. There were, however, exceptions. 'If one had to pick a single Labour MP in whose social conscience one would trust it would be Mrs Shirley Williams.' Observing how government office could make a woman unattractively aggressive as she held her own with the men, it went on:

> Shirley Williams is not a bit like that, she is one of those very rare women who could become Prime Minister (and perhaps should) without losing a scrap of her good nature and charm; and without thinking any the better of herself for it ... It will be a great loss to the new Parliament if Mrs Williams is not returned to it.[22]

The editorial caused quite a stir and some difficulties for her opponents. The Conservative agent in Hitchin admitted that she was a very nice person and quite a good MP, but scoffed at the idea that she was prime ministerial material, and Shirley, while grateful to *The Times* for marking her card, felt its rather curt dismissal of Labour's compassionate credentials a regrettable error.

The campaign nationwide, played out in glorious weather, was a dull affair with Wilson in presidential pose projecting a statesman-like image and deliberately avoiding undue controversy. His ploy, which in retrospect seemed unduly complacent, appeared to be working as the polls consistently gave Labour a comfortable lead. A rogue set of bad trade figures for May, announced during the final week, caused something of a minor flurry, giving some credence to Heath's repeated claims about Labour's deception over the real state of the economy, but not enough to suggest anything untoward. It was thus something of a genuine shock to almost everyone when the first results recorded a significant swing to the Conservatives. Despite the recent improvement in the economy the electorate remembered their loss of spending power over the previous few years. More important, for all the talent arrayed in the Wilson Cabinet, their collective failure to live up to the high ideals of 1964 had cost them dear. By the time Shirley's result was announced the next morning it was clear that the Conservatives were returning to government and Luce recalls seeing her in tears as she learnt of the defeat of good friends such as David Ennals on the radio. Her own majority was slashed by some 6,000 to 3,674 on a 4.4 per cent swing, one of the smallest in the region, the effect in all probability of her strong personal following. It was small consolation for a minister who days earlier had been predicting a Labour majority of between thirty and fifty, and who could conceivably have expected promotion to the Cabinet.

Yet she could look back at her first few years in Parliament with satisfaction. In an administration that had generally disappointed she was fortunate that her main contribution had been in one of its most successful areas: education. By her commitment to comprehensive schools she had helped implement one of its big ideas to such a point that it appeared unstoppable; equally, her passion for expanding the boundaries of higher education had helped make the Robbins Report of 1963 a reality, tempered by the subsequent need for readjustment when the purse strings began to tighten. The failure of many universities to face up to the hard choices with which she and her successor confronted them came back to haunt them thereafter.

As a minister she had been dedicated, approachable and proficient. Vice-chancellors and academics were often dazzled with the ease with which she mastered the intricacies of their block grant. Civil servants liked her, appreciated her openness to ideas and admired her command of a brief, though her failure to delegate clogged the wheels of government. It was this failure that caused Crosland to raise doubts about her effectiveness, but all the other ministers under whom she served rated her, with Callaghan telling her that he looked forward to seeing her hold high office in a future Labour Cabinet.

In Parliament she won respect on all sides for her competence and charm, with one Tory MP telling Robin Douglas-Home of the *Daily Express* that Shirley was not only the most attractive woman in the House, she was also the nicest. While no Churchill with soaring flights of eloquence or Bevan with a biting wit that could destroy an opponent, she spoke with authority, her clarity reinforced with an abiding sense of moral conviction. Unlike some of her colleagues she treated her opponents with courtesy, rarely stooping to partisan joust or personal barb in the course of her exegesis. Sir Edward Boyle, a liberal-leaning baronet who was her shadow at Education, considered her one of the most distinguished minds and delightful personalities that he had encountered in his twenty years in politics. She in turn admired him not only for his commitment to learning but also for defying his party over comprehensive schools, immigration and capital punishment. To be known as the Edward Boyle of the Labour Party was an accolade she wouldn't mind having, she told her father. It was a revealing comment, given her own propensity to dissent.

For all Shirley's immense popularity with the press and public, the high esteem in which she was held wasn't entirely shared by all those MPs who worked closely with her, chiefly because of her quixotic streak. Politics is the art of the possible but Shirley was more flexible than most in her tactical manoeuvring, with a tendency to depart from an agreed script, not least in a radio or television studio or on a political platform. Whether this inconsistency was down to absentmindedness, self-interest or a reluctance to court controversy, it was a trait that lingered throughout her career. Many readily forgave her but some of her fellow rebels on issues such as immigration or Rhodesia were less understanding when abandoned at the eleventh hour. Even over Europe, a cause which she often fought with great courage, her failure to resign over Labour's commitment to a referendum in March 1972 (of which more later) made her a rather more detached figure than met the eye, an important fact given the divisions on Labour's centre-right during the 1970s.

This detachment wasn't merely the result of her unwillingness to fully conform to the rules of the political club; there were extenuating reasons. Aside from the fact that female MPs generally felt out of place at Westminster, she was also the victim of circumstance. The break-up of her marriage to Bernard, which was to come in December 1971, would, aside from its personal trauma, leave her with the practical problem of having to combine her onerous responsibilities as shadow Cabinet minister and constituency MP with those of a single parent tending to her young daughter. What free time she did have was spent with Rebecca rather than socialising with colleagues. The lack of a permanent partner in her life during her remaining years in Parliament was a loss which diminished her self-confidence at a time when she sorely needed it.

**Endnotes**

1   *Observer*, 8 August 1965
2   *Hertfordshire Express*, 19 November 1965
3   GC diary, 6 January 1967
4   SW to VB and GC, 6 December 1967
5   Richard Crossman, *The Diaries of a Cabinet Minister, Vol. 2, 1966–1968*, ed. Janet Morgan, Hamish Hamilton and Jonathan Cape, 1976, p.681
6   A parliamentary convention whereby two MPs from opposition parties – mainly for convenience – agree to mutually refrain from voting.
7   SW to Harold Wilson, 16 February 1968, SW Papers (personal collection)
8   Hansard, 15 March 1968
9   SW to GC, 28 April 1968
10  *Teacher*, 1 August 1969
11  Richard Crossman, *The Diaries of a Cabinet Minister, Vol. 3, 1968–1970*, ed. Janet Morgan, Hamish Hamilton and Jonathan Cape, 1977, p.681
12  *Times Educational Supplement*, 31 October 1969
13  *Times Educational Supplement*, 17 October 1969
14  *Morning Star*, 1 May 1968
15  SW to Harold Wilson, 4 November 1968, SW Papers (private collection)
16  *Guardian*, 24 January 1969
17  Harold Wilson to SW, 30 January 1969, PRO PREM 13/2710
18  *The Times*, 16 December 1969
19  SW to GC, 14 April 1970
20  SW to GC, 14 April 1970
21  SW to GC, 5 May 1970
22  *The Times*, 4 June 1970

# 8

# PRIVATE LIVES

Ever since earliest times Shirley had fallen for the lure of politics, completely at home on the public stage, her genuine desire to serve matched by her love of the limelight, a trait she has never lost, so that even by the standards of leading politicians her life-style has always been a frenetic one. Some of her friends suspect that this lifestyle has helped compensate for a certain void in her personal life that can be traced back to earliest times and a rather dysfunctional upbringing. These theories are given some credence by Shirley herself in a letter to her parents confessing that out of the various people who needed her there would be fewer of them 'if in some bizarre way I didn't need them to need me'.[1] Whatever the reason, the absolute priority she gave to her political commitments meant less time with her family. It proved to be a costly oversight.

From the moment she entered Parliament Shirley was a woman in a hurry. Although endowed with an exceptional constitution that enabled her to survive on a few hours' sleep, she always maintained that time was the one commodity of which she never had enough. Incorrigibly optimistic as to what she could achieve during the day she was often rushing breathless to meetings or to stations to catch trains. Even after the Commons had risen late at night, her day wasn't yet done as she grappled with red boxes (when in government) and reams of correspondence. The weekend brought little relief as Friday and Saturday were spent attending to the constituency and Sunday often entertaining at home.

With her public life so all-consuming, there was little time for household chores and private relaxation. Never one to be preoccupied by possessions or mementoes, her London home was surprisingly austere, with cardboard boxes, filing cabinets and briefing papers littering the drawing room. Living frugally was the norm. Despite possessing a healthy appetite, Shirley normally made do with just a sandwich for lunch, travelled to the Commons by public transport, shunned the high life and rarely spent money on herself. (She did buy a new dress to visit the Queen in 1968, although typically she played it fine, arriving at Buckingham Palace from Harrods with two minutes to spare). The one indulgence she and Bernard allowed themselves was adventurous holidays, with France, Italy and the US among their favourite destinations. While they enjoyed visiting museums, art galleries and ancient churches on the Continent, the US gave scope for more robust activity such as riding, canoeing and hill-walking.

From early adolescence Shirley had formed a love of the hills, spurred on by their enticing combination of natural beauty and physical challenge. Learning from the expertise of her childhood friend, Robert Bruce, who taught her how to rock-climb, she repaired to Snowdonia and Scotland thereafter to put theory into practice, invariably opting for the most challenging route to the summit. Occasionally her adventurous instincts and flawed naviga-tion left her very much at the mercy of the elements. Once when climbing Goat Fell, the highest peak on the Isle of Arran, with Robert Bruce, they missed the last ferry back to the mainland and were forced to walk miles in the driving rain to stay with a friend of Bruce's. On another occasion, on Skye, Shirley's lone assault on the Cuillin, one of the most hazardous mountain ranges in the country, ended with a perilous descent at night before she sought refuge in the tent of her friends David and Dickie Ennals.

Friends and family have always been important to her and soon discovering that 'public life isn't a good context for deep friendships though it is a greenhouse for shallow ones', Shirley fell back on her wide circle outside Parliament.[2] A magnet for attracting admirers whenever she went, she rarely turned her back on friendship. ('She wants to be liked by everyone, even those she dislikes,' Bernard used to remark with a laugh.) According to her old friend John Spencer, it was an exceptional set of qualities which the Good Fairy bestowed on her. Aside from her infectious warmth, her fierce intelligence and generosity of spirit, he singled out her abiding optimism and the good cheer she radiates in others. His conviction is echoed by Marian Burnett, the daughter of Amy and Charlie Burnett. Their close friendship sheds light on another of her most attractive traits: treating everyone the same regardless of their background. Marian recalls Shirley's fury when her brother introduced Marian to some eminent guests of their parents as the butler's daughter.

In line with her upbeat personality, she tends to see the best in people and make light of their defects. Even those who have fallen short or upset her (she has a volcanic temper if stirred) can work their passage back, since she isn't one to bear grudges. To her good friend Ben Hooberman, her reluctance to speak ill of others makes her someone special, while to Peter and Barbara Metcalfe her warmth readily compensates for her foibles. (She can be quite demanding of her friends, especially the errands they undertake on her behalf.) Her general benevolence has been the source of help, advice, inspiration and sympathy to many, not least to the bereft. When Larissa and Alexander, her niece and nephew, were left orphans during their teenage years Shirley stepped in and acted as a surrogate parent thereafter. Like her parents, she has always been the soul of generosity not only as a host but also in her willingness to give financially to her extended family, her church, her party and her many charities. (Even as a political novice she used to donate her television appearance fees to Oxfam or Save the Children.)

There have also been the countless good turns, such as an invitation to lunch at the House of Commons, a glowing reference for a colleague, or a roof for those who have needed it. Marian Burnett recalls staying at Shirley's home in her absence at a time when politicians such as Shirley were potential targets for the IRA. One night she had just gone to bed when there was a knock at the door. Going downstairs to investigate she found a bright torch being shone in her eyes and two policemen inquiring who she was as their colleagues searched the garden. When she later told Shirley that two of them had stayed in their car all night outside, she replied, 'Oh Mav, how terrible. Why didn't you ask them in?' According to Marian, her inability to say no has been exploited by some. Enid Howard, a friend for over sixty years, believes that Shirley's constant loyalty is her foremost quality. She has never forgotten the immense effort Shirley made to journey to Suffolk to comfort her husband Trevor as he lay dying. Her unexpected arrival was one of the most uplifting moments of his life.

Shirley also gave much time to her parents during their final years. As Vera entered her seventies, her writing and lecturing, while still prolific for a person of her age, assumed a lesser place in her priorities compared to her family. She found increasing pleasure in George's company and in June 1965 they celebrated their ruby wedding. She was also a devoted grandmother, plying her grandchildren with gifts and affection, but her relationship with John had become increasingly taut as he struggled to find his true vocation.

His cause hadn't been helped by contracting tuberculosis in Egypt in 1946 when serving in the RAF, in an era before BCG and other drugs enabled TB to be cured. This illness not only necessitated a long spell of convalescence and caused subsequent ailments, it also had a significant effect on his character. At Oxford he had incurred his mother's disappointment by achieving only a Third, but had compensated somewhat by meeting the intelligent and beautiful Jennifer Manasseh, daughter of wealthy parents, an alumnus of St Paul's and an Oxford undergraduate like Shirley, although their marriage in 1951 meant that she completed only one year of her degree. Within weeks of the wedding Jennifer was to prove her worth by nursing John devotedly throughout a virulent lung affection which he sustained on their honeymoon in France and which necessitated six weeks of recuperation in Brompton Hospital on return. Sadly, her loyalty was never properly reciprocated because, as he later admitted in his book, *Family Quartet*, John was quite unprepared to face the demands of marriage and to fully consider the interests of his wife and three children, Daniel, Timothy and

William. While capable of considerable charm and vivacity, which in time won him a devoted circle of friends, his mercurial temperament and demand for attention made him an uneasy companion. Once his plans to be an artist had been quashed by his parents on grounds of financial insecurity he embarked upon a career as a freelance property developer. Thereafter he was persistently chivvying Vera to give financial backing to his various companies. That meant her dissolving the Brittain trust and giving him a disproportionate amount of her spare capital at a time when her own income had all but dried up. Her generosity did little to erase John's long-standing grievance that she had put her work before her children, together with his own realisation that he had failed to live up to family expectations, especially in comparison with Shirley.

While exasperated by John's extravagance, Vera continued to act more in sorrow than anger, justifying her continuing indulgence towards him on the grounds of a lingering guilt about sending him to the US. Yet for all her indulgence even her patience was stretched to breaking point when John's marriage, insecure for some time, eventually foundered in 1966, and she described his treatment of Jennifer as disgraceful. 'It is terrible that so kind and conscientious a person (to say nothing of her ability and good looks) should have had to endure so much adversity.'[3]

John's volatility was also a source of bemusement to Shirley. While they had gone their separate ways after university (John had shown little interest in politics) they rarely fell out when they met and Shirley was close to both Jennifer and the children. Although chiding her mother for continuing to bail John out, believing that he would bankrupt her, she had been more than generous herself and was most sensitive to his setbacks when set against her own success. She did, however, like her parents, draw the line at his treatment of Jennifer and his comparative neglect of his children, so that when the break came she too sided with her sister-in-law, especially since she disapproved of John's new love, his secretary Elaine Drakeford.

As Vera's problems with John mounted, her dependence on Shirley became ever greater. She revelled in seeing her elected to Parliament and followed her progress with great pleasure and pride, believing that there were no peaks beyond her reach. In October 1966 Vera suffered a cruel misfortune. When setting out one night to give a talk at St Martin-in-the-Fields she tripped on some scaffolding left in the street and broke an arm. More important than the physical pain the accident destroyed her vigour and confidence. 'My little bird with the broken wing is very far from well,' George confided to his diary, and certainly the psychological effects lingered.[4] For not only was she increasingly susceptible to sleeping disorders, falling on the floor and lapses in memory, she felt finished as a writer, fuelling in turn premonitions of mortality. In March 1967 she told Shirley that she was clearly 'approaching the end of her journey' and was grateful to Providence 'because you are here to continue so much of what I started and because you are what you are'.[5]

Later she was even more effusive about her when looking back over her life.

I can only thank God that you have come so near to fulfilling all my dreams for you – indeed, you have gone right beyond fulfilling them, for when you first went to Somerville after I had asked you at least to try for the scholarship – I never thought of you as a Minister, and even soon in the Cabinet. If my shoulders have been welcome as something to climb on, I have been only too glad. I have always known that as a member of the breakthrough generation, I could never achieve what I wanted for myself, and it means a great deal that what I have done in the world has been of some use to you.[6]

On 27 March 1968, at Central Hall, Westminster, Vera, despite her infirmity, made her last public appearance, appropriately enough to mark the fiftieth anniversary of the Act introducing women's suffrage for those over the age of thirty. On an occasion suffused with tributes from all three leaders of the main political parties and from a host of female luminaries, Shirley helped Vera onto the platform and made a well-received speech herself about giving women opportunities in industry. She then helped her mother down and ran all the way back to the Commons to vote. 'The darling girl almost makes me weep,' Vera told George. 'She is so conscientious.'[7]

Shirley visited Vera almost every day while George was away lecturing in the US and thereafter she kept a protective eye on her whenever time permitted. Vera's frailty not only inspired great loyalty from Amy Burnett, but also brought the best out of George. Grateful in one sense that he had now come fully into his own he showered her with devoted care and no small measure of veneration. 'Vera is still so beautiful, so unchanging from the young woman I have always known,' he wrote in October 1969.[8] He was delighted to have her still at home as he felt a nursing home would break his wife's heart. Unfortunately, her condition became so serious that there came a time when he could no longer cope. In January 1970 Vera was admitted to a nursing home in Pimlico and in March, with the end in sight, she was transferred to one in Wimbledon. George and Shirley were regular visitors, but found that only her eyes were capable of responding.

'I loved her with a fierce, protective love,' Shirley later recalled, 'and felt angry that someone who had given so much to the world should face such a prolonged and cruel death. It was agonising to see the slow ebbing of her faculties. She died on Easter Sunday, 1970. It seemed an appropriate day.'[9]

At a private funeral at St Martin-in-the-Fields, Shirley read from the Beatitudes and later, in accordance with her mother's wishes, she, Bernard and her loyal friend Paul Berry scattered her ashes on Edward's grave in Italy.

Vera's death left George bereft. When, on a brief lecture tour to the US shortly afterwards, he learnt that he had been awarded a knighthood for his services to Anglo-American relations, his pleasure was tempered by his sadness that his wife wasn't there to share the news. Increasingly he thought of Shirley as an alter ego and it was she, along with Charlie Burnett, who accompanied him to Buckingham Palace in May for his investiture by the Queen

Mother. Yet amidst his desolation, help appeared from afar. Delinda Gassmann was a vivacious thrice-married hotelier (all her husbands had predeceased her) who had first met George in London in 1950. Thereafter they saw each other quite frequently when he and Vera used to dine at her hotel, The Griffin, close to Charing Cross. In 1956 she and her husband had departed for New Guinea and after five years there went to Australia. During this time she kept closely in touch with George and although they hadn't met for nearly two decades, a spark had been lit because as her third husband, Bert Gassmann, lay dying, he told Delinda that she should marry George.

When she wrote to tell him that she was coming over for a holiday and would appreciate his company, he happily rose to the bait. She arrived in late July full of anxiety as to what she had instigated, but she need not have worried. They clicked immediately and for the next two weeks they lived life to the full, visiting the theatre and meeting many of George's friends, including his farewell party at Whitehall Court. By the time she returned to Sydney the deal had all but been sealed. They married the next April at George's church in Chelsea, followed by a reception at the National Liberal Club and a honeymoon in the Mediterranean.

And yet for all the joy of a late harvest, marriage didn't rid George of his melancholic temperament. Despite his substantial achievements as a political scientist, his failure to enter either the Commons or the Lords, where Lord Longford had lobbied on his behalf, still rankled. He continued to bombard leading Labour figures with missives, especially Wilson and Callaghan over Anglo-American relations, but their civil responses couldn't disguise their indifference. He even managed to cross swords with Shirley over the Common Market, not surprising given their opposite positions. 'I have little patience if she chooses to vote to keep Heath in and against Party Conference,'[10] he wrote in his diary several months before the vote. Thereafter, he refrained from discussing politics with her for some time. In any case there were more serious matters to confront.

When Shirley became engaged to Bernard, Vera wondered how they would cope with setbacks, given their successful lives to date. Although their intense lifestyles and lengthy absences from each other (Shirley was living in London and Bernard in Oxford) told of an unconventional marriage it seemed to work. On one occasion when Shirley had mislaid her house keys, Bernard drove all the way to London to give her his. 'He really is a natural don; I think meditation, discussion and writing give him almost complete satisfaction,' Shirley informed her parents. 'He likes wit and cultivated living and love, but not, I should guess, power. I thank my stars and angels often that I married him and not the others. Each day seems to bring greater understanding.'[11]

As a philosopher of unusual brilliance and teacher of true originality much revered by his students, Bernard dazzled Oxford before his move to University College, London in 1959, motivated partly by the presence of Freddie Ayer, the celebrated British philosopher, in the capital (Ayer soon disappointed him by returning to Oxford) and partly by a desire to accommodate Shirley's political ambitions. Revelling in London's open, worldly atmosphere Bernard was riveting company as he sparkled with scintillating conversation, fresh ideas and irreverent wit.

With their penchant for intellectual curiosity, their loyal circle of friends and their willingness to expand their horizons – Shirley prised Bernard out of the narrow world of academia, he introduced her to opera – they neatly complemented each other. Their joy was complete when Rebecca was born in 1961 and although Shirley's work restricted her maternal role, the communal ethos of Phillimore Place helped compensate. While Rebecca merged seamlessly into the Rubinstein household (becoming particularly attached to their third child, Mark) Bernard played his part too, readily adapting to domestic duties in addition to more public ones.

As a fervent believer in equal opportunities, he was fully supportive of Shirley's political activity, lending a hand by lecturing at Fabian summer schools, campaigning with gusto and mixing easily with all comers, his lighter touch a ready foil to her earnest idealism. 'She could never have done what she did without Bernard's help,' Vera wrote to a friend after Shirley's election to Parliament, 'he is a splendid and most unselfish young man ... He looks after Becky like a mother, baths and dresses her and helps in the house as well as drives for Shirley.'[12]

'They are a very rare couple amongst young politicos today in that they are plain living and high thinking,' observed Godfrey Smith in a *Sunday Times Magazine* profile that went on to describe them as 'the New Left at its most able, most generous and sometimes most eccentric'.[13]

'We don't believe in gracious living; we are too busy,' Shirley told *The Times*. 'For six months there was no curtain on the bathroom window because I just could not find the time. Bernard did not mind; too bad if the neighbours did.'[14]

As Shirley's political career began to flourish, the strain on family life became ever greater as Bernard's output as a philosopher was reduced by his duties at home. Vera used to worry that when Shirley was away on some parliamentary delegation he was unsure as to her whereabouts and when she was due back. 'I feel instinctively that I ought to warn her not to immerse herself too completely but no one can say such things at the right moment,' she confided to George.[15] He agreed, aware of Bernard's misgivings about the inordinate time Shirley devoted to her constituency and her propensity to accept every invitation. On one occasion an interminable local meeting prevented Shirley from taking over child-minding duties from Bernard, much to his fury since he was forced to miss an important dinner in Shrewsbury. On another occasion, at Sunday lunch with the Metcalfes, Bernard tried to stop her going to Liverpool to talk at some inconsequential educational seminar that evening. They went for a drive around the block to discuss it, but Shirley wouldn't be dissuaded. 'We will have a divorce over this,' he jested on his return.' It was an ominous comment from a man increasingly unhappy about his lot, not least at the rather caustic references to him as 'Mr Shirley Williams'.

In 1967 Bernard's career took a major step forward when he was appointed Knightbridge Professor of Philosophy at Cambridge, one of the most prestigious posts in the country. His change of location led to the purchase of a lovely old house in an east Hertfordshire village complete with a manor house and thirteenth-century flint-faced church. Here, in these attractive surroundings, they entertained family and friends at weekends, but Shirley's fears about Bernard's move to Cambridge proved well founded. Once ensconced there, he developed new friendships (he joined the Board of English National Opera), dressed more fashionably and became more detached.

Shirley later recalled,

> Ours was a very alive marriage, but there was something of a strain that comes from two things. One is that we were both too caught up in what we were respectively doing – we didn't spend all that much time together; the other, to be completely honest, is that I'm fairly unjudgmental and I found Bernard's capacity for pretty sharp putting-down of people he thought were stupid unacceptable ... He can be very painful sometimes. He can eviscerate somebody. Those who are left behind are, as it were, dead personalities. Judge not that ye be not judged. I was influenced by Christian thinking, and he would say, 'That's frightfully pompous and it's not really the point.' So we had a certain jarring over that and over Catholicism.[16]

There was another reason, which she omitted but later included in her autobiography, and that was Bernard's lack of faithfulness, a situation exacerbated by her increasing absences and idiosyncratic lifestyle which didn't equate with his more conventional tastes. Once, when returning from lecturing abroad, he found that all their electricity had been cut off because of Shirley's repeated failure to pay the bill. Feeling a trifle neglected when he needed bolstering, it wasn't long before he found love elsewhere.

Whatever the potential for trouble, Shirley was slow to detect the signs. After seeing in 1968 alone at Carradale while Bernard was lecturing in the US, she told him how much he meant to her. The next two summer holidays passed off happily enough in the US and the Antipodes, but the one after that on a ranch in Wyoming in August 1970 was less satisfying. Apart from all three of them being subjected to a terrifying ordeal on the Santa Fe trail when one of the two hitch-hikers to whom they had given a lift produced a gun (he was eventually persuaded to put it back into his knapsack before he fell asleep), Bernard wasn't himself. Instead of his usual good cheer he became increasingly impatient and irritable and Shirley told him that he was acting like a stranger.

During the autumn of 1970, Shirley's doubts grew as Bernard retreated further into his shell. Finally, almost casually, she asked him if he was in love with someone else. He hesitated and admitted he was, his new love being Patricia Skinner, the attractive young wife of the intellectual historian Quentin Skinner, whom he had met at a function at King's College, Cambridge, the previous year.

The discovery that her husband not only loved another woman was bad enough, but that he had kept the liaison from her made it all the more devastating. She accepted that the pattern of their working lives was far from ideal, but for all the enforced absences she loved him unreservedly and had endured much, not least the pain of previous liaisons and the four miscarriages. As a Catholic who believed firmly in the sanctity of marriage as a lifelong commitment, the idea of being left alone with Rebecca in a house without his company and support was a prospect too bleak to contemplate. The roof of her world had caved in around her.

One wintry evening before Christmas, Barbara and Peter Metcalfe had just gone to bed when the telephone rang. It was Shirley, asking whether Peter could come up to London and collect her from the Commons. He assented and as he was about to drop her at home in Hertfordshire she told him that she and Bernard were to part. The next Sunday, Barbara Metcalfe spent much of the morning trying to persuade Bernard to stay, while he asked her to talk to Shirley. When the four of them met together he reiterated his resolve to leave and get divorced but agreed to stay for another year.

He was as good as his word. He came home at weekends, went on holiday to Cyprus and supported Shirley in her fracas with her local party over Europe, but was immune to her efforts, and those of Quentin Skinner, to save their respective marriages. Even her offer to give up politics was to no avail. An appeal by Shirley to Bernard's parents to persuade him to think again proved fruitless, for although sympathetic to her plight, they felt unable to intervene. On 1 December 1971, after a long period of silence, Shirley telephoned her father to tell him that she and Bernard were separating. When George wrote to commiserate and suggest she renounce her surname, she was the very essence of restraint in reply.

> Whatever may have happened I'm at least equally responsible. I love Bernard and have loved Bernard more than anyone else in my life and I don't wish to deny his name or the years of our marriage. It is very bitter for me that it should end as it has done...

She confessed to finding no pleasure in life at all and that politics was a great grinding bore she would rather be shot of.

> The next few months, like the last, fill me with horror because I cannot bear having my private life become public. Unlike some film stars, it is what I detest about my job. I suppose one grits one's teeth and just waits for the interest of the press to blow over.[17]

While close friends digested the news with shock and sadness, Christmas was spent with the Spencers at their cottage near York. It was a miserable time, with Shirley spending much of it in bed. John Spencer recalls that everyone was friendly on the surface, but Bernard was due to leave the next day. Before he left, he wrote Shirley a heartfelt letter in which he thanked her for the many good times they had enjoyed together and wished her every future happiness.

As Shirley grappled with the calamity that had befallen her, she made every effort, with Rebecca in mind, to keep on civil terms with Bernard, acknowledging that unpleasant legal arguments about custody 'would be nothing short of catastrophic'.

She also chose to live out in Hertfordshire and send Rebecca to the local school, thereby bringing fifteen years of sharing with the Rubinsteins to an end. Given their reassuring support it seemed a curious time to be parting company, but Shirley hankered after some space to rebuild her life. She managed to lean on her former daily, Mrs Curry, for help. Margaret Curry and her recently retired husband moved in to look after Rebecca when Shirley was detained at Westminster. There was also the unstinting support of the Metcalfes, but the situation wasn't ideal. With her shadow Cabinet and NEC responsibilities on top of her constituency work, and a seventy-mile return commute, this arrangement couldn't last for long, especially with the Currys keen to return to Ireland. Consequently Shirley bought her sister-in-law's house in Brook Green, Hammersmith, when Jennifer moved to Scotland, and sent Rebecca to school close by.

Amidst the gloom there was one ray of light. Tony King was a renowned Canadian political scientist and broadcaster four years Shirley's junior. A Rhodes scholar, he taught at Magdalen College, Oxford, before becoming Professor of Government at the University of Essex. Having first met at the Labour Party conference in 1959, their friendship developed out of their television work, and in the summer of 1971 their respective families holidayed together in Corsica, with Shirley forming a close rapport with Tony's wife, Vera, who had battled unavailingly against ill health. Her death that October from cancer had left him bereft.

On 28 December, two days after Bernard left, Shirley on some whim drove over to Tony's home near Colchester. Over the course of the next few days they spent much time in each other's company, comforting each other in their respective losses and listening to music, of which Tony was something of a connoisseur. It was the beginning of a heartfelt romance, their need for each other underpinning their mutual interest in politics. While Tony was attracted to her warmth and vivacity, Shirley found him to be a quiet, strong and trustworthy man who excelled at being a father figure to Rebecca, cooking for her, helping her with her homework and bringing the sparkle back into her life.

After an enjoyable holiday in Portugal and the Pyrenees that summer they were resolved to marry. In August 1974 Shirley and Bernard were officially divorced on the grounds that the marriage had irretrievably broken down because they had lived apart for more than two years, but Shirley's hopes of marrying Tony were dashed by the Roman Catholic Church's teaching on divorce. Given her reluctance to be excluded from a Church she believed in she had to submit herself to its elaborate process of inquiry to assess whether her marriage was a binding Christian contract, a process that took until July 1980, when a marriage tribunal in Dublin returned an affirmative decision in favour of nullification.

By then the opportunity to marry Tony had passed. Although they shared many of the same values, they were essentially different people with different friends and those differences were accentuated once Shirley became a Cabinet minister. The pressure of work, the long hours and late nights all conflicted with Tony's more ordered, conventional lifestyle (he didn't particularly like London). Aware that both of them had forceful personalities, his increasing tendency to defer to her wishes left him feeling inhibited and unhappy.

In September 1977 he began a year's sabbatical at Stanford University, California, and once there felt it better if they went their separate ways. His decision upset Shirley just at a time when the pressures of government weighed heavily upon her. She understood his concerns and felt any difficulties could be ironed out, but Tony wasn't for turning. His time in California had confirmed him in his original intentions and two years later he married Jan Reece, a former social worker.

On top of Shirley's problems, her father was becoming more mercurial with old age, and relations were periodically tense. When he began to have second thoughts about his marriage, she buttressed Delinda by extolling 'her gaiety and gallantry' and urging him to respond more positively, not least by giving her a holiday. She also warned him that because of her constituency and shadow Cabinet responsibilities, she was no substitute. Her first priority had to be Rebecca.

There was also the vexed question of money. With Vera's nursing fees having cost some £75 per week (Shirley contributed over £1,000 towards these) and with overheads of nearly £800 per year, remaining at Whitehall Court wasn't an option. George and Delinda moved into a seventh-floor flat in Swan Court, Chelsea, a retrograde step as both felt miserable there. Confronted with her father's predicament, Shirley told him that having run up an overdraft in recent years she couldn't afford to finance a full-time flat in London, but she was willing to give them Allum Green for life once she got it back from her tenants.

In April 1976 George and Delinda finally moved in to the cottage, but while it proved a godsend to his wife, it did little to raise George's spirits since his absence from the hub of the capital left him feeling intellectually starved – not helped by his decision to give up reading – and prone to depression. Aside from his conviction that his life had been a failure, he brooded incessantly about his frayed relationship with John and the hefty sums John owed him. Shirley tried to raise his spirits by reminding him of his past achievements and telling him of all the people she had met who had asked fondly after him. She also advised him to stop pursuing John, who had suffered enough losing his job, his home and his second wife, and in any case it would achieve little other than expending precious capital on lawyers' fees.

In March 1978 George gave an interview to the *Daily Express* in which he spoke with touching pride about the daughter he still believed could become Prime Minister. It was his last public pronouncement, for despite being well cared for by Delinda, he was beginning to fade, afflicted by pneumonia. On 30 January 1979 he was admitted to a hospital in Southampton to give her a rest and Shirley wrote to him to say that she was looking forward to seeing him on Friday 9 February. Three days before that she was fending off an opposition motion critical of her handling of the school caretakers' strike when a note was placed on the despatch box that said, 'Your father is dying – leave immediately.' Having made her apologies to the Conservative front bench, she made for Southampton as quickly as possible and reached her father's bedside in time to be with him as he slipped peacefully away. He was aged eighty-two and was laid to rest beside his father in the Holy Trinity churchyard at Old Milverton in Warwickshire.

George's death marked the end of an era and yet the beginning of another, for that autumn a much acclaimed BBC production of *Testament of Youth* helped contribute to the resurgence of Vera's reputation just when her writing was attracting a new following. The previous year the republication of the book by Virago Press had turned out to be a commercial masterstroke. Now, over thirty years later, the interest in her life and work has shown no sign of abating, helped by the publication of her biography in 1995 by Paul Berry and Mark Bostridge.

With Shirley preoccupied by affairs of state and the death of her father, there remained her responsibility for Rebecca. Despite being devoted to her daughter, giving her the time and care she needed was a constant challenge that she was never quite able to fulfil. During the early years she had struggled home in the evening traffic to give her supper, but once in the Cabinet this was no longer possible and although Rebecca was now old enough to fend for herself, it was a small consolation for a diffident teenager still missing her adored father.

In 1977 Rebecca moved to Camden High School for Girls and continued to excel academically, with top-class A levels in English, History and French. She now decided to try Oxbridge, but in awe of living in her parents' shadow she kept the news from them, Shirley only discovering once she had gained a place at Wadham College, Oxford, to read Law. It was a telling gesture, for while close to both her parents and sympathetic to their ideals, Rebecca would tread her own path as a lawyer away from public view, a course from which she has never deviated.

## Endnotes

1   SW to VB and GC, 22 September 1967
2   SW toVB and GC, 22 September 1967
3   VB to SW, 5 September 1966
4   GC diary, 12 January 1967
5   VB to SW, 21 March 1967
6   VB to SW, 2 July 1967
7   VB to GC, 29 March 1968
8   GC diary, 11 October 1969
9   *Climbing the Bookshelves*, p.213
10  GC diary, 30 July 1971
11  SW to VB and GC, 6 February 1957
12  VB to Miss Latchmere, 17 October 1964
13  *Sunday Times Magazine*, 17 April 1966
14  *The Times*, 20 September 1967
15  VB to GC, 4 October 1965
16  *Guardian*, 30 November 2002
17  SW to GC, 4 December 1971

# THE BATTLE FOR EUROPE

After the party's shock defeat Labour MPs returned to Westminster dejected. While Wilson was re-elected unopposed, there was plenty of carping about the smug complacency of the election campaign. An early indication of the left's growing influence over the party was the surprise election of its great tribune, Michael Foot, to the parliamentary committee (better known as the shadow Cabinet), which is elected by the PLP when Labour is in opposition. His success overshadowed that of Shirley, who came seventh, leapfrogging over senior colleagues such as Barbara Castle, Ted Short and, more surprisingly, Michael Stewart, one of four ministers in the previous Cabinet who failed to be elected. Undecided about standing, as she feared the worst, she had been talked into it by Pat Duffy, and her reluctance to do any campaigning, she told George, actually played to her advantage. 'Poppy's policy is delectably similar to FDR in his Albany days', he later wrote in his diary, 'to love all and to offend none.'[1]

As Shirley expressed amazement at her promotion on the eve of her fortieth birthday, *The Observer* speculated as to her future destiny, reviving all the talk about her becoming Britain's first woman Prime Minister. Under a heading 'Labour's leading Lady', the paper commented that she was the only member of her political generation to be elected to the shadow Cabinet.

A practising Roman Catholic, Mrs Williams belongs to a tradition of plain living and high thinking. Almost uniquely among female politicians she can speak without rhetoric in public and yet deeply move an audience. She is a convinced European; if the

English Left is to make real headway with the European Left, her contribution will be invaluable.[2]

Another accolade came her way soon afterwards with her election to the NEC, a body to which she was returned each year thereafter until her resignation in February 1981. Having narrowly missed out the three previous years to Judith Hart, the MP for Lanark, in the women's section, she came in third out of five, her cause helped by the retirement of two incumbents, Alice Bacon and Jennie Lee. With Barbara Castle and Joan Lestor, the MP for Eton & Slough, elected in the constituency section, it meant that all seven women on the NEC were university educated and all but two of them former journalists.

In her autobiography, Shirley made great play of the camaraderie between women MPs, especially their refusal to disparage each other, but for all her sympathy for anyone singled out for unfair treatment she wasn't close to any of them. Certainly not her three colleagues during her two stints at the DES, Lee, Bacon and Margaret Jackson (later Beckett), nor those on the NEC, although she admired Castle, and when she stood for the deputy leadership of the Labour Party in 1976 she was supported by only one other of its eighteen female MPs, probably Betty Boothroyd, the future Speaker of the House of Commons.[3] Admittedly many of these women were on the left of the party, but those on the centre-right included Shirley Summerskill, a near contemporary of hers at both St Paul's and Somerville, Helene Hayman, a neighbouring MP for whom she canvassed in 1974, and Gwyneth Dunwoody, one of the 1966 intake.

Although reared in a feminist stable and a strong advocate of female advancement, Shirley herself was never a feminist, telling her mother that it was an outdated concept. Ignoring parental advice to keep her maiden name, she was fully at ease in male company, late-night revelry in Parliament excepted, drawing most of her friends from its ranks. (Most of her closest female friends, such as Helge Rubinstein, Eileen Spencer, Barbara Metcalfe and Enid Howard, happened to be married to some of her closest male friends.) It helped of course that she was physically attractive, but much of her allure was down to her warm, down-to-earth temperament that shunned the shrill militancy and raw emotion often associated with female politicians of that era. 'Many men find Shirley irresistible,' Marcia Falkender later recalled. 'To some, her untidiness seems a challenge. They realize, very correctly, that her attitude to life is almost totally cerebral, they listen to that soft, seductive voice – and they feel that if only they got the chance, they could introduce her to a whole new world.'[4]

Soon the darling of the media, flattering profiles of Shirley were featured periodically, depicting her as the modern professional woman. 'Shirley Williams makes light of difficulties in being wife, mother and politician,' commented the *Shropshire Star* in January 1966.[5] 'It is this capacity for energetic compartmentalisation that makes her a popular MP and a force in that overlooked Centre of Labour's Establishment.'

Weeks later, in an article in the *Daily Telegraph* highlighting the hazards facing women seeking election to Parliament, there was the same reassuring message that 'Shirley Williams has found she can combine politics with caring for a 4-year-old (with the help of a nannie)'.[6] Her claim that women now faced little prejudice might have contained an element of bravado, but it didn't necessarily resonate with female colleagues less fortunate than herself. According to Melanie Phillips, this wholesome image riled a number of them and probably contributed to the rivalry played out each year in elections to the women's section of the NEC. Personal ambition aside, the fact that many differed from her not only in temperament but also in attitude would only have widened the gulf between them. Such a gulf was only to be expected from those on the left such as Renée Short, Judith Hart and Joan Lestor, but even those on the centre-right might well have found Shirley's views on abortion and divorce out of keeping with the spirit of the age. This isn't to suggest that Shirley wasn't sympathetic towards the advancement of women. She cared profoundly about equal pay, maternity rights and maintenance payments for single mothers, but, like Castle, she believed that equal opportunities should form part of a wider programme of social reform.

In time and perhaps in response to the very poor level of selection of women in the SDP and later the Liberal Democrats, Shirley did become more responsive to the idea of positive discrimination, insisting that the SDP constitution contain a commitment to equal rights and supporting the idea of quotas for Liberal Democrat women candidates. She also began to develop closer friendships with women, coming to feel that they were less selfish than men, but interestingly most of those friends were of a younger generation such as Helena Kennedy, the leading human rights QC, Julia Neuberger, a senior female rabbi, and Carol Bracken (now Savage), her former personal secretary, who looked up to her as an iconic figure. According to Lesley Abdela, a Liberal Democrat activist and leading women's rights campaigner, Shirley was rather distant towards Liberal Democrat women of a similar age. She was much better with younger women. Having worked extensively with her in Central/Eastern Europe during the 1990s, training women there for public life, Abdela noted that Shirley would always take the lead in public but would happily relax in private. In her estimation Shirley was a role model for many women of her vintage, the 1960s generation, for the way she had conducted herself in public life rather than for her political activity.

In a shadow Cabinet which saw Jenkins (re-elected deputy leader), Callaghan and Healey shadow the three great offices of state, Shirley was disappointed not to receive an economic portfolio. She briefly held the shadow Health and Social Security portfolio and was promoted to shadow Home Secretary in October 1971 – a testament to her ability given her leading role in Labour's bitter rift over Europe.

While the centre-right was the predominant faction within the PLP, this curious coalition of middle-class intellectuals and trade union loyalists was by no means as united or powerful as it appeared. Not only was it strongly associated with the perceived failures of the Wilson government, notably its failure to attain sustained growth – the Crosland panacea for greater equality – but it had been racked by division over industrial relations. This clash of cultures was to be further exacerbated over Europe when important questions about Britain's place in the modern world became entangled with arguments about the future direction of the Labour Party.

The pro-European right, which comprised most but by no means all of the intellectuals, found their inspiration in Roy Jenkins, Labour's newly elected deputy leader in succession to George Brown, who had lost his seat in 1970. Not only was he a man of impeccable European credentials, Jenkins had emerged from government with his reputation enhanced and was feted among the British Establishment and the press as Labour's leader-in-waiting. Yet much as he was revered by his followers in Parliament, a number of whom shared his predilection for sophisticated living, he lacked a base within the wider party, with some blaming his austere economic policies for Labour's defeat in 1970.

While there had always been conflicting views within the party over Europe, the Wilson government's application to join the EEC in 1967 had aroused relatively little controversy, perhaps because its chances of succeeding were so remote. This all changed once President de Gaulle, the architect of the French veto, had departed the scene and Ted Heath, an avowed European throughout his career and the chief negotiator during the Macmillan government's abortive attempt to join in 1963, began to pursue his own terms for entry. Although his negotiating brief was very similar to that which Wilson would have employed had he won the election, the Labour Party rediscovered its anti-European voice as principle merged with political opportunism. Convinced that they were being bludgeoned into a European capitalist club with its unappetising diet of higher prices, fewer jobs and rule from Brussels, opposition to the EEC became the great rallying cry of Labour activists and trade unions, not least as a means of getting rid of the Conservatives. They had resolute allies on the NEC such as Barbara Castle, Michael Foot and Tony Benn, all of whom were determined to move the party to the left.

After a sluggish start the government's EEC negotiations took a massive step forward on 20–21 May 1971 at an Anglo-French summit in Paris when the French removed their previous resistance to British membership. This development brought a public backlash from Callaghan, who in a speech in Southampton deployed crude nationalist rhetoric to demonstrate a new-found opposition to the European idea. His remarks served to unnerve Wilson, who up to then had adapted a fairly relaxed approach to the issue, confident that he could get the party to support entry or, at the very least, accept a free vote. Remembering Callaghan's challenge to him over *In Place of Strife*, Barbara Castle's attempt to restrict the power of unofficial strikes, he now began to drift with the anti-European tide as Callaghan's words resonated with many in the party's mainstream, notably Healey and Crosland. Both concluded that the benefits of joining the Community came at too high a price for the party.

At a meeting of the NEC in June an amendment from Barbara Castle calling for a special conference to determine delegates' feelings was passed by thirteen votes to eleven by dint of Shirley's surprising support. (She later claimed that her vote was predicated on the assumption that Conference's decision wouldn't be binding.) Her decision dismayed Wilson, concerned that such a conference would expose Labour's rift in public, and irritated her allies. Days later when speaking to a Labour Party gathering in Blyth she went some way towards restoring her credibility by publicly aligning herself in favour of the terms of entry, which at first reading 'looked like very favourable terms'. There were many facts about the EEC that the Labour movement should admire. Wages were higher, pensions more generous, holidays longer and unemployment, Italy aside, much lower.

> … I do not believe we will wield much influence outside the EEC, as a country of 50 million people in a world dominated by great powers…

But I do believe we would add strength to democracy and
social justice in the EEC, and act as an influence towards a generous trading policy of building bridges with the Commonwealth
and the developing countries, if we decide to enter.[7]

At Labour's special conference on 17 July, Wilson, in a lacklustre
speech, poured scepticism on the terms that Heath had obtained for
entry, despite the suggestion by George Thomson, a leading Labour
pro-European, that such terms would have been perfectly acceptable
to Wilson had *he* negotiated them. His words helped strengthen
his leadership, but elicited contempt from the pro-marketeers. Their
effusive support for a rousing response by Jenkins to a shrill anti-
European tirade from Barbara Castle at a meeting of the PLP two
days later served only to heighten the tension between the two sides.
When the NEC followed up the verdict of the special conference
by voting sixteen to six to oppose entry on the existing terms, it
was left to Shirley to act as the standard-bearer for the European
cause. Reading from a prepared text, she referred to the meeting as
a sad and tragic moment for her. She had been proud of the Wilson
government when it had applied for membership. She agreed with
George Brown that the terms were adequate and unlikely to be renegotiated. The party had to face the fact that it had turned its back
on its social democrat comrades in Europe at a crucial moment in
history. Together they could have won the continent of Europe for
socialism. According to *The Guardian*, both pro- and anti-Europeans
agreed that her contribution was the most moving and effective
statement of the pro-European case they had heard in months.

Alongside other leading pro-Europeans, Shirley continued to
fight her corner, not least in her constituency (renamed Hertford
& Stevenage at the February 1974 election) where the majority
of her local party was opposed to entry. In August, after a series of
fractious meetings at which she was heckled as she put the case for
Europe, she wrote to her good friend Peter Metcalfe to apologise
for reproaching him for the failure of local members to stand firm
in the eye of the storm.

I'm sorry if I got angry at the time. You are the last person I would ever want to go on at, and I am very conscious that you are one of the very few who battle to keep the Party reasonably sensible. I do feel very grateful, even if I sometimes forget to say so, so please don't ever think otherwise![8]

On the eve of Conference she caused a flurry of disapproval by appearing on a television debate with Harold Lever and Michael Stewart against Barbara Castle and Peter Shore, thereby flaunting Wilson's stipulation that Labour members would be free to air their views on the issue provided they refrained from doing so in public. When at the next meeting of the shadow Cabinet she joined forces with Thomson in support of a pro-European motion, she raised the ire of both Callaghan, who warned that defiance of Conference would cause consternation in the constituencies, and Wilson. His proposal that the shadow Cabinet should recommend opposing entry to the PLP was comfortably carried, although as a sop to the pro-marketeers it was agreed that members of the former could vote according to their convictions at that meeting.

Labour's growing hostility to the EEC helped, paradoxically, solidify support for entry within the Conservative Party, but unrest still smouldered on its backbenches, where implacable opponents such as Enoch Powell viewed the loss of national sovereignty as non-negotiable. With the government's majority now down to twenty-five and the parliamentary arithmetic uncertain, Heath couldn't be certain of victory when Parliament voted on the principle of entry on 28 October. Unwilling to rely on stragglers from other parties to get his precious legislation through, his inclination was resolutely in favour of a whipped vote. That remained his conviction right up 'til the eve of the six-day debate, whereupon he bowed to the calculations of his Chief Whip, Francis Pym. Aware that a free vote would entice many more Labour pro-Europeans into the 'yes' lobby than Conservative anti-Europeans into the 'no' one, Pym finally convinced a reluctant Prime Minister to change tack. The announcement of a free vote by the government side on 18 October caught Labour off guard. Wilson, anxious as ever about party unity, minded to do likewise, but he ran into a wall of resistance from Benn and the left. Determined to use this prime opportunity to eject an unpopular Conservative government over a cause about which they cared passionately, they insisted on maintaining the status quo.

The NEC's resolve upset many beyond the circle of committed marketeers. An amendment for a free vote by Willie Hamilton, one of Labour's more independent backbenchers, was only narrowly defeated at a meeting of the PLP the next day. Once the historic six-day debate began, Jenkins, Shirley and other pro-Europeans in the shadow Cabinet were barred by collective responsibility from speaking. On the eve of the vote Shirley told the party that it couldn't stand on its head an issue to which Labour had been committed in power. Some people felt that she might be wavering on whether to abstain, but her remark, 'We will have to suffer', left the NEC in no doubt about her dissenting tendencies. When the vote came she joined Jenkins and sixty-seven other Labour MPs in the government lobby. (Twenty others, including Crosland, abstained.) Their courage won them no favours from many of their colleagues, some of whom vented their spleen, since with their help the government secured a comfortable majority of 112. Britain had voted to join the EEC, but the wording was merely one of principle and now needed to be given legality. This created the dilemma for the Labour rebels of whether they incurred odium by continuing to vote night after night in the government lobbies or whether they risked inconsistency by now opposing what they had supported in principle.

The bitterness wasn't just confined to Parliament. Among the Labour rank and file the mood remained distinctly anti-European, especially in Lincoln and Dundee, where Dick Taverne and George Thomson respectively faced bitter opposition from their local parties, but also in Stevenage. On 11 November, at an acrimonious meeting which brought her to the verge of tears, the only time that Peter Metcalfe ever saw her in such a state, Shirley was reprimanded by her GMC for flouting the party whip and was asked to give an assurance that she would in future abide by the discipline of the party in all ways. She in turn reminded the GMC of her lifelong commitment to the European cause and its knowledge of her views when it had selected her for the new constituency the previous April. She also rounded on a small coterie within the party whose contribution, she averred, consisted of constant denigration of her and the previous Labour government. 'They do no good at all for the very party they claim to support.'[9] So despairing was she of the situation and the irreconcilable differences between the party and herself over Europe that she seriously contemplated retiring from Parliament and accepting a job with the Community Relations Centre. 'I share the Party's urgent desire to get rid of the Tory Government,' she wrote to John Tye, the Stevenage party secretary, in a letter that was never sent. 'I cannot, however, bring myself to believe that the right way to do so is to defeat legislation to take this country into the EEC.'[10] It needed another meeting two weeks later to heal the breach. In return for Shirley accepting the reprimand and promising to liaise with her local party if she ever felt compelled to break ranks again, the GMC unanimously expressed its full confidence in her.

For all her travails, Shirley climbed four places to third in the shadow Cabinet rankings, helping her to land the portfolio of shadow Home Secretary. An additional boost was Jenkins's re-election as deputy leader, but the next few months were taxing as the European Communities Bill, incorporating EC law into the domestic law of the UK, wended its tortuous way through the Commons. The vote on second reading (17 February 1972) was particularly traumatic, with Jenkins and Rodgers recalling it as a day of misery, and David Owen as one of shame as Labour's pro-Europeans, aside from a faithful few who abstained, reverted to type as the government's majority fell to eight. The announcement of the result caused uproar as Labour's anti-Europeans erupted in unrestrained fury, much of it directed against the unfortunate Liberals because five of their six MPs had voted with the government. On leaving the chamber in a state of uproar Owen went to Jenkins's room, where he found Shirley, Harold Lever and a few others all dejected, scarred by having voted against a Bill they passionately believed in. 'It seemed that Harold and Shirley both wanted to resign immediately and this was the general mood,' he later wrote.[11] They agreed to think it through over the weekend. They duly did and returned to Westminster the following week still members of the shadow Cabinet, but yet undecided as to whether their commitment to Europe took priority over the unity of the Labour Party. Their conundrum would be further compounded during the coming months as the question of whether a future Labour government should pledge itself to withdrawal now dominated.

It was at this point that Benn's proposal of a referendum began to assume a greater significance. When he had first mooted the idea back in 1970 it had attracted scant support, but as the rifts became ever greater many previous sceptics began to be won over. On 15 March 1972 the shadow Cabinet rejected it by eight to four, but President Pompidou's announcement of a referendum in France over European enlargement the very next day gave Benn's campaign additional credibility. At the NEC the following week he managed to win support for a motion that asked the shadow Cabinet to reconsider the question (Wilson, Jenkins, Callaghan and Healey were away). Consequently, on 29 March, just two weeks after having rejected the idea, the shadow Cabinet did precisely that. Jenkins, as ever, remained resolutely against, regarding it as a device that undermined parliamentary democracy, but more importantly he feared it jeopardised the gains already made, as well as fracturing the Labour Party in the process. The crucial intervention came from Wilson who, in the middle of a bitter diatribe against the pro-marketeers, placed his vote, and his authority as leader, in favour of a Tory backbench amendment calling for a referendum, justifying his volte-face on the decision of the NEC. With Healey and Willie Ross, the shadow Secretary for Scotland, both of them previous opponents of referendum from different perspectives, absent, and Callaghan, Mellish and Short defecting to the

pro-referendum lobby, Shirley and Jenkins now found themselves
in the minority. Defeated by eight votes to six, they retreated to
Jenkins's room, Shirley, according to Jenkins, 'torn between disapproval of the tactical cynicism of the reversal of the previous
decision and her democratic populist feeling that it was difficult
to oppose a referendum'.[12] After contemplating his future over the
Easter recess Jenkins returned to Westminster resolved to resign
as deputy leader. For him the referendum vote was the point of
no return. Having felt like an impostor when voting against the
European Communities Bill at second reading, he wasn't prepared
to risk yet further humiliation at the hands of his opponents.

The news drew somewhat different reactions from his leading
supporters. Bill Rodgers and Dick Taverne were very understanding,
Roy Hattersley accepted it with regret and Shirley was rather more
non-committal, although, according to Jenkins, she intimated that
she would probably resign too. He appeared less than convinced,
because when he saw Wilson the next day he indicated that she was
likely to stay. For a leader confronted by the resignation of not only
Jenkins but also Lever and Thomson from the shadow Cabinet, as
well as four junior shadow ministers, and keen to stave off a full-
scale revolt this news came as a genuine relief. In a public letter to
Wilson, Shirley explained that the only reason she wasn't resigning
lay in her support, albeit qualified, for a referendum. For while she
disliked it as a constitutional device she accepted that there was a
case for consulting the public again before a final decision on the
Common Market was reached, although she would have preferred
a general election prior to ratification. What did greatly disturb her
was the growing anti-Europeanism of the shadow Cabinet and the
depressing sight of witnessing the PLP voting week after week with
right-wing Tory MPs opposed to Europe. She continued to believe
that cooperation with European socialists and trade unionists offered
the best way forward of advancing their socialist objectives.

Therefore, while I am not resigning at this time, I am bound to say
that if the Shadow Cabinet refuses to adopt a more constructive

approach towards the issue of British entry into the EEC, one which reflects the party's official policy of support in principle combined with re-negotiation of certain of the terms, I will find it impossible – and indeed hypocritical – to continue as a member.[13]

Shirley's unwillingness to resign, while unpopular with some of her pro-European colleagues who felt it undermined their collective strength, caused her little harm compared to Hattersley, the party's new shadow Defence Secretary, who became the butt of much vitriol for his perceived opportunism.

Jenkins's resignation was a defining moment not only in his own career but also for the social-democratic right of the Labour Party. Whatever its merits – and most questioned his judgement in choosing this issue on which to resign – it certainly diminished his standing among a number of his parliamentary colleagues and activists. As Healey and Callaghan took up their new positions as shadow Chancellor of the Exchequer and Foreign Secretary respectively, they became the heirs apparent to Wilson, whose own position had been enhanced by the disarray of his fiercest critics. Their divisions were all too evident over their refusal to support Crosland for the vacant deputy leadership because of his unwilling- ness to support Jenkins both over the principle of entry to Europe and over the referendum. Up against Michael Foot from the left and Ted Short from the centre-right, Crosland in normal circum- stances would have rated his chances of success, but these weren't normal circumstances. Susan Crosland recalls how Shirley rang her husband at home from a callbox at Westminster to say, 'We think you shouldn't stand.'

'Who is we?' Crosland replied.[14] Shirley was evasive, but she spoke for the Jenkinsites as they lined up behind Short, despite him being Crosland's inferior in every sense, and this unexpected backing helped him beat both Foot and Crosland, the latter coming a poor third.

In contrast to the travails of the Jenkinsites, Callaghan, by cannily aligning himself once again with the prevailing consensus within

the party, enhanced his prospects for the leadership should a vote
for withdrawal at Conference precipitate Wilson's resignation. In
the months leading up to it Wilson, while not advocating outright
opposition to the principle of entry, continued to express reservations. His stance wasn't heroic but it proved increasingly effective as
leading spokesmen on both sides of the argument figured that he
was a safer option than anyone else. In the event, his compromise
motion at Labour's 1972 conference proposing the renegotiation of
the government's terms subject to a referendum was comfortably
carried, much to general relief.

Shirley's promotion to shadow Home Secretary had come at a
time when the ideological gulf separating her from her opposite
number wasn't a wide one. For, despite pressure from the Tory right,
Reginald Maudling, the Home Secretary, had no intention of turning his back on the social reforms of the Wilson government. A
genuine libertarian, he viewed the growth of the permissive society
with equanimity and advocated penal reform rather than retribu-
tion as the preferred solution to rising crime. After his enforced
resignation in July 1972 over his links with the disgraced architect
John Poulson, his successor Robert Carr was of a similar liberal
persuasion and someone whom Shirley both liked and respected.
Throughout the two turbulent years she shadowed this portfolio
she was often willing to adopt a bipartisan approach, while reserv-
ing the right to criticise where appropriate. An early clash came
over the emergency caused by the miners' strike of February 1972,
when workers picketed power stations to prevent the movement
of coal by road, a crisis which she attributed to the government's
obstinacy and complacency. She appealed to it to abandon the
industrial brinkmanship that had created the chaos, something to
which the government reluctantly consented soon afterwards once
the Wilberforce Inquiry had conceded most of the miners' demands.
    Another area in which she was able to score points was the

government's failure to combat the rise in crime. In a debate on police manpower in July 1973 she reminded the Commons of the claim made by the then shadow Home Secretary, Quintin Hogg, back in 1970 that 'the permissive and lawless society is a by-product of socialism'. His attitude, she declared, often smacked of over-simplification. Claiming that society was more lawless than in 1970, she said that no party had simple answers to the problems of law and order.

Shirley's previous exposure to Northern Irish affairs at the Home Office helps explain her measured approach in opposition as the province became increasingly ungovernable, the introduction of internment (imprisonment without trial) merely delivering a spectacular propaganda coup to the IRA. The Republican cause was further boosted by the shocking events of 30 January 1972, when thirteen civil rights demonstrators were shot by the British army on the streets of Londonderry. The level of slaughter served only to heighten tension yet further and the IRA gave notice of its intent by detonating a bomb in Aldershot, killing seven, the first attack of its type on the mainland, forcing the British government into drastic action. The Government of Ireland Act was suspended and the Northern Ireland Temporary Provisions Bill reimposing British rule was rushed through Parliament at the end of March with minimum opposition.

Direct rule didn't stem the flow of violence, but it did at least set in motion a number of constitutional initiatives aimed at improving links with the Irish Republic, and established a new system of government for the province. While Shirley supported the withdrawal of the Special Powers Act and the end to internment, she wasn't dismissive of the Unionist case. Given its particular vulnerability to terrorist attacks and the difficulties confronting the police in breaking the conspiracy of silence, she backed an impartial judicial commission to recommend how best to replace the Special Powers Act. She also accepted that, for all its merits, a united Ireland had to appeal to Unionists as well as Republicans. At Conference that year, in what the *Daily Telegraph* called a skilful and sincere speech, Shirley, on behalf of the platform, criticised the lack of reference to a union by consent in the emergency resolution. Without dissent Conference approved an NEC statement regretting continuing violence and calling for all-party talks.

She was also supportive of the government following the brutal expulsion of the East African Asians from Uganda by President Idi Amin in September 1972, not least the courage of the Home Secretary Robert Carr in placing principle above popularity. Waving aside the bitter protests of the Powellite right and the public, he supported Heath's commitment to honour its obligation to admit the 57,000 Ugandan Asians with British passports.

It so happened that Shirley was on holiday in the Pyrenees when the crisis erupted and with no one else deputed to speak for the opposition its lack of a clearly defined view didn't pass without comment. When tackled about this on return in a radio interview she called the criticism 'a little hard', especially as her remote location made her oblivious to world events and thus to the gravity of the crisis.

When Shirley brought the matter before the NEC, it urged the government to adopt a more active resettlement programme by increasing funding to overstretched local authorities. During the following weeks, as refugees lingered in camps near airports amidst mounting doubts about the adequacy of the funding, Shirley suggested extending loans to refugees. Her proposal that Stevenage should take fifty families to give an important lead to the nation won support from local churchmen, but, overall, caused unrest in the locality. With a growing number of families to accommodate, the Stevenage Development Corporation urged that priority should be given to those with jobs. Eventually it agreed to house five families, the first arriving by the end of October, as 28,000 Ugandan Asians eventually settled in Britain.

Aside from the divisions over Europe, Shirley became increasingly preoccupied by the leftward drift within the Labour Party. In line with its democratic tradition, the party's 1918 constitution had divided power between the parliamentary party, the constituency parties and the trade unions. It wasn't unusual for the left to find its voice at Conference, but its impact on policy was slight as the right-wing trade union bloc vote invariably shored up the leadership. This gradually began to change during the late 1960s, when discontent with the Wilson government became ever more vocal both from party workers and from the trade union movement. While the new radicalised middle class often became the dominating faction within local parties, especially in a number of inner-city constituencies, the growing militancy on the shop floor and general disillusion with wage restraint had thrown up a new generation of trade union leaders in league with the left. Men such as Jack Jones, general secretary of the Transport and General Workers Union, and Hugh Scanlon, president of the Amalgamated Union of Engineering Workers, weren't committed to the strike weapon only to achieve higher wages; they made frequent inroads into the political domain to ensure Labour satisfied its sectional interests.

The growing extremism of the NEC was given additional momentum by the election of Benn as party chairman in 1971 and chairman of the influential Home Policy Committee in 1972. One of the most able and charismatic politicians of his time, well versed in the art of media presentation, the privately educated Benn was an unlikely champion for the new left. A pro-European and dutiful technocrat in the 1964 government, he experienced a Damascene conversion to ideological socialism after the 1970 election and pursued his new faith with undisguised zeal. Having been one of the prime instigators of the new anti-Europeanism he now used his position as shadow Industry Secretary and chairman of the NEC's Industrial Policy to promote a radical new programme featuring compulsory planning agreements and an interventionist National Enterprise Board which would take a controlling interest in twenty-five leading companies.

As the left mobilised, the right was slow to respond both intellectually and politically, its plight compounded by its growing isolation on the NEC, where Shirley, Healey and Callaghan of the shadow Cabinet moderates formed a distinct minority. At a six-hour shadow Cabinet meeting on 14 May 1973 when the major policy document, 'Labour's Programme 1973', was discussed, Shirley warned that it would damage Labour's electoral prospects. In concert with Crosland and Harold Lever she called full-scale industrial intervention undemocratic and argued for a Keynesian policy of demand management as an alternative to one-party socialism. She and Crosland were to the fore at a joint meeting of the shadow Cabinet and NEC two days later when they opposed a programme of excessive nationalisation, but Healey's later amendment at the NEC to stop the commitment to nationalise twenty-five leading companies was defeated by a single vote. Wilson tried to limit the damage by claiming that he would veto it, but the press were on to a good thing and wouldn't let the matter drop.

The question of the twenty-five companies continued to preoccupy the party. While the familiar arguments added little to what was already known, the discussion did reveal substantial differences over where power lay, with the right invoking the sovereignty of the PLP and the leader's right to the veto, while the left championed the authority of Conference. The row dragged on at Blackpool that October. Reg Prentice, the abrasive MP for East Ham North, thought it disgraceful that the NEC had refused to meet the shadow Cabinet and felt that MPs should have the final say, while Shirley believed the NEC had to be confronted. 'Harold, I'm very depressed,' she said. 'We have got to face this one. You will have to say at the Conference on Tuesday what you have said about the Twenty-five in the past. You must sort this out. You've got to do it right.'[15]

Benn in turn told Shirley to be less alarmist in her approach. 'If we have this psychology of confrontation, we really miss the mood of the Party.' In their desire to meet radical expectations of their supporters the left overreached themselves by recommending the nationalisation of 250 major monopolies, enabling Wilson to appear more responsible with his selective approach. He also restored links with the trade unions which had been severely fractured over *In Place of Strife* by committing the party to repeal the Conservatives' Industrial Relations Act and entering into a social contract which, in return for responsible wage demands, promised price controls, industrial democracy and generous increases in welfare spending.

Despite her favourable reception and her success in being re-elected to the NEC at the top of the women's section, Shirley found Blackpool a troubling experience as Conference overwhelmingly endorsed a programme of massive state intervention. At a meeting organised by *Socialist Commentary*, the social-democratic periodical, she pleaded for more realism in presenting Labour's future programme. 'If we do not succeed in bridging the gap between the views of the electorate and the views of our own party activists', she concluded, 'Dick Taverne (the former Labour MP who had won a resounding by-election victory at Lincoln earlier that year on a pro-European manifesto) will become the leader of an important breakaway movement, and even more than that, I believe that the Liberals will tend to benefit as well.'[16]

Her words had a prophetic touch when, days later, the Liberals won the Berwick-upon-Tweed by-election in which Labour was relegated into third place, and the following month Labour lost the safe seat of Govan to the Scottish Nationalists (SNP). In face of these setbacks she told George that she didn't think the party would win the next election because it lacked time in which to explain the complexities of its new economic policy. Her pessimism was understandable and yet the government remained all at sea, buffeted by economic and industrial storms. The success of the 1972 miners' strike, which led to a substantial increase in their pay, and a rapid deterioration in the balance of payments, had made inflation the foremost dragon to slay. So concerned was the government by its explosive effects that it too fell prey to an incomes policy. Stage one of the ninety-day price and wage freeze helped to reduce unemployment. Stage two introduced greater flexibility, but stage three foundered on the rock of external events.

Its genesis in October 1973 coincided with the Yom Kippur War between Egypt and Israel, which precipitated a fourfold increase in the price of oil. This in turn exacerbated inflation and strengthened immeasurably the miners' hand as the dependence on coal, a cheap form of energy, became all the greater. The National Union of Mineworkers submitted a wage claim well in excess of stage three and signalled their intent by imposing an overtime ban beginning on 12 November. The next day the government, desperate to avoid another humiliation by the miners, announced a state of emergency in order to limit fuel consumption. To Shirley such a development smacked of overreaction. No government should ask for such powers, she declared, unless the case was an overwhelming one. Placing the blame on certain trade unions struck her as shoddy practice, especially when the emergency applied not just to Britain but also to the wider world.

And yet for all her barbs about government provocation, Shirley knew that the issue of trade union militancy on her own side had to be faced down. Not only did she support her shadow Cabinet colleague Reg Prentice after his denunciations of union militancy had landed him in trouble, she warned her party that the retention of voter confidence called for restraint over industrial disputes, in particular strikes for political ends. That meant obeying the law until it was in a position to change it.

In the midst of a crisis which had brought out the best in her, Shirley fell victim to the internal politics of the Labour Party. With his resignation as deputy leader having achieved little aside from causing resentment among the grassroots, Jenkins was under pressure from his supporters to raise his profile. Ruling out a challenge for the leadership as politically unfeasible, he opted for the safer course of standing for the shadow Cabinet, coming a respectable fifth, three places above Shirley, who had fallen from equal first the previous year to eighth, likely the result of her pro-European sentiments. With Wilson reluctant to move Callaghan and Healey from shadow Foreign Secretary and Chancellor respectively, the only obvious portfolio that he had at his disposal for a man of Jenkins's stature was the Home Office. Jenkins was reluctant to be the cause of Shirley's demotion to shadow Prices and Consumer Affairs, but ultimately didn't let sentiment intrude on his comeback. Although she was unhappy with the outcome she accepted it with good grace, which was more than could be said for her father. 'Poppy conspicuously failed to display ruthlessness against her dear false friend the high-minded, ambitious Mr Jenkins,' he wrote.[17] It was a common enough refrain. In a major interview in *The Observer* magazine weeks earlier she admitted she hated the infighting within her party and hated upsetting people. Her consensual approach towards the Heath government whenever she felt it merited support was out of kilter with the raw tribalism of many of her colleagues. 'Shirley represents everything that is most agreeable, most civilised about English life,' opined one Labour MP. 'She's liberal, rational, intelligent, concerned. The trouble is that she does not understand that politics here aren't about those things. They're still about class, the unequal distribution of wealth.' Another doubted her capacity for leadership. 'Everyone votes for Shirley for the Shadow Cabinet because they like her. No one objects to her. How could they? But there are probably 10 people whom they would prefer to see as leader of the party.'[18]

With negotiations between the government and the NUM mired in deadlock, Heath announced the introduction of a three-day week from 1 January 1974. The dire repercussions predicted at the time never materialised as the long hours worked by many firms for the three days they had power meant that output barely suffered. While Heath and his ministers became embroiled in fruitless negotiations with the TUC, Shirley berated them for their economic incompetence. 'The Government, by financing Budget deficits and public expenditure out of inflation, have placed the maximum burden on those less able to afford it.'[19] Privately, she placed Heath and the union militants on an equal footing when it came to obstinacy. 'I think myself if the miners' strike isn't settled next week we'll have an election on a "Who Governs Britain?" basis', she wrote to George, 'and it could be very nasty indeed, especially if the strike is going on and there are pickets out etc.'[20]

On 7 February, after a miners' ballot revealed overwhelming support for a strike, Heath duly called the election for the 28th of that month along the lines that Shirley had predicted, but thanks to Wilson's adroitness it didn't turn into a showdown between government and miners. Instances of union aggression were almost non-existent and when Wilson did mention the dispute it was to highlight his role as a national conciliator well able to work with the unions to bring about industrial peace and social progress.

In the new Hertford & Stevenage constituency, Shirley's Conservative opponent was Vivian Bendall, a former Greater London Council (GLC) councillor who later became MP for Ilford North. He tried to make hay out of Labour defence cutbacks and the effect that this would have on job losses at Hawker Siddeley Dynamics and BAC. Shirley in turn focused on the trebling of rents and mortgages since 1970 and the four-year waiting list for a council house. She also decried a Conservative Party political broadcast which depicted Labour harbouring a hidden army of extremists as shameful lies and half-truths.

For all Bendall's bullish noises about victory it was Shirley who had the last laugh as many Conservatives, conforming to national trends, defected to the Liberals. Her victory, on an 85.4 per cent turn-out, saw her majority rise to 8,176 amidst claims that the seat would remain Labour for as long as any of them could see.

Despite the consensus that Heath would be returned to power, a general disenchantment with his government's running of the economy was more than enough to offset the lack of enthusiasm for Labour and some of its more extreme policies. In an election which saw the votes of the two main parties drop quite considerably, mainly to the Liberals (whose 19 per cent of the vote only gave then fourteen seats due to the vagaries of the electoral system) and SNP, the Conservatives, although winning slightly more votes than Labour, ended up with four fewer seats. Heath tried to stay in office by entering into coalition with the Liberals, but the obstacles were insurmountable, and it was Wilson who went to Buckingham Palace on the evening of Monday 4 March to form a minority government. That afternoon the shadow Cabinet had met for the final time, after which Jenkins saw Shirley in his room in the Commons. She was unhappy to hear that Wilson hadn't offered him the Treasury and talked defiantly about them staying out of the government, but Jenkins wasn't convinced. He did, however, in further conversations with Wilson, make his acceptance of the Home Office conditional on a suitable placing in the Cabinet for Shirley. Although her portfolio of Prices and Consumer Affairs wasn't among the most glamorous it nevertheless meant a seat at the top table for a woman still aged only forty-three. Once again the distant peaks beckoned.

### Endnotes

1 GC diary, 25 October 1970
2 *Observer*, 19 July 1970
3 Information cited in Elizabeth Vallance, *Women in the House*, The Athlone Press, 1979, p.96
4 Marcia Falkender, *Downing Street in Perspective*, p.253
5 *Shropshire Star*, 29 January 1966
6 *Daily Telegraph*, 10 March 1966
7 *Daily Telegraph*, 26 June 1971
8 SW to Peter Metcalfe, 13 August 1971, Peter Metcalfe Papers (private collection)
9 *Stevenage Gazette*, 18 November 1971
10 SW to John Tye, undated and unsent, SW Papers (private collection)
11 David Owen, *Time to Declare*, Penguin Books, 1991, p.188
12 Roy Jenkins, *A Life at the Centre*, Macmillan, 1991, p.344
13 SW to Harold Wilson, 11 April 1972
14 Susan Crosland, *Tony Crosland*, Jonathan Cape, 1982, p.241
15 Tony Benn, *Against the Tide: Diaries 1973–76*, Hutchinson, 1989, p.63
16 *The Times*, 3 October 1973
17 GC diary, 23 November 1973
18 *Observer* magazine, 16 September 1973
19 Hansard, 21 January 1974
20 SW to GC, 2 February 1974

# 10

# THE HOUSEWIVES' CHAMPION

There were few surprises in the Wilson Cabinet. Fourteen had served in his previous ones and all the old warhorses were back in prominent positions. Callaghan became Foreign Secretary, Jenkins Home Secretary and Healey Chancellor of the Exchequer. The left was represented by Foot at Employment, Benn at Industry and Castle at Health and Social Security. With Wilson no longer the dynamo of old, there was less intensity within government this time as ministers were given greater leeway to run their departments free of interference, while the Prime Minister concentrated on keeping the party together. The fact that he presided over a minority government wasn't entirely to his aversion as it helped him rein in the extremists. Left-wing policies which had largely been foisted upon him in opposition could be substantially modified or quietly shelved for more immediate priorities. He quickly settled with the miners, ended the three-day week and saw Healey introduce a redistributionist budget, but short-term industrial peace was partially bought at the cost of hyper-inflation. 'Mrs Shirley Williams has been given responsibility for prices which are absolutely certain to rise fast whatever she does,' warned the *Financial Times*. 'It is a pity that male Prime Ministers tend to think of women in terms of the shopping basket and it is particularly a pity for Mrs Williams to have been handed a booby-trapped shopping basket.'[1]

The Department for Prices and Consumer Protection (DPCP) was formed out of the Department of Trade and Industry (DTI). Among its responsibilities would be the supervision of the Price Commission, established by the previous government as a semi-independent agency to regulate prices, as well as monopolies and mergers and the Office of Fair Trading. According to Patrick Shovelton, the deputy secretary with responsibility for consumer protection, the DPCP was a ridiculous department created by Wilson to give Shirley a seat in the Cabinet. His view was broadly endorsed by Peter Hennessy, the leading Whitehall historian, who considered it a nonsense to split up the DTI, and John Burgh, the DPCP's Deputy Secretary, who thought the new department had an impossible brief since inflation couldn't be restrained by imposing price controls; it could only be accomplished through wage control.

Shirley's reaction to her new portfolio was lukewarm. She admitted to her local paper that she would have preferred the Home Office and called the DPCP 'a bed of fairly sharp nails'. To her father she referred to it as 'one of the two or three toughest jobs in the Government', her success largely dependent 'on luck and hardly at all on me...'[2] By some fairly astute bargaining, however, she managed to recruit two of Whitehall's finest civil servants, Kenneth Clucas and John Burgh, to head up her department. The three of them made a formidable team. Clucas, the Permanent Secretary, was a man of sharp intelligence, impeccable judgement and unswerving principle, with a deep appreciation of how the civil service should operate. When he spoke, Shirley listened. She equally valued Burgh's wisdom and integrity, qualities that later saw him become Director General of the British Council, the first Jew to be accorded the distinction. At one important meeting with the Confederation of British Industry (CBI), when tired and keen to excuse herself, she had no hesitation in asking Burgh to chair the rest of the meeting, knowing that his views were in sympathy with hers.

She also used him in her abortive efforts to rid herself of Arthur Cockfield, the chairman of the Price Commission. Cockfield was a man of immense ability, but his vanity shone through every pore and he became a great thorn in her side, not least the way that he upset the CBI over his inflexibility over price control. Having toyed with replacing him when she first became the minister, she soon wished that she had, and sent Burgh to see him to persuade him to resign. Burgh was suitably diplomatic, but Cockfield was deeply offended by the mere suggestion. He complained bitterly to Shirley, not least about the impropriety of a civil servant communicating such a message, and she thought better of it, inviting him out to lunch. On reconsidering his position she came to the conclusion that she should keep him, appreciating that a loyal Conservative as Price Commissioner would be more effective in dealing with the Retail Consortium and the CBI than someone who was a Labour supporter, not that Cockfield ever allowed party considerations to interfere with what he thought was right.

Shirley was on good terms with Patrick Shovelton, who handled a long-standing case of price-fixing which had originated with the previous government. The dispute centred on the pricing policy of Roche Products Ltd, the British subsidiary of Hoffmann-la-Roche, a Swiss-based global health care company. Following a scathing report by the Monopolies and Mergers Commission in 1973 into the pricing of its drugs, Librium and Valium, the company was ordered to reduce its prices by 50 to 60 per cent on these drugs and repay excess profit.

The company then took the Crown and MMC to court, claiming a natural breach of justice, but in April 1974, following a change of government, out-of-court negotiations began to try and reach a settlement over the pricing of drugs. After months of wrangling between Shovelton, leading for the DPCP, and Roche, they reached a settlement. He recalls taking it to Shirley one day and saying, 'I think you'll need to take it away over the weekend and read it.'

'Oh no,' she replied. 'I'll look at it now.'

Within a few minutes she had made up her mind. 'Patrick, I can't possibly accept this,' she told him.

Devastated by this rebuff after all his months of toil, Shovelton went back to Roche and found them amenable to his demand for further concessions. Under the terms of the settlement reached in November 1975, the company withdrew its legal action against the Crown and MMC, repaid £3.75 million to the government and accepted a price for Librium and Valium at half their 1970 level. Years later Shovelton tackled Shirley about the settlement and asked her how she knew she could extract more from Roche.

'Oh, that was easy,' she retorted. 'The Papal Nuncio had come to see me the weekend before and told me what marvellous fellows they were. I smelt a rat.'

'How disgraceful,' remarked Shovelton.

'Yes, I know,' she said. 'I don't support my church all the time.'

Shirley's excellent rapport with her leading officials, her political adviser, John Lyttle and her junior minister, Bob Maclennan, an upright, conscientious Scot with responsibility for competition policy, set the tone for the rest of the department. According to Peter Hennessy, everyone liked working with her because of her glowing temperament. She was always very appreciative, avoided apportioning blame and could express herself candidly without causing offence. Shovelton recalls discussing consumerism with her one day and letting slip the remark that people should shop around to get the best prices. 'Patrick, do you really think young mothers or working women have time to shop around?' she rebuked him, the clear implication being that the senior civil service was out of touch with the world.

Within a week of taking office, Shirley gave notice of early legislation to fulfil the government's undertakings to introduce stricter price controls. She thought it right to retain the Price Commission as an independent agency to control prices in accordance with a general price code, but wanted to impose a general reduction of 10 per cent on retailers' profit margins and to introduce subsidies on basic foodstuffs such as bread, butter, cheese and sugar.

As Shirley began a round of intense consultations with industry and retailers their general reaction to her proposals was one of dismay. Lord Redmayne, the chairman of the Retail Consortium, called the Prices Bill a horror. At a time when many retailers were struggling he feared it could precipitate a liquidity crisis which could force many small shops out of business. They had hoped to persuade the government to reduce the proposed cut in gross margins from 10 to 5 per cent, but Shirley wasn't for turning. She did, however, suggest that in return for entering into a voluntary agreement to reduce profit margins on essential goods, the government wouldn't use its statutory powers to regulate particular food prices and other household necessities. (The price-cutting orders under the Prices Bill could not come into effect until November.) It would also continue to exclude small traders below a £250,000 annual turnover from the 10 per cent reduction in gross margin and introduce a new profit margin safeguard of 25 per cent for distributors in respect of the food distribution trade.

Faced with this pistol pointed at them the larger retailers reluctantly agreed to cooperate and, led by the Food Manufacturers Federation, they gradually signed up to price curbs. The Conservatives called it a cynical charade designed to fool the British people in the short term, but Shirley refuted their charge, pointing out that it would hold down the prices of essential foodstuffs, especially for the poor.

Shirley's reassuring performance at the DPCP during the government's first few months won her pride of place in Wilson's estimation. At an address to the PLP on the eve of the recess he singled her out for repeated praise for the way she had closed the loopholes on repricing, subsidised essential foodstuffs and negotiated a voluntary agreement with retailers on a number of the most basic items in the shopping basket. With Terence Lancaster in the *Daily Mirror* building her up as the court favourite and potentially the next Prime Minister, not all of Shirley's colleagues were as generous in their compliments. 'What on earth is Harold up to?' declared Castle in her diary. 'I haven't had a word of recognition from him about my efforts in the last three weeks.'[3]

With Labour remaining comfortably ahead in the polls and the Conservatives lumbered with an unpopular leader, Wilson not surprisingly sought a fresh mandate in September with the election to take place on 10 October. The campaign itself produced little of novelty as Wilson stressed the experience of his team, the restoration of normality after the turmoil of the three-day week and the increase in benefits. With her innate warmth and broad-base appeal, Shirley was given a prominent place in its election team, posing as the housewives' champion against inflation. It was therefore ironic that Wilson's campaign should be temporarily blown off course by the hand he trusted more than any other at the tiller.

For the previous year or so, Europe had been the dog that had failed to bark as Labour's astute policy of 'renegotiate and decide' had kept its fissures in check. The only real trouble had come at the NEC in July, when Benn's motion calling for a special conference on the Common Market was carried against the wishes of the pro-marketeers, and at the joint Cabinet–NEC meeting on 16 September to draw up the manifesto, when Jenkins spoke forcefully against a referendum. A concession to use the phrase to 'consult the British people at the ballot box' as opposed to a referendum wasn't enough to persuade him to appear at Labour's initial press conference, but the incident aroused little comment. Nine days later it was a different matter. It so happened that Shirley had just cleared up an earlier gaffe from Healey about the rate of inflation having fallen to 8.4 per cent when the focus switched to Europe. After a previous question about whether a referendum should be binding on the government, Christopher Jones of the BBC asked Shirley whether in those circumstances she would remain a member of a government committed to leaving the Common Market. He was interrupted by a flustered Prime Minister who said that they weren't there to take questions as individuals. They were a united team with a manifesto that was binding on all of them. Any member of a government who didn't agree with a major decision of the Cabinet on which they felt very strongly would leave that Cabinet.

As another journalist began a question, Shirley, brushing aside Wilson's efforts to stop her answering, said:

Can I just add one thing to that. I think it's a fair question

ABOVE Shirley, aged six, with her mother at Glebe Place. From the earliest of times Vera Brittain predicted great things for her daughter and encouraged her to work on behalf of the underprivileged.

LEFT Shirley, aged twelve, during her last year in the US, with her two cats. She has remained a great lover of animals.

LEFT Shirley's father, George Catlin. A distinguished academic who never realised his ambition of becoming an MP, he was Shirley's great political and spiritual mentor.

RIGHT Vera Brittain in her dotage. Her reputation as a novelist has grown posthumously. Few mothers and daughters have achieved the eminence that Vera and Shirley have attained.

Shirley and her daughter Rebecca at the installation of the plaque at 117 Wymering Mansions, commemorating Vera Brittain's years of residence there.

ABOVE Shirley in familiar pose during the 1964 election. She has that great ability to listen intently and make each person feel they matter.
© Peter Metcalfe

LEFT One of the few occasions when Shirley hasn't drawn an audience. Outside the BAC factory in Stevenage during the 1964 election.
© Peter Metcalfe

Shirley addressing her local Labour Party at Boxwood. Note the Thatcher-type handbag! A marvellously fluent speaker, she always appears to have something of interest to convey. © Peter Metcalfe

LEFT Shirley with her husband Bernard and daughter Rebecca on a victorious tour of her constituency after holding Hitchin in the 1970 election. Their reception was more enthusiastic in Labour Stevenage than in Tory Royston. © Peter Metcalfe

RIGHT Shirley on the stump in Stevenage town centre during the February 1974 election. A consummate campaigner, she came across so naturally with the microphone. © Peter Metcalfe

Shirley with her close friend and colleague Peter Metcalfe, a stalwart of the Stevenage Labour Party and later the SDP. © Peter Metcalfe

LEFT Shirley on the picket line at the Grunwick film processing plant in 1977 with fellow Labour MPs Fred Mulley and Denis Howell in support of trade union rights for its workforce. As a Cabinet minister Shirley's presence attracted much coverage and when the dispute turned violent weeks later, she was accused, unfairly, of fanning the flames.

© Press Association

LEFT The Gang of Four: Shirley with (L–R) Bill Rodgers, David Owen and Roy Jenkins during the early days of the SDP. Although very different personalities, together they made a formidable team. © Press Association

RIGHT Shirley with George Robertson (right), a future Secretary-General of NATO, at the Iguazu Falls on the Brazil–Argentine border, 1984, on a mission to restore relations with Argentina following the Falklands War.

Shirley and Roy Jenkins on a cruise in the Peloponnese after a conference in Athens, autumn 1984 – a brief respite from the internecine travails of the SDP.

LEFT Shirley trying to stump David Owen at the SDP party conference, Torquay, 1985. A more than useful hockey player in her youth, Shirley had her teeth knocked out in a mixed hockey match at university. © Press Association

RIGHT Shirley with her second husband, Dick Neustadt, an eminent American political scientist and most amenable of men. In his obituary for *The Independent*, his friend Tony King described him as a man without enemies. © Elaine Lockerby

Shirley at Gull Pond, Dick's much-loved holiday home on Cape Cod, November 1990.
© Peter Metcalfe

Shirley rafting the Colorado River in 1994 – her ideal type of holiday, combining natural beauty with strenuous physical activity.

Women at the Crossroads Conference, Cape Town, 1999. A popular speaker at conferences the world over, Shirley is in her element on these occasions.

directed at me. I didn't resign on the basis that the Common Market should go the ballot box because I have always felt that on a matter of crucial importance there ought to be an effective test of the people's opinion.

But speaking for myself, I would not remain in active politics if that referendum went the wrong way from my point of view.

When asked whether her colleagues shared her view, Shirley replied that she couldn't speak for others, but she thought the position was really well known. Her intervention visibly irritated Wilson and afterwards he upbraided her for the embarrassment that she had caused. Sensing the biggest story of the campaign to date, the media were out in force that evening at Shirley's adoption meeting at Stevenage. She sought to play down talk of a split, telling them that her European views were well known and she had done little more than retread old ground. 'There is, of course, no question whatever of my getting out of the Labour Party.'⁴

The next day her defiance made the headlines and won her many an accolade in the editorials. 'She has, at a stroke,' reported David Wood in *The Times*, 'opened out all the questions that Mr Wilson understandably has tried to smother ... In an important sense, Mrs Williams redeemed politics and electioneering from the contempt into which it is said to have fallen.'⁵

Jenkins's admission that he too would resign from a government that withdrew from Europe kept the story running for another twenty-four hours. Thereafter it ran out of steam as other issues predominated. With few questioning the general assumption that Labour would be returned with a decent majority, the rest of the campaign offered little in the way of excitement. Up against Vivian Bendall once more, Shirley duly increased her majority to 9,046, but her party's expectations of capturing a slew of Tory marginals never materialised. On an overall 2.2 per cent swing it only secured an overall majority of three over all other parties, which now included eleven Scottish Nationalists.

Despite this minuscule majority, Labour introduced an ambitious

Queen's Speech, which included the phasing out of private practice from the NHS, the abolition of selection in secondary education and more rights for trade unions. Dwarfing all the controversy over the left-wing legislation was the faltering economy as inflation continued its remorseless upward spiral, courtesy of the world oil crisis and excessive pay demands. As Prices Minister, Shirley had an important role, along with Foot and Healey, in persuading both sides of industry to show restraint over wages and profits. It proved an exacting assignment.

Although on good terms with most of the union leaders – Jack Jones she admired, Hugh Scanlon rather less so – she viewed the TUC–Labour Party Liaison Committee, by which the former approved every piece of the latter's legislation, as a constitutional outrage. Governments, she professed, were accountable to Parliament, not to outside pressure groups. Yet at the same time she recognised the imperative of keeping the unions satisfied if wage restraint was to work.

After the Prices Bill became law in July, Shirley initiated a review of the price code with a view to stimulating investment by manufacturing and the service industries. She received a great many submissions about the plight of British industry, some of which described the situation as desperate. The CBI had constantly called for the end of price control to enhance profits, boost investment and ease the cash crisis afflicting companies. That was out of the question, she told its leaders. She believed that price control had to be semi-permanent in a world of high oil and raw material prices, but there seemed a strong case for stimulating investment relief and allowing companies to reap greater benefits for improved efficiency.

Shirley's proposals won the backing of Healey. He thought them sensible and would limit the Retail Price Index (RPI) to a maximum of 1 per cent. He suggested that they should reach no formal decision on the figures to be inserted into the consultative document, which should be left to the two of them to decide at a later date.

When Shirley published the review of the price code on
12 November, she indicated that the most important change to the
code related to a new investment relief. Manufacturing, service and
distribution companies could recover 17.5 per cent of budget capital
expenditure through increases in profit margins and prices. She
also allowed companies to pass on a bigger share of wage increases
in higher prices, although these concessions weren't enough to
satisfy the CBI.

With the unions determined to extract every ounce of flesh from
the social contract, especially during Labour's first year in office, the
cost came in the excessive wage claims that ran close to 30 per
cent. This inevitably fuelled inflation and with the public sector
borrowing requirement spiralling out of control, Healey's April
1975 Budget was deflationary as he increased taxation. The medicine was unpleasant, but it did nothing to rehabilitate the stricken
patient and with inflation reaching a staggering 26 per cent in June,
Shirley felt bound to raise the alarm. She told the National and
Local Government Officers' annual conference at Blackpool that
'the cancer of inflation is destroying our currency, our willingness
to invest, our savings and pension funds. If it rages on unchecked, it
will surely destroy our democracy and ourselves.'[6]

On 20 June, at an all-day Cabinet on economic strategy at
Chequers, Healey painted a bleak picture of the national economy
and declared the need for a credible policy by the end of July. For his
part, he wanted a maximum £5 wage rise per week. In the discussion that followed, Shirley thought that Healey's timetable was too
relaxed. An increased norm of 15 per cent for the next pay year was
much too high. The figures provided by the Treasury suggested that
the country couldn't afford a wage increase higher than 10 per cent.
She conceded that a tighter control of wages would mean a similar policy towards prices, but warned that the scope for squeezing
profit margins in many industries was very limited. Any thought
of a price freeze was an illusion given the intolerable strains this
would place on a firm's liquidity and the government should make
this clear to the TUC. She questioned whether it was possible to

avoid a statutory policy, but accepted a voluntary one was better than nothing.

Clearly any change in government policy would be highly unpopular with the unions. At the Liaison Committee three days later, Jack Jones attacked the government over its wages policy before taking aim at Shirley, berating her for relaxing the price code at the behest of the CBI. She returned fire by telling him that, despite its relaxation, profits were in freefall. Attempts to impose a price freeze would lead to bankruptcy – some leading firms in food production and manufacturing were teetering on the brink – and the only hope for strengthening price control was by a slowing down in the flow of cost pressures.

On 30 June, in response to growing pressure from the markets, Healey pronounced himself in favour of a 10 per cent statutory policy to be accompanied by major cuts and price controls. Such a move brought the threat of resignation from Foot, and Wilson, having apparently given Healey his support, retreated in the face of a paper from Bernard Donoughue, his chief political adviser. There then followed a week of intense deliberation between the government, CBI and TUC as they tried to cobble together a deal which was acceptable to all sides. With Jones playing a crucial role in winning union consent for a flat rate £6 a week increase limit on all those earning up to £8,500 a year, Shirley's role, according to Healey, was equally significant. For the unions, in return for pay restraint, looked to the government to keep prices as low as possible by using the penal clauses of the price code against private sector firms who tried to breach it.

On 8 July, when Healey confirmed that the unions were now willing to accept reserve powers, Shirley and Crosland, according to Donoughue, were all for implementing sanctions in general but less willing to apply them to their own departments. It needed a narrow vote in favour of the £6 norm by the TUC's General Council to convince her that Healey was right about reserve powers. At a six-hour Cabinet on 10 July, she insisted that the government should be absolutely clear about where it stood. If it failed to get a voluntary pact it should be prepared to impose a statutory one. With six ministers opposed to reserve powers, including Foot, who had been toying with resignation, it was agreed that they would only be introduced if the voluntary approach broke down. The next day Wilson unveiled the new policy in the Commons in a White Paper, 'The Attack on Inflation', which for all its semantics amounted to something close to a statutory policy.

With the fight against inflation the government's overriding priority Shirley began to look to new ways to protect the least well-off from its ravages. She asked manufacturers and retailers to coop-erate voluntarily in a price restraint scheme. Although its effect on the retail price index would be insignificant it was seen as a neces-sary palliative to persuade the trade unions to accept another round of pay restraint when the £6 freeze expired the following July. As autumn brought the first signs of a drop in inflation and a modest improvement in profit margins and corporate liquidity, she made it clear to retailers that restraint had to be shown by both sides. With profit margins remaining very low and cash flow deteriorating even further in the food trade, the CBI and the Retail Consortium were reluctant partners in the scheme, signing up for a maximum of six months. When the government published its plans in October it comprised some seventy-seven items, but as negotiations continued the number began to steadily diminish.

By the time Shirley formally unveiled her programme in February 1976, it included about forty items in normal household use accounting for between 15 and 20 per cent of total consumer spending. The government spent some £500,000 on publishing the scheme and providing window stickers featuring a red price check triangle for those cooperating, but its enthusiasm wasn't shared by others. Sally Oppenheim, the shadow Prices Secretary, called it a cosmetic exercise and *The Guardian* commented that:

> Mrs Shirley Williams has just unleashed a new and impressively elaborate way of spending public money ... The justification for the scheme is that it may persuade the trade unions to accept a

lower limit to pay rises in the second stage of the incomes policy. If it really helps achieve that, it will not have been a completely futile exercise. But as a direct way of tackling the problem of inflation, the scheme (alas) is pretty irrelevant.[7]

Outside her department Shirley roamed widely across broad acres of government policy, joining forces with Jenkins and Prentice to withstand the challenge from the left. Not surprisingly, her consensual approach pitted her against Benn. A relationship which was once personally and politically compatible deteriorated abruptly post-1970 as Benn moved sharply to the left. A particular bogey was Benn's Industry White Paper which promoted economic planning through a powerful National Enterprise Board. It was subjected to Shirley's rigorous scrutiny at every stage through Cabinet committee and by the time she and Callaghan had finished, the project had been reduced to a pale shadow of its original intention, with co-planning agreements voluntary not obligatory, and no further extension of nationalisation during the next Parliament. 'Shirley is, without doubt, the most reactionary person I know,' Benn complained afterwards.

She gives the impression of being so nice yet she feels society is crumbling and she herself has no confidence in any of our policy. But she is now being built up as the great heroine: 'Shirley keeps our food prices down, Shirley protects our shopping baskets' and so on when she is, in fact, doing nothing beyond doling out money to industry.[8]

In May the following year they were involved in heated exchanges at the National Economic Development Council (NEDC) when Shirley advocated a measure of consensus between the parties over economic management to enable it to plan ahead with more confidence. The warmth that her words engendered failed to impress Benn. He intervened to disassociate himself from her views, accusing her of wanting coalition government, a taunt that goaded her into a furious denial amidst fresh headlines of government splits.

The row came just when the cross-party coalition over the EEC referendum had attracted talk of a government of all the talents to cope with the recession. Once Labour had been re-elected on a manifesto promise to consult the people 'through the ballot box' within twelve months, the business of proper renegotiation commenced. Throughout that winter Callaghan was locked in exhaustive deliberations in Brussels that touched on such sensitive issues as high food prices, reform of the CAP and Britain's budgetary contribution. Both he and Wilson had from the outset resolved to stay in Europe, but with a divided Cabinet and hostile party, they had to tread carefully.

At the end of November 1974, the Labour conference, postponed because of the general election, heard a bravura speech from West Germany's new Social Democratic Chancellor, Helmut Schmidt, in which he flattered his audience and invoked the socialist ideal of solidarity. More important, his constructive talks with Wilson afterwards paved the way for the successful European Council in Paris at which Wilson relayed his positive intentions for the future. On 20 December Jenkins told Wilson he would accept the principle of a referendum provided that the government's recommendation was a positive one, but Benn wasn't quite so accommodating. His New Year letter to his constituents expressed unreserved misgivings about continued membership, whatever the outcome of the negotiations.

Throughout the whole dispute over Europe, Wilson's overriding priority was to keep the Cabinet and party together and avoid the fate which had befallen Ramsay MacDonald in 1931 when his Labour government had folded over proposed draconian cuts in unemployment benefit. If the price for that unity meant a touch of constitutional tinkering then that was a price Wilson was quite prepared to pay. On 21 January 1975 he informed the Cabinet that, drawing on the 1932 precedent of the National Government's right to differ over the introduction of import duties and imperial preference, he was willing to suspend the convention of collective responsibility in regard to the referendum so that ministers would be free to campaign on either side of the argument.

Aware that the government's credibility was being weakened by every growing spat, Wilson and Callaghan vowed to bring the negotiations to a conclusion at the next European summit. In Dublin, on 10–11 March, after winning some minor concessions over the British budgetary contribution and cheap New Zealand butter imports, they pronounced themselves satisfied with the renegotiations.

When Cabinet came to consider them at an exhaustive two-day session the following week, each member was invited to have his or her say before a final decision was taken. Most of the leading campaigners on either side had little new to contribute and when the vote came on the second morning it was sixteen to seven in favour of continued membership, a better result for the leadership than might have been anticipated. Wilson reiterated his earlier commitment sanctioning the right of dissident ministers to differ from their colleagues during the referendum campaign provided they desisted from personal attacks on each other.

That afternoon Wilson gave a humdrum statement to Parliament outlining the government's recommendation to accept the terms just as the battle lines were being drawn up. Jenkins informed him that he would be heading up 'Britain in Europe', the pro-European organisation comprising many Conservatives and Liberals, while the Cabinet anti-marketeers were orchestrating an anti-government campaign around an inflammatory NEC motion that condemned Wilson's terms and urged withdrawal from Europe. According to Ben Pimlott, the effect on the Prime Minister was like a match to a powder keg. He was incensed that his generous gesture was being undermined by both wings of the party. He rang up Castle later that night in blind fury and then accused Jenkins of consorting with the enemy. The next day he warned Cabinet about avoiding a 1931-style split and a Tory-led coalition, before withdrawing angrily to his study, his gesture, according to Donoughue, conveying a willingness to resign. His various protests worked. Foot persuaded the left to moderate their activities and Shirley rallied the right. The final NEC motion, while opposed to continued membership, did not commit the party organisation to campaign against the government; it simply allowed Labour members the same freedom to support or dissent as had been given to ministers.

Given the fractious state of the party it wasn't hard to understand Wilson's fraught condition. On 7 April, 145 Labour MPs rejected continued British membership of the EEC, the first time that the majority of the party had deserted him since becoming leader, forcing him to rely on opposition support. Not surprisingly he played a low-key role during the campaign, leaving the likes of Shirley, Jenkins and Hattersley to make the Labour case for Europe.

Although Shirley had become a vice-president of Jenkins's all-party Britain in Europe reluctantly, as campaigning with Conservatives and Liberals was something that didn't really appeal, though she spoke at a number of its rallies, she reserved most of her activity for the Labour Campaign for Europe (LCFE), of which she had become chairman. According to Jenkins, an occasional participant of LCFE, its semi-sectarianism sat ill with the spirit of the referendum, its atmosphere less stimulating than his own organisation, which not only contained the cream of the British Establishment but also played to larger audiences.

Yet despite this, Shirley's role and that of her organisation shouldn't be discounted, especially since most converts to the 'Yes' cause during the campaign were mainly sceptical Labour voters. At a news conference announcing her chairmanship of LCFE, she attacked those who referred to the Common Market as a rich man's club. She was confident that it was outward-looking and was pioneering links with the Third World. Later she told a Labour audience in Manchester that the higher standard of living and welfare in the EEC justified continued membership.

The country's first referendum took place against a background of depression and decline, giving an additional frisson to all those concerned about inflation, unemployment and national sovereignty. Blaming Europe for national ills became the guiding force of the 'No' campaign, posing something of a dilemma for the pro-Europeans. Determined to destroy the myths about rocketing food prices, Shirley accused her opponents of living in a fantasy world and distorting the true picture. She didn't believe that life outside the EEC would once again provide access to cheap food such as Jamaican sugar and New Zealand dairy commodities. She was particularly dismissive of the claim of Christopher Frere-Smith, the leader of Get Britain Out, that continued membership would see food prices rise by 40 per cent, calling it 'unadulterated tosh'. She accepted that some foods such as dairy products were more expensive, but others such as cereals and sugar were cheaper. At a time of escalating world food prices, the cost of food, on balance, had been slightly lower inside the EEC than outside.

On the 'No' side, Benn injected some real spark into the campaign with his repeated contention that entry into Europe had cost 500,000 jobs. While Jenkins retaliated with a scathing personal attack, infuriating Wilson in the process, Shirley weighed in with hard facts. In a *Panorama* appearance with Enoch Powell, she remarked that Benn's argument linking job losses to the trade deficit was a very odd one because the UK's trade deficit with the rest of the world had risen considerably faster over the previous two years than it had with Western Europe. Firms with a selling market of 250 million people within a tariff wall were clearly better placed to invest. Later that week, in a speech at Hertford, she warned that leaving the EEC would be a 'stupendous act of folly' as it would exacerbate unemployment. At present it was the only large industrial market for British exports that was still growing.

Although Europe had never been a leading issue to preoccupy voters at general elections there was little popular affection in favour of it. Polls throughout the two previous years had consistently shown a narrow majority for coming out, but when asked if renegotiated terms were successful enough for the government to recommend continued membership, the mood changed. Approximately two out of three supported this proviso and throughout 1975 in the months leading up to the actual vote these figures remained fairly consistent. The British, as later attitudes would suggest, hadn't come to love Europe, but they recognised that in a more turbulent world in which their voice counted for less, the Community offered stability. These attitudes if anything intensified throughout the campaign as Labour sceptics, following in the footsteps of the pragmatists led by Wilson and Callaghan, embraced the 'Yes' cause. Certainly the pro-Europeans held all the cards. Not only did they have the support of pro-Labour moderates, most Conservatives, the Liberal Party, the CBI, the City of London and the press, but they were, as the columnist Hugo Young wrote, the acceptable forces of British public life. The 'No' campaign, in contrast, was an uneasy coalition including the far left and much of the far right led by the likes of Foot, Benn, Powell and Ian Paisley, their perceived image of intemperate extremism carrying little popular appeal. For the moment, the people had spoken by 17.3 million in favour compared to 8.4 million against, but Labour's anti-marketeers refused to let the matter drop, as subsequent events were to prove.

After the satisfaction of the referendum campaign, returning to the narrow sectarianism of domestic politics was something of an ordeal for pro-Europeans such as Jenkins and Shirley. They fought unavailingly against Foot's introduction of the closed shop, especially in journalism, where they saw it as an affront to press freedom, and against the massive bailout of the stricken company, Chrysler UK, believing that it set a dangerous precedent for other loss-making industries.

Shirley did manage one success during the final days of the Wilson government when she combined with Harold Lever to help block Barbara Castle's proposals for phasing out the treatment of private patients in NHS beds, believing it would discourage the consultants from working in the NHS and privately as well. (At the time the NHS depended upon doctors who worked in both.)

It was Castle's last battle, because days later she was axed from the Cabinet by her old adversary Jim Callaghan. Out of all the many letters of commiseration she received, few matched Shirley's in grace and generosity. Despite their differing brands of socialism, they always admired each other and Shirley was forever grateful for the lead that Castle had given her. Even the trauma of divided loyalties caused by the emergence of the SDP never entirely severed the bond that linked the two leading ladies of the left.

Labour's return to power had, if anything, exacerbated the tensions between the leadership and the NEC as each departure from the manifesto by the former was greeted with derision by the latter. According to Pimlott, Wilson had developed a loathing for the NEC and avoided attending its meetings if at all possible. As one of the very few government ministers on the committee, and a moderate on a body that had become ever more extreme, Shirley found the ordeal increasingly taxing. It wasn't simply the fact that people held contrasting views to her own that exercised her; she was, after all, on good terms with left-wingers such as Castle, Foot and, more surprisingly, Eric Heffer. What galled her was the meanness of spirit in which they conveyed those views, coupled with the personal antipathy of those such as Ian Mikardo, a leading power broker on the back benches, and Renée Short, the fiery MP for Wolverhampton North East. For years Shirley's eloquence and charm had cast their spell on even the most implacable of opponents, but up against unbending ideologues immune to the warmth of the human spirit, these attributes now counted for nothing.

Late one evening in July 1975, over a glass of wine in Bill Rodgers's room in the Commons, she encouraged him to lead a counter-offensive against the extreme left. Rodgers wrote,

> For Shirley Williams to raise such matters was itself unusual, because in the past she had chosen to stand a little aside from the roughness of internal troubles. But she was incensed by the behaviour of the National Executive Committee, on which she sat, and was finding problems in the constituencies – including Stevenage, her own – where she had once been sure of a wholly friendly welcome.[9]

Rodgers was sympathetic, but said it needed a minister of Cabinet rank to raise the standard. He would follow, but she must lead, and in a way she did, not least in standing up for Reg Prentice, by no means a natural soulmate.

Reg Prentice had represented the east London seat of East Ham North (renamed Newham North East in February 1974), a socially deprived inner-city area, since 1957. His appointment to the Cabinet as Education Secretary in March 1974 saw him become Jenkins's most dependable ally as he spoke out against the left in a way that irritated Wilson, so much so that he demoted him in his post-referendum reshuffle and only kept him in the Cabinet on pain of Jenkins's resignation.

Wilson wasn't Prentice's only problem. He had become the victim of an extremist constituency clique determined to oust him, despite an impressive record as a local MP and loyal party member. His cause hadn't been helped by the decision of the NEC in 1973 to scrap the party's list of proscribed organisations. Any number of these organisations now emerged, the most menacing of which was Militant, with its own structure, publication and programme. While at one with the others in its disdain for democratic institutions and commitment to intimidation, it alone believed that capturing control of the Labour Party was the necessary prelude to establishing the revolutionary society. Deploying considerable energy and commitment, it began to mobilise in a number of inner-city constituencies such as Newham.

In March 1975 the Newham North East executive passed a motion of no confidence in Prentice and in July he was deselected, much to the horror of many in the PLP, 180 of whom signed a declaration of support. Furthermore, Jenkins, Shirley and Tom Jackson, the moderate leader of the Post Office Workers, organised a meeting at Newham Town Hall on the evening of 11 September in a show of solidarity. It wasn't an occasion for the faint-hearted. Events soon turned exceedingly rowdy as extremists of both the left and right gathered to vent their spleen over conflicting agendas. (The far right was bitterly opposed to Jenkins's race relations proposals announced earlier that day in his capacity as Home Secretary.) Against a background of constant abuse both Jenkins and Shirley were shouted down by the mob, and Jenkins was hit by a flour bomb from a middle-aged woman.

Undaunted by the violence and obscenities, Jenkins, red in the face, yelled at an audience of 500, 'I hope you will ignore this tiny intolerant, undemocratic claque.'

Shirley declared that she was there simply to support a comrade whom she respected. 'Sometimes he can be an uncomfortable colleague – blunt, even tactless, unsmooth. He is also honest, capable and brave. There are not enough such men and women in politics.'[10]

Any constituency party had the right to dispense with MPs who were lazy or foolish, but it was quite another matter when challenged about their opinions. The referendum on the Common Market had demonstrated how the sentiments of the activists didn't represent mainstream Labour supporters.

The uproarious nature of the meeting made dramatic headlines and provided the most glaring example yet of the kind of internal feuding which blighted a number of Labour constituencies over the course of the next decade. Disgusted by his treatment, Prentice wasn't going to take it lying down. He appealed to the NEC, alleging that his only crime had been to have fallen foul of a Trotskyist clique within his local party. When the inquiry committee unanimously found that the local party had acted within its constituency rights, Prentice denounced it in public and demanded to address the NEC in person.

On the day before its November meeting, when the question of extremism was set to dominate, Shirley met Wilson to discuss tactics. She was reassured by his willingness to fight. At the Labour conference weeks earlier he had referred to the extreme left as subversives and troublemakers, and now, in a statement he read out at the NEC, he not only denounced extremism but warned it was getting out of step with the PLP.

Wilson's words had little effect as Shirley's attempt to overturn Prentice's dismissal was roundly defeated. His intemperate reaction on hearing the result and his refusal to cooperate with Ron Hayward, the general secretary of the Labour Party, appeared to lend substance to those like Crosland who questioned why Shirley had rushed to his defence. Later, when Prentice defected to the Conservatives in 1977, accusing the NEC of cowardice, Shirley wrote him a private note reminding him of her efforts on his behalf. To be branded a coward she thought 'a bit tough'.

On 11 February 1975, the Conservative Party made history by electing not only a woman leader but one from a modest background. Peter Hennessy recalls being with Shirley in her office when she heard the news. Her delight that a fellow woman had won was tempered by her concern that politics would become increasingly polarised as Margaret Thatcher's election signalled a shift to the right.

The two didn't know each other well but maintained civilities, Shirley admiring of her resilience and ability. When she discussed the inadequacies of Tony Barber, Heath's Chancellor of the Exchequer, with her old friend Peter Parker, she surprised him by suggesting that Thatcher should replace Barber.

Thatcher in turn had been understanding over Shirley's separation from Bernard and rated her enough to tell her that they were the only two women MPs that really counted. 'You did well,' she complimented Shirley after her spirited performance at the despatch box in the early stages of the 1974 Wilson government. 'After all, we can't let them get the better of us.'[11] Yet amidst the female solidarity there was some ideological and personal rivalry. There had been one major parliamentary clash after the 1970 election when Shirley had berated her Conservative counterpart for her support for selective education, a source of tension thereafter given Thatcher's touchiness about Shirley's privileged upbringing. 'People know I have a sizeable house in the country and they confuse size with wealth,' she complained in a newspaper interview. 'Shirley Williams came from a much better background than I did and she also had a nanny for her children but she was never accused of half the things that I am.'[12]

Raised by a fiercely ambitious father, Thatcher's attempt to escape provincial Grantham set her apart from her contemporaries. At

Oxford she was shunned by her fellow undergraduates and patronised by the dons for political views at variance with Somerville's progressive tradition. Although president of the Conservative Association, her time there passed in the shadows compared to Shirley's, and while her rise up the Conservative Party was solid enough, she never seemed destined for the highest peaks. In Heath's Cabinet she was treated with some disdain by her colleagues, so that even as calls for his resignation reached a crescendo after the October 1974 election, there were few who touted her as his successor. Her brazen courage in mounting a challenge changed all that as many Conservatives, disillusioned with Heath, rallied to her cause.

Once established as leader, the comparisons with Shirley gathered pace. Both were steeped in politics from early childhood and at Oxford they achieved the unusual distinction of leading their respective party groups. With their good looks, acute intelligence and flair for public speaking, both courted the media to good effect, appreciating the value of the photo call. Yet beneath the glamour there was the hard graft, as each laboured for a full decade trying to get into Parliament. It would have been enough to deter those of lesser grit, but not these two exceptional women endowed with immense stamina and an insatiable appetite for politics. While both were moral crusaders out to regenerate society with their respective panaceas of free enterprise and social democracy, each was able to relate their high-flown principles to everyday concerns. What's more, their grasp of the issues, their tireless electioneering and their willingness to engage with all comers made them not only formidable campaigners but also outstanding representatives for Finchley and Hitchin respectively.

Once elected, they shunned the social life of Westminster and dedicated themselves to the interminable round of meetings, speeches and correspondence, working into the small hours to stay on top of their brief. Their assiduity soon paid off as junior office beckoned, each impressing with their competence. The fact that they happened to be women did them no harm. It won them additional columns in the press and Shirley told the *Daily Telegraph* in March

1966 that there was very little prejudice against women compared to yesteryear. In her autobiography she came to revise that opinion, but at that time, with every paper depicting her as prime ministerial stock, it was perhaps inopportune to quibble. Certainly the focus on her rather than Thatcher appeared eminently justified. Aside from her breadth of vision, her warmth and humanity had won her many admirers that extended well beyond traditional party loyalties. Her courage in confronting her party in opposition over Europe won her more glowing opinions in the editorials and when Labour returned to government in 1974 she was *The Sun*'s Woman of the Year.

A natural performer both on the platform and in the television studio, she had become indispensable to Labour's election campaign. In contrast to Shirley's natural charm, Thatcher came across as unduly combative, so that even many of her closest colleagues failed to warm to her. On television, instead of engaging with the audience she tended to lecture it. In Parliament her lack of a strong voice and inability to think on her feet accentuated her shrill stridency as she struggled to land a blow on either Wilson or Callaghan at Prime Minister's Questions. With her jarring personality and prim suburban ethos, it wasn't only her political opponents who were ready to write her off. Not for the first time they underestimated her unflinching determination to succeed. While fairly dismissive of personal popularity (unlike Shirley, she rarely read what the press wrote about her), she was fully alive to the importance of a leader's image, especially a female one, in the modern media age and leaned on her trusted advisers to broaden her appeal. She courted the tabloid press, modernised her wardrobe, lowered her voice and projected the image of the meritocratic housewife in touch with the household budget, despite being married to a millionaire husband. This and her clever exploitation of the 'Iron Lady' epithet to her own advantage enabled her, according to her biographer John Campbell, to appeal to greater sections of the electorate than either Barbara Castle or Shirley.

Such cosmetic tinkering was anathema to Shirley. For years her refusal to bow to sartorial convention or political subterfuge had cemented her reputation for natural informality that formed so much of her general appeal. Now, in comparison to Thatcher, the crumpled dresses and dishevelled appearance told of a disorganised lifestyle that seemed inappropriate for political leadership. It was something that her father had fretted about during the previous Wilson government when Shirley was temporarily out of the limelight.

> Perhaps you don't dress well enough or adequately attend to good photographs being available. Judith Hart and Barbara [Castle] and Jenny [Lee] all attend to this. One must not look like Mrs Mopp aged 50. One must not expect to escape … journalistic comment if one travels to Party Conferences with holes in one's stockings. My mother did this. But Ministers mustn't. Even Soviet Ministers don't.[13]

The warning went unheeded, much to the regret of Bernard Donoughue, who thought Shirley's image did her no favours. 'The fact that she dresses, stands, walks and sits like an over-full sack of cabbages does not help. In fact she has pretty eyes, a pleasant open face and a lovely open smile. If she could get herself "organised" … she would have to be taken very seriously indeed.'[14]

It was a prospect that held no terrors for Thatcher. She once remarked that she would always beat Shirley because she was better organised. Many years later, when asked by the journalist and broadcaster Andrew Neil why Thatcher rather than she had become the first female Prime Minister, Shirley conceded that she was too disorganised. This was true but it wasn't the whole story.

Like any politician of note, Shirley hankered after high office and enjoyed the limelight, not least her countless appearances on radio and television. She also appreciated the opportunity to sit on influential committees and flourished in the collective leadership of the SDP's Gang of Four in 1981–2, but she was much more ambivalent about becoming *primus inter pares*, let alone *maximus optimus*. As a young woman she used to tell her mother that she

disliked responsibility because it restricted her freedom and independence, and now, as a prominent public figure, the likelihood
of extensive media intrusion into her personal life diminished the
attractions of becoming leader. More important was her lack of
confidence compared to Thatcher in coping with the less forgiv-
ing side of political leadership, be it ousting rivals, disciplining
colleagues or taking unpopular decisions. At no stage did she court
elements of the press, build up a following of close-knit supporters
or preside over a sophisticated private office (despite giving gener-
ously to party funds), and when the opportunity came to seize the
hour she procrastinated. In 1976 she kept her supporters waiting
'til the last minute before agreeing to oppose Michael Foot for the
deputy leadership of the Labour Party, a contest she probably could
have won had she gone all out for victory, and in 1982 she didn't
even stand for the leadership of the SDP despite the crown being
in her grasp. By then Thatcher's victory in the Falklands, the greatest gamble of her premiership, had transformed her fortunes and
assured her place in history, while within a year Shirley was out of
Parliament never to return.

※

On Tuesday 16 March 1976 Harold Wilson astounded the political
world, including most of his Cabinet, by announcing his resignation. His decision attracted the usual number of conspiracy theories,
but the plain truth seems to have been that he had had enough.
He had been leader of the Labour Party for thirteen years, Prime
Minister for nearly eight and lacked the energy and focus of his
prime. There were also the first signs of the various ailments that so
afflicted his final years.

Wilson, it appears, had returned to office in 1974 resolved to do
just two more years and in December 1975 he formally notified the
Queen of his intention to quit the following March. One or two
close friends were in the know, but otherwise, despite the odd public
hint, the secret remained watertight. Most of his Cabinet appeared

stunned when they heard the news. After receiving instant accolades from Ted Short and Callaghan, Wilson withdrew, at which point Cabinet agreed to Shirley's suggestion that they formalised their thanks. 'While Shirley and I were drafting upstairs,' Castle wrote in her diary, 'I asked her what she thought. "Very sad," she said and I think she meant it, though I didn't think she was heart-broken.'[15]

As the jostling began in earnest to succeed Wilson, Shirley quickly ruled herself out on grounds of age and inexperience. Her decision was a cause for regret for her local newspaper, but *The Guardian*, while calling her thoroughly decent and honourable, was rather more circumspect about her leadership potential, questioning her toughness and sound judgement.

Shirley's unwillingness to stand didn't mean she was indifferent to the outcome. As Callaghan, Foot, Crosland, Jenkins, Benn and Healey all entered the contest the danger for the centre-right lay in a split vote among its foremost figures which would let in the left by proxy. While Callaghan started as overwhelming favourite, Shirley and most of the pro-Europeans placed their hopes on Jenkins despite his diminishing stature within the party as his detachment from its grassroots had become ever greater. Needing every vote going, his candidacy would receive some impetus if Crosland chose not to run. With this in mind Shirley paid Crosland a visit at his home to try and dissuade him from standing. He accepted her candour in good heart, unlike his petulant reaction to Hattersley when he proffered similar sentiments.

The fact that Crosland did stand was ultimately of little consequence since his pitiful tally of nineteen could not be held responsible for Jenkins's failure. After securing a measly fifty-six votes and finishing a poor third behind Callaghan and Foot he withdrew, leaving Healey to fight on despite performing even worse than Jenkins. In the third ballot on 5 April, Callaghan, now the standard-bearer of the centre-right, saw off a spirited performance from Foot to win by 176 to 137 to become Prime Minister at the age of sixty-four. As he worked on the composition of his government that evening, Shirley told him that she would appreciate a move from the DPCP and fancied an economic portfolio (according to Marcia Falkender, Wilson had envisaged her as a future Chancellor of the Exchequer). What she didn't want was the Foreign Office, since all the travelling would detract from her maternal responsibilities, or Health and Social Security, because of her opposition to the 1967 Abortion Act.

When the reshuffle was finalised several days later, Callaghan dispensed with the services of Castle, Short, Bob Mellish and Willie Ross and promoted Crosland to the Foreign Office, thus depriving Jenkins of the one position that would have kept him in the government. As Shirley waited to see Callaghan, Donoughue told her that the Prime Minister wanted to promote her and make greater use of her talents. She replied that she was more worried about the rumours that Jenkins would not be getting the Foreign Office than her own fate. She had already intimated to Callaghan that she wouldn't wish to serve under him if there was a lurch to the left, only to have been rebuffed by Callaghan's reply that he made his own Cabinet. While keeping her at the DPCP for the time being, he did confer upon her the additional portfolio of Paymaster General with responsibility to chair several important Cabinet committees. With Jenkins on borrowed time as a minister, his departure to Brussels as president of the European Commission would not only deprive the government of one of its most formidable talents, but also the pro-European right of its most outspoken champion. With that wing of the party losing ground in Labour's ongoing war it was now up to Shirley, or one of her ilk, to step into his shoes and rally the demoralised troops. The stakes could hardly be higher.

**Endnotes**

1  *Financial Times*, 6 March 1974
2  SW to GC, 18 March 1974
3  Barbara Castle, *Diaries 1974–76*, Weidenfeld & Nicholson, 1980, p.168
4  *Guardian*, 26 September 1974
5  *The Times*, 26 September 1974
6  *Guardian*, 12 June 1975
7  *Guardian*, 12 February 1976
8  Tony Benn, *Against the Tide*, p.212
9  Bill Rodgers, *Fourth Among Equals*, p.155

10  *The Times*, 12 September 1975
11  *Climbing the Bookshelves*, p.148
12  *Sunday Express*, 16 January 1972
13  GC to SW, 16 January 1969, SW Papers (private collection)
14  Bernard Donoughue, *Downing Street Diary*, Vol. 1, Jonathan Cape, 2005, p.434
15  Barbara Castle, *Diaries 1974–76*, p.690

# THE GREAT DEBATE

Jim Callaghan's accession to the premiership was significant in more ways than one. At sixty-four he was one of the oldest and most underprivileged to have entered No. 10, with roots deep in the Labour movement. He always regretted his lack of a university education, but compensated with his immense guile, grit and experience, having previously held the three great offices of state. If his time as Chancellor of the Exchequer was less than auspicious he grew considerably in stature at both the Home and Foreign Office, so that becoming Prime Minister in no way fazed him.

Although older than Wilson, Callaghan immediately brought a new vitality to the office and restored the smack of firm government after a period of drift. Bolstered by a happily enduring marriage, a firm set of values inherited from his Baptist youth and unencumbered by a scheming inner circle of courtiers, his leadership lacked the paranoia of his predecessor. He looked to his Cabinet as a genuine team rather than a collection of rivals and was happy to give them their heads provided their efforts were directed towards the common good.

Although Shirley's relationship with Wilson had blossomed over time it was never especially close. With Callaghan it was always warmer. Ever since she had entertained him at Oxford as chairman of the University Labour Club there had been a genuine affection between the two of them. Years of mutual hospitality at the Mitchison home at Carradale had enhanced that friendship (Shirley also liked Callaghan's wife, Audrey), and when she entered the Home Office under his tutelage their respect for each other grew despite their widely differing philosophies. The 1971 vote over the Common Market when Labour was in opposition caused some tension, but once back in government they were more often than not allies, primarily in their resistance to the left.

On becoming Prime Minister, Callaghan was determined to make full use of Shirley's many gifts, not least her unique appeal to the wider public, which professional politicians such as Wilson and himself could never hope to emulate. 'Shirley was a very good platform speaker, both in the Commons and the Lords,' he later recalled. 'She was extremely popular in the Party and would have been a strong candidate as Leader of the Labour Party, if a vacancy had come. Her gifts were such that she was possibly better as a politician and member of the Cabinet than as a Department Minister.'[1]

In addition to her departmental responsibilities, Callaghan asked her to chair several contentious Cabinet committees, knowing that she had the healing touch to bring warring factions together, and he also trusted her to be his eyes and ears on the NEC when unable to attend himself. Although he could pull rank if she became too feisty in Cabinet, and he reprimanded her for her Education Green Paper, these were but passing squalls in a warm-hearted relationship that survived the pressures of office. Donoughue recalls that when Shirley went through a spell of falling asleep in Cabinet during the summer of 1977, Callaghan fretted about her personal welfare and hoped there was nothing untoward in her personal life. After she had lost her seat in the 1979 election he confessed to feeling heartbroken and even after the pain of separation when Shirley joined the SDP, the old bonds weren't severed. They continued to enjoy each other's company and on Callaghan's death in 2005 it was Shirley who gave one of the tributes at his thanksgiving service at Westminster Abbey.

After remaining at the DPCP for another five months, during which she made further relaxations to the price code, Shirley was promoted to the DES in the September 1976 reshuffle. According to her successor, Roy Hattersley, her departure was much lamented by her officials despite their open criticism of her record.

Shirley's move to the DES was something of a surprise as she had expressed no particular wish to return there and according to Donoughue, Callaghan had earmarked Hattersley for that portfolio. Donoughue also thought that, in line with press speculation, the Prime Minister was planning to send her to the Home Office, but was forced to think again when she told him that it was one of three portfolios she didn't want because of her unhappy experiences there as a junior minister. There is some evidence from Shirley herself that she did try setting out her stall before reluctantly taking Education, although there is nothing to suggest that she turned down the Home Office. It was, after all, one of the great offices of state and one that she had shadowed for two years. Had she been that unhappy with her lot she surely would have shown less reluctance in relinquishing the portfolio to Jenkins in November 1973, and refrained from expressing regret about not becoming Home Secretary the following March.

The DES ranked as one of the less prestigious departments in Whitehall and was rarely at the heart of government initiatives. Wilson never took much interest in Education, appointing six Secretaries there in eight years, and Shirley's two predecessors, Reg Prentice and Fred Mulley, were both way down the Cabinet pecking order. The 1964–70 government, it is true, had given Education a higher profile than hitherto as it looked to schools and universities to help build the meritocratic society, but Labour's return to power wasn't accompanied by any new educational philosophy. Much of what it accomplished between 1974 and 1976 was unfinished business. The arrival of Callaghan as Prime Minister gave Education a greater priority, giving its Secretary of State a touch more kudos. Yet appearances were deceptive. A weak government engaged in drastic cutbacks was hardly the ideal backdrop for a portfolio that traditionally lacked real clout and was at the mercy of a myriad of powerful interest groups.

Shirley's move to the DES had been preceded by the appointment of James Hamilton, a civil engineer by profession, as Permanent Secretary to help galvanise a department that had been notoriously inert and insular. He was at one with his political masters in their belief that it had to assume a more proactive, centralising role in allocating ever scarcer resources and raising standards in schools, but, temperamentally, he was very different from Shirley, his robust managerial style at odds with her more persuasive one. Their differences surfaced over her 1977 Green Paper, which Hamilton thought far too accommodating towards the local authorities and teaching unions.

She wasn't entirely comfortable with her team of ministers either. Gordon Oakes, the Minister of State responsible for higher and further education, despite improving adult literacy, was prone to idleness and capriciousness; Margaret Jackson, her Under-Secretary of State, was able and industrious but her Bennite loyalties created a sense of mistrust between the two of them.

More to her liking was the Arts Minister, Jack Donaldson, and her successive PPSs, John Cartwright, Giles Radice and Bob Mitchell, all loyal, genial, exceptionally able and ideologically compatible. Aside from helping her to prepare speeches, and giving her advice on party policy, their main task appeared to be getting her to Parliament in time for crucial votes.

She was also well served by her succession of private secretaries: Clive Booth and Stephen Jones, strong supporters of comprehensives, and Philip Hunter, a zoologist by training, later to become chief schools adjudicator.

Closest of all were her two political advisers, John Lyttle and Stella Greenall. John Lyttle was a native of Merseyside who grew up there during the Depression. A great admirer of Gaitskell when a student and an implacable opponent of discrimination of any kind, he made his name as chief officer of the Race Relations Board before joining Shirley at the DPCP in 1974. Politically astute, he understood the civil service as few did and knew what was needed to get a ministerial decision implemented. A past master of the workings of the Labour Party, he used his many contacts to advance

Shirley's interests and those of her wing of the party, urging her, for instance, to run for the deputy leadership in 1976. He also took issue with those who pried intrusively into her personal life or subjected her to unwarranted slurs, such as over her supposed incitement of violence following her appearance on a trade union picket line at the Grunwick film processing firm in May 1977. Given also his involvement in her constituency work, Shirley became ever more dependent on Lyttle's loyalty if not his strictures. Never one for being corralled by her officials, or anyone else for that matter, her propensity to act on impulse and alter her schedule helped precipitate tension. 'He was totally devoted to Shirley,' commented Carol Bracken, 'and although he could be icily critical of her in a wonderfully tongue-in-cheek sort of way, I believe the problem at least in part was that he was suffering from unrequited (neo-Platonic) love.'[2] This may well help account for the subsequent rupturing of their friendship following the formation of the SDP. Lyttle proved a highly accomplished press officer for the party, but Shirley's unwillingness to use her influence as chairman of the Communications Committee to support his candidacy for the role of chief media officer, knowing his contempt for television, was a slight he never forgave.

Less prominent than Lyttle but no less dependable was Stella Greenall. A widely respected NUS officer for many years, credited with creating the universal student grant, she went to work for Fred Mulley in 1975 and transferred her loyalty to Shirley when she succeeded him. With her assiduous research, mainly on higher education, and disinterested advice, the popular Greenall proved to be a model adviser as well as a loyal friend.

Whatever Shirley felt about being back at Education, her enthusiasm was infectious. She used to clamber up the stairs to her ministerial suite on the twelfth floor of Elizabeth House, home to the DES, dictating as she went. Working for her was both personally rewarding and intellectually stimulating, albeit a trifle fraught when her overstretched schedule, the result partly of her accepting too many invitations, caught up with her. Stephen Jones remembers one Friday when she was due to fly to Strasbourg that evening to give a major speech at the European Council. As the time for departure drew ever closer, Shirley, catching up on a backlog of work in her office, dismissed repeated warnings from her secretary about the time, reassuring him that everything would be fine. Finally, in desperation, Jones rang the Metropolitan Commissioner of Police to advise him of their predicament and request a police escort to get them to Heathrow. The commissioner was reluctant, but eventually agreed provided they got themselves to Hyde Park Corner. They did, whereupon they met a police car. 'You are the ones who need to get to Heathrow?' the driver said. 'Just follow me,' and taking off at breakneck speed they made it there in record time as Shirley sat in the back of her official car signing papers, oblivious to the commotion around her.

For all the considerable demands that she placed on her staff, Shirley, unlike some ministers, retained her personal touch. Stephen Jones was once working with her late one evening at her flat when she volunteered to cook him dinner. Besides admiring her empathy with strangers he thought her capacity for winning over an audience unrivalled. He recalls how on one particular occasion, when her message had fallen flat, she changed tone and without altering policy managed to sound much more appealing. Yet for all her capacity to listen and to consult he dismissed the idea that she was indecisive. He acknowledged that her active mind could take her off at a tangent, thereby reducing her effectiveness, but once set on a particular course she wouldn't be shifted.

His views were echoed by his successor, Philip Hunter. His experience of giving advice both to Shirley and to Margaret Thatcher when she was Education Secretary provided an interesting contrast. True to form it was Thatcher who would challenge, hector and harangue, whereas Shirley would always listen sympathetically, but when it came to decision making, Thatcher was the one more likely to absorb the advice. The fact that Shirley didn't make greater headway with her proposals for educational reform, he felt, wasn't down to a lack of clarity on her part, but rather to the political realities of the time. Others were less generous in their assessment. The educationalist Brian Simon wrote that 'procrastination, indecision, delay at all costs' marked Shirley's term of office[3] and even Callaghan regretted that she didn't 'push harder to get reforms moving after my Ruskin speech [launching the Great Debate on education in October 1976] ... so we did not get very far before the 1979 election'.[4]

Callaghan's emphasis on educational reform stemmed from a growing national concern about eroding standards in basic literary and numeracy skills, increasingly attributed to the onset of comprehensive education.

Although secondary reorganisation had raised the hackles of many on the educational and political right, it had progressed reasonably smoothly 'til 1974, by which time some 60 per cent of schools had gone comprehensive. Thereafter the media changed tack and highlighted the failings, real or imaginary, of a number of London comprehensives. That these deficiencies were highlighted at a time of acute economic crisis merely added to the sense of malaise. A fourth instalment of the *Black Papers*, a series of pamphlets written by right-wing academics and politicians denouncing the excesses of progressive education, advocated a restoration of traditional educational standards, the Bennett Report called for a return to formal methods in primary education and leading employers blamed schools for the shortage of skilled workers in industry. Even *The Guardian*, no friend to outmoded tradition, demanded a more rigorous preparation of students for the world of work.

All this was fuel for the Conservative Party, which, under its trenchant new leader, a devotee of the grammar school ethos, set out to challenge the prevailing educational consensus with a rash of ideas that blended tradition with innovation. For alongside a trumpeting of age-old values such as discipline and testing, there emerged a new emphasis on parental choice. Leading the charge was Norman St John Stevas, a junior education minister under Heath, and his deputy, Rhodes Boyson, a former secondary headmaster who had contributed to the *Black Papers*. Theirs wasn't an easy relationship, but their joint emphasis on selection, excellence and parental involvement gave Conservative educational policy a cutting edge, placing additional pressure on the government to act.

Callaghan's own disadvantages in life made him a passionate believer in education as a means of a passport to better times. He worried that the growing neglect of literacy and numeracy was not only performing a massive disservice for many underprivileged pupils, but was also handing the Conservatives valuable ammunition. With the support of the Policy Unit and James Hamilton, both keen to make the educational Establishment more accountable to the public interest, he resolved to take action. His celebrated Ruskin speech in October 1976, calling for an educational system which provided a basic curriculum and universal standards, and which equipped children with the vocational skills for the ever changing workplace, gained widespread coverage, prompting the great debate he had intended to provoke.

Callaghan's sentiments chimed in with Shirley's for the most part. Fully alive to the value of a well-ordered school with specific rules, strong pastoral care and a sound learning environment which included the setting and marking of homework, she knew that some teachers fell far short of general expectation. Their shortcomings and the methodology that informed their approach would need to be addressed. She told Donoughue that she intended to pursue a hard line at Education. At the same time she had to tread carefully since the running of schools and the means of assessment were very much in the hands of the local authorities and teaching unions. The two largest, the National Union of Teachers (NUT), which contained a younger radical element, and the National Association of Schoolmasters/Union of Women Teachers (NASUWT), often fought their own turf wars, but much resented any intrusion by stray predators into their territory, as Callaghan discovered in the build-up to Ruskin.

The spirit of Ruskin very much shaped Shirley's time at Education as her department came under the critical gaze of a Prime Minister who saw this as his 'big idea'. The day after the speech he wrote to her to say that, having raised certain questions, she should follow these up by bringing forward specific proposals for publication. He wanted her to publish a Green Paper before Christmas. She agreed on the need to move quickly, but preferred to postpone publication until such time as she had held a series of consultations with the interested parties in the New Year.

Her procrastination frustrated No. 10. Convinced that 'the rats have been getting at your initiative', John Meadway, the Prime Minister's Private Secretary, pressed him to get her to reconsider. On 22 November Callaghan wrote to Shirley to express his concern that delay risked losing the momentum of Ruskin as public interest waned.

> My view is, therefore, that the document to be issued at the turn of the year should be a Green Paper. It is, after all, inherent in the concept of a Green Paper that the Government is not committed to the proposals in it, and if particular aspects run into difficulty they can be modified or dropped as seems best. The regional conferences you envisage would then be based on the Green Paper as a formal expression of Government proposals on which it is inviting the widest comments.[5]

He hoped it would be possible for the results of the consultations to be assimilated in time for ministers to take the necessary decisions before the summer recess.

Conscious of Callaghan's criticisms, Shirley replied that it would be 'premature and unhelpful' to issue a Green Paper before the regional conferences. She assured him there had been no erosion in public interest towards their proposals. On the contrary, requests to participate in the conferences had grown daily. 'We would lose a lot of goodwill (and perhaps special knowledge) if we tried to move too quickly to a Green Paper.'[6] To discuss its content at these conferences ran the risk of becoming weighed down by undue detail and lacking any clear consensus. She felt confident that she could deliver what the Prime Minister wanted by the end of May.

Her words won her time as Callaghan was advised to hold his fire. 'I do not think Mrs Williams's arguments are convincing,' advised Meadway, 'but there comes a point at which it does not seem sensible for you to press a point as she is so much closer to the issue.'[7]

The regional conferences began at Newcastle upon Tyne on 18 February, and proceeded through various centres to address the underlying concern of where schools had fallen short. After chairing the first of these conferences, Shirley pronounced herself well pleased with what she had heard, but *The Times* was rather more sceptical in its post-Bradford editorial. The debates had thrown up some useful discussion on the curriculum and attainment, but their weakness lay in the refusal of teachers to accept public concern about falling standards. 'There is a whiff of complacency about the education groups,' it concluded, a view that riled the teachers, as they made clear to Shirley at their Easter conferences.[8]

The Green Paper went through about fifty drafts, in which Shirley took a close interest, not least in a number of its compromises to accommodate the views of the various educational pressure groups. This conciliatory approach was to prove its most glaring weakness, especially the lack of any mention of a core curriculum covering 50 to 60 per cent of the school timetable. When it reached the Policy Unit, Donoughue found it sparse and deeply complacent in tone. On 15 June he went to see Margaret Jackson to discuss it. 'She was fairly scathing,' he wrote in his diary. 'Claims that Shirley was not sure what to say in it, especially after the PM's Ruskin speech had pre-empted the ground.'[9] Donoughue told Callaghan that he didn't think it met the substantial expectations aroused by Ruskin and the ensuing debate. The paper, he felt, contained little about the range of problems facing the schools regarding standards, discipline and teaching accountability. It seemed too slanted towards the education lobby rather than parents, and made only scant reference to the Great Debate.

Donoughue's findings coalesced with those of Callaghan. He thought the paper too general, especially over the core curriculum, and asked the Policy Unit to 'stir things up'. On the evening of 21 June, Donoughue met Shirley, but while making a number of constructive concessions she baulked at radical proposals to raise standards and improve discipline. She also resisted any attempt to rewrite the document in a less turgid style, arguing that many of the sentences reflected long discussion with various interested parties and rewriting it might alter the agreed balance.

She enlarged on this theme in Cabinet. Her need to proceed cautiously in light of her limited powers won her some sympathy, but the general mood was one of hostility to a document deemed too long, too imprecise and too unresponsive to the public mood. The Prime Minister himself didn't hold back. When everyone had had their say he asked her to draft a considerably shorter document, taking account of the points made, and to lay much more stress on the proposals for action.

Donoughue recorded,

> I met Shirley Williams coming out of Cabinet. She looked a bit down. She clearly thought I was behind the criticisms, but was very friendly. She said that on reflection it was probably a good thing not to publish it, since it was not well written. She had been too busy chairing the subcommittee on industrial democracy and had left a deputy secretary to write the main body of the work, and he had compromised with everybody, in true Civil Service fashion. Now she would have to 'pretend to be sick' and take off four days to rewrite it properly.[10]

She did precisely that, following discussions with James Hamilton and other members of the Cabinet such as Shore, Hattersley and Ennals. By the time Donoughue saw it he thought it 'read extremely well'. It 'no longer fudged the issues of general concern' and had taken fully into consideration all the suggestions made. When Cabinet met the next day it agreed to publish it. Callaghan congratulated Shirley on a good paper worthy of the public debate about education in schools. Her pleasure was somewhat tempered by a leaked report in *The Times*, which referred to the rejection of the Green Paper by the Cabinet, believing this to be unprecedented.

She conveyed her dismay to Donoughue, pointing the finger at No. 10 as the source of the leak, since no one in her department knew about it, a claim that he disputed as he knew that his Private Office had spoken to hers. 'It shows how ministers are ignorant of the machine. It is curious that Shirley thought it was possible that the decision of Cabinet could have been kept secret from her department.'[11]

Having raised expectations at Ruskin of an educational renaissance it was now time for the government to deliver. Shirley had been sent to Education precisely because she had the personality to inspire the public and persuade the teaching profession to reform itself. Civil servants liked her receptiveness to new ideas. 'But it is precisely this open-mindedness, this refusal to strike dogmatic attitudes that makes Mrs Williams a weaker minister when it comes to forcing through her decisions and identifying priorities,' noted Peter Wilby, the *Sunday Times*'s education correspondent. 'What she still has to prove is that she also has political muscle and single-mindedness.'[12]

After a tussle with the teachers over a core curriculum which, after a long consultation exercise, produced little of substance, Shirley found herself at loggerheads with them over exams. Since 1970 the teacher-dominated Schools Council had been investigating the possibility of a single exam at sixteen to replace the dual system of O level taken by the top 20 per cent and the lower standard CSE. Not only did the Council believe that sixteen-plus would more positively reflect the comprehensive principle, it would be administratively advantageous for schools, and spare teachers hard academic choices at too early a stage. It also devised a Certificate of Extended Education, a new exam for less able sixth-formers unable to cope with the demands of A levels.

The Schools Council proposals, presented to the DES in July 1976, were given a mixed response, the enthusiasm for its rationale among many teachers offset by the doubts of traditionalists, who feared that the new exam lacked rigour for the intellectually able. These doubts were similar to ones that Shirley shared herself. Pupils had widely differing abilities, she told the chairman of the Schools Council, and the examination system should continue to reflect those differences.

She thus sought a second opinion from a committee under Sir James Waddell, a former deputy under-secretary at the Home Office. After a year-long investigation it broadly endorsed the sixteen-plus. Shirley publicly accepted the bulk of Waddell's findings, but with further delays pending, such as the need for rationalisation among a number of exam boards, the decision to go ahead with GCSE in 1987 was left to her successor.

At a time when growing affluence was generating greater consumer choice, its relative absence in the educational system convinced the Wilson government that parents should be consulted more widely. It thus established a committee under Tom Taylor, the former chairman of Blackburn education committee, to look into school government. When he reported in 1977, Shirley gave a broad welcome to his proposals that each school should have its own governing body and that representatives of parents, teachers and the local community should have a statutory right to membership of that body. (In secondary schools, representation should also include employers and trade unions given the importance of the transition between school and work.) Consequently, legislation was prepared to this effect in a major Education Bill, but it never saw the light of day as opposition from Benn (see below) and other government priorities such as its major Devolution Bill postponed it for another year.

The question about choice of school in the state sector was one much peddled by the Conservatives. In a memorandum submitted to a Cabinet committee in September 1977, Shirley and John Morris, the Welsh Secretary, recognised the widespread dissatisfaction regarding the then law over school admissions. The extent to which parents could express preferences varied from one part of the country to another, but essentially 80 per cent had no choice at all. They proposed that local education authorities should be required to take into account parental wishes in the allocation of places and to bring the unsatisfactory authorities into line with their more enlightened counterparts. Legislation would compel them to set out admissions procedures clearly and provide for local and national appeals.

Their proposals not only alarmed the teaching unions, who feared that popular schools would be overcrowded while the unpopular ones would go under, it also brought Shirley into conflict with Tony Benn. It so happened his wife Caroline, a leading educationalist and ardent supporter of comprehensive schools, had advised him that parental choice would reintroduce selective education, as well as placing greater pressure on to local authorities. 'Prime Minister, I think this is going to be a very controversial bill as far as the Party is concerned,' Benn warned Callaghan at Cabinet on 20 October when Shirley wondered why it hadn't been included in the Queen's Speech.

> 'Absolutely untrue,' said Shirley.
>
> I went on, 'I am not arguing the case now but I think it ought to come to Cabinet.'
>
> Shirley said that it had been to the Home Affairs Committee of the Cabinet and no one had raised any query – to which I replied that I wasn't a member of that committee.
>
> 'If Tony wants to raise it in Cabinet, he is entitled to do so,' said Jim.
>
> So I stopped the Bill going into the Queen's Speech.[13]

The 1974 Labour manifesto had pledged greater opportunities for sixteen- to nineteen-year-olds either at school or in further education, especially those from low-income families, by redressing the inequities of the grant system. Compared to the help given to those in higher education, where 50 per cent of students received a maximum award, only 2.5 per cent of those in school and 7 per cent in further education received help, and that was fairly measly. It helped explain why Britain had one of the worst participation rates of sixth-form education in Western Europe, but when Fred Mulley tried to give substance to the manifesto commitment by extending educational maintenance allowances (EMAs), he faced stiff resistance from Joel Barnett, the Chief Secretary to the Treasury. Aside from his reluctance to countenance further public spending commitments, Barnett questioned the cost-effectiveness of a scheme which he felt would do little to keep alienated youngsters at school. Eighty per cent of the grants, he argued, would go to students who were likely to stay on in any case. He remained wedded to these convictions as EMAs continued to consume much time and debate over the course of the next three years.

It was a scheme to which Shirley was strongly committed. After exhaustive discussions with local authorities and after winning her case in committee she made her pitch to the Cabinet on 11 May 1978. In order to improve the vocational education of sixteen- to nineteen-year-olds, especially those from low-income backgrounds, these people needed an incentive to stay on at school. She proposed a weekly means-tested grant of £7 for those at school and £9 for those at college. The Cabinet approved in principle, but with Callaghan sharing Treasury reservations about the cost of the scheme, some £100 million per year, the final decision was shelved 'til the autumn.

When the Cabinet met that October to discuss public spending for the forthcoming year it was decided that EMAs wouldn't be provided for in the White Paper, but Shirley would be free to make the case for them in an enabling provision in the forthcoming Educational Bill. Despite continuing opposition from the Treasury, a pilot scheme, to be run in selected areas of high unemployment at a cost of £10 million in 1979–80 and £15 million in 1980–81, to be funded by the MSC and DES respectively, and to commence in 1979, was approved. Yet even this modest victory proved a hollow one as the Education Bill hadn't materialised by the time the government fell, and with it went the scheme itself.

For all Shirley's efforts to reform the state sector her time at the DES will chiefly be remembered for her battle with the grammar schools as Labour's hostility to selective education became all the more pronounced. The attempts of the 1964 Labour government to integrate the independent sector within the state one had come to nothing, and its manifesto in February 1974 merely contented itself with a commitment to end its charitable status and all forms of tax relief. Even this proved elusive, owing partly to the inability of two committees to unravel the complexities of the law relating to charities and partly to the European Convention of Human Rights, which ruled out any attempt to abolish fee-paying schools. Shirley also tried to chip away at their financial resources by ending the subsidy given to military and diplomatic personnel and reducing local authority grants to independent school places, but was blocked by David Owen at the Foreign Office. Only on the reduction of local authority grants to fee-paying school places did she make some progress.

Aside from the nation's prestigious fully fee-paying schools, there were the remaining 174 direct grant schools (selective day schools funded partly by the DES for pupils from low-income backgrounds and partly by fees) and the maintained grammar schools (funded by the local authorities). Together these schools had been the means by which many a leading Labour politician had risen from modest beginnings, a fact that had helped preserve them hitherto, but with selection increasingly seen as undermining the comprehensive ideal their days appeared numbered.

The 1970 Donnison Report, welcomed by the outgoing Labour government, had advocated the integration of the direct grant schools into the local systems and when it returned to power in 1974 it duly withdrew financial support to these schools, forcing them either to go comprehensive or become fully fee paying. While fifty-one, almost all of them Roman Catholic schools, opted for the former (and several closed), 119, including Manchester Grammar and Bradford Grammar, chose the latter, an ironic twist as it merely strengthened the fee-paying sector by making it even more elitist. It also galvanised the Conservative Party towards a greater defence of selection. One such case revolved around St Marylebone Grammar School in central London.

St Marylebone GS, founded in 1792, was a top-flight academic school with a proud history. Yet despite its reputation its future had been shrouded in doubt for a number of years as its governing body, the Inner London Education Authority (ILEA), mainly Labour-controlled, planned to amalgamate it with a neighbouring secondary modern.

The plans met with fierce resistance from the parent body at a time when ILEA was attempting to outlaw selective education in the capital's state schools. Following Fred Mulley's approval of its proposals for a newly enlarged merged school, they took it to court and won an injunction that stopped it proceeding. Confronted with this setback, ILEA, rather than appealing to a higher court, asked Shirley to use her powers under the 1944 Act to enforce closure, a request which she obliged.

Her decision, announced at the end of January 1977, sparked fresh outrage. The local MP, Kenneth Baker, tried to force an emergency debate in the Commons, claiming that Shirley had used her powers previously reserved for administrative purposes only 'to attain a political end, namely the destruction of a fine school with a great scholastic tradition'.[14]

The Parents' Association once again resorted to the courts. They were granted an injunction, restraining ILEA from implementing its proposals, but ILEA's appeal was upheld, thereby consigning the school to its fate, much to the fury of the *Daily Mail*. Once, the diversity of the British educational system was a cause of admiration the world over, declared its education correspondent, Christopher Rowlands. 'Now if the dogmatic Socialists have their way, the classroom diet will be chips with everything.'[15] The article went on to raise the delicate topic of Rebecca Williams's schooling, implying that by sending her daughter to a private school, Shirley had been guilty of double standards. This wasn't quite the case.

Back in 1972 Shirley, now living in Brook Green, had been delighted when Rebecca passed the eleven-plus and was accepted by Godolphin and Latymer, an ILEA voluntarily aided girls' grammar school in Hammersmith. There, in this studious atmosphere, she settled in nicely, becoming popular and successful in turn as the school led resistance to ILEA's determination to withdraw support for selective schools. The ILEA decision was endorsed by Fred Mulley, the Education Secretary, and by Shirley, whose stance angered some parents when she attended a meeting at Godolphin to discuss the issue. With the school's governors concerned that going comprehensive would erode academic standards, the decision was taken in December 1975 to go independent from September 1977. Parents with children already in the school would escape payment, but new arrivals would be charged £810 per year.

For nearly a year after the school had opted for independence Shirley held her fire, wanting to do what was best for Rebecca. On becoming Education Secretary in September 1976, the pressure to move her from Godolphin mounted, but in the end the decision to leave at the end of the school year was primarily Rebecca's. It was a decision that the school understood, although they did quibble with Shirley's public declaration that she had originally sent her daughter there on the understanding that Godolphin would go comprehensive, only for the governors to change their mind. The governors had done nothing of the sort, the chairman assured her, they had always kept their options open, but this minor altercation aside, Shirley's association with the school was a happy one.

Rebecca's new school was Camden High for Girls, a former voluntary-aided school that began the process of going comprehensive in 1976, but the furore over her education wouldn't abate, so much so that Shirley felt compelled to issue a circular to SDP candidates during the 1987 election to help counter allegations that she had sent her child to a fee-paying school.

In April 1974 Reg Prentice reasserted the government's determination to end selection but with progress slow, a more statutory approach was required. The Education Bill, introduced by Mulley in December 1975, required local authorities to complete reorganisation, an edict which prompted a robust reply from the grammar school lobby, parents' organisations and the Conservative Party. The latter were particularly supportive of the newly elected Conservative authority of Tameside in Greater Manchester in its fight to abandon its Labour predecessor's proposal for secondary reorganisation – due for September that year. On 26 July 1976 the Appeal Court ruled that Mulley had greatly exceeded his powers under Section 68 of the 1944 Act in trying to foist comprehensives upon Tameside. (This was before the 1976 Act based on Mulley's Bill had come into effect.) When its ruling was upheld by the Law Lords, their judgment based on the fact that the Conservatives had come to power in Tameside on a mandate for selection, Shirley called it misconceived, misguided and wrong. It could do lasting damage to a generation of children in the area. No reasonable authority would wish to override the will of Parliament. Her frustration was understandable enough. Tameside not only fuelled further resistance to reorganisation, helped by large Conservative gains in the 1977 local elections, it also compelled her to proceed carefully in dealing with recalcitrant authorities, fearful that the vagaries of the 1976 Act made another Tameside quite possible.

The Education Bill was one of five controversial Bills that had been subjected to a hostile grilling in both houses, the Conservatives fighting it tooth and nail in committee. When the Commons considered three crucial Lords' amendments to the Education Bill in November 1976, Shirley alleged that the Tory emphasis on parental choice was a device by which to maintain the principle of selection. As far as the government was concerned, comprehensives substantially widened choice, not least over choice of courses. For the Conservatives, St John Stevas denied they were opposed to comprehensives, only to their imposition as the only type of school. He wrote in the *Sunday Telegraph*,

By rejecting the eminently reasonable amendments passed by the Upper House, Mrs Williams showed herself every bit as rigid, although undoubtedly more charming and skilful, than her immediate predecessors. There has been a change of style but none of substance. The hoary old Labour preoccupation with organisation to the exclusion of action to raise standards remains as obsessive as ever.[16]

Once the Education Bill had become law in November, Shirley wrote to eight rebel authorities, Bexley, Buckingham, Essex, Kingston-upon-Thames, Redbridge, Sutton, Trafford and Tameside, all Conservative, asking them to submit effective plans for secondary reorganisation and giving them six months to comply. The following January she followed suit with another thirty who had only partially complied because of their failure to mention a date for reorganisation. By the time of the 24 May 1977 deadline, only Tameside had refused to submit anything at all, but many other schemes proved unsatisfactory either by retaining some form of selection or by prolonging the date for reorganisation to well after the next election in the hope that a Conservative government would be re-elected in the meantime. As Tameside continued to delay, claiming it needed more time to consult, its protestations won little sympathy from Shirley. She told it that it had been given ample time and she expected compliance by 26 September – uncompromising language that did little to quell the mood of disillusion of the Tameside Labour Party. Frustrated by her failure to turn words into action, it passed a motion highly critical of her as other Conservative authorities opted for resistance.

In June, Birmingham, now again in Conservative hands, acting on legal advice, had declared her letter of 17 January 1977 invalid, claiming that under the 1976 Act the Secretary of State couldn't require reorganisation of individual schools; she could merely specify areas or parts of areas where change was needed. Shirley rejected its claims and started proceedings to take it to court. She also asked Bexley to make a further submission by 20 October and told Trafford, Sutton and Kingston-upon-Thames to stop procrastinating.

Labour assaults on selective education posed a dilemma for the Conservative opposition. With the vast majority of the nation's children enrolled in state schools there was no question of undoing the work of the past two decades. Equally, as the party of choice, they ardently supported the right of all existing selective schools to be free of state interference. A pledge to repeal the 1976 Act, maintain grammar schools and restore direct grants through what became known as the assisted places scheme became the flagship educational policies around which the party could unite.

Their continued defiance frustrated Shirley. At the 1977 Labour conference she excoriated Tory promises to restore direct grant schools as a most cynical interpretation of parental choice. Taxpayers' money would be distributed to the privileged few at the expense of the many and comprehensives would be deprived of their most able pupils, placing in jeopardy everything that Labour had achieved. One of the strongest reasons for re-electing a Labour government was to prevent a return to the educational deprivation of the previous era. The choice would be back to the 1930s with Norman St John Stevas or to the 1890s with Rhodes Boyson with a vengeance. Her outburst induced a spirited riposte from Margaret Thatcher in her leader's speech at the Conservative conference the following week. 'People from my sort of background needed grammar schools to compete with children from privileged homes like Shirley Williams and Anthony Wedgwood-Benn.'[17]

Shirley's attempts to enforce compliance ran into further trouble. A QC advised Bexley that she had exceeded her powers in demanding that the council submit alternative plans for reorganisation, because she had failed to give a full explanation as to why the original plans, a mixture of eleven-to-sixteen and eleven-to-eighteen schools, were unsatisfactory. Then North Yorkshire became the first council to take her to court after she had rejected its provision for two Ripon schools having sixth forms. With Tameside retaining grammar schools as sixth-form colleges, Redbridge resolutely refusing to dismantle its two surviving grammar schools and Sutton unwilling to reorganise before 1984, the struggle seemed never-ending. By the spring of 1978 thirty-eight local authorities, including many of the larger ones, hadn't yet signed up to full-blown reorganisation. Shirley's desire to proceed carefully was understandable given the fate that had befallen her predecessor over Tameside and her fear that history would repeat itself, but her caution cut little ice with Caroline Benn. In the winter 1977–78 editorial of *Comprehensive*

*Education*, a journal for pro-comprehensive parents and teachers, Benn alleged that government legislation to abolish grammar schools had failed partly because of Shirley's reluctance to turn words into deeds. When Shirley next met Callaghan she showed him a copy of the offending article, complaining that it was very unfair given the imperfections of the 1976 Act. Callaghan agreed that it wasn't the appropriate way for a colleague's wife to behave, but admitted that there was nothing that could be done. At the NUT conference in March, its secretary, Fred Jarvis, an old friend of hers from Oxford, warned her that she must not allow those delaying tactics by one device or another to thwart the will of Parliament. She assured him that she was contemplating legal action against all those authorities resisting full reorganisation, a threat which earned her the sobriquet of a tyrannical bully girl from St John Stevas. A Conservative government, he promised, would restore to the local authorities the freedom to organise their own schools.

With the summer proving little respite as Kirklees joined Sutton and North Yorkshire in taking Shirley to court for acting *ultra vires*, the Labour tribe was getting restless. Speaker after speaker at Conference denounced the government for a failure of political will in the fight against selection and demanded immediate sanctions against the rebel authorities. In reply Shirley reminded her audience that 83 per cent of children were now state educated and 503 proposals for reorganisation had been accepted since 1974. She asked it to remember Tameside. The fate of what happened rested with the courts and it was something over which she had no jurisdiction. Nevertheless, the government was pressing as hard as it could and would be renewing battle with the likes of Sutton, Birmingham and North Yorkshire in the courts. In a fiercely partisan speech she lacerated the Conservatives' 'scurrilous' campaign against comprehensive education. As for their education spokesmen, she derided 'the Blessed Norman', who winked to the comprehensive lobby and 'Stone Age Boyson', who played to the grammar school gallery. Only two things united them, she averred: selection and the desire to be the next Education Secretary.

That same month the High Court declared for Shirley against North Yorkshire, ruling that the 1976 Act took precedence over the 1944 one which gave the government the right to require local authorities to provide proposals of a kind it favoured, a judgment that deterred Kirklees from mounting a similar challenge. She rejected Tameside's new proposal for reorganisation, claiming that it would perpetuate inequalities, berated Kingston-upon-Thames's refusal to reorganise before 1982 and declared Bexley in default of its statutory duty to end selection by 1979. Only the imminence of the general election prevented her from initiating legal proceedings against the latter two, but as the government entered its dying fall few of the recalcitrant authorities had given up the ghost. The return of the Conservatives meant that 400 grammar schools lived to fight another day.

Shirley's fight to raise standards was made no easier by the austerity of the times. For years Education had pocketed a growing share of the nation's wealth, but in the harsh economic climate of the 1970s and a rapidly declining birth rate, it couldn't escape its share of the pain. Reg Prentice had closed thirty teaching training colleges. Now, with birth projections set to fall even further, a government advisory committee in November 1976 downgraded the number of teachers required for 1981 from 57,000 to 45,000, 12,000 fewer than the most recent estimate, and a long way short of the 117,000 originally planned. The teaching unions were far from happy, but after a couple of meetings with Shirley they accepted the inevitable, leaving her to decide which colleges to close, one of the most painful decisions she ever had to make. In January 1977 she announced the closure of another thirty colleges, subject to further consultations between the DES and the local authorities, consultations which led to five colleges being reprieved. She accepted her proposals were severe, but in the face of opposition taunts about an educational holocaust she remained defiant, claiming that she wasn't prepared to train thousands of people for inevitable unemployment. She considered that the debate over reorganisation of teacher training was over for the time being, although at local level the resentment lingered as the cuts forced schools to adapt to fewer teachers and larger classes.

Universities, after years of expansion, also underwent contraction. Following severe cuts by the Heath government, the Cabinet in December 1975 agreed to increase charges on overseas students from £250 to £320, a decision influenced partly by the rapidly growing number studying in Britain, many from rich countries. Six months later, under pressure from the Treasury for further savings in the education budget, Fred Mulley announced swingeing fee increases for both undergraduates and postgraduates. Undergraduates, then paying £182 per year, would now be expected to pay £650 per year, most of which would be covered by local authorities, while post-graduates (also paying £182 per year) and overseas students would pay £750.

With the UGC concerned about the adverse effect the rises would have on university finances and the local authorities regarding the number of discretionary awards they would be able to give, Shirley, on succeeding Mulley, decided to reduce the proposed rise for British undergraduates to £500. She offered no such concession, however, to postgraduates and actually increased the fees of overseas students to £850, citing the loss of the pound's value during the previous few months.

Reaction to these increases was swift and bitter. At the NUS conference that December, the president, Charles Clarke, a future Education Secretary in the Blair government, denounced Shirley for her hostility towards the Third World. At Newcastle upon Tyne in January, 250 lecturers and students greeted her arrival at the first of her regional conferences with cries of 'Shirley Out', while February brought mounting unrest on campuses, with occupations at the LSE and elsewhere. As the police moved in to eject the ring-leaders, she told Clarke that she was happy to mediate, although demonstrations were hardly the best way to advance the student case. She agreed that overseas students enriched their educational system and that Britain had an obligation to help the poorer ones. 'But I see no reason why this obligation should extend towards countries better off than ourselves or why the British taxpayer should heavily subsidise students from those countries.'[18] She made it clear that there was no question of the government reneging on its commitment to raise fees that September, although she later asked a government committee to help poorer overseas students. When interrupted at that year's NUS conference by hecklers she calmly reminded them that students were the most privileged group within the educational system, privileges that would become less apparent to future generations of students weighed down by rising living costs and tuition fees.

Against a constantly depressed economic backdrop, the vexed question of pay proceeded to impinge on Shirley's tenure at the DES. In March 1978 she had to settle an acrimonious teachers' pay dispute and months later followed suit with the university lecturers. That wasn't the end of the unrest, because her final weeks in office were engulfed in further spats with the teachers over pay, culminating in an unedifying war of words between her and the leaders of the teaching unions. It was an unfortunate end to her time at Education, which had promised so much. *The Times* had greeted her appointment by declaring her the minister with the greatest potential, but two and a half years later her halo had slipped. In January 1979, her record at the DES came under scrutiny from the *New Statesman*. 'Her humanity and warmth have given her a comparatively easy ride,' it wrote, 'but her persistent failure to deliver has left many patiences wearing thin.'

There had been successes, such as maintaining central funding for adult literacy, approving the early retirement schemes of teachers and giving an unexpected endorsement to parent governors.

She had been handicapped by education cuts and the exacting brief given her by the sheer ambition of the Prime Minister's agenda, which had 'brought out her tendency to scatter herself too widely'. Her scattiness had helped account for her indecisiveness, and that combined with her fear of the unknown had been her undoing. It concluded, 'She has done the easy part well – listening, caring – but, like the true conservative she is, she has failed to move on from caring to curing.'

In some ways it seemed a harsh verdict, but one, nevertheless, that has stood the test of time.

**Endnotes**

1   Jim Callaghan to Mark Peel, 9 September 2003
2   Carol Bracken to Mark Peel, 21 June 2010
3   Brian Simon, *Education and the Social Order 1940–1990*, Lawrence and Wishart, 1991, p.454
4   Jim Callaghan to Mark Peel, 9 September 2003
5   PRO PREM 16/1238, 22 November 1976
6   PRO PREM 16/1238, 6 December 1976
7   PRO PREM 16/1238, 8 December 1976
8   *The Times*, 28 February 1977
9   Bernard Donoughue, *Downing Street Diary*, Vol. 2, Jonathan Cape, 2008, p.119
10  Bernard Donoughue, *Downing Street Diary*, Vol. 2, p.204
11  Bernard Donoughue, *Downing Street Diary*, Vol. 2, p.215
12  *Sunday Times*, 27 November 1977
13  Tony Benn, *Conflicts of Interest: Diaries 1977–80*, Hutchinson, 1990, p.232
14  Hansard, 2 February 1977
15  *Daily Mail*, 21 July 1977
16  *Sunday Telegraph*, 14 November 1976
17  Quoted in John Campbell, *Margaret Thatcher*, Vol. 1, Jonathan Cape, 2000, p.408
18  *Daily Telegraph*, 9 March 1977

# 12

# AGAINST THE TIDE

From the outset Shirley's elevation to the Cabinet had apparently been seamless as she rapidly won Wilson's esteem not only for her work at the DPCP but also for her general contribution towards government policy. As a unifier she was in her element, but even when putting a partisan view she could be equally effective. Jenkins was full of admiration for her defence of press freedoms, while her textual critique of Benn's Industry White Paper greatly impressed Donoughue. Even Benn, no admirer of Shirley, conceded that everything she said contained something of interest, while another left-winger, Castle, paid tribute to her all-round ability.

On becoming Prime Minister, Callaghan enhanced her stature by giving her the chairmanship of several important committees, including the one on devolution (she was in favour of a Scottish Parliament having limited tax-raising powers but found herself in a minority). In an institution traditionally riven by factional discord and crude one-upmanship, Shirley, while a zealous champion of her department's interest, refrained from undermining her colleagues. Indeed, she genuinely liked a lot of them and worked harmoniously with those such as Foot and Healey over prices-and-incomes policy. 'She was spontaneous in manner, unaffected, open-hearted and generous,' recalled Callaghan.

> She usually arrived in a rush and we were never surprised if she was a little late, but she had a grasp of the central meaning of problems as they arose. She did not confine herself to Departmental issues, but would bring a broad approach to Cabinet discussions on both domestic and especially on international affairs.[1]

He did, however, harbour reservations about her ability to deliver, which perhaps explains why he failed to promote her to a senior Cabinet portfolio.

For all the many personal qualities that made her such a formidable campaigner, Shirley was less assured in the corridors of power, where establishing priorities, building alliances and brokering deals was common currency. According to Bill Rodgers, she lacked political judgement. Her great skill was in synthesis – bringing things together – not analysis. She listened to others but when obliged to make a decision from the cold she was often found wanting. In his opinion she never lived up to her billing as Roy Jenkins's true heir in Cabinet by failing to rise to the occasion on the major issues, partly because she was too preoccupied by departmental matters not least during the IMF cuts. To Joel Barnett, its Chief Secretary, her repeated attempts to browbeat the Treasury into providing additional resources for education in the 1978 Spending Review proved counterproductive. His view was supported by Sir John Hunt, the Cabinet Secretary, who advised Callaghan that she had probably spoilt her case with the other colleagues by protesting too hard. When Callaghan came to discuss EMAs, he expressed his irritation with Shirley for lobbying the press in support of her proposals, about which he remained lukewarm. He was also unsympathetic to her efforts to place the teachers on an equal footing to the civil servants in the 1979–80 pay round despite the merits of their case.

It was Crosland's view that her approach to Cabinet was flawed.

> 1 Spends her time on detail that a civil servant should be handling when she ought to be applying herself to *policy* decisions. 2 Takes far too much to Cabinet. Why can't she make decisions by herself instead of having to be reassured? 3 Has some deep psychological need to show she's familiar with every subject under the sun, knows the name of the Foreign Minister of every underdeveloped country. *Finally* Harold is winding up Cabinet after four and a half hours, everyone longing to get back to their own work, and

Shirley says: 'Prime Minister there's just another tiny point I'd like to raise' – Enough to make one weep.[2]

According to Bob Maclennan, Shirley wasn't a skilful operator in her own interests. Aside from her tendency to jump to conclusions too easily without a thorough appraisal of what needed to be done, a propensity to meddle in too many areas expended vital political capital so that her own initiatives sometimes lacked support. He recalls her great astonishment when her proposal to end corporal punishment, a matter about which she cared passionately, was defeated in Cabinet committee.

As a woman operating in a man's world (she was the only female minister in the Callaghan Cabinet), Shirley was something of a loner, deterred by the collegiality of Westminster, especially when she had family responsibilities to attend to without the support of a husband. She was never part of Wilson or Callaghan's inner circle and, according to Donoughue, 'suffered a bit as a woman' from male colleagues slightly envious of her golden reputation. She also neglected to build a body of supporters around her, depriving her of valuable advice and reducing her political effectiveness as the capricious dynamics of the centre-right in Cabinet showed all too clearly. Over Europe, trade union power and taking on the extreme left, her alliance with Jenkins detached her from potential allies such as Callaghan, Crosland and Healey. Later in the summer of 1978 she appears to have fallen out with Owen and Hattersley, two leading moderates, for when complaining to Jenkins about her colleagues, she singled them out for particular censure: the former had opposed her attempts to end boarding school allowances for diplomatic personnel; the latter had been a leading critic of her proposed Education White Paper, giving a glimpse of her predicament at that time.

Of all the difficulties that had confronted Callaghan, the economy was the gravest. With inflation still excessive and the public finances greatly in deficit, the pound had come under immense pressure as investors cast doubt on the country's economic stability. Increasingly at the mercy of foreign markets, Healey felt obliged to seek further painful cuts of £1 billion in July 1976, together with an additional £1 billion from an increase in employers' national insurance contributions, but despite these measures, the currency markets remain dissatisfied. They wanted more. On 27 September, with Healey about to leave for a Commonwealth finance ministers' conference in Hong Kong, the pound's continuing plunge caused him to cancel his trip and return to the Treasury. There he formally applied to the IMF for a conditional loan of £3.9 billion, the largest ever sought from it.

As Healey became immersed in negotiations with the IMF, he increasingly accepted the need for further cuts in order to satisfy the markets. His prognosis won him little sympathy from Callaghan, whose bruising experiences at the Labour conference had conveyed to him all too clearly the likely reaction to further retrenchment. Like Wilson over Europe, he saw the ghost of Ramsay MacDonald hovering over him and, determined to save the government and party from another 1931, he favoured caution. His efforts to enlist the support of the US and German governments, however, had come to nothing and, forced to bend to the prevailing gusts, he began the painfully slow process of guiding his Cabinet towards a settlement that would be acceptable to all sides.

On 18 November the Prime Minister informed Cabinet that the Chancellor wouldn't enter into an agreement with the IMF unless he had their approval. The price, though, would be a heavy one and this was enough to galvanise both the left, with its alternative economic strategy, and the centre-right, led by Crosland. At a meeting on 22 November (at which Crosland was absent because of government business), Shirley, Lever, Hattersley, Rodgers and Ennals, for a variety of differing motives, agreed to resist public expenditure cuts.

The next day in Cabinet, after Healey had made his pitch for the loan and outlined the IMF's position, which amounted to cuts of some £3 billion, he was pulverised by Crosland. The Foreign Secretary argued that public sector borrowing forecasts were far too high, that the balance of payments would be in surplus by 1978 and that unemployment wouldn't rise any further. The economic case for further retrenchment was unproven, while, politically, it would be disastrous. He accepted the need for a loan, but advocated a reduction in the country's defence commitments in Germany should the government be pushed any further into a corner. With ten members of the Cabinet speaking against the cuts and only two rallying to his defence, Healey was given an early warning of the treacherous waters through which he would have to navigate. A clear majority were against the Treasury position, but any attempts by the Crosland group to make common cause with the left were firmly rebuffed.

At the European summit at The Hague on 29 and 30 November, Callaghan's ongoing efforts to secure help from the Germans came to grief as Helmut Schmidt told him to reduce his borrowing and settle with the IMF. With Crosland present at these discussions, Callaghan took the opportunity on the flight home to confront his Foreign Secretary with the dilemma in front of them now that German assistance was no longer an option. He told him he would be supporting his Chancellor and asked him to give great thought to where his responsibilities lay.

That same evening at 10.30 Crosland convened a meeting of his supporters to reconsider tactics. While Shirley and Ennals, buoyed by a partial reprieve to their departmental budgets, stayed non-committal on the side, he, Lever and Hattersley remained hawkish in their opposition, brandishing the threat of withdrawing troops from Germany and Cyprus in order to place pressure on NATO. Their brinkmanship alienated Rodgers, a resolute supporter of NATO, who now changed sides. He later told Donoughue that for all Crosland's and Lever's apparent resolution, he felt they would fold in the end.

The next morning Benn's paper on import controls was subjected to a grilling by all and sundry. His failure to cope adequately with the range of questions badly damaged his credibility and although Shore was more persuasive over his plan for temporary import controls, he too wilted before the Chancellor's forensic interrogation. Even Crosland's call for the maintenance of the economic status quo failed to grasp the significance of international confidence and the need to convince the markets. He was also under fire from within his own camp as Shirley and Lever, an avid free trader, were implacably opposed to his import deposit scheme not only because they felt it too protectionist but also because it would damage the Third World. That evening, on the way to a meeting with Crosland, one of Shirley's colleagues had seen her writing furiously. 'I knew that she was lost,' one of the group advisers later commented. 'Whenever Shirley resorts to paper you know she's trying to work out a compromise.'[3] Indeed she was, as she attempted to find a way of acceding to IMF public sector borrowing targets while inflicting minimum damage on public spending and jobs. By the end of their deliberations Crosland could count on the support only of Hattersley.

Thursday 2 December was, according to Callaghan, 'the moment of decision'. Healey explained that the price for the restoration of the government's credibility with the markets would be cuts of £1 billion for 1977/78, along with the sales of BP shares of £500 million and £1.5 billion for 1978/79. With the Prime Minister finally declaring his hand and coming down firmly on the side of his Chancellor it was time for the dissidents to call a truce in hostilities. Crosland, in one final note of defiance, declared continuing scepticism about the economic case for retrenchment but accepted that, for the sake of party unity, the Prime Minister must be supported. He was – by eighteen to five – and although some of the left remained unconvinced none of them seriously contemplated resignation.

After three more meetings haggling over where precisely the axe should fall, the Chancellor was able to announce the details of his programme to the Commons on 15 December. It wasn't the government's finest hour, but the way in which Callaghan had steered the ship of state safely into port was a tribute to his stoical calm in the eye of the storm. Unlike 1931, the Cabinet and party had survived intact and the economic tide soon began to turn.

Yet despite the upturn, the government remained vulnerable. In February it had suffered the untimely death of Tony Crosland from a severe stroke. His replacement as Foreign Secretary was the able David Owen, but the loss of Crosland following that of Wilson, Castle and Jenkins over the previous year deprived the government of much of its aura. Its minority status in the Commons meant it lacked control over its legislative agenda and in March 1977 it looked all set to lose a no confidence motion until rescued by the Liberals, whose inclination for an early election was no greater than the government's. In return for the right to be consulted on government legislation, progress on devolution and direct elections to the European Parliament, with a free vote on the voting system, the Liberals would sustain the government in Parliament. On the morning of the debate of the no confidence motion, Callaghan briefed the Cabinet on his negotiations with David Steel, the Liberal leader, and won their assent to the agreement. With Callaghan and Steel establishing a good rapport the pact worked surprisingly well and although Liberal MPs were rather more lukewarm about it, it was renewed, come the summer, for another year.

Aside from her departmental duties, Shirley's most thankless task in government was her chairmanship of the Cabinet Committee on Industrial Democracy, since it involved her in much work for no ultimate purpose. The idea of industrial democracy had always figured more prominently in countries such as West Germany, Holland and Sweden than in Britain, but in 1975, follow-ing pressure from a number of trade unions, a committee under the Oxford historian Alan Bullock was established to explore the matter further. The committee struggled to find a consensus, but ultimately its report contained two major proposals. First, company boards of over 200 employees should have an equal number of workers and shareholder representatives, with all the worker-directors chosen by their union. Second, the directors of all companies should take an equal account of the interests of employees and shareholders.

Bullock's proposals, made public in February 1977, unleashed a volley of opposition from the CBI, who objected to the union single channel (workers' representatives being nominated by the trade unions) and the downgrading of non-union employees, fearing it would herald an era of industrial collapse. It had supporters in Cabinet such as Shirley and Edmund Dell, who thought union power to be excessive, in contrast to those such as the Employment Secretary, Albert Booth, who favoured the single channel.

From the outset Callaghan, recognising that industrial democracy was a divisive issue, counselled a gradualist approach, hoping that consultation would help win over the CBI. Time, however, brought a scant meeting of minds and it was with a view to reconciling these differences that Callaghan asked Shirley in May to head a new ministerial group comprising the interested parties.

She reported the next month that they had made some progress but significant differences remained. Legislation to provide a right to representation would struggle to get through Parliament during the next session. A better alternative would be to persuade the TUC to proceed on a voluntary basis.

For the rest of the year and into the next, negotiations dragged on interminably with little headway being made. Prior to publication of her White Paper in May, Shirley showed both the CBI and TUC draft copies. Neither side affected great enthusiasm for the content, with the TUC unhappy about only one-third board representation. She told it that the government had gone a long way towards meeting its demands by requiring a company of over 500 employees to discuss company strategy with its workforce and by giving employees in firms of over 2,000 the right to ballot to ascertain whether they wanted board representation. Her views were endorsed by the Cabinet. Parity would not only have jeopardised the chances of attaining a lasting solution, it would also have had an adverse effect on investment, although as a sop to the trade union movement it didn't rule it out in the future.

The publication of the White Paper in May 1978 drew a fairly measured response, with *The Times* commending it for its 'moderate and constructive proposals', but it left unresolved the fundamental issue of whether the unions should be the sole channel for the election of employee representatives. With the CBI and TUC drifting ever further apart, the Cabinet's commitment to legislation during the forthcoming session of Parliament seemed unduly optimistic. When the committee eventually reported in March 1979 the differences remained as glaring as ever, not least the vexed question of board representation. While a minority opted for the single channel, the majority, led by Shirley, favoured a German-style election of directors by the whole workforce as the most democratic method. With the Cabinet equally divided it is not surprising that industrial democracy ranked a low priority in the party's manifesto before the new Conservative government consigned it to oblivion.

While Shirley tried to grapple with the intricacies of Bullock, she became embroiled in a bitter industrial dispute that left her personally tainted. Grunwick, in north London, was one of the biggest film processing firms in the country, employing a largely female Asian workforce. Its owner, George Ward, was a redoubtable Anglo-Indian entrepreneur whose abrasive style of management was a source of some tension. In August 1976 these tensions boiled over when 137 out of the 480 workforce demanded union recognition, an act of defiance that led to their dismissals. Their cause was taken up by the Association of Professional Executive, Clerical and Computer Staff (APEX), the moderate white-collar union, who persuaded the Union of Post Office Workers to boycott the company's mail, a dangerous threat to a company which relied overwhelmingly on mail orders, but this show of trade union power brought about the intervention of the National Association for Freedom (NAFF). It quickly helped Ward gain an injunction against the postal boycott under the 1953 Act, which made it a criminal offence for post office workers wilfully to delay the delivery of mail.

With the initiative slipping from the strikers, Shirley and her ministerial colleagues, Fred Mulley and Denis Howell, all APEX members, decided to visit the picket line on Thursday 19 May 1977 to draw attention to the workers' grievances. They stayed for some thirty minutes talking sympathetically to the picketers and spoke out against the management. Howell said that some workers had been humiliated, while according to Shirley, Grunwick was 'guilty of as bad a case of exploitation as you could find', comments which led to her being successfully sued for libel by Ward, along with the BBC, which reported them.[4]

The appearance of Shirley and her colleagues on the picket line brought Grunwick back into the public domain as their judgement was called into question by the Tory press. 'Mrs Williams, Mr Mulley, and Mr Howell are paid to govern the nation,' protested the *Daily Mail*. 'Not to cavort on picket lines for the gratitude of their trade union sponsors.'[5]

On 13 June APEX called a mass picket, setting the scene for a summer of bitter confrontation during which hundreds of police faced down the striking employees, supported by an assortment of sympathisers outside the factory gates. Soon the stand-off turned violent and the raucous scenes accompanying the arrival of the strike-breaking buses, relayed on television day after day, did lasting damage to the trade union movement.

As the violence intensified, so did the political battle. Sir Keith Joseph, the shadow Industry Secretary, in a speech in Doncaster on 24 June accused Shirley and her colleagues on the picket line of leading a Trojan horse through the gates. Did they not owe it to the public to speak out against violence? 'Is not silence cowardice? Let me ask the so-called moderates how they can exist with the Marxists and thugs? *Quo vadis* Shirley?'[6]

In a speech in her constituency later that day, Shirley stood by her action. She joined the picket line because her union was right about the merits of the dispute. She still held that view. 'But I do deplore the intervention of the far Right and the far Left, who have no useful place in this dispute, and whose arrival on the scene – very late in the day, I might say – has done no good to the cause my union is fighting for.'[7] There was no better alternative but to get both sides back around the table.

Certainly Ward was in no mood to compromise and although the strikers continued to hold out throughout the winter and into the spring, support whittled away, not least from APEX. On 14 July 1978 the strike was officially wound up. Two days earlier, in a deeply caustic article in *The Times*, Bernard Levin tried to insinuate that Shirley and her colleagues had been responsible for much of the violence that had occurred. 'Do you remember the face of Mrs Williams as she was photographed on the Grunwick picket-line? It was the face of a democrat who has thrown in her lot with a cause supported by thugs, and is rightly ashamed of herself for so doing.'[8]

His words caused Shirley deep offence. 'It seems to me that the logic of your position,' she wrote, 'is that no reasonable person should ever express support for any cause just in case at some later date the same case should receive support from unwelcome quarters. I trust that you will now retract what you said about me.'[9] To his credit Levin did unreservedly, but others were less obliging. 'In the context of a growing level of industrial strife, I was marked by the Grunwick affair as if it was a tattoo,' she later recalled. 'Failure to anticipate what the Tory press might make of my intervention was one of the biggest mistakes of my career.'[10]

Throughout the 1974–79 governments Shirley continued to be preoccupied by Labour's internal feuding. The change of leadership didn't usher in a more harmonious atmosphere between the government and the wider party, since Callaghan was even more contemptuous of the left than Wilson. At his first party conference as Prime Minister he warned about political extremists infiltrating the party and using it for their own ends, but his concerns weren't shared by the majority of the NEC. As the burdens of office began to weigh more heavily upon him, he increasingly looked to Shirley, his leading Cabinet ally on the NEC, to fight his corner on those occasions when he was absent. She willingly consented, but was under no illusions about the difficulties they faced.

In contrast to the iron grip of the left, Labour's centre-right had been badly undermined by the battles over Europe, the death of Crosland and the departure from Parliament of Jenkins, leaving it bereft of both leaders and ideas. The failure to construct a new policy for growth and a continual reliance on incomes policy did nothing to restore its relations with the trade unions and party activists. As Shirley's allies on the NEC were reduced to a hard core such as the trade unionists Russell Tuck and Bryan Stanley and MPs such as Tom Bradley and John Cartwright, she found serving on it ever more harrowing. Even worse than the political divisions was the personal abuse directed against her from those like Dennis Skinner. John Cartwright recalls how left-wingers rushed into London traffic after an NEC meeting in order to avoid being seen with her.

In October 1976 Ted Short decided to quit politics to become chairman of Cable and Wireless, leaving vacant the position of deputy leader. In terms of seniority the obvious successor was Foot, especially after his creditable performance in the leadership election a few months earlier. Although a man of the left, he was popular across the party and had formed an excellent relationship with Callaghan since the latter had become Prime Minister, despite the fact that the two weren't close personally. At the same time Foot's leadership of the Commons, most notably his determination to dragoon it into accepting contentious left-wing legislation without adequate debate, hadn't been to everyone's taste and the right needed to put down a few markers against the left's growing influence. With Healey too embattled at the Treasury, Shirley now seemed the ideal candidate. Aside from her recent promotion within the Cabinet, she was a member of the NEC and, like Foot, reached out beyond her core constituency. The only problem was her apparent reluctance to run. Having told John Lyttle she would do so, she began to have second thoughts, citing unwelcome publicity and pressures of work. Lyttle assured her that this wouldn't be the case with the publicity as he urged her to reconsider in order to rally the centre-right.

As Shirley continued to haver, Phillip Whitehead, the moderate MP for Derby North, asked Donoughue to have a word. When he did he found her reluctant, aware that Callaghan wanted Foot to have the position unopposed in the interests of party unity, and feeling that she would lose in any case. At the same time she didn't want to be seen as opting out, especially given the undeniable fact that she, more than any other moderate, stood the best chance of winning. Eventually she allowed her name to go forward, but on the strict understanding that she wouldn't actively campaign against Foot with interviews and briefings etc., a truce to which Foot was only too happy to agree, especially as he was holed up in hospital with shingles for much of the campaign.

Shirley's decision to run was widely welcomed, not least by the Tory press, who viewed her as the very essence of moderation, and after a most decorous contest Foot won by 166 to 128. 'Mrs Williams came out of the contest with considerable credit,' opined James Wightman in the *Daily Telegraph*.[11] The paper wasn't alone in thinking that the result had enhanced her credentials as a future leader, although few stopped to consider whether this was in reality a missed opportunity. Had she really gone for the prize it may well have been within her grasp and would have done wonders to both her confidence and that of the centre-right as it remained under siege from the left.

The charge of extremism erupted once again over the appointment of Andy Bevan, a well-known Militant supporter, as Labour's National Youth Officer in September 1976. The decision sparked uproar, not least from Callaghan, who spoke of the deep disquiet caused by his appointment, but despite the reservations the NEC wouldn't budge. It passed a resolution that December castigating the scurrilous press campaign against Bevan and rejected what it called a further descent into McCarthyism, while Benn claimed that Marxism was one of the many sources that flowed into the Labour movement.

The Bevan controversy and the NEC's riposte caused Shirley much consternation. In a speech to a Labour gathering at Belper in January 1977 she took issue with Benn's contention that Marxism was a reputable train of thought. Someone who wasn't prepared to abide by the principles of liberal democracy had no place in the Labour Party.

'The party may, as Sir Harold Wilson likes to say, be a broad church', opined the *Guardian* editorial, 'but even the broadest church must draw the line on atheism. That, precisely, is the challenge thrown out – belatedly, it may be said, but powerfully and impressively by Mrs Shirley Williams in her speech in Derbyshire last night.'[12]

Faced with a renewed media campaign against Militant, the NEC felt compelled to establish a subcommittee under Michael Foot's chairmanship to re-examine the Underhill Report against entryism.

Back in November 1975 Reg Underhill, the party's National Agent, had compiled a report alleging Trotskyist infiltration within the party, singling out Militant in particular. The NEC's organisation committee refused to publish the report or take any further action against extremism, Ian Mikardo declaring that there had been Trotskyists in the Labour Party for thirty years – whereupon Shirley, in conjunction with Russell Tuck of the National Union of Railwaymen, tried to reverse the decision at the NEC. They had the support of Wilson, who launched a bitter diatribe against all types of extremism, but it was all to no avail as their motion was defeated by sixteen to twelve.

It was a similar story eighteen months later. Foot's subcommittee did find Militant to be in breach of the rules, but advocated no disciplinary action, arguing that extremism was best countered by free debate. On 25 May 1977 its recommendations were accepted by the NEC, despite Shirley and Bryan Stanley's efforts to publish.

'I was outraged by this cavalier dismissal of Reg Underhill's report,' she later wrote.

> Here was a man of impeccable loyalty and integrity, as everyone on the NEC knew, and who had given his life to the Labour Party. That his report was not even considered by the NEC, the body responsible for the health of the Party, and that we could not rally a majority of its members to insist on doing so, appalled me. The key issue, as this instance demonstrated, was not Europe, nor public ownership, but representative democracy. The hard left and in particular the Trotskyites regarded representative democracy as a sham, a way of disguising the interests of the property-owning classes. They shared with the Communists the belief that it was the Party, not the public, to whom elected politicians should be accountable.[13]

The year 1978 brought further setbacks to the moderates, particularly the mandatory reselection of MPs by their constituency parties during the lifetime of each parliament, one of the means by which the left hoped to gain control of the party. Although a resolution to that effect had been rejected by Conference in 1977, the NEC decided the following September to set up a working party on reselection. Shirley was predictably scathing about such a decision which, if implemented, could have permitted a small clique to overrule the wishes of the electorate and seriously impede the work of government. 'If we want to write in advance the epitaph of the Labour Party as a future party of Government this is the way to do it.'[14]

Her dismay was easy to understand as a combination of personal and political factors had led to one of the most turbulent periods in her life. While she continued to rue the absence of someone to love following her separation from Tony King, she found the political landscape increasingly barren both at Education, where she was assailed on all sides over the grammar schools, and within the party. Flak from the left was only to be expected, but it was in the darker recesses of the Labour right where the knives were out in force. According to Hugo Young she was the despair of the moderates for her apparent irresolution, rather unfair given her ongoing struggle for moderation in near-isolation on the NEC. Her disillusion with her colleagues, especially their lack of trust and crude one-upmanship, was such that she told Donoughue on 13 July of her readiness to quit. Three days later, 'Cross Bencher' in the *Sunday Express* carried an unflattering profile, depicting her as a burnt-out meteor, a waning force in Cabinet and a ditherer at Education in the face of robust opposition attacks, especially over comprehensives. 'Even among the Labour faithful, Shirley recognises that her appeal is fading. Her enthusiasm for the threadbare cause of Europe loses her friends with every new diktat from Brussels.'[15]

Her mood didn't lighten when she was forced to return from an important state visit to China after two nights to vote because of the Conservatives' refusal to pair her. She slammed them for their foolishness before returning to China to oversee the establishment of a scholarship scheme for several hundred Chinese academics to study at British universities over the next few years, the first act of cooperation in education and research between any Western country and post-Mao China. Then after holidaying in Aspen, Colorado, with Rebecca, she seemed more upbeat when she lunched with Roy and Jennifer Jenkins at the end of August. While not denying her general disenchantment, not least with most of her Cabinet colleagues, she appeared intellectually engaged as she discussed European monetary union. According to Jenkins, she was in favour of a spring election rather than an autumn one, although not very certain about this. A week later she had opted unconditionally for October.

From the dark days of the IMF there had been a gradual upturn in the economy as two years of wage restraint and the proceeds of North Sea oil began to make a difference. If 1977 laid the foundations of recovery, 1978 was even better, with the public finances seeing a dramatic improvement and inflation dropping to below 8 per cent by June. This economic revival brought with it political dividends. The large Tory leads of the two previous years had disappeared and the Prime Minister's personal ratings towered over Margaret Thatcher's as he seemed the very essence of avuncular moderation.

With Labour inching ahead in the polls by August, the case for an autumn election gained currency, especially given the appearance of two black clouds lurking on the horizon. The first concerned the government's precarious position in Parliament now that the Liberals had ended their pact, and the second, the rumblings of discontent from the unions over wage restraint. With Jack Jones and Hugh Scanlon, the architects of the social contract, now retired and replaced by lesser men, the chances of holding the unions to another year of restraint were fast diminishing.

As Callaghan digested the polling data during the summer recess it didn't make for comfortable reading. For whatever the national polls might suggest, the situation in the marginals was less encouraging and the best that Labour could reasonably hope for was another minority government. Already wearied by months of haggling with the minority parties, Callaghan thus opted for delay in the hope that something better might turn up. His instincts were reinforced by Foot and the whips' office, but their caution contrasted with the majority of the Cabinet and TUC leadership, who were all for an autumn election.

As polling fever continued to mount, Callaghan's jocular references to an election at the TUC conference on 6 September did nothing to quell it. When Cabinet gathered the next day, the sense of anticipation was evident as it awaited the call to arms. Instead it listened in astonishment as the Prime Minister explained why he wouldn't be raising the standard. Shirley and Peter Shore both begged to differ, but were sharply slapped down by the Prime Minister, who told them that the timing of the election was his prerogative and his alone. The disappointment of many a minister wasn't hard to gauge as they trooped out of Cabinet – and for good reason, given the subsequent turn of events.

Whatever the justification for Callaghan's caution, his maladroit handling of the timing of the 'election' alienated many within the

trade union movement who felt deceived by him. In these circumstances his confidence that he could hold them to another year of
wage restraint – this time at 5 per cent – smacked of hubris. An
early warning of their pent-up anger came at the Labour conference
several weeks later when the 5 per cent norm was decisively voted
down. The result infuriated Shirley, who had been instrumental
in trying to make the unions withdraw their opposition. She told
a meeting of the Campaign for Labour Victory (CLV), a group
formed in 1977 to revitalise the party's moderates, that the pay vote
had been 'aimed at the heart of the Labour Government, but I don't
believe Conference yet understands that. They will not help us in
any way in winning the next election.'[16]

They didn't. The government's attempts  to impose penal sanctions on the Ford Motor Company for breaching the pay policy was
narrowly defeated when five left-wingers abstained in deference to
the Labour conference's resolution to abandon pay restraint. This
serious setback brought home to Shirley not only the likelihood of
an early election but an escalation in industrial strife as one union
after another queued up to cause trouble. 'It's funny – somehow the
1960s seem like a time of astonishing calm,' she wrote to her father,
'I don't suppose they actually were, given the Vietnam War and so
on. It does not seem the human lot to have a quiet life.'[17]

Events were soon to bear out the wisdom of her words. Wednesday
3 January 1979 marked the beginning of a nationwide strike by road
hauliers and tanker drivers, accompanied by secondary picketing and
violence as the country endured one of the coldest winters on record.
The dispute soon spread to the public services as refuse collectors,
sewerage staff, hospital porters, school caretakers and grave diggers
demanded a £60 per week minimum wage. In freezing conditions,
the sight of roads going ungritted, hospital patients unattended,
rubbish uncollected and, most appalling of all, the dead unburied
inflamed public opinion. It also seriously jeopardised Labour's claim
to be the party of industrial peace and national solidarity.

A mood of depression and inertia descended upon Downing
Street as Callaghan's tough talk wasn't supported by action. With

a number of exceptions, such as Owen and Rodgers, the Cabinet proved fairly supine in accommodating the exorbitant demands of public sector workers. As its pay policy collapsed before its eyes various efforts were made to revive the social contract in the form of national guidelines, but the government–trade union accord of 14 February was barely worth the paper it was written upon. The damage had been well and truly done.

At Education, Shirley became embroiled in the prolonged public sector dispute which closed a number of schools. As the disruption spread, she fretted about the damage done to children and urged schools to shorten their half-term or extend the school day to compensate those affected by the strike. None of this was good enough for the columnist Paul Johnson, once a leading polemicist of the left but now very much of the right. In a searing article in the *Evening Standard* he compared Shirley's failure to ensure half a million children received schooling with her willingness to act against Conservative authorities over grammar schools.

His words were given some weight by the unilateral action of Haringey Council in north London. Its compliance with the demands of the public sector unions to close its schools saw 37,000 children deprived of teaching for five weeks. While Shirley was inundated with requests from anxious parents to intervene, she wrote to them to inform them that the council hadn't failed to discharge its duty. In the Appeal Court the Master of the Rolls, Lord Denning, ruled otherwise. He declared that 'the unions had no right to ask the council to close the schools and the council had no business to agree'. He criticised Shirley for being badly briefed. 'If she thought that the duty of the borough council was only to provide the school buildings and no more I think she was badly advised on the law.'[18]

No sooner was Shirley rid of the school caretaker dispute than an even more serious threat loomed, fuelled by a gnawing sense of injustice. Ever since their generous pay award back in 1974 following the Houghton Report, the teachers had seen the value of their salaries regress by 36 per cent compared to other public sector workers. This shortfall the NUT set out to recoup, hardly music to the ears of the government's Policy Unit, who considered teachers very well paid, compared to nurses. Following the collapse of the 5 per cent pay policy the government had set up the Standing Commission on pay comparability under Professor Hugh Clegg of Warwick University to ensure fair remuneration for all public sector workers. This initiative, while commendable on grounds of equity, spelt potential danger should the teachers gain any mention of Houghton in their terms of reference since it could precipitate another explosion of pay in the public sector.

Having sought guidance from Shirley on what was available, the local authorities duly offered 8 per cent when they met the teachers on 21 March. Not surprisingly, it was brusquely rejected, especially since the civil servants were about to gain a massive 26 per cent. Such a settlement Shirley branded irresponsible, especially since it would exacerbate her task of settling with the teachers. At Cabinet on 22 March she argued very strongly against the civil servants' pay award being backdated to 1 April 1979. When her colleagues wouldn't accede to this, she declared that she felt honour-bound to support the claim from the teachers for equal treatment, and that any such settlement should be funded from the government's share of the Rate Support Grant (RSG). So concerned was she about this that a serious threat of substantial shortfall of RSG would cause her to consider whether she could remain a member of the Cabinet.

Soon it appeared that there would be no Cabinet to belong to as the travails of minority government overcame them all. Driven by political necessity as much as constitutional ideals, the government, with some reluctance, had embarked upon a devolution bill for Scotland and Wales setting up a parliament in Edinburgh and an assembly in Cardiff. After a prolonged struggle through the Commons the Bill finally passed in 1978 subject to an affirmative vote by referenda in both countries, and with approval of at least 40 per cent of the registered electorate. This latter amendment by a Labour backbencher proved to be the sting in the tail, for when the referendum took place on 1 March 1979 Scotland, while narrowly voting in favour, fell short of the 40 per cent level necessary for implementation. (In Wales the referendum was overwhelmingly lost.) The SNP responded by signalling its support for a Conservative motion of no confidence in the government. When the vote took place on 28 March, the government lost by one, so becoming the first government to be brought down in the Commons since Ramsay MacDonald's in 1924. An election was called for 3 May, the longest campaign since 1945, the hope being that Margaret Thatcher would be more vulnerable to a marathon than a sprint.

Labour's election procedure dictated that the drafting of the manifesto was the joint responsibility of the party leadership and NEC, with no guidance as to who should prevail should their views differ. With senior ministers at an impasse over a left-wing draft from the previous December, it needed an acrimonious meeting on 6 April between leading representatives of the Cabinet and NEC to bring the left to heel. By threatening resignation, Shirley helped omit the more offensive anti-European comments in the manifesto, while Callaghan used his veto to keep out any proposal to abolish the House of Lords. The finished article very much bore his own stamp, but the failure to include more radical measures embittered many activists, which they cannily exploited in the months ahead.

Labour entered the campaign in poor heart with an indifferent record and a mountain to climb if the opinion polls were to be believed. Stressing 'fairness for all', Callaghan fought a plucky, dignified campaign, with Shirley at his side at press conferences to contrast her warmth with Margaret Thatcher's stridency. Their attacks on Conservative tax-and-spend policies had some effect, but Thatcher's emphasis on trade union reform and tax cuts struck a chord with the electorate as the 'winter of discontent' remained uppermost in the minds of many. This feeling was given added substance by the simmering dispute between the government and the teachers.

The failure of the Burnham Committee, the committee overseeing teachers' salaries in England and Wales, to agree on terms of reference to Clegg – the employers wanted to include teachers' fringe benefits while the unions insisted on adhering to Houghton in relation to other workers – signalled apparent deadlock. With the average teacher £2,500 the poorer since 1974, there was overwhelming support for the various forms of industrial action mooted by their union executives at their Easter conferences.

On 24 April events took an unexpected turn when the NUT accepted wider terms of reference that included reference to Houghton, much to the fury of the NASUWT, who felt they would receive better terms at arbitration. They weren't the only ones to feel aggrieved, since Callaghan rang Shirley the following day to express his displeasure at the terms of reference, especially so close to the election. When she said that they were better than they might have been, he replied that they simply weren't good enough, an uncompromising line that caused Shirley some disquiet, concerned that she was letting down the NUT. She dutifully drew up a statement suspending the negotiations but felt impelled to warn Callaghan of the furore it would create when they spoke again the next evening. Callaghan accepted this, but said he wasn't prepared to see the government held to ransom by union blackmail and he didn't think the electorate would stand for such behaviour.

Amidst the predictable outcry that greeted the suspension of the talks, Jarvis deplored Shirley's 'ill-advised' intervention and her accusation that teachers wanted to be treated as a special case. What they wanted, he insisted, was comparable treatment with groups such as nurses and civil servants. He strongly urged her to reconsider her position and lift the embargo on further negotiations before the election.

In her reply Shirley denied having placed an embargo on the negotiations. 'I said that it would not be appropriate for the Government to come to a hasty decision on matters which would have implications for the working of the Standing Panel.'[19] In particular it was the insistence of the teachers to terms of reference radically different from those agreed for the manual workers and nurses which had delayed negotiations. If the teachers had agreed to terms of reference similar to those of other groups, negotiations on other aspects of the claim could have been concluded by now.

She hoped that negotiations would resume as soon as possible after the election and that teachers would refrain from disruptive action in the meantime.

None of this satisfied the teaching unions as once again they resorted to industrial action, forcing many a school to close early. The NASUWT took the unprecedented step of seeking a High Court injunction, with Terry Casey, its general secretary, accusing Shirley and the government of breaking the law by their interference over the pay negotiations.

Jarvis, for his part, accused the government of reneging on its commitment to the Houghton relativities (a commitment that Shirley had never given). By discriminating against the teachers she had achieved the unique distinction of uniting the whole profession against her more effectively than any other education minister since Florence Horsbrugh twenty-five years earlier. When Shirley countered by insisting that they had been offered the same as other groups such as nurses and civil servants, Jarvis dismissed this as untrue in pre-election headlines that depicted her as a liar.

'My immediate reaction was one of disbelief and then of indignation,' Shirley later wrote.

> I had known Fred for thirty years. We had campaigned together for comprehensive schools. Nothing was to be gained for the teachers by such denunciations, nor for the children they taught. I was already angry that children had been prevented from going to school by caretakers' obstructiveness and the willingness of the teachers to hide behind them. But then I reflected on the situation we faced. Moderate and sensible leaders like Fred were being harried by their extremists. They were becoming desperate. Like drowning men, they grappled with their government and took it down with them.[20]

Shirley's absence from her constituency for much of the campaign reflected confidence at party headquarters that nothing untoward could happen to her. When her good friend Barbara Metcalfe went to Transport House to collect some leaflets, she was told that Hertford & Stevenage wasn't a marginal. When she assured them it was, they glared at her before giving her the leaflets. With a majority of over 9,000 and a flattering profile as an exemplary MP, Shirley could be forgiven for thinking that she was safe, but aside from national trends there were local forces at work that played to her disadvantage. The boundary changes in 1974, it is true, had given her her biggest majority yet, but on balance they hadn't helped her cause, since Hertford, Ware and the surrounding villages weren't fertile Labour territory. Hilda Lawrence, a Labour activist in Stevenage, recalls Jim Caldwell, Shirley's agent, pressing her to spend more time canvassing these villages when she felt they should be focusing their attention upon Stevenage, especially since it was more vulnerable than usual. Aside from some divisions within the local party, and a rather lacklustre campaign, they were up against an energetic Conservative opponent in Bowen Wells, who had courted the constituency assiduously. For the previous two years he had harried Shirley over Grunwick, and throughout the campaign highlighted tax cuts and home ownership, the latter an alluring promise in a town where the council houses were of high quality. 'You are a good MP, Mrs Williams,' remarked one constituent to her, 'but you aren't worth £5,000 to me.'[21]

Although Shirley detected a general sense of disillusion, especially with the excesses of the trade unions, and some antipathy from teachers over their pay dispute, few doubted that she would be re-elected. On the day of the election, much of which she spent on the phone to the DES over the teachers' dispute, she predicted a close result nationally and a majority of 5,000 for herself. When participating in a television panel on election night she seemed genuinely astonished that she might lose. Later on the Friday morning, by which time it was clear that the Conservatives were returning to government, Brian Hall, the leader of Stevenage Council, recalls Shirley coming up to him at her count in Stevenage and telling him that there was a chance of her losing. He assured her that the pundits were wrong because the bundles of votes had her well ahead, but when she returned from a cup of coffee he was shocked to see that the Conservative bundles had inched in front. On an 80.9 per cent turn-out and 8.1 per cent swing, more or less the norm for that area, they had polled 31,739 votes to take the seat with a 1,296 majority. While Shirley's vote had increased by 895 from the previous election theirs had shot up by 11,237 as ex-Liberals (their vote was down by nearly 4,000) and floating voters turned out for them in large numbers. Given the narrowness of the Conservative majority, Jim Caldwell begged her to ask for a recount, but she refused. The result, announced shortly before 3 p.m., caused pandemonium. There were howls of disbelief from Labour supporters while their Conservative counterparts clapped, cheered and embraced each other.

As Bowen Wells beamed his delight, Shirley, dressed in bright pink, smiled bravely, congratulated him on his 'remarkable success' and said that she was placing the constituency in his trust. She remained philosophical when speaking live to Robin Day and Norman St John Stevas on television; then on her return to the count for the Borough Council elections, where Labour strengthened its control over Stevenage Council, she was accosted by countless people who shook her hand and offered their commiserations, all of which she accepted with good grace. Her defeat, the one Cabinet minister to suffer this fate, was the defining moment of the 1979 election, similar to the Defence Secretary Michael Portillo's shock defeat at Enfield Southgate in 1997. The Prime Minister was on his way to Buckingham Palace to tender his resignation when he heard the news. Later he confessed to being 'heartbroken', describing Shirley as 'a woman with a great heart and intellect, imagination and sympathy to match. But she is very young and she will be back again. I believe there is a most distinguished future for her.'[22]

Callaghan's distress was echoed elsewhere, not least at the Department of Education, where she was a much-loved minister, and among the public at large as callers jammed the election lines of the *Stevenage Comet* to express their shock. 'Mrs Williams's reputation has transcended party politics,' the paper averred in its post-election editorial. 'We were proud to be represented at Westminster by an intelligent and fair-minded MP whose very honesty and lack of political guile were said, astonishingly, to be her biggest handicaps in high office.'[23] Messages also flooded in to the local Labour headquarters from voters of all persuasions and at a party wake at the Council Chambers on the Saturday evening she was plied with flowers and accolades. There was plenty of brave talk about her return, but in truth it was the end of an era as Margaret Thatcher began to undo the post-war consensus to which Shirley had been so attached. Yet for all her concerns about the free-market nostrums of the new government, a more pressing challenge lay closer to home as the party she loved seemed intent on self-destruction. Could she halt the rush to the precipice?

### Endnotes

1   Jim Callaghan to Mark Peel, 9 September 2003
2   Quoted in Susan Crosland, *Tony Crosland*, p.298
3   *Sunday Times*, 28 May 1978
4   *Daily Mail*, 20 May 1977
5   *Daily Mail*, 20 May 1977
6   *The Times*, 25 June 1977
7   *The Times*, 25 June 1977
8   *The Times*, 12 July 1978
9   SW to Bernard Levin, 13 July 1978, SW Papers (personal collection)
10  *Climbing the Bookshelves*, p.238
11  *Daily Telegraph*, 22 October 1976
12  *Guardian*, 22 January 1977
13  *Climbing the Bookshelves*, p.264
14  *Guardian*, 3 October 1978
15  *Sunday Express*, 16 July 1978
16  *Guardian*, 3 October 1978
17  SW to GC, 14 December 1978
18  *Daily Telegraph*, 14 March 1979
19  SW to Fred Jarvis, 28 April 1979, SW Papers (private collection)
20  *Climbing the Bookshelves*, p.250
21  *Climbing the Bookshelves*, p.254
22  Quoted in *Hertfordshire Mercury*, 11 May 1979
23  *Stevenage Comet*, 9 May 1979

# 13

# JUMPING SHIP

On Saturday 5 May 1979, Shirley awoke from a good sleep and began singing in the bath. Defeat, for all its disappointment, brought certain consolations, not least a break from a life of sustained pressure and the chance to spend more time with family and friends. There was also the opportunity to pursue other fields of interest as offers of alternative employment poured in. She rejected overtures to become Vice-Chancellor of both Lancaster and East Anglia Universities. (The idea of fundraising didn't appeal, nor being a big fish in a small pond.) She also turned down an offer to become General Secretary of Amnesty International, and the possibility of becoming an EC Commissioner. She did, however, accept a research fellowship at the newly established Policy Studies Institute of London, a think tank funded by the Rowntree Trust, and worked there intermittently for the next six years on a series of studies on youth unemployment for the Organisation for European Cooperation and Development, a body which represented all the industrial Western countries.

She also accepted an offer from the Institute of Politics at the Kennedy School, Harvard, to go there for a semester as a Fellow in the autumn of 1979. Aside from teaching an undergraduate course on the EEC, it gave her an opportunity to reflect on the industrial–political malaise then afflicting Britain. Much of that thinking was to emerge in her book *Politics is for People*, published in April 1981.

Accepting that the corporate bureaucratic state had become ever more remote, she looked to curb its power and bring it closer to the people. Industrial regeneration would be achieved by introducing greater democracy in the workplace, as well as promoting better educational and training opportunities for the young and more tax incentives for expanding firms.

Her emphasis on popular participation extended to the public services, with self-governing schools, hospitals and housing establishments and, above all, to government. Recognising that institutional remoteness had accounted for much public disillusion, Shirley sought a panacea through greater local accountability, freedom of information and parliamentary control of the executive.

Yet for all her frustration at the failure of socialism to extend individual freedoms, she concluded that decentralisation and individual participation weren't conducive to creating equality. Full employment, redistributive taxation and a more generous provision of welfare had to continue, while the abolition of private education would go some way towards eradicating class inequalities.

For all its commercial success, the reviewers weren't entirely convinced by *Politics is for People*, not least by the lack of rigour and a want of originality in some of its solutions. 'What can sound profound and original in Shirley's fine voice can read flat and ordinary,' opined Bernard Crick in *The Guardian*. 'She is clear that she is still a socialist, but neither principles nor theory are defined clearly.'[1]

Shirley's absorption with academia hadn't removed her from the political stage. She remained an important figure on the NEC and a staunch defender of social democracy as others threatened to replace it with something more extreme. The failure of the 1974–79 government to bring about real social progress and its drubbing in the 1979 election not only caused bitter disillusion among Labour activists, it also gave them further ammunition to fire at the embattled leadership. Using its powerbase in the constituency parties and trade unions to enhance its position, the left was relentless in its pursuit of constitutional change, its cause aided by Tony Benn. Increasingly an isolated figure in the Callaghan government, he lost no time after the election in disassociating himself from its record and galvanising the NEC into action. In June its Organisation Committee voted to waive the rule that a constitutional issue, once decided, couldn't be debated again for another three years, which effectively would allow the forthcoming conference to debate mandatory reselection. Two weeks later, at the full NEC, Shirley, supported by Eric Hammond, a leading moderate in the Electrical Trades Union, tried to reverse this decision, but their motion was easily defeated.

This set the scene for several years of intense wrangling as the left tried to break the PLP's domination over policy. Callaghan's pre-election veto on the pledge to abolish the House of Lords formed a bitter backdrop to the battle over who controlled the manifesto. Up to that point responsibility had rested jointly with the NEC and shadow Cabinet, but in July the NEC chose to defy Callaghan and give itself the final say. Objecting to the fact that the PLP was being sidelined despite 11 million having voted for Labour MPs, Shirley served notice that she would fight to maintain the concept of representative democracy. The proposals for changing the party constitution were 'reactionary and absurd', she told a Fabian meeting during the TUC conference, and she accused the NEC of being completely out of touch with Labour voters. It wasn't too little socialism that had cost them the election, as the left had argued, but rather too much trade union power. She declared that the unions needed to find ways of penalising the employer rather than the public, even if that meant limiting the use of the strike weapon.

She returned to the attack during the Labour conference in early October as delegates gathered at Brighton in vindictive mood. Taking their cue from the party's General Secretary, Ron Hayward, they availed themselves of every opportunity to vent their spleen at Callaghan and his government for selling out the rest of the party. Determined to make the leadership more accountable to the Party activists, they carried resolutions calling for the mandatory reselection of MPs during the lifetime of each Parliament and transferring control of the manifesto to the NEC – subject to confirmation at the 1980 conference.

Shocked by the climate of hatred, not least by the unwarranted personal attacks on Callaghan by Hayward and that year's Conference chairman, Frank Allaun, Shirley rallied to his defence both at the NEC and on the fringe. She told a CLV meeting that 'the new history of the Labour government is being written at this conference and it is a kind of Soviet rewriting of the truth'.[2] The next day, after Callaghan's speech, she was greeted with rapturous applause when she declared that time was short and that the counter-attack against the left must begin. 'I say to my erstwhile colleagues, for God's sake stand up and start fighting for yourselves. The Parliamentary Labour Party has a right to be heard before it agrees to its own castration.'[3] In these circumstances she felt a moral obligation to renew her struggle against the left, but her demand for a sizeable PLP representation on the new Commission of Enquiry to recommend constitutional changes to the 1980 conference was flatly rejected by the NEC as it shaped the new body very much in its own image.

These developments spelt trouble for Labour's moderates, who still comprised the majority of the PLP, even allowing for the more radical intake of both 1974 and 1979. No one was more dismayed at this turn of events than Bill Rodgers, a veteran of battles past with the left. On 30 November 1979, in a speech at Abertillery, he warned the Labour Party that it had a year – not much longer – in which to save itself and predicted a split if it didn't. His speech was the prelude to lunch the next day with Roy Jenkins and Shirley, at the Jenkinses' home near Oxford. The meeting was significant because days before, Jenkins, still president of the European Commission, had won glowing reviews for his recent Dimbleby Lecture, 'Home Thoughts from Abroad', in which he had attacked the rigidities of the British two-party system and raised the possibility of a new centre party under his aegis. 'Shirley, no more than Bill,' wrote Jenkins in his memoirs, 'had not been frightened off by Dimbleby, and she, almost, but not quite as much as Bill, was prepared in certain circumstances to contemplate a break from the Labour Party. But they both wanted plenty of time in which to convince themselves that those circumstances had arrived.'[4]

The slow countdown towards midnight edged that bit closer when further allegations of Trotskyist infiltration resurfaced. A letter from Neville Sandelson, one of those Labour MPs affected, demanding the publication of the Underhill Report was discussed at the Organisation Committee on 7 January, but Shirley's endeavours and those of John Golding, the feisty MP for Newcastle-under-Lyme, on his behalf were in vain. The report remained suppressed. Her ongoing battle against extremism was very much to the fore when she dined the next evening with Giles Radice.

'She is as charming and beguiling as ever,' he recorded in his diary, 'but all she wants to talk about is the Labour Party and the NEC – and how to expose the Militants ... Lisanne [his wife] comments afterwards that Shirley is obsessed by politics and that she is certain that she will come back.'[5]

Following the refusal of the NEC itself to change tack, despite pressure from Underhill himself, and a call from Eric Heffer to those who couldn't accept socialist principles to leave the Labour Party, Shirley declared war on Militant at a CLV meeting in Leicester on 1 February. It had to be expelled. In all but name it was a separate organisation within the party and thus ineligible for affiliation under its constitution. Labour couldn't turn its back on its internal rows, not least because many of its best workers were leaving.

> Speaking for myself, I do not want a new centre party. I want a Labour Party, the Labour Party, refreshed by new thinking and able to offer a convincing and attractive alternative to the Tories ... But if nothing is done by the legitimate left to fight the depredations of the Militant Tendency, the Labour Party will split or the support for a party of the centre will grow and grow. Our survival is in our hands.[6]

With Callaghan and Healey becalmed in the face of the machinations of the left, the Labour centre-right's morale was low when Shirley addressed a meeting of its Manifesto Group on 21 May. She refused to entertain the idea of forming a new party, dismissing it as nonsense. 'I am not interested in a third party. I do not believe it has any future,' a reference to Jenkins's hopes of launching something new. A better alternative was for the Labour Party to change some of its attitudes. Her words reassured her large audience, though her failure to respond to the repeated calls for her return to Parliament disappointed many. More than one speaker threw up the scenario of her becoming the leader of the party if she moved quickly.

On 31 May 1980, a special Labour conference was staged at Wembley to approve an official policy document entitled 'Peace, Jobs and Freedom', opposing membership of the EEC and advocating unilateralism and protectionism. Once again, the atmosphere was acrimonious as the 1974–79 government was subjected to ridicule, while moderates who dared speak out were heckled and abused. 'A lot of the usual claptrap – crisis of capitalism etc.' was Shirley's verdict of the conference. 'Only a couple of forward-looking speeches. The whole thing is terribly flat and pointless – it only shows the NEC should have had the guts not to do it.'[7] The next few days brought no relief. She branded Benn's speech at a trade union conference denigrating an incomes policy as 'utterly irresponsible', chided the PLP for its failure to send a letter to the NEC expressing its unease with Wembley and baulked at Barbara Castle's call for Benn to be leader. By the time David Owen rang her on 4 June to arrange a meeting she felt utterly deflated. 'What a bloody mess,' she wrote.[8]

Owen, too, had been in the wars. Ever since addressing the Hornsey Constituency Labour Party the previous September when Trotskyites had given full voice to their venom, the former Foreign Secretary had been leading the resistance to the left in both Parliament and the country. Then as the defence issue moved centre stage with the Thatcher government's decision to deploy Cruise missiles in Britain, he vowed to fight the growing unilateralism within his party. Such convictions came at a cost. The crude treatment meted out to him at Wembley during his speech defending Labour's defence policy left an indelible impression upon him. Appalled by the animosity on display and disgusted at the pusillanimity of his colleagues for failing to speak out, he resolved to

launch an immediate counter-attack. Three days later, his resolve
was stiffened when, en route to the House of Commons, he was
apprised by a journalist of a demand by John Silkin, the shadow
Industry Secretary and anti-marketeer, for an incoming Labour
government to withdraw unconditionally from Europe. At a chance
encounter with Bill Rodgers immediately afterwards, Rodgers
informed him that he was shortly to meet with Shirley at her flat
and suggested that he came along too. Owen concurred and asked
Rodgers for her telephone number, a telling request that underlined
the distance between them despite their similarity of views.

When the meeting took place Shirley, beside herself with anger
at Silkin's demand, insisted they respond in kind. They decided to
issue a joint statement for the benefit of the Sunday papers declaring their total opposition to the reopening of the European question
and branding a future Labour manifesto commitment to leave the
Community as irresponsible, opportunistic and short sighted. They
concluded on a defiant note: 'There are some of us who will not
accept a choice between socialism and Europe. We will choose
both.'[9] The implication was clear. 'That was the first indication I
had ever given that I could contemplate leaving the Labour Party
for a new social democratic party,' Owen later wrote.[10]

The statement caused ripples in the Sunday press and at the next
meeting of the shadow Cabinet Owen and Rodgers faced a broadside from Peter Shore, a leading anti-marketeer, forcing Callaghan
to intervene as peacemaker.

The row over Europe ironically coincided with a major speech
that Jenkins was about to give to the Parliamentary Press Gallery,
in which he was expected to raise once again the possibility of a
new centre party. Although he had been buoyed by the positive
response to Dimbleby, he soon discovered that turning enthusiasm
into something more tangible proved a formidable task, especially
since he was still based in Brussels. Between their November 1979
encounter at East Hendred and the following July, he and Shirley
had met only once and that meeting in Brussels in March was,
according to Jenkins, more about reliving the past than shaping the

future. For the next three months they didn't even speak on the phone ... until Sunday 8 June. With the newspaper headlines that day full of fresh Labour divisions over Europe, Shirley had given a radio interview in which she had raised the possibility of leaving the party should it vote to leave the Community. At the same time she had once again ruled out the possibility of joining a new centre party which would have 'no roots, no principles, no philosophy, and no values'. What she and her colleagues wanted, she said, was to fight for a Labour Party which was 'democratic, representative, parliamentary', and, most important for her, 'an international party'.[11]

Minutes after the interview went out on the BBC's *World at One*, she rang Jenkins to minimise any offence that she might have given by her ringing renunciation of a centre party. As it was, Jenkins hadn't heard the interview and was more concerned to win her approval for his speech the next day, so he never did discover from her what she had actually said. In his memoirs he records that they rang off on the best of terms. 'She said she was sure we would all be together in six months or so.'[12]

The next weekend, as Shirley was telling Rodgers's local party in Stockton that it had to fight the left's undemocratic and unrealistic constitutional changes, Labour's committee of enquiry held its final meeting at Bishop's Stortford. It agreed by a seven to six majority to recommend a future leader be elected by an electoral college comprised of MPs, trade unions and constituency parties. These proposals outraged Owen in particular. He expressed bewilderment as to why Callaghan and Healey should have endorsed something which so compromised the integrity and independence of the parliamentary party. He and Rodgers exchanged angry words with Callaghan the next day at shadow Cabinet, accusing him of appeasement.

Shirley, too, had her say on Bishop's Stortford, telling a regional party conference that the Commission of Enquiry had left behind some very pertinent questions. The leader had to have the confidence of the PLP. It wasn't clear that the Commission's proposals met that stipulation. She returned to this matter at the NEC in July when she, along with Foot and John Golding, put the case for the status quo, but their attempts to defeat the electoral college failed by fourteen votes to eleven. At her fiftieth birthday party, attended by leading Labour moderates and journalists, there was an elegiac air to proceedings. John Cole, then deputy editor of *The Observer*, recalled that as Shirley showed him and his wife to the door at the end of the evening, she said with a sad smile, 'You have just witnessed the wake of Labour's old establishment.'[13]

For some time Shirley, along with Owen and Rodgers, had been preoccupied with drafting the comprehensive policy statement they considered necessary if they were to stand any chance of rallying the centre-right, since Europe by itself wasn't a prominent enough *casus belli*. Consequently, following a series of meetings mulling over different drafts and whether they should explicitly raise the question of an alternative socialist party, the 3,000-word statement was published in *The Guardian* and *Daily Mirror* on 1 August. The opening sentence read: 'The Labour Party is facing the gravest crisis in its history – graver even than the crisis of 1931.' Having outlined their traditional programme, the mixed economy, British member-ship of NATO and the EEC, they ended with a call to arms which, through a careful choice of words, managed to reconcile Shirley's oft-repeated rejection of a centre party with her growing accept-ance that a new party might be necessary should the NEC fail to change course.

> We have already said that we will not support a centre party for it would lack roots and a coherent philosophy. But if the Labour Party abandons its democratic and international principles, the argument may grow for a new democratic socialist party to estab-lish itself as a party of conscience and reform committed to those principles.[14]

'Twenty years later,' Rodgers wrote in his autobiography, 'our *Guardian* letter stands up remarkably both as a warning to the Labour Party on the brink of self-induced disaster and as a manifesto for a social democratic party in the closing years of this century.'[15]

The letter generated much interest and support in the press, who dubbed them the Gang of Three after the notorious Gang of Four in China a few years earlier, compared to the contempt it received from the left. According to the socialist publication *Tribune*, it exposed the paucity of thought which had been evident on the right for some time. Its present predicament was of its own making. Even many moderates who supported Shirley, Owen and Rodgers in their aims were less than sympathetic to their timing, believing that it undermined Callaghan's call for unity. They did at least find some reassurance from their curt dismissal of David Steel's blandishments in *The Guardian*, imploring them to 'end their dialogue with the deaf' and enter into talks with the Liberal Party with a view to creating a radical coalition.

After a lull during August, battle was resumed at a CLV meeting during the TUC conference, when Shirley launched a scathing attack on Benn for his disloyalty towards the Callaghan government. She had been particularly incensed by his recent denunciation of its incomes policy, which he had dubbed 'Stalinist', and its meek acceptance of the IMF's ultimatum on cuts in public expenditure. If he felt so inclined, she declared, he should have resigned from the Cabinet or kept his views to himself. According to the *Daily Telegraph*'s James Wightman, Shirley looked and sounded like a potential candidate for the Labour leadership. 'It is often said in her criticism that she lacks political ruthlessness, but she did not display such a weakness last night. The only point on which she held back was in actually naming Mr Benn.'[16]

Shirley's combative demeanour was even more evident during Labour's conference at Blackpool. In a week brimming with raw antagonism, the fist-clenched ranks of the Bennite left stood at their zenith as they worked closely with leading trade unions such as the TGWU to chalk up a number of significant victories. On the opening morning Benn himself set the tone by declaring to rapturous applause that an incoming Labour government within a month would nationalise leading industries, restore to Britain all the powers transferred to Brussels and create 1,000 peers if necessary to abolish the House of Lords.

The debate, aside from its compelling viewing, brought all the internecine strife of the previous months and years to the surface as moderates, appalled by the day's events, resolved to fight back. Seething at the hatred she had encountered in the hall and outside, where she had been spat at, Shirley used a CLV meeting that evening, to excoriate the left for its fantasy programme which she claimed bore little resemblance to the modern world, and was positively vitriolic towards Benn and his demagoguery. Recalling his three legislative commitments that morning to be enacted within a month, she wondered why he was so unambitious. 'After all, it took God only six days to make the world.'[17] Decrying the fascism of the left, Shirley silenced the dozen or so Militant hecklers by her uncompromising stance. 'We are going to fight to save this party – and, by God, we can.'[18] Her references to the deafening silence of many of her colleagues on the party's moderate wing and to the fascism of the left caught the mood of the evening. 'The CLV meeting is a terrific success,' enthused Radice in his diary. 'Shirley, David Owen and Bill speak superbly, particularly Shirley,' but it couldn't lift the gloom that had descended over the centre-right.[19]

Later that evening, many moderates gathered in Shirley's suite at the Imperial Hotel (one of the privileges bestowed on members of the NEC) to watch the day's proceedings on television and contemplate the future. For the first time MPs talked openly about leaving the party without qualifying what they were saying.

The next day, in his leader's speech, Callaghan attempted to paper over the cracks and reconcile different factions by reminding delegates of the growing crisis in unemployment and asserting that only a united Labour Party was capable of offering hope to the younger generation. 'Nobody here, I think, talks about centre parties,' he said with Shirley in mind. 'It is dead as a dodo. Mere fluff.'[20] His words elicited the biggest cheer of the afternoon in what was otherwise the speech of a leader past his prime.

Wednesday, referred to by Benn as a 'thrilling day', saw Conference vote to leave Europe, remove all American bases, ratify compulsory reselection of MPs and accept the principle of the electoral college, although its precise composition remained unclear after two amendments were voted down. As the vote on Europe was announced to loud cheers, Shirley pointedly left her seat on the platform to sit next to Owen in the main body of the hall. When the NEC met that evening, she was unsparing in her contempt for Conference, not least the shenanigans over its support for the electoral college, and refused to attend its hastily convened meeting the following morning at which it would try to frame a resolution to put to Conference.

The final setback to a disastrous week for the moderates came on Thursday with the passing of a motion supporting unilateralism, despite a courageous speech from Rodgers, who, like Owen the previous day over Europe, was heckled for his pains. At a fringe meeting Shirley denounced the NEC, calling the proposed electoral college 'a travesty of democracy' going beyond even all the travesties that they had seen that week, and lambasted the miners for having their Communist vice-chairman, Mick McGahey, preside over their lunchtime caucus. 'What I am bloody well not going to have is the situation where the Communist party determines the leadership of the Labour party,' she remarked.[21] In a sign of her frustration at Callaghan's lacklustre efforts at combating the left, she contended that the main reason for the party's current plight lay in the continuing uncertainty about the leadership. It was vital that he, Callaghan, made his intention clear.

Days later he did. Amidst the growing carnage he retired, leaving his successor to be elected by the PLP as the new electoral college wouldn't be in operation until after a Special Conference in January had finalised its details. Four candidates put themselves forward: Healey, Foot and two outsiders, Peter Shore and John Silkin. Healey, the preferred choice of the centre-right, was the obvious man in terms of stature and experience, but at this critical juncture in the party's history this great warrior of battles past was found wanting. Apparently unwilling to rock the boat in his attempts to court the centre, a number of whose votes he needed, and cheerfully assuming that the right would automatically back him as it had no other option, his undue passivity merely succeeded in alienating a number of his natural supporters. Up against the much-loved figure of Foot in the final round, Healey discovered that his defects, most notably his abrasive personality and breezy overconfidence, took precedence over his many virtues, so that certain MPs whom he assumed would vote for him didn't. (The fact that several right-wingers bizarrely voted for Foot in order to further accentuate party divisions and bring a split ever closer also appears to have undermined him.) His defeat by 139 to 129 was another prominent milestone along Labour's road to ruin, since Foot, for all his gifts as a crusading journalist and parliamentarian, wasn't leadership material, especially in the mass media era. Aside from his age and eccentricities on camera, his outdated views and failure to keep the far-left in check made him a fatal liability.

Within days of his election, Shirley, in a speech in Glasgow, complimented Foot on his impeccable democratic credentials, while casting aspersions on many of his supporters for their contempt of Parliament. Claiming that the doctrinal left was wrecking the party's hope of winning an election, she warned Foot that he had to decide whether the democratic left would prevail or in turn be destroyed.

She repeated her public warning in private to Foot on several occasions thereafter. While there had never been much love lost between Foot on the one hand and Owen and Rodgers on the other, dating back in Rodgers's case to the defence battles of the Gaitskell era, the opposite was the case with Shirley. Like Healey, Foot had worked closely with her in government and, besides warming to her intelligence and charm, was well aware of her revered status within the Labour movement. At a time when the party's image had never looked so sinister, the loss of one of its most attractive personalities would be nothing short of catastrophic. Yet despite the high stakes pending upon their discussions they proved curiously unsatisfactory as Foot made little headway with his appeals to party unity and talk of a glittering future if she stayed, while Shirley found him unresponsive to her very real concerns. The fact that he seemed to accept blithely the erosion of democratic forces within the party and was unable to fathom the gravity of Labour's plight increasingly convinced her that time was running out for her and her fellow moderates.

Owen, too, had his reservations. Disillusioned by Foot's election and Healey's undue willingness to be his deputy, alongside the refusal of both the shadow Cabinet and PLP to fight for the principle of OMOV (One Member One Vote) in the electoral college, he was beginning to contemplate life outside the Labour Party. When he met Shirley and Rodgers at Shirley's flat on 18 November to discuss recent developments, he told them that he was resigning from the shadow Cabinet. His decision stunned the other two. They urged him to stay. According to Owen, Shirley initially felt honour-bound to stand for Stevenage again and said that they should all act in unison, but after hearing him out, she quietly said, 'If you don't stand for the shadow Cabinet, David, I'm not going to stand at Stevenage.'[22] Her sudden change of heart was greeted with scepticism by Rodgers, who told Owen as they left that years of knowing her had convinced him that she would renege on her commitment.

Ten days later in Stevenage, Shirley proved as good as her word. In an emotional meeting she informed her local party that nothing had ever given her a greater sense of achievement than her fifteen years as MP for the constituency. Claiming that it was the party that had changed rather than herself, she told them she couldn't 'honestly expound or defend, as I would rightly be expected to do as a parliamentary candidate, the policies conference agreed at Blackpool'. Dismissing the idea of joining any other *existing* party today (a carefully chosen form of words), she confirmed that she would remain a member of the NEC and continue to fight for change from within.

'Her speech last night', wrote James Wightman, 'can legitimately be interpreted as another warning that her membership of Labour is not open-ended,' and when taxed on *The World This Weekend* about the formation of a new party, she didn't discount the possibility. Yet who would join it and what kind of party it would be was far from clear given Shirley's clear repudiation of both the Liberals – 'not a serious alternative' – and Jenkins's centre party – 'I could not belong to a party that is not Socialist' – alongside her continuing scepticism about Owen's social-democratic alternative.[23] In her hour of doubt she turned again to Healey for support, hoping that he might now provide more of a lead than he had done hitherto.

Although they were very different characters, Shirley had always enjoyed an easy relationship with him and his wife Edna. As the party stumbled from one crisis to another it was natural that she, like Owen and Rodgers, should flock to his colours to fight for social-democratic ideals. The fact that Healey had barely responded had disillusioned all three of them. At a meeting in Shirley's flat before the party conference and in subsequent phone calls, they had tried to impress upon him the urgency of the situation, but with a leadership election to win he didn't respond to the tocsin. Even the shock of his defeat had failed to drag him out of his slumber to lend a helping hand. What's more, he felt that not only were their repeated ultimatums to the party premature, but also they were counterproductive, as his letter of 3 December makes clear.

My dear Shirley,

I am really grateful to you for your letter although I am deeply saddened by recent statements and, particularly, that Bill, David and yourself keep sounding off and making announcements without any consultations with your friends. Whether the future keeps us within or without the Party we shall be a rabble if we act in an incoherent and uncoordinated manner.

As I see it at present our generals have marched the troops into an exposed position and left them there totally exposed to the enemy.

You may be interested to know that at my ultra loyal constituency gathering on Sunday all your friends were dismayed and encouraged only by my decision to stand for the Parliamentary Committee, which they took to be a sign that I wish to continue the fight within the Party but that I had not deserted the war against the Tories.

With respect, what you should have said to Stevenage on Friday night is that 'my beliefs are as follows … and the stand I intend to take within the party is … and if, fully understanding that you wish to select me I shall be very happy to serve you!'

We must all judge these matters to ourselves and it may well be that there is no future for us within the Party, although I detect possibilities which you apparently discount, but that moment of crisis must not be brought about by isolated actions but as a natural development following a collective situation affecting our many friends. We cannot ask our friends to stand and be counted then fail to do so ourselves.

In my own case, I cannot possibly desert so many loyal colleagues who have stood by me in many battles, both in Apex and in the party, who believe in me and still believe in the party. As far as I am concerned that is the essence of the matter.

Having assured her that he didn't believe in the proposals for the electoral college and regretted the loss of Owen from the shadow Cabinet, he concluded:

However, the point I want to make is that none of us should indulge our own positions and disregard our friends and I certainly have no intention of doing that so far as you, Bill and David are concerned. We should meet and talk with our friends – often.

Whatever you do – all of us still love you dearly but for goodness sake do let us try to influence you occasionally.

Yours ever,

Denis[24]

Healey's sentiments were broadly echoed by Callaghan.

> I do wish you had said to your GMC, 'Here I am. You know my
> views and policies. Do you wish me to be your candidate?' I bet
> they would have said, 'Yes' – and then you could have thumbed
> your nose at the NEC – with the best of all political bases under
> you – namely your constituency workers.
>
> This party belongs to all of us – not to the NEC or the so-called
> militants. I shall go on expressing my own views and will stand
> as a Labour Candidate whatever may be in the Manifesto. They
> would have to kick me out before I would cease to say that I was
> of the Labour Party – because it is my Party. I hope very much
> that you feel the same.[25]

This was the question she increasingly pondered as she inched ever
closer towards Jenkins, Owen and a new party.

For years Roy Jenkins had been one of the towering figures on
the British political landscape, but had been increasingly estranged
from Labour over its class-based politics and anti-European priorities. The fact that his leadership bid in 1976 had attracted a mere
fifty-six votes, and that he had decamped to Brussels the following
year, had only enhanced his sense of detachment as Labour crashed
to defeat in 1979, an election in which he couldn't even bring
himself to vote for his party. The change of government rekindled
his political spark, however, and his Dimbleby Lecture calling for
a realignment of the party system served notice of his intent. In
league with David Steel he decided that, rather than joining the
Liberals, a new party would be the best vehicle to attract disillusioned MPs, and, helped by some of his most trusted followers such
as David Marquand and John Harris, he began to prepare for
such an eventuality.

Jenkins's vision was greatly aided by Labour's growing drift to
the extremes, and a Conservative government presiding over mass
unemployment and social dislocation, but if his new party was to
get airborne it would need some eminent names in the cockpit.

Bill Rodgers had probably been his greatest friend and admirer over twenty years, as together they had fought for a modern, revisionist, pro-European party. Although less charismatic than Shirley, he was able and experienced and as mentor to a number of young MPs from the north-east, he could deliver several additional recruits, but Rodgers wasn't yet ready to desert. A Labour man to the core, he was, unlike Owen, prepared to give Foot one final chance to restore order to the ranks. He also hoped to get promotion in the shadow Cabinet, but Foot's failure to oblige on either score cast him into a giant valley of despair as he nursed a chronic back complaint over Christmas.

As for David Owen, the cordial relationship that Jenkins had formed with him between 1970 and 1976 somewhat cooled once the latter went to Brussels, since the former's style as Foreign Secretary was too Gaullist for his taste. Aside from his dismissive approach to Dimbleby, Owen harboured scepticism about Jenkins's leadership prowess, especially given his abject showing in 1976, his patrician personality and his Whiggish views. A new party, Owen insisted, had to be firmly left of centre. In the four-hour meeting he had with Jenkins on 29 November 1980 he informed him that he thought that Shirley would join and that she should be the leader not only because of her immense popularity, but also because of her classlessness and commitment to the new politics.

As a fellow liberal-internationalist, Shirley found much to admire in Jenkins. Europe brought them closer together and after Reg Prentice she became his firmest supporter in the 1974–76 Cabinet when he led the fight to stay in Europe and oppose the more extreme parts of the party's manifesto. Yet despite voting for him in 1976 and admiring his political accomplishments, she kept her distance personally. According to Bill Rodgers, she never fully knew or understood Jenkins, appearing uneasy in his company and that of his immediate circle, especially when mixing with Conservative grandees at his Oxfordshire home. (Aside from William Rees-Mogg, an Oxford contemporary whom she saw occasionally, Shirley had no Conservative friends, although there were a number, such as

Iain Macleod, Robert Carr and Sir Geoffrey Howe, she respected politically.) Never one for London clubs, she avoided the exclusive milieu in which Jenkins mixed, her open informality sitting uneasily with his more elitist tendencies (she once splashed out £20 for a bottle of wine for his benefit which he failed to appreciate) and as a convinced egalitarian she rejected his idea of a centre party. Thus, while his supporters paid court to the 'prince across the water', clamouring for his return from self-imposed exile, Shirley was more guarded in her response. Dimbleby she dismissed as a mildly interesting academic lecture, not much more, and thereafter when Jenkins pressed his suit he never came away from an encounter with her without being totally mystified about what she was going to do next. That remained the position during the closing weeks of 1980, when he talked up his similarities with her and played down his claims for the leadership. 'Much, I believed, would depend on Shirley,' wrote Rodgers. 'I doubted whether she would help start a new party unless I committed myself, but she might draw back at the last moment even then.'[26] The feeling was mutual given Rodgers's own uncertainty. At lunch with Jenkins over Christmas and when hosting Shirley and Owen at his home on 4 January, he was still havering.

Shirley had received a boost from two leading psephologists, Tony King and Ivor Crewe, who back on 10 December had outlined the potential for a new centre party in alliance with the Liberals. Her failure the following week to get fringe organisations outlawed by the NEC, despite the support of both Foot and Healey, could have acted as the catalyst for a final break, yet still she hesitated. Thus when Owen met up with a group of potential defectors on 5 January he could report only that 'Bill's backing off, and Shirley is dithering.'[27]

On 11 January Shirley took part in a five-hour meeting with Jenkins and Owen at East Hendred (Rodgers was too ill to attend), when she seemed more inclined to make the break. Three days later, at her flat, with Rodgers now on board, the Gang of Four met all together for the first time and agreed to work on a statement in response to Wembley if, as expected, the electoral college without OMOV was passed. They also agreed to consider Shirley's proposal for a council of democracy to be established once Owen and Jenkins had been assured that it would constitute the first step along the road to a new party, and to meet again in private at Jenkins's home the following Sunday. Unfortunately, *The Observer* got wind of the summit and depicted it as a summons by the imperious Jenkins to the other three to help him form his new party. When Shirley read this she was absolutely livid. Suspecting that Jenkins or his acolytes had leaked the story, she rang Jenkins to inform him that she wasn't coming. It took several calls from Jenkins to persuade her to think again, helped by a rescheduling to Rodgers's house in north London to dupe the press. Even then there were further hitches. Arriving late, Shirley was further enraged to discover a posse of photographers and newsmen confronting her. Hiding her face from the cameras like a criminal entering court, she was unusually coy when asked about the purpose of the meeting. 'I am visiting the sick. I am visiting Bill Rodgers,' she muttered, referring to Rodgers's chronic back trouble, now fully healed.[28]

Once inside, Owen recalls the steely anger on her face as, letting out her frustration at the morning's events, she admonished them for briefing the press, and her rage barely assuaged even after Jenkins had offered a half-hearted apology. 'I am sorry that this great enterprise of ours is starting up in the same spirit as the worst of the Wilson Cabinets.'

'Look, I'm not prepared to be pushed out of the Labour Party by anyone,' Shirley retorted.[29] Eventually, the mood relaxed and work on the joint statement proceeded apace. The main impediment was Shirley's reluctance to accept the phrase 'a realignment in British politics', since it implied an absolute commitment to leaving Labour, a Rubicon she wasn't yet prepared to cross.

The next day Shirley dined with her three former PPSs, John Cartwright, Bob Mitchell and Giles Radice, and reiterated her sentiments. According to Radice, she said that a breakaway party would emerge later that year, but she and Rodgers hadn't yet decided whether to join, a surprising comment in the case of Rodgers. The possibility of Foot and Healey holding the party together still existed if they took a stand against Militant. After she left, Mitchell told the others that he had formed the impression she was reluctant to leave, an astute observation given some credence from other sources.

When Mike Thomas, the MP for Newcastle upon Tyne East, and a group of like-minded MPs ready to defect, had met Shirley on 13 January, he was led to believe that their collective sticking point was an electoral college involving the block vote, and should the Wembley conference endorse that, they would definitely leave. A week later, it now appeared she was having second thoughts and was willing to compromise with Foot, which would enable her to stay. Having reminded her that, unlike her own prospects of finding alternative employment, he and his colleagues were risking everything by leaving Labour, Thomas warned her that her external credibility had become increasingly fragile. She had been very fortunate that the enormous reserves of goodwill towards her had enabled her 'to survive the perceptible shifts of view and evident uncertainty of your position over the past twelve months. Another phase of public shilly-shallying will damage it terribly.'

> There are millions of people in Britain who desperately want our kind of people and our kind of politics. They still associate what they want with you and Roy and David and Bill. If we throw that away by failing to bite on the bullet this weekend we will have betrayed everything we stand for. We will be seen as being prepared to wound but not to strike.[30]

On the same day as Thomas's letter, Shirley, Owen and Rodgers held another unproductive meeting with Foot. Quite apart from his failure to concede OMOV, the ideological gulf between them was too great, and his promise of tolerance for the expression of minority views seemed a forlorn one in that climate. Now it really did appear that Wembley would be the point of no return.

Although the mood was less rancorous than previous conferences, Wembley excelled itself in procedural confusion and sleight of hand as several of the largest unions rebuffed Owen's call for OMOV and Foot's plea to give MPs half the votes in the electoral college. The conference opted instead for a system which gave 40 per cent of the vote to the unions in comparison to 30 per cent each for the MPs and constituency parties. This additional power for trade union leaders seemed to vindicate everything that the right had been saying about union chicanery and the inexorable rise of the left. On a day of chaos and conspiracy, with much of the action taking place away from the conference floor, Geoffrey Goodman of the *Daily Mirror* recalls visiting his newspaper's suite in the afternoon in search of Tony Miles, its editorial director, and Terence Lancaster, its political editor. Entering a room at the back of the suite he stumbled across a secret conclave between Shirley, Rodgers and senior *Mirror* executives at which the former two were trying to persuade the latter to support the formation of a new party. Several of the latter, notably Tony Miles, according to Goodman, were sympathetic, but in the end they failed to take the bait.

Shirley was equally unsuccessful in her attempts to woo the unions. Previous attempts to win over Alan Tuffin of the Postal Workers had failed. Now, during the closing stages of the conference, she sidled up to Bryan Stanley, the general secretary of the Post Office Engineering Union, who was sitting with his fellow delegates, and requested a word. She conveyed to him her firmly held belief that the Labour Party had become unelectable. It was time now to look anew at a party based on social-democratic ideals.

'Shirley then asked me if I would be prepared to support such a move,' Stanley recalled.

> I was deeply disappointed to hear these things coming from Shirley, as we had worked together on the NEC in opposition to the crazy ideas of some of the more extreme left-wing members. I respected her intellectual ability and I did not want to see the Labour Party losing her support.

I told her that I had been a member of the Labour Party for over thirty years and that I would never leave. There were things that were wrong at this time, but that we had to work together to change things for the better. However, she took the view that it was already too late, and pointed to the absolute chaos so evident that day at the Conference and expressed grave doubts about whether moderate trade union and Party Leaders would ever be able to work together to save the Labour Party from further disintegration and decline.[31]

In his leader's speech after the result was announced, Foot made another appeal to the potential defectors to stay. Then afterwards, in a personal capacity, Terry Duffy, the right-wing president of the AUEW, pleaded in similar vein, telling Shirley that she was one of the finest female politicians he had ever encountered, but it was all to no avail. Radice recalls going to the *Daily Mirror* party afterwards and Shirley saying goodbye to him as if she really meant it. That evening she, Owen, Jenkins and their main supporters gathered at Rodgers's house delighted with the day's events.

The next morning the four of them met at Owen's dockland home in Limehouse to finalise the Declaration. Shirley still resisted the word 'realignment', but her case was rather undermined by a BBC interview she gave that morning in which she was unfailingly precise about her commitment to leave the Labour Party, a point the others gleefully seized upon as they listened to the recording over lunch.

At 4 p.m. the world's press was summoned and the Gang of Four (Shirley in a borrowed blouse) posed for photographers against a background of a desolate east London street as their establishment of a Council of Social Democracy (CSD) made front-page headlines the next day. No questions were taken, but copies of the 500-word 'Limehouse Declaration' were distributed. As to its content, it reiterated rather well-worn social-democratic goals, but its greater significance lay in the meaning behind the message. Shirley's objection to a centre party was specifically acknowledged, yet having raised the social-democratic standard they ended with an appeal to fellow moderates in the Labour Party. 'We recognize that for those who have given much of their lives to the Labour Party the choice that lies ahead will be deeply painful. But we believe that the need for a realignment of British politics must now be faced.'[32]

Only a miracle, it seemed, could now prevent a split, as nine other Labour MPs placed their support behind CSD and Rodgers resigned from the shadow Cabinet. The meeting of the NEC on 28 January was particularly acrimonious, with Shirley, according to John Golding, extremely uncomfortable and behaving very strangely. The main motion on the agenda – the need for a Labour government to be re-elected and the NEC's pledged support for the programme, principles and policies of the party – was originally drawn up by Benn as a form of loyalty test. In response Shirley moved two amendments, making clear that she couldn't support Labour's programme as it then stood. She took exception to an inquisition about the activities of CSD when Militant operated as a party within a party. Foot then said that the real question was whether she was forming another party. It would be quite intolerable for her to sit there if she was planning to join another one.

'I say directly to Shirley, it is a matter of morality and we have the right to ask you that straight question,' added Benn.

'You will only get that answer when you put that question to all the groups in the party,' she responded.[33]

Clearly shaken by the tone of the meeting and the remarks directed against her, Shirley told waiting reporters that she would have to consider her future in light of what had happened. Following another unproductive meeting with Foot and Healey on 2 February ('David Owen and Rodgers already decided to leave. Shirley unsure but still agonising', Healey wrote in his diary), she duly resigned from the NEC a week later.[34] 'You have tried to dissuade me from this course,' she told Foot, 'and I would like to say that you have spoken to me directly, fairly and in a spirit of friendship.'[35] She wasn't quite so charitable in her letter to Ron Hayward. In it she accepted that she would face criticism over her failure to stay and fight on, but claimed that after years of trying to combat the leftward surge with minimum support she now regarded defeat as total and unmitigated. In taking issue with those who still argued for compromise on the question of the leadership she deemed it unacceptable that a potential Prime Minister should be elected by a block vote or a mandated vote. The only genuinely democratic method was a secret ballot of MPs elected by the people or of individual Party members.

> Politics is the art of compromise, and compromise must be based on give and take. I have found, however, that compromise in the NEC is just another name for endless retreat...
>
> The party that is now emerging is not the democratic socialist party that I joined but a party intent on controlling those of its members who are elected to public office by the people of Britain. I believe that to be incompatible with the accountability of MPs to their electors which lies at the heart of parliamentary democracy.[36]

Her parting words of regret weren't reciprocated by Hayward, who dubbed her decision 'ill advised and one which you will regret'. He ridiculed her denunciation of the block vote as it was that same block vote that had elected her as a member of the NEC for the previous decade, and reminded her that her membership of the party had given her the opportunity to serve the country in high ministerial office. He added: 'I regret that the way in which you have resigned from the NEC, with full aid from the media, can only have been designed to give the maximum aid and comfort to our political opponents.'[37]

Others joined in the war of words as things turned personal. John Golding accused Shirley of deserting her allies in the heat of battle. 'There are some of us who have had a gentle upbringing, and faced with a crisis are not able to stand the rough and tumble like those of us who are used to scrapping in working-class organisations.'[38]

He was followed by Foot, who, in a speech at Nelson, firmly rebutted Shirley's charge that Labour had grown intolerant over the previous decade and abandoned its commitment to parliamentary democracy. She had been in a minority in the debate over Europe, but her right to dissent from the party line had been respected.

On 30 January Owen had forfeited his links with Labour by telling his Devonport constituency that he wouldn't be standing for it again and by 2 March all thirteen of the SDP supporters in the Commons had resigned the Labour whip. Such a parting of the ways often came at a considerable cost as much of the traditional point-scoring was now fuelled by personal acrimony, as cries of 'traitors' emanated from the Labour benches. Even away from Parliament traditional civilities weren't always observed as some former friends and colleagues simply shunned them or kept their conversation to the most mundane of matters. Owen was all but ignored by Foot, who, in a rare act of petulance, informed him, Shirley and Rodgers that they would no longer be welcome at the dinner to be given by the Callaghan cabinet for Jim and Audrey. The three of them responded by sending the Callaghans an Ackermann print of Oxford University as a token of their continuing friendship. Callaghan, who had been in Australia when the formal break came, wrote to thank them, but was much troubled by political developments while he was away. He wrote to Shirley,

> I am told that you will be leaving the Party, and if you have made up your mind, I know nothing will stop you – because you have a stubborn sense of what is right. But I do not believe the break is for ever. I very much hope that in the fullness of time we shall be working together again.[39]

It proved wishful thinking, for despite their continued friendship their political bond had been well and truly severed.

## Endnotes

1 *Guardian*, 10 April 1981
2 *Guardian*, 3 October 1979
3 *Guardian*, 3 October 1979
4 *A Life at the Centre*, p.520
5 Giles Radice, *Diaries 1980–2001*, Weidenfeld & Nicholson, 2004, p.5
6 Speech, Leicester, 1 February 1980, SW Papers (private collection)
7 SW diary, 31 May 1980, SW Papers (private collection)
8 SW diary, 4 June 1980, SW Papers (private collection)
9 *The Times*, 9 June 1980
10 David Owen, *Time to Declare*, p.439
11 Interview quoted in *The Times*, 9 July 1980
12 Roy Jenkins, *A Life at the Centre*, p.525
13 John Cole, *As It Seemed to Me*, Weidenfeld & Nicholson, 1995, p.213
14 *Guardian*, 1 August 1980
15 Bill Rodgers, *Fourth Among Equals*, p.197
16 *Daily Telegraph*, 2 September 1980
17 *Daily Telegraph*, 29 September 1980
18 *Guardian*, 30 September 1980
19 Giles Radice, *Diaries 1980–2001*, p.15
20 *Guardian*, 1 October 1980
21 *Daily Telegraph*, 3 October 1980
22 Andrew Stephen, 'The Kicking, Squealing Birthpangs of the SDP', *Sunday Times Magazine*, 27 September 1980
23 *Daily Telegraph*, 29 November 1980
24 Denis Healey to SW, 3 December 1980, SW Papers (private collection)
25 Jim Callaghan to SW, 17 December 1980, SW Papers (private collection)
26 Bill Rodgers, *Fourth Among Equals*, p.200
27 Andrew Stephen, *Sunday Times Magazine*, 27 September 1981
28 *Daily Telegraph*, 19 January 1981
29 Andrew Stephen, *Sunday Times Magazine*, 27 September 1981
30 Mike Thomas to Shirley Williams, 20 January 1981, SW Papers (private collection)
31 Quoted in John Golding, *Hammer of the Left*, Politico's, 2003, p.162
32 *The Times*, 26 January 1981
33 *The Times*, 29 January 1981
34 Diary quoted in Edward Pearce, *Denis Healey*, Little, Brown, 2002, p.552
35 SW to Michael Foot, quoted in Mervyn Jones, *Michael Foot*, Victor Gollancz, 1994, p.460
36 *Daily Telegraph*, 10 February 1981
37 *Guardian*, 12 February 1981
38 *The Times*, 10 February 1981
39 Jim Callaghan to SW, 20 February 1981, SW Papers (private collection)

# 14

# BREAKING THE MOULD

Limehouse had clearly caught the mood of the nation, as messages of goodwill and offers of money poured in following support from a hundred luminaries and a number of prominent journalists, businessmen and academics in a full-page advertisement in *The Guardian*. Opinion polls suggested massive support for a new Liberal–SDP alliance, much of the media comment was favourable and after all the heartbreak of leaving Labour, the exhilaration of forming a new party had a bracing effect. Never one to sit still, Shirley's days became ever more intense as she fielded calls from well-wishers, encouraged friends to sign up (many did) and dashed from meeting to broadcasting studio, sheaves of paper under her arm, reading and signing documents while she travelled. So great was the avalanche of letters that littered her small flat she was up half the night trying to answer them.

Starting a new party is an exacting business, but within a couple of weeks of Limehouse, temporary offices were found in Queen Anne's Gate, volunteers were in ready supply to deal with the mass of correspondence and trustees were appointed to handle the incoming funds. The Gang of Four chose to meet informally once a week at L'Amico, an Italian restaurant in Westminster, and soon agreed to a division of responsibilities: Jenkins to be in charge of coordinating policy, Rodgers the party organisation, Shirley communications and publicity and Owen to lead the parliamentary group. At the same time a Steering Committee (later the National Committee) of fifteen was established to meet once a week and be chaired in rotation by one of the Gang of Four, followed soon afterwards by the parliamentary committee of the SDP.

Originally the launch of the SDP was expected to be in the autumn, but with party and press keen to maintain the early momentum, it was decided to bring the date forward. Jenkins and Owen wanted it to be within two months, as opposed to Shirley and Rodgers, who favoured delaying it until after the local elections in May. Eventually, given the rise in expectations, they settled for 26 March.

For the launch of the first major British political party since Labour in 1900, 500 of the world's press crowded into the Connaught Rooms in Covent Garden. Against a compelling background of their new red, white and blue logo, each of the four, in a deliberate show of collective leadership, stressed the new type of politics they offered and their left-of-centre credentials. The launch, expertly masterminded by Mike Thomas, was generally reckoned to have been an unqualified success. The massive publicity it generated brought an additional 43,000 members over the course of the next ten days and raised more than half a million pounds. Public meetings, echoing the politics of a previous era, became commonplace as hundreds, disillusioned by the failures and extremism of the two main parties, flocked to hear these new apostles of hope expound their gospel of consensus.

In 1979 Jenkins had begun a series of discussions with David Steel, a friend of his whose political philosophy was similar to his own. Although some twenty years junior to Jenkins, Steel was in no sense the political novice depicted by the media; rather he was a wily and clear-sighted tactician determined to make a difference. On succeeding to the leadership of the Liberal Party in 1976, Steel immediately faced down his rank and file at his first conference by indicating his willingness to cooperate with other parties as part of his desire to bring in the Liberals from the cold. Not for him the icy wastes of interminable opposition for no purpose. While the Lib–Lab Pact delivered little of actual substance to his party, it at least gave him a fleeting glimpse of power with all its possibilities and enhanced his reputation as a formidable negotiator, endowed with a clear-sighted strategic vision. Like Jenkins, Steel wanted a realignment of the centre-left of British politics along radical, non-socialist lines and both had agreed that Jenkins should try to create a new party with close links to the Liberals. In this way, they reasoned, he would attract a number of Labour dissidents, enabling them to mount a challenge to the Labour Party in its heartlands in a way that had previously eluded the Liberals.

In contrast to Steel's friendship with Jenkins, his links with Shirley, Owen and Rodgers were few, although Rodgers had acted as an intermediary during the Lib–Lab Pact and, like Shirley, had cooperated with leading Liberals during the European referendum. She, too, had been a keen advocate of the Lib–Lab Pact, but she didn't mix with the Liberals socially and had no particular affinity with their leaders. Jo Grimond she felt was clever but untrustworthy, Jeremy Thorpe, whom she had known at Oxford, was a brilliant actor rather than a serious politician, and Steel had sponsored the Abortion Bill, which she had resolutely opposed. As to the wider party, she certainly could identify with a number of its progressive values but regarded them as political innocents reluctant to slug it out with the big battalions in the heat of battle. 'The Liberals, meanwhile, make their enlightened speech-day speeches,' she had written back in 1965. 'Somehow it all seems rather academic and remote.'[1] Describing their constituency workers as nice people but rather lacking in common goals, she figured that until they had rid themselves of their heterogeneous tendencies and secured a national identity, they would continue to struggle. The fact that they remained, despite 1974, a minority party meant that she continued to view them as something of an irrelevance and certainly not worth joining.

Her views were broadly shared by Rodgers and even more by Owen, who had observed them at close quarters in the West Country, one of their strongholds. His experience of fighting a pro-armament Liberal in Devonport, a dockyard seat, when neighbouring Liberals stood for something very different, brought home to him all too clearly the ambivalence of a third party with scant control over its grass roots. Such a party, he figured, with its minority vote, fissiparous tendencies and parochial mentality appeared unable to make the great leap forward towards the kind of historic realignment that the SDP was seeking. He recognised that some form of informal accommodation with them was necessary, but beyond that he wasn't prepared to go.

After the Gang of Three's open letter to *The Guardian* in August 1980, Steel replied with some asperity in the same paper, taking issue with Shirley's central contention that any new centre party would lack roots or a coherent philosophy. His appeals, both public and private, to enter into talks went unheeded. He did, however, have two meetings with the three of them and Jenkins in mid-January 1981 and one with Shirley and Jenkins in early March. Otherwise, there was little discussion until the annual conference of the Anglo-German Association at Königswinter in early April, when Shirley, Rodgers, Steel and Richard Holme, the president of the Liberal Party, were among the guests. On the final day, before walking up the Drachenfels, Shirley and Rodgers, as previously arranged, had lunch with Steel and Holme, and the conversation soon turned to coopera-tion between the two parties. As Steel outlined his strategy, Shirley and Rodgers found that they were broadly in step, accepting the need for a joint statement of principles and agreement on policy, the prel-ude to an electoral pact and division of seats. The meeting, both on a personal and political level, was most productive. As they left the hotel, Steel has recollections of Shirley sweetly inquiring of Holme, 'Does this mean I'll have to support proportional representation?'

Königswinter prompted much disquiet within a section of both the SDP Parliamentary and Steering Committees, not least Owen himself, at a special joint meeting two days later. This was partly because the talks hadn't been authorised, but, more importantly, due to the general mistrust of Liberal designs on the SDP's independ-ence. A number of SDP MPs, mainly from northern working-class areas, maintained that whereas the Liberals were tainted with fail-ure, their party's appeal was in its novelty. With its capacity for reaching out beyond traditional class boundaries it should have time to build up its organisation and establish its own identity so it could negotiate with the Liberals from a position of strength. Conscious of the mood of the meeting, Shirley promised to try and persuade Steel to establish a moratorium on the selection of Liberal parliamentary candidates, but made the case for proceeding harmoniously, as Liberal cooperation in the event of a by-election would be essential.

When Shirley and Rodgers next met Steel he was disappointed by the tepid response from the SDP. Fully aware that many in his own party, including the likes of Grimond and Cyril Smith, the staunchly independent MP for Rochdale, viewed the SDP with scepticism, he needed joint agreement to a short policy statement which he could then recommend to his conference. Without that he could do little to stop the adoption of Liberal candidates. After some discussion Shirley and Rodgers said they would try and steer their colleagues down that particular route in return for Steel using his authority as leader to place a curb on local selection. This was agreed and from mid-May representatives from both parties met under Shirley and Steel to draft a statement of principles upon which the two parties could work together. On 16 June *A Fresh Start for Britain*, a brief seven-paragraph document outlining the main areas of agreement, was published. It also set out to consider ways of cooperating electorally, including an allocation of seats, something Steel accepted could be problematic. As he and Shirley posed benignly in Dean's Yard, Westminster, with the document, the press had a field day comparing them to two superannuated lovers. More seriously, the agreement, besides reassuring the Liberals, marked a step away from the social-democratic principles around which the new party had been formed in March.

At the end of May, Sir Thomas Williams, the Labour MP for Warrington, resigned to become a judge. The news wasn't entirely a surprise and Owen recalls raising it in the Steering Committee having previously discussed it with the rest of the Gang of Four over lunch. The general assumption was that Shirley would be the SDP candidate, but she had her doubts and it was all Owen could do to stop her closing the option there and then.

Warrington, halfway between Manchester and Liverpool, industrial, working-class and Labour, was hardly ideal territory for a new party which had no local organisation and where the Liberals had traditionally polled badly. Yet, for all the potential pitfalls, the SDP's claim to be a national left-of-centre party rested on creditable performances in seats like this. Shirley's classlessness, popularity and Catholicism in a constituency where the Catholic vote was strong made her by some way the most powerful weapon in the SDP armoury. Her appeal was confirmed by a poll in *The Sun*, which showed her with a massive lead over Labour, and a front-page headline proclaiming 'You Can Do It Shirl'. Yet far from encouraging her to stand, this development appears to have had the opposite effect. Once apprised of it, she rushed out a press release confirming that she wouldn't be standing and that she would be of better service to the party by helping to establish it throughout the country. Having consulted Tony King and friendly journalists, she had decided that Warrington was a constituency too far and that another defeat post-Stevenage would be a serious blow to her credibility. Not even a late-night call from Mike Thomas begging her to reconsider – academic research on polling, he reminded her, didn't allow for the constant changing momentum of politics, and the Alliance had momentum – could make any difference. The result was some of the most unflattering headlines that ever came her way.

'There must be many people,' wrote Robin Oakley in the *Daily Mail*, 'who have worshipped her as the madonna of moderation, who, perhaps, recognise for the first time that the one quality she does not possess is the vital one of political courage.' Referring to Jenkins's experimental airborne plane, and the need for the people behind it to believe in its capacity to soar, he continued: 'It is at precisely this moment that Mrs Williams, everybody's choice for the test pilot's job, has stepped down from the cockpit at the end of the runway, and said: "Let someone else do it. I'm needed back in the laboratory."'

Speculating on whether Shirley's withdrawal had dealt the Social

Democrats a blow from which they would never recover, he went on to place her decision in context.

> Is it not the whole pattern of her career? Mrs Williams's qualities are not a myth. She really is one of the warmest, nicest people in politics, ever open to reason … She has a first-rate brain and a burning sense of justice. But the great drawback is her fatal indecisiveness … The flaw, some say, is that she likes being liked and making decisions makes enemies.

Oakley accepted that standing at Warrington would have been a gamble, but 'to win in politics is to gamble'. That, surely, was what distinguished the new politics from the old. 'The trouble for the Social Democratic airplane is that Shirley Williams's good common sense and instinctive caution makes her keep two feet firmly on the ground. That way you don't crash … but you don't fly either.'[2]

'It was the worst decision Shirley has ever made in politics, and certainly the most damaging single decision for the future of the new SDP,' Owen wrote in his memoirs. 'It effectively put paid to Shirley's chances of becoming Leader of the SDP and ensured that Roy would be its first Leader. I have no doubt that Shirley could have won Warrington, with dramatic consequences for the SDP and the country.'[3] Even allowing for Owen's own agenda, there is no doubt, as Shirley later admitted, that she was badly damaged by her failure to run. ('I did not dither. I quailed.')[4] Mutterings began to surface about her indecision and lack of resolution, assisted, she believed, by members of Jenkins's entourage. 'One wag made an anagram of my name: "I whirl aimlessly". I had to agree that it was both wounding and clever.'[5]

Once Shirley had opted out of Warrington, Jenkins felt obliged to put himself forward, which at first glance wasn't conducive to his patrician style. However, once into his stride, he settled into a spirited campaign which belied his reputation for aloofness and caught the imagination of the locals. Helped by an influx of supporters, which included many Liberals, and by several mass meetings addressed by the Gang of Four and Steel, morale began to grow, and although no one expected him to win, Jenkins's narrow defeat by less than 2,000 won him the most appreciative of reviews. Apart from being a humiliating setback for Labour, it gave credence to the new party, strengthened its bonds with the Liberals and enhanced his chances of becoming the SDP's first leader.

With the Alliance riding high in the polls, the opportunity beckoned for the SDP to win the Conservative marginal of Croydon North West, which had fallen vacant in late June following the death of its MP, Robert Taylor. Both the SDP high command and Steel wanted Shirley to fight it, and she was happy enough to oblige. For not only was Croydon close to her London home, its small majority was ripe for the plucking. Yet as she confirmed her intentions at a lunch at the Press Club in London she hadn't reckoned with the determination of the Liberal candidate, Bill Pitt, a local government officer, to remain entrenched, despite three failed attempts and a lost deposit in 1979. Unhappy about Shirley eyeing Croydon without any prior consultation with him or his association, he resisted all blandishments, including a private appeal from Steel, to step aside in favour of her. His position was strengthened by an informal agreement between the two parties that, in return for Jenkins fighting Warrington, the Liberals would have prior claim at the next by-election, and once it became clear that Pitt wasn't for turning the SDP quietly fell in with his wishes. In retrospect, Owen felt their compliance was a massive mistake. They should have faced the Croydon Liberals down even if that meant jeopardising the Alliance.

Such shenanigans were soon forgotten at the Liberal Party assembly at Llandudno in September. There was some concern that the renowned independence of the party's activists might reassert itself against their leader's realignment strategy, and so on the night before the crucial debate, Steel cunningly organised a 'fringe' meeting, to which Shirley and Jenkins were invited to speak, hoping that the enthusiasm engendered would help sway the delegates. In the event, his hopes were more than fulfilled, as in a series of rousing speeches the elated audience were allured with enticing visions of the future. Breaking the rigid mould of British party politics was within their grasp, Shirley told them, if the two parties made the alliance work, although that would require mutual forbearance and trust, a reference to the ongoing delicate negotiations over the allocation of seats. Her words proved a real tonic. The delegates took her and Jenkins to their hearts and the vote endorsing the electoral pact the next day was little more than a formality. Another important staging-post on the journey towards closer Liberal–SDP union had been reached – much to the displeasure of Owen, the one member of the Gang of Four not present at Llandudno.

As discussions about the leadership of the SDP began to gather pace, the party, with its flair for novelty, refrained from visiting Blackpool or Brighton for its conference. Instead it established a rolling conference, beginning in Perth before heading in their special train to London via Bradford. In the days leading up to Perth there came news of the death of Sir Graham Page, the long-serving Conservative MP for Crosby. With a majority of over 19,000, this wasn't the ideal territory for a major Alliance assault, so Shirley could be forgiven for having mixed views about standing.

Stung by the accusations of dithering over Warrington and determined that such charges wouldn't be levelled at her yet again, she indicated her willingness to run following an informal approach from the SDP constituency association there. Over a meal with her co-leaders and Steel in Perth, there was unanimous support for her candidacy, even though Liberal sentiment in Crosby would have to be appeased. It so happened that the day before Sir Graham's death, the Liberal Association had selected its chairman, Anthony Hill, as its candidate. A pillar of the local community and a respected local councillor, he had fought the seat to good effect in 1979, winning some 9,000 votes, and was now relishing the opportunity to have another crack in much more favourable circumstances. Soon he was fielding calls from all and sundry asking him about his intentions once Shirley had launched her kite into the Crosby sky. In initial discussions with Steel he indicated a willingness to stand aside for either Shirley or Jenkins provided they were genuinely interested in fighting the seat and that his local party was in agreement. The negotiations were proceeding amicably enough until Steel was upstaged by Owen and Rodgers at Bradford. Anxious that Shirley might have second thoughts in response to Liberal rumblings, they pressed her to declare her hand despite her announcement on *Panorama* the previous evening that she would say nothing further about her intentions until the end of that week. Rodgers recalled,

> Although David Owen and I tried to persuade her to fight, she began her keynote speech to our Bradford conference with no more than a weary half-promise that she would do so and, as the speech progressed, it looked dangerously as if she would not. I was sitting next to her on the platform and, appalled that the moment might pass, I printed in block letters on a scrap of paper: Say, 'so I am willing to fight Crosby', and propped it against a glass of water in her line of vision.[6]

When she eventually succumbed her words generated ecstatic applause but also considerable consternation to many a Liberal, not least Steel as he battled to avoid another Croydon, a seat which the Alliance was about to win with another massive swing, but fortunately for him Hill was no Bill Pitt. Following discussions that evening with David Alton, the Liberal MP for Liverpool Edge Hill, Hill travelled to Bradford the next day for a brief meeting with Shirley during which he presented her with a letter inviting her to stand in Crosby. It was a gesture as gracious as it was courageous, since he had to withstand a number of barbs from his own executive for acting unilaterally. That weekend Shirley also felt the chill winds blowing up the Mersey as Crosby Liberals accused her of being a carpetbagger. It needed all of her charisma at a special meeting to quell the tempest and turn their gaze to the sunnier climes ahead. With the Area Party of the SDP intent on nominating her, and local opinion fast warming to the idea of her candidacy, the tide had turned in her favour. On 18 October she gained the overwhelming endorsement of the Crosby Liberal Association, leaving the resignation of its local treasurer as the only casualty, the prelude to her formal adoption the following evening when Hill appeared on the platform with her. From then on throughout the campaign he rarely left her side and his support not only provided her with useful local intelligence but also helped win over other Liberals to her cause, most notably their formidable Liverpool machine.

The Crosby constituency, sandwiched between the northern fringes of Liverpool and the affluent resort of Southport to the north, consisted of three main towns, Crosby, Maghull and Formby, separated by flat fertile farmland and small outlying villages. With its 83,000 electorate it was the second largest constituency in the country, and its grand opulent mansions, links golf courses and fee-paying schools made it classic Tory territory. A Conservative seat ever since its inception in 1918 (then known as Waterloo), its share of the vote had only once ever fallen below 50 per cent, and in 1979 its majority was one of the largest in the country. With the working-class vote confined to the housing estates of Seaforth and Waterloo close to the Bootle docks, there were few obvious areas of support for John Backhouse, the amiable, far-left Labour candidate to tap. With his party still in the throes of division and despair following Benn's acrimonious challenge to Healey for the deputy leadership, there was no chance of him winning. The real question was whether Shirley could win over enough Labour defectors and make substantial enough inroads into the solid Tory vote to emerge victorious.

The great unpopularity of the Thatcher government as high interest rates, rocketing unemployment and inner-city turbulence, not least in neighbouring Toxteth, began to bite deep was all grist to her mill. She was also helped by the low esteem for the Conservative-controlled Sefton council with its penny-pinching ethos, and the unhappy choice of her main opponent, John Butcher, a Cheshire accountant unfamiliar with the local terrain and unwilling to trim his Thatcherite sails to the prevailing economic breezes. His insistence on reading a prepared statement at his daily press conference and stalling on many of the questions won him few friends from the hardened Westminster press corps, and in no time he became an inviting target as they harried him mercilessly.

Shirley, in contrast, was riding a tide of goodwill, with the Alliance then at the peak of its popularity as support reached an incredible 50 per cent. Before the campaign began in earnest, Alec McGivan, her agent, travelled with her back to London by train and recalls the surge of people who greeted her as they made their way through to the refreshment carriage, so much so that they never did get their drink.

Having sounded the trumpet she threw herself into the campaign with gusto, bolstered by many volunteers, SDP and Liberal alike, who descended on Crosby to do battle on her behalf. Keen to capitalise on her personal popularity, Shirley opted for a high-profile campaign which brought her into contact with vast swathes of the electorate. Perched on the back of an open truck in her trademark khaki trench coat to cope with the incessant rain, and accompanied by Bill Rodgers and his megaphone and their *Chariots of Fire* theme tune, they repeatedly criss-crossed the constituency, conversing with groups as they appeared. On her walkabouts in the streets and shopping malls it was exactly the same, as locals strained to shake her hand or exchange brief pleasantries. Her twelve evening rallies were full to capacity, beginning with the opening night, when 500 had to be turned away, and when numbers exceeded capacity at the Hightown Hotel two meetings were carried out in simultaneous rooms, with Shirley dashing from one room to the other.

Alongside the glamour there was a lot of hard graft since Shirley, ever the consummate politician, went in search of every vote as people engaged with the issues in a way she had previously never known. Dru Haydon, the SDP secretary in Formby, canvassed with her on many an evening in the town and recalls the looks of astonishment on people's faces as they opened their doors to see her standing there. Only Shirley Williams could win votes in rock-solid Tory Formby, because of her ability to relate to them, she opined. 'The charm of Mrs Shirley Williams is famous,' observed Charles Moore in the *Daily Telegraph*. 'The friendly woman stumping the respectable streets of Crosby, grinning and cocking her head on one side, and listening to everybody else's point of view, is widely believed to be that rare thing, the human being in politics.'[7] Such warmth embraced all types. Owen admired the brilliant way she attracted Labour voters on the council estates in Bootle, while David Alton, one of her leading campaigners, thought she was a stunningly good candidate, not least the way she won over many Liberals by her common touch.

Yet for all the goodwill, Shirley had to navigate the treacherous shoals of education and abortion. In a constituency where 11 per cent of the children went to fee-paying schools and where the prestigious Merchant Taylors' School and St Mary's College, a Roman Catholic foundation, had recently lost their direct grant status, her hostility to private education troubled many. Independent Schools Information Service, a pressure group representing the private sector in education, leafleted every home in the constituency, reminding voters of her desire to abolish such schools, and when the press latched on to the issue she was reluctant to discuss it, dismissing it as a 'blue herring'. Eventually, under constant pressure, she relented. She admitted that the SDP's adherence to the European Convention of Human Rights, with its commitment to parental choice, placed her in something of a quandary. Good as many independent schools were, she declared, they were also a cause of persistent social division. She accepted that they couldn't be abolished by law, but she wanted to drive them out of existence by making the maintained sector so good that parents would no longer feel the need to go private. Her views caused some embarrassment at a press conference with Jo Grimond when those present savoured the opportunity of drawing a wedge between them. 'I suppose I do find it rather hard to believe, as an OE, that Eton was a charity,' he conceded, but his claim that Shirley and he agreed on the aims of education lacked conviction, especially as he had just publicly lauded the virtues of private education. 'Independent schools, you know, are able to experiment; they set a certain standard,' he explained, much to her silent embarrassment.[8]

Well aware that education was damaging her attempts to win over a number of wavering Tories, Shirley opted to take her case into enemy territory and managed to secure an invitation to speak at Merchant Taylors' (Boys). Even this sparked controversy. The president of the old boys' association objected to an 'abolitionist' visiting the school, and at an extraordinary meeting of the governing body, the decision to allow Shirley to address the sixth form was only narrowly approved. When she did, she wisely kept off education and talked about the values behind the formation of the SDP. Her audience was impressed and she in turn warmed to it. They were very bright pupils, she said – adding hurriedly, just as they were at the Sacred Heart Comprehensive down the road.

At a special seminar on education at Sacred Heart, in front of an invited audience of teachers, school governors and parents, Shirley once again promised that the SDP wouldn't ban private schools. They would, however, try and promote closer integration by abolishing the government's assisted places scheme and ply the state sector with extra resources, something the Conservatives had singularly failed to do.

Abortion also courted controversy. Although a Roman Catholic herself who had opposed the Abortion Act of 1967, Shirley's refusal to give the Society for the Protection of the Unborn Child, a Roman Catholic pressure group, the uncritical support it demanded over amendments to that Act greatly upset it. It mounted a furious campaign against her, but its militant tactics backfired, for no sooner had news reached the Bishop of Liverpool, Derek Worlock, than he rang David Alton, a fellow Catholic and good friend, to establish the full facts. Having received a thorough briefing from Alton and being assured of Shirley's pro-life convictions, the bishop wrote to all the churches in his diocese instructing them to desist from supporting a particular candidate in the by-election.

With the rest of the Gang of Four and David Steel on hand to help emulate the revivalist atmosphere of Warrington, the campaign continued to gather momentum. 'Whether canvassing, speaking at meetings or facing up to her morning press conferences,

Shirley Williams gives the impression of one sure she is going to win,' wrote Diana Pulson in the *Liverpool Echo*. 'She's tough and swift in answer, slams anyone who starts to be critical, and all in all behaves like the seasoned campaigner she is.'[9] *The Times*, in a thoughtful eve-of-poll editorial, advised its readers that the voters of Crosby didn't have to decide whether Shirley would make a good Prime Minister or leader of her party; rather, whether she had more to contribute to Crosby compared to the other candidates.

> The distinction is particularly important ... Mrs Williams's capacities are considerable but uneven. Few politicians today are her equal at charming an audience, whether at a public meeting, on television or in person on the doorstep. She has a remarkable eloquence that depends partly on her facility with words and partly on her ability to convey both earnestness and strength of feeling. She is not humorous or witty, but she does seem to understand the anxieties and aspirations of most of those to whom she speaks. She is thoughtful without being decisive.
>
> These are not qualities that would be likely to make her an effective party leader. Her judgement is not so good as her intentions. She lacks the necessary power of decision and would tend to shrink from the unpopular acts that are required of someone who is to lead any party with success, especially a party that is embarked on such a daring enterprise as the Social Democrats.
>
> ... But Mrs Williams nonetheless has a great deal to contribute to the party and to Parliament. It is hard to think of any other politician today who can inspire the warmth and trust that she does. Her party will be the stronger and political life in this country will be healthier if she is once again in the House of Commons – good enough reasons for the voters of Crosby to send her there tomorrow.[10]

Come polling day, informed opinion was predicting a comfortable SDP victory, but the actual result exceeded expectation. On a 69.8 per cent turn-out Shirley overturned a Tory majority of 19,272 into a SDP one of 5,289 on a swing of 25 per cent, 2 per cent less than the 27.6 per cent swing recorded at Warrington. While the Tory vote had held up relatively well, Labour's collapsed completely, with 70 per cent of it going to the SDP, enough to consign its candidate to political oblivion as he lost his deposit. In her victory speech Shirley depicted the election of the SDP as the beginning of a great movement that would culminate in an Alliance victory at the next election. Then, after greeting the cheering crowds outside and leading an emotional rendition of 'We Shall Overcome' at her 600-strong campaign party, it was on to the Blundellsands Hotel for a 4 a.m. champagne breakfast and a kiss from the head waiter. The next morning she toured her new domain to convey her thanks as horns blew and people hung from bedroom windows blowing kisses. Some were in tears. It was as if people felt liberated, recalled Anthony Hill.

The following Tuesday Shirley returned to Westminster as the SDP's first elected MP and amidst the general climate of goodwill even a number of Labour MPs appeared pleased to see her back, led by Jim Callaghan, who took her to one side to congratulate her. 'Mrs Williams arrived at the Bar of the House,' commented *The Times*'s columnist Frank Johnson. 'She was looking very smart. This meant that she had sacked Oxfam as her couturier.'[11]

The heady period post-Crosby saw the Alliance at its apogee as it continued to bask in its stupendous poll ratings and dreams of major gains at the next election. *The Economist* even led with a photo on its cover of Shirley, Jenkins and Steel captioned: 'Her Majesty's Opposition'.

Yet amidst the sunshine dark clouds were gathering as the negotiations between the SDP and Liberals over the allocation of seats at the next election had reached a particularly fraught stage. The latter, with their proud traditions of grassroots campaigning, resented the assumption that their local organisations should be placed in the hands of political novices. Only they could win certain seats, they argued. Their intransigence so exasperated Bill Rodgers, the SDP's chief negotiator, that he contrived a showdown in early

January by very publicly suspending talks. After some heated words on both sides the bargaining soon resumed and a deal that provided for parity of representation accrued. It was a formidable achievement, but by then the damage had already been done, since the public tiff had not only sullied the new politics of consensus, it had also raised echoes of the old politics it had vowed to replace.

It was against this less than promising background that Roy Jenkins had staked his claim for Glasgow Hillhead in a by-election caused by the death of the Conservative MP, Sir Thomas Galbraith. Although the Liberal vote at the previous election there had been a paltry 14 per cent, and Jenkins's Scottish connections were minimal, it was the one constituency in Scotland where a challenge from an outsider might work. And with his leadership ambitions dependent on a quick re-entry to Parliament, this was an opportunity he could hardly afford to reject.

With Steel's help, Jenkins persuaded the Liberal candidate to stand down in his favour and took to Hillhead, the Conservatives' last stronghold in the city, with considerable gusto. Yet for all his affinity with the cultural milieu of Glasgow's West End, he found it an uphill struggle. On 14 March, eleven days before the election, an NOP poll in *The Observer* had him trailing the other two candidates, causing despondency in the camp. That same poll galvanised Shirley. Aside from conducting a series of small early evening meetings on her own in some of the constituency's less salubrious parts, she joined the rest of the Gang of Four for an exceptionally large and vibrant meeting at Hyndland Secondary School. (They took it in turns to address the left-out hundreds in the frosty playground outside.)

The unprecedented activity began to bear fruit and, as the campaign entered its final stages, morale improved. On election night Jenkins won with a majority of some 2,000 over the Conservatives, with Labour a close third. It was a considerable personal triumph for a man who now became the pundits' favourite to lead his party as Steel called on the SDP to bring forward its election contest – originally scheduled for September.

The onset of that contest coincided with the gradual decline of the collectivist ethos of the Gang of Four. Their weekly lunches had become increasingly infrequent as battle lines over ideology, relations with the Liberals and the leadership became more pronounced. When Owen had first discussed with Jenkins the composition of the new party back in November 1980, he thought that he had received an assurance that the leader would be elected under the format of OMOV. He was thus visibly seething when Rodgers, with Jenkins's approval, proposed the following September that the method of election should be solely in the hands of the MPs, especially as this would be playing to Jenkins's core constituency. Shirley, too, was unhappy about the apparent abandonment of OMOV by the Steering Committee, and conveyed her concern to Owen afterwards. Their one consolation lay in an important concession they extracted. In conjunction with its recommendation to the forthcoming constitutional conference of Rodgers's proposals, the Steering Committee agreed that the party membership would be the ultimate arbiters of the type of system used. Presented with three options, the membership, in line with Shirley and Owen's wishes, narrowly opted for OMOV in a ballot, declared in May 1982, and brought forward the election from that November to July.

The ramifications of the new system were considerable. According to Owen, Jenkins and his supporters were intent on avoiding a fight with Shirley. 'They began to woo Shirley with the idea of a dual leadership – Roy as Party Leader, her as President. This two-leader scenario was assiduously run for the next few months and Shirley became progressively more attracted by it.'[12] Yet if that was the case why did Jenkins's entourage continue to undermine her with snide briefings about her disorganised lifestyle? There is no evidence to suggest that any of these briefings emanated from Jenkins himself, but he had irritated her the previous autumn when, grinning broadly, he had attributed her non-appearance at a press conference to her catching the wrong train. (Jenkins, like Owen and Rodgers, was highly efficient.)

She wrote in her autobiography,

David had been scornful of my reluctance to run against Roy for the leadership. He acknowledged, as I did, that my high recognition and popularity among Labour voters were a crucial factor in the appeal of the new Party, more so than Roy's political eminence. What he failed to recognise was my lack of self-confidence. I readily conceded, publicly and privately, that Roy was a greater person than I was. I shared the judgement, on this, of the Jenkinsites. I was also concerned about making enemies, something that troubled David not at all and Roy much less than me. I doubt whether that would have mattered so much to me if I had then the love and support of a spouse like Dick Neustadt, who believed in me more than I believed in myself.[13]

Yet despite her retrospective appreciation of his qualities, especially in comparison to her own, Shirley's reservations about a full-blown Jenkins leadership were genuine enough. For all their shared experiences and the occasions when she had deferred to him, she was in no sense his lackey. She hadn't joined him in resignation from the shadow Cabinet in 1972 over the European referendum and throughout 1980 she failed to march to his drumbeat as he tried to enlist her in his new party. Once reunited, her doubts persisted, believing that his best days were behind him. Rodgers recalls how she and Owen bemused him with their suggestion that Jenkins should be in charge of fundraising rather than taking a more prominent role when the four of them came to share out the responsibilities of their collective leadership, a suggestion that, he, Rodgers, wouldn't countenance. Jenkins, of course, was their potential rival for the leadership, but it did nothing to alter their conviction that his obsolete style, out of kilter with the television age, made him eminently unsuitable to lead a dynamic movement for change.

Even his victory at Hillhead changed nothing. Immediately afterwards, Shirley, with Owen's support, had submitted a proposal to Jenkins that in return for him becoming Prime Minister in the event of the Alliance forming a government, the leader of the party should be one out of Owen, Rodgers and herself. Days later she went public when, in a speech to the Epping Forest SDP, she warned that the party 'must not now slip towards a hierarchy dominated by a single person, however wise or brilliant', which was her way of saying that under Jenkins the SDP would fail to win potential Labour support. The plan found little favour with either Jenkins or Steel, but Shirley continued to wax lyrical about the virtues of collective leadership as she ran into another round of hostile briefings.

While the manoeuvring for the leadership continued in the background, Britain was now at war with Argentina over the Falkland Islands and the stirring victory brought a considerable boost to the Thatcher government. The crisis also elevated Owen, the SDP's foreign affairs spokesman, into a figure of some prominence as his polished media performances managed to combine staunch patriotism with constructive opposition. Now, with added support from the back benches, he was even more adamant that Jenkins's candidacy for the leadership and his plans for closer links with the Liberals should not go unchallenged. He initially hoped that Shirley would be the candidate, figuring that her chances of being elected ranked higher than his own, but despite wooing her throughout mid-May he failed, much to his consternation, to dissuade her from having second thoughts.

With Shirley not for turning, Owen now stepped forward himself, armed with a promise of her support (in return he supported her bid for the party presidency) in the belief that his Kennedy-style aura and dynamic radicalism could reach out to voters beyond Jenkins's grasp. Her apparent volte-face mystified Rodgers, Jenkins's closest ally, who wrote to her in some indignation.

> You agreed that at Aspen in August last year you said to me that Roy would make the best leader and you would not challenge him. You added that you changed your mind in December in view of a campaign on the part of some of Roy's friends that was personally damaging to you. How is the matter relevant to the choice of leader? We need someone to pull the party together,

achieve a working relationship with the Liberals and lead us in Government if we win. Why should anything that may have been said by Roy's friends – however mistaken and hurtful to you – invalidate the qualities that at Aspen led you to support him?

Rodgers accepted that the contest wouldn't necessarily be acrimonious, but it would predominantly focus on the personality of the two men.

Given David's style and mood and his personal antipathy to Roy, his behaviour is at least predictable. I had hoped that you would see matters in a different light.

I appreciate that you may decide not to stand against Roy, although you would be a stronger candidate than David. But, if you nominate David or otherwise support him, it will still be a clear breach of our understanding of last summer.

The Gang of Four has been a remarkable achievement and much good has come out of it. As I told you when we drove to Cambridge, I agree with what you said in your controversial speech about the need for a continuing collective leadership. This is now likely to be much more difficult. For the first time since the party was launched I am profoundly depressed.[14]

In her reply, Shirley assured Rodgers that she had kept her word and wouldn't oppose Jenkins. She both liked and admired him.

But one cannot wholly divorce anyone from their friends and supporters. After all, they are the people who will influence him most...

I'm not wholly certain that he would not be more influenced by them than by the rest of the Four – and that's why I've consistently argued for a collective style of leadership.

Frankly, I believe there is a perfectly legitimate right for any of us to stand as leader, and there isn't an adequate consensus in the party to select a leader without an election. I believe many Party members would believe they had been led up the garden path at the time of the vote on the method of election otherwise.[15]

Shirley's support and that of eleven other MPs, and Owen's impressive campaign weren't enough to bring him victory, but his creditable showing in gaining 20,900 votes to Jenkins's 26,300 raised his stature within the party. This he wasn't slow to exploit as Jenkins's leadership faltered not only in the Commons, which he had once so effortlessly commanded, but also on television, where his answers appeared wooden and ponderous. Predictably his stock began to fall among the public and his backbenchers just as the Alliance's support had faded quite dramatically in the post-Falklands euphoria. What's more, he was, according to Rodgers, struggling to work with Owen, whose black moods began to concern him. The tension between the two men surfaced all too publicly at the SDP's rolling conference at Great Yarmouth, when the leadership suffered a major defeat over a statutory incomes policy, a defeat which infuriated Shirley as much as it did Jenkins. The fact that one of Owen's assistants happened to play a leading part in the opposition only added fuel to the fire. 'The debate is narrowly won by David's faction (after much lobbying behind the scenes),' Shirley recorded in her diary.

On hearing the result, David makes a thumbs-up sign to the TV cameras. I'm furious. On the way to the afternoon session, I tell David that I'm disgusted with him, and if he doesn't make a generous speech about Roy that afternoon when he's due to speak I will publicly denounce him. He goes white and then says 'You're right. I will. I'm sorry.' He does just that, winding up the afternoon with a gracious tribute to Roy.[16]

It wasn't just Jenkins's star which was on the wane. Although Shirley had easily seen off Rodgers for the post of party president, a sign of her immense popularity with party members, there was increasing scepticism among colleagues about her alchemist's touch. According to Rodgers, her re-entry speech in the Commons had been rather superficial and *The Guardian* reported that she had made far less impact at Westminster than might have been expected, partly because she had had little to say about the Falklands. There were also her outspoken comments about the leadership, which had alienated Jenkins's supporters. An *Observer* profile entitled 'Whatever became of Shirley' conveyed the same message. 'The cheers for her, as she presides this week over the second annual roadshow of the Social Democratic Party, will be warm and genuine. Yet within the inner circle of the party her standing is lower now than seemed possible back in the heady days of the SDP's launch.'[17]

Shirley's standing may have dropped within the inner counsels of the SDP, but it remained sky-high on Merseyside. Aside from the time devoted to the local party, she threw herself into the life of Crosby much as she had done in Hitchin.

In addition to reading every letter (on average there were 300 per week) and signing each reply personally, she was assiduous at holding surgeries. As a general rule, she would travel up from London once a fortnight and conduct surgeries in Crosby and Maghull on Fridays and in Formby on Saturday morning. Doreen Service, who became liaison officer for Maghull, arranged for Shirley to see constituents in the informality of her lounge, while she dispensed refreshments for those waiting in her kitchen. 'Don't turn anyone away,' Shirley would instruct her, despite some people coming just to meet her, and, having immediately put them at ease, she would listen intently to their problems, giving them as much time as necessary. Then once back in London, and with the aid of her secretary, she would, as far as possible, turn words into deeds.

In line with her communal ethos, Shirley would carry out as many engagements as possible, particularly visiting schools, colleges and hospitals. En route to an unfamiliar institution, Doreen would brief her on its history and character, offering her notes as an aide de memoir. 'Now I have the background,' she would reply and, utilising her memory to the full, she wove it all seamlessly into her speech, before conversing with all and sundry afterwards.

The only problem with all this frenetic activity was the age-old one of keeping to schedule. Shirley had a touching faith in her drivers getting her to her next destination on time, and more often than not her optimism was well founded, for people would go the extra mile on her behalf. Doreen Service's husband, Civ, was one such person. Normally a great stickler for the rulebook he would even break the speed limit to ensure that she wasn't late.

A willing conduit to all those who nursed grievances, Shirley found that her crusading activity on behalf of her constituents, especially the poorer ones, brought her into conflict with the Conservative-controlled Sefton council. Used to ruling its own fiefdom in the manner it saw fit, it was somewhat affronted by the constant chivvying it now endured from a popular outsider. Its refusal to allow her use of council premises to conduct her constituency surgeries on the grounds that large public buildings shouldn't be specifically open to minor political parties prompted a dramatic response. With three Alliance councillors, Shirley staged a protest on the steps of Bootle Town Hall by holding an open advice centre for local ratepayers. The media were there to record the event and the council soon relented.

Publicity aside, there were serious clashes over policy, with Shirley berating the council for its neglect over the deplorable state of much of the public housing in Crosby and Seaforth – attacks that did bring about some improvement but won her few friends with the local Tory Establishment. A series of unpleasant personal attacks surfaced in the local press denouncing her record over Grunwick, private education and capital punishment as her opponents eyed the coming election with steely determination.

In August 1982 Shirley gave serious thought to a proposal from Peter Metcalfe and the officers of the Stevenage SDP that she become their candidate at the next election. With a good organisation, a home close by, plenty of friends in the vicinity and an excellent chance of being elected in light of the party's success at the local elections, the idea was an alluring one. Crosby she genuinely cared for, but the electoral mountain she faced in holding it had become that bit steeper given the pending boundary changes that would play to her disadvantage. Yet after consulting Jenkins, Owen, Tony King and John Spencer, she reluctantly concluded that deserting Crosby for Stevenage would send out the wrong message for the new politics she claimed to represent. 'The party would be accused, however unfairly, of carpet-bagging,' she informed Metcalfe. 'Other SDP MPs might excuse leaving their own constituencies because I had; and the essential belief that some of us put principle ahead of political advancement would be destroyed. I'm so sorry – but I'm clear that I must stay and fight Crosby, however hopeless.'[18]

With the solid Conservative lead extending into 1983, and with Labour registering a modest recovery, the Alliance began the New Year in a rut. It took a stunning by-election triumph at Bermondsey in south-east London for the Liberals' Simon Hughes, the result of local Labour divisions and its unpopular candidate, Peter Tatchell, to revive spirits. Seeing her own chances of re-election come to life again post-Bermondsey, Shirley was in buoyant mood at the Scottish SDP conference at St Andrews. She told the cheering throngs that many other 'crumbling and derelict bastions of the Conservative and Labour citadels' were vulnerable to an Alliance assault, but a poor third by the Alliance at Darlington placed them back on the ropes. Following spectacular gains for her party in the local elections in May, Margaret Thatcher went to the country a year early, her re-election never seriously in doubt. The interest centred on whether the Alliance could win enough seats to give it a real presence in the next Parliament and establish a firm enough bridgehead to eventually overtake the Labour Party, tethered to the most extreme manifesto in its history.

The initial runes were unfavourable. Alliance poll ratings remained well below 20 per cent and despite some well-attended rallies there was little momentum over the first couple of weeks of the campaign. The one glimmer of hope seemed to lie with the assured performances of Steel, especially on television. Were he rather than Jenkins to lead the Alliance campaign the prospects seemed much brighter, but his hand had been tied by the conundrum of its dual leadership. In order to get around this concept, Steel, back in March 1982, had privately agreed with Jenkins that they should fight the election as joint leaders, with Steel in charge of the campaign and Jenkins the Prime Minister designate. When the agreement became public in April 1983 the emphasis of the media was naturally upon Jenkins, but as his ponderous public appearances became an increasing liability, pressure grew from within Liberal ranks for a change in leader, especially given their man's greater popularity and aptitude on television. Twice during those first two weeks Steel raised the matter with Jenkins, who, understandably, was reluctant to consider such a drastic change of direction in mid-stream.

With the Alliance ratings remaining flat, the plotting continued behind the scenes as its leaders headed for Steel's home in the Scottish borders on Sunday 29 May for a prearranged summit. On the way up, John Pardoe, the former Liberal MP for North Cornwall, informed Owen that he was planning to raise the question of the leadership. Owen, although no admirer of Jenkins, demurred, believing that the recent discussion between the two leaders had laid the matter to rest.

With bad weather causing havoc to the travel arrangements, the meeting started late in ill humour as the leading figures in both parties, crouched around Steel's kitchen, began their deliberations in earnest. After some initial random remarks about the precise state of the Alliance's health given the conflicting message from the polls and the more buoyant mood on the ground, Pardoe duly raised the leadership. His tirade against Jenkins and his alleged deficiencies was the signal for Steel to weigh in with a draft statement which, he suggested, should form the basis of a press release afterwards. The gist of it was that, owing to a mutual recognition of their lacklustre campaign hitherto, Steel would replace Jenkins as leader of the Alliance and spearhead the rest of it.

As Jenkins recoiled from the shock of this attempted political assassination, and while Owen unusually kept his own counsel, Rodgers and Shirley sprang to his defence. Rodgers began by objecting to the underhand manner in which the matter had been raised, before going on to decry the sheer idiocy of a plan which, apart from dividing the Alliance, would merely bring succour to their opponents. Shirley was equally vehement, claiming that it would do immense harm and invite ridicule from the media ten days before the election. She did, however, suggest that Steel might reasonably be given a higher profile on television.

Her proposal attracted some favourable response, but Pardoe wasn't to be fobbed off with this compromise. He again went straight for Jenkins's jugular and with Steel also returning to the fray as he relayed the reservations of many of his activists, the Liberals seemed determined to have their pound of flesh.

As the atmosphere became increasingly fraught and Jenkins's resilience began to weaken, Shirley stared at him intently until he looked back at her. She then mouthed silently, 'No.' He said nothing. She meanwhile stressed that she would desist from further campaigning if Jenkins were forced out. She conceded that he was less effective on television than Steel and that Steel should do rather more of it for the rest of the campaign, but no more than this. When Jenkins eventually did speak he calmly reiterated his belief that a change now would be to the detriment of all and with Steel finally sensing that the game was up, the meeting broke for lunch. An alternative press release was cobbled together which indicated a greater prominence for Steel in the campaign, before both Alliance leaders faced the media in the village hall, where, miraculously, news of the bloodletting had failed to seep out.

After lunch Rodgers drove Shirley and Owen to Berwick-upon-Tweed, where they caught the train to London, a journey Owen recalled with bittersweet memories.

> Bill, I think, knew he was going to lose, Shirley was very worried and I was far from certain that I was going to win. But there were no recriminations as we re-lived the last three years from the moment in June 1980 when we had first got together as the Gang of Three. I look back on this now as the last truly happy time that we all had together.[19]

Back in November 1982, in front of 250 enthusiastic party supporters at Liverpool's Adelphi Hotel to celebrate the first anniversary
of her by-election triumph, Shirley insisted that it was perfectly
possible for the Alliance to form a government at the next election.
Yet, whatever the state of the parties nationally, the task of retaining
Crosby was always fraught with difficulty, especially given changing local circumstances. One hurdle to overcome was the boundary
changes that removed the overwhelmingly Labour–SDP voters
in Seaforth's Church ward into the Bootle constituency, while
including in Crosby the Tory-voting Aintree-Melling ward from
Southport. The ruling left Shirley feeling aggrieved because she
believed she had fallen victim to a joint submission by the other two
parties. Yet whatever fickle hand fate had dealt her she continued
to play fair by instructing her activists to refrain from canvassing her new ward until such time as it officially became part of
her constituency.

Another hurdle lay in the selection of Malcolm Thornton, a
former river pilot on the Mersey, a Wallasey councillor and MP
for Liverpool Garston, a seat that was to disappear under boundary
changes, as the new Conservative candidate for Crosby. He had
spent much time in the constituency during the 1981 campaign and
learnt much from that debacle. An able and experienced politician, he was bound to offer a stiffer challenge than the unfortunate
John Butcher as he built on substantial Tory gains in the recent
local elections.

Most telling of all was the handicap of fighting a general election against a revitalised Conservative Party. For all the fillip of
her personal popularity, and the help of celebrities such as the film
director Richard Attenborough, who spoke at a packed meeting in
Maghull, it was hard for Shirley to recreate the mood of euphoria
of the by-election, especially when deprived of her army of outside
supporters. When Steel came to Crosby to lend his support they
found the streets embarrassingly deserted, not helped by it being
Bank Holiday Monday, and the opening of a local supermarket
never took place owing to a misunderstanding with Sainsbury's,

who had it earmarked for the following day. ('I suppose it is just Shirley,' shrugged Steel.)[20]

During the campaign she was subjected to some snide letters in the *Crosby Herald*, not least about her views on education, and a vitriolic editorial in *The Sun* which, even by the standards of political knockabout, was deeply offensive. Entitled 'The two faces of Sister Shirl', it accused her of a failure to speak out against extremism when in government and of fomenting industrial strife on the picket line at Grunwick, allegations which her solicitors successfully contested through their complaint to the Press Council.

As she entered the last few days, Shirley conceded it was neck and neck in Crosby, but even a late surge in the national polls for the Alliance, mainly at the expense of Labour as its campaign stumbled from one crisis to another, wasn't enough to save her. 'Now I don't want you to be disappointed. The boundary changes have beaten us and the cameras mustn't catch us with long faces. We must lose in style,' Shirley told Doreen Service before the count. Although her vote had held up well, Conservatives who had stayed at home during the by-election returned to the fold, giving the Tories a majority of 3,405. In her concession speech she said that, by any standards, the result was a moral victory. She thanked Thornton for a decorous campaign and wished him well. 'I consign to him, at least temporarily, the lovely and well-humoured people of Crosby and ask him to look after them as I am sure he will endeavour to do.'[21]

After the formalities, and a word of consolation from the presiding officer, Shirley was driven home by the Services, giving the media the slip as they pursued her. Next morning, as she caught up with some sleep, Doreen discovered them congregated outside her home and fended them off until such time as Shirley was ready to face them. She then fulfilled a long-standing engagement at Maghull High School, which she discharged with her customary grace, before taking leave of a constituency she had served all too briefly. Letters poured in to the local paper lamenting her loss. One talked about the unprecedented sense of community she had brought to

Merseyside, another said they would never see her like again, and the passing of the years has in no sense diminished the affection accorded her whenever she returns to Crosby. Anthony Hill recalls Shirley appearing at a press conference several years later during the local elections, when a worker in dirty overalls strode up to her, put his arm around her and exclaimed, 'Shirley, what have we done? Why did we let you go?'

Overall, the election had produced the much-trumpeted Conservative landslide, but although the Alliance had performed creditably, getting to within a couple of points of Labour, it was ill served by the vagaries of the electoral system. Not only had its 26 per cent earned it a derisory twenty-three seats compared to Labour's 209 on 28 per cent, but SDP MPs had fared particularly badly. Aside from Shirley, Rodgers had lost in Stockton and only six of them, including Owen and Jenkins, had been elected.

As its leaders mulled over their disappointment, the pressure for Jenkins to quit became ever greater, not least from Owen, who feared for the continuing independence of the SDP should Jenkins remain as leader. In a brutally frank exchange on the phone he told Jenkins that unless he went quickly, he, Owen, was ready to force the issue. On the Monday after polling day, Jenkins convened a gathering of his main advisers at East Hendred and announced his decision to resign. The news shocked Shirley and Jack Diamond, the SDP leader in the Lords, who had coordinated the campaign. Unaware of Owen's earlier threat they implored him to think again, or at least to leave it to the summer recess so as to erase the impression that his departure was linked to a poor election result, which, Shirley argued, was not the case, but Jenkins was adamant. As the news was made public later that evening, she discovered the real reason behind his sudden departure. 'So David will get the leadership,' she wrote in her diary, 'because none of the six SDP MPs will oppose him or nominate anyone else. It's a small kingdom, but David is head of it now.'[22] With Jenkins something of a diminished figure and Shirley and Rodgers out of Parliament, the era of the Gang of Four was well and truly over.

## Endnotes

1  *Guardian*, 23 September 1965
2  *Daily Mail*, 5 June 1981
3  David Owen, *Time to Declare*, p.520
4  *Climbing the Bookshelves*, p.289
5  *Climbing the Bookshelves*, p.299
6  Bill Rodgers, *Fourth Among Equals*, p.217
7  *Daily Telegraph*, 24 November 1981
8  *Daily Telegraph*, 20 November 1981
9  *Liverpool Echo*, 24 November 1981
10 *The Times*, 25 November 1981
11 *The Times*, 2 December 1981
12 David Owen, *Time to Declare*, p.544
13 *Climbing the Bookshelves*, p.300
14 Bill Rodgers to SW, 13 May 1982, Bill Rodgers Papers
15 SW to Bill Rodgers, 22 May 1982, Bill Rodgers Papers
16 SW diary, 17 October 1982, SW Papers (private collection)
17 *Observer*, 10 October 1982
18 SW to Peter Metcalfe, 13 September 1982, Peter Metcalfe Papers (private collection)
19 David Owen, *Time to Declare*, p.582
20 *Daily Telegraph*, 23 May 1983
21 *Crosby Herald*, 10 June 1983
22 SW diary, 13 June 1983, SW Papers (private collection)

# 15

# THE WILDERNESS YEARS

On 21 June 1983 David Owen was unanimously elected leader of the SDP, and so began a turbulent four years with him in charge. Throughout his career he had aroused strong reactions from supporters and detractors alike. One thing that few disputed was his immense ability. Appointed Foreign Secretary at the age of thirty-eight, he appeared to have the political world at his feet until Labour's internal feuds threatened to condemn him and his colleagues to years in opposition. Determined to fight for his brand of social democracy, he was nothing if not robust in squaring up to the far left, and once he had given up on the Labour Party, he became the galvanising force behind the SDP. Content to participate in a collective leadership at first, his acclaimed performances during the Falklands War boosted his credentials and gave him the confidence to challenge Jenkins for the leadership. Jenkins won, but the failure of the ageing maestro to perform as of old enabled his ambitious understudy to push him aside.

In many ways Owen, with his youth, glamour, energy and ambition, was ideally suited to lead this new party, as he was at one with many of its members. Politically active for the first time, they were first-generation students made good who wanted a Britain that was open, innovative and meritocratic, combined with a strong social conscience, and in Owen they found their champion. A naturally domineering figure, he was determined to halt the element of drift and inject a more dynamic edge to the party commensurate with the 'can do' ethos of its members. With phenomenal energy and no little skill belying his status as the leader of a minority party of six MPs, he thrust himself into the limelight and attained real stature with the quality of his pronouncements on a whole range of issues. His success in eclipsing both Neil Kinnock, the new leader of the Labour Party, and Steel, who took a three-month sabbatical after the election to recover from exhaustion, helped consolidate his hold over the party as he remoulded it in his own image. When Jenkins visited Salford for their first post-election conference he detected a changing of the guard as the National Committee became more rigid and fractious in its approach compared to the upbeat mood of 1981. Little was to change thereafter as the shadow of their relationship with the Liberals continued to hang over them.

Totally devoted to the SDP, Owen was determined to fend off the many attempts within the Liberal Party for closer cooperation at best and merger at worst. Although he recognised the progress that it had made under Steel, he still viewed it as essentially a party of protest. If it were to make the great transition to being a party of government it would need to follow in the SDP's footsteps. Presented with an opportunity to relaunch his party, he moved it to the right, taking as his model the Democratic Party in the US, accepting the Thatcherite emphasis on competition and deregulation in the modern economy. (He would have been more radical than the Conservative government in breaking up private monopolies.) He also gave a high priority to protecting the nation's defences, alongside his continuing commitment to the politics of redistribution and constitutional reform, the latter sentiments often overshadowed by his conversion to the social market economy.

Owen's detachment from the Liberals helped undermine his own relations with the rest of the Gang of Four, all of whom were better disposed towards their Alliance partners. This was partly down to their similar philosophical outlook and partly to personal chemistry on the campaign trail. Owen, in contrast, was more removed. His main interaction with the Liberals was with its parliamentary party, a party whose MPs had only survived by placing their constituency interests above anything else – hardly a model of discipline and unity which would appeal to his regimented instincts.

When he met Steel for the first time after his election as leader

Owen emphasised his total opposition to merger (while agreeing not to rule it out indefinitely), and the need to return to the original concept of the Alliance, with each party complementing the other's appeal. His views weren't shared by all his members. A substantial minority who had worked closely with the Liberals during the election advocated much closer relations with them through joint selection of local, parliamentary and European candidates, and Jenkins, in a speech to an SDP conference, refused to rule out merger indefinitely.

Such talk raised Owen's hackles amidst mounting tension before the party's conference at Salford. In her pre-conference presidential report, Shirley tried to reconcile the two sides by urging them to spend less time looking inwards and more time establishing themselves as the only alternative to the Conservatives. That meant avoiding a headlong rush towards merger, while continuing to forge bonds with the Liberals. 'It is therefore our responsibility to work out a satisfactory way of bringing the two parties closer together, and of involving members of both in joint social and political activities without destroying our separate identities and our distinctive appeal.'[1]

She enlarged on this theme when she opened the party conference with a fighting speech in which she gave notice of the Alliance's potential. It had won more votes than any third party since 1923. The political structure was shifting and rocking 'as if an earthquake were grumbling beneath its foundations'. No one believed that the 'so-called dream ticket' of Neil Kinnock and Roy Hattersley, its new leader and deputy, would rescue Labour from its own self-inflicted wounds.

With his inbuilt support on the National Committee, Owen had his way over joint selection and merger, but the debate left a festering resentment within the party and caused friction with the Liberals, who felt the cooler breezes blowing in from Salford. In order to mend fences Shirley paid a flying visit to the Liberal assembly to tell delegates that a split over the selection of candidates was not a catastrophe. She conceded that her party's opposition to joint selection wasn't simply confined to the leadership – it was the view of the majority of the membership – but stressed that the Alliance wasn't primarily about constitutional haggling. It was essentially about friendship and matching the expectations they had aroused. She won cheers when she asked delegates not to underrate the extraordinary achievement of their joint efforts throughout the campaign.

Joint selection, despite Owen's antipathy to it, wouldn't go away, since it was favoured by almost all Liberals and quite a few Social Democrats. What's more, the former, relishing their additional bargaining power by virtue of having nearly three times as many seats at Westminster than the latter, began to reclaim a number that the SDP had fought in 1983. Amidst growing acrimony between the two parties over seat distribution, Rodgers told Owen that he should place greater confidence in Shirley's team of negotiators and stop being so obsessed with the Liberals. He also told him to be more collegiate in his approach, tolerant of opposing views and avoid Alliance divisions. After several hard months of bargaining between the two sides, agreement was reached in January 1984. It allowed for more local decision making than hitherto, but decreed that joint selection should only take place in exceptional circumstances. Herein lay a problem, since the phrase was loose enough to be open to conflicting interpretations. Confronted with a rash of proposals for joint selection from SDP local parties during the course of the following year, they consumed much time and caused acrimony at the National Committee. Fearing that joint selection was the Trojan horse for the gradual absorption of the SDP by the Liberals, Owen and his supporters resisted them, not always with success. Only after a general settlement masterminded by Rodgers in July 1985, which conceded twenty cases of joint selection in return for rough parity of all seats (and winnable ones) for the next election, did the storm begin to subside.

As this row was rumbling on, Steel wrote to Owen and Shirley in April 1984 to express his concern about the diffident relationship between the two parties. Merger he was quite prepared to rule out for that parliament, but he definitely wanted closer cooperation, a sentiment Shirley shared. She told Steel she felt the Alliance's image had become blurred in the public mind. She felt it imperative that it should distance itself from the government and emphasise the plight of the disadvantaged to attract moderate Conservatives and floating voters. 'You and David [Owen] are the Alliance's most precious assets ... Both of you are immensely able, energetic and compelling. But here too lies one of our greatest problems. The Alliance looks like a two-man band.'[2]

She enlarged on these concerns in a further letter to Owen, first of all reproving him for his support for market forces.

Our economic policy statements have favoured income policies, though voluntary rather than statutory, they have not come out for privatisation. There seems some divergence here between your own position and that so far endorsed by the CSD. I believe, as I've said in my letter, that there is great appeal and great relevance in the economic policies we originally adopted and I want to see us stick to them. I believe they will be justified by future events.

She then raised the question of his leadership.

You have been amazing in your energy, your new ideas and your brilliant exploitation of political openings to advance the SDP cause. But democratic governments aren't formed by one, or even two, people. I myself believe – and here I expect we disagree – that Presidential government in Britain does not last long: there is a tendency to revert to Cabinet government. Furthermore, the SDP is rich in talent, including the expertise of many of our members in diverse fields. We haven't adequately used that resource, though I know you consult some of them. But you do so as an individual, their advice is not available to other Party spokesmen.[3]

She finished by warning him of mutterings in both the Liberals and SDP about their troubled relationship. She hoped he would deign to meet Steel and suggested that Geoff Tordoff, the president of the Liberals, and herself had something to contribute.

Shirley's frustration at feeling excluded from the inner sanctum was all the more intense given her formative role in the establishment of the SDP, her closeness to Owen during 1981–82 and her position as party president. Some of this exclusion could be attributed to Owen's naturally domineering style and some to his brooding sensitivity that his ousting of Jenkins would come back to haunt him, especially since Shirley and Rodgers had cavilled at the brutality of it. For a man obsessed with loyalty and who repaid it in droves to those he trusted, the doubts began to surface about his co-founders, especially as differences mounted over policy. In his mind a challenge from one became a challenge from all three. In these circumstances he wasn't amenable to Shirley and Rodgers's desire to restore the old collective leadership of 1981–82, believing such a concept to be obsolete, especially now that both of them were out of Parliament and newer faces were clamouring for recognition. He also thought Shirley held delusions of grandeur over her role as party president, investing it with a prominence that didn't equate with reality.

There were also personal forces at work. Shirley's failure to show political mettle over Warrington and the party leadership caused her to fall rapidly in Owen's estimation. Accordingly, he often failed to consult her, something he later regretted, and could be brutally dismissive of her views. It is true that she remained in her element at party rallies, where she continued to be a prime attraction, or during by-elections such as Portsmouth South, won by the SDP in June 1984, but, no longer in Parliament, she cut an increasingly forlorn figure. Her growing disenchantment with Owen became evident to Jenkins when he stayed with her in Hertfordshire later that month. 'Probably for the first time she spoke to me in terms of unhappy complaint against the sheer abrasiveness of David Owen, buttressed by some emerging worry about his policy positions,' he later wrote.[4] In early October they both addressed a conference in Athens and thereafter, in conversation on a cruise around the Peloponnese, the criticisms surfaced ever stronger.

Jenkins later confessed,

I remember with mild guilt that I received them with satisfaction, whereas I suppose in the interests of the future of the party I ought to have received them with dismay. But I think that, in view of David Owen's persistent offensive/defensive attitude to me and of Shirley Williams's position in 1982, I would have needed to be super-human to have done so.[5]

Prior to this, at the SDP conference at Buxton, she and Jenkins tried to rein Owen in, Shirley telling delegates that it was inaccurate to describe the party as a one-man band. Rather, the SDP had 'abundant talent in the ranks of its MPs, previous MPs and among its members', while Jenkins cautioned against alienating the Liberals by adopting policies they couldn't support. His sniping infuriated Owen and widened the gulf between them. That in turn might have accounted for Owen's professed desire to see Shirley back in Parliament, but with consecutive defeats behind her she understandably wanted to bide her time until the right seat became available.

The year 1985 proved one of steady progress for the Alliance, but the SDP conference at Torquay reignited latent tensions within the Gang of Four over the future direction of the party – evident during the year-long miners' strike when Owen had been considerably more supportive of the government's stance than Shirley. A motion from the Stevenage area party calling for the continuing adhesion of the SDP to many of the traditional values of the Labour Party brought matters to a head. Despite support from Shirley and Rodgers, the National Committee chose to oppose it. Even worse, the motion received short shrift on the conference floor as delegate after delegate dismissed the idea of any association with Labour. Instead they wished to emphasise their genuine radicalism as a party that cut across traditional ideological and class boundaries. The motion was withdrawn in favour of something more anodyne.

That wasn't Shirley's only setback. Her contention in a television interview that the leader of the Alliance party with the most seats would head the negotiations with other parties in a hung parliament was directly contradicted not only by Owen but also by Steel. They stressed at a joint conference that both leaders would conduct the negotiations since both parties would be involved in the coalition.

It was perhaps with this confusion in mind that her address at the Liberal assembly highlighted the perils of division, given the media's propensity to turn a rift into a chasm. Her words had their desired effect on her audience, but the failure of all sides to pay heed to them the following year cost them dear.

Given the emotions aroused by the issue of defence and the immense damage inflicted on Labour during the previous election by its unilateral stance, the Alliance leadership, well aware of the potential for trouble within its own ranks, had decided in 1984 to establish a Joint Commission on Defence and Disarmament to help forge a defence policy acceptable to both parties. The commission, which included Rodgers, John Cartwright and John Roper for the SDP, was very much multilateral in character and gave little quarter to the vocal unilateralist minority within the Liberal Party.

As the commission deliberated behind the scenes it secured consent on all important questions such as British membership of NATO, American bases in Britain and even the maintenance of Cruise missiles, the cause of an embarrassing defeat for Steel at the 1984 Liberal assembly. Even the most delicate issue, the future of the British independent nuclear deterrent, which it had deliberately left to the end, proved less divisive than imagined. While setting itself against the purchase of Trident, partly on grounds of cost, it agreed to maintain Polaris until the end of its lifespan in the mid- to late 1990s and to defer a decision about its replacement in the light of international developments.

The commission's conclusions were much closer to the SDP view of defence than the Liberal one, but a journalistic sleight of hand helped turn a potential tiff between the two parties over the alternative to Polaris into a full-scale crisis. On Friday 16 May, David Steel was having lunch with two *Scotsman* journalists when, in a reply to a question about the commission, he let slip the fact that it didn't commit the Alliance to the replacement of Polaris. His reply, stripped of its important rider about postponing the decision to a later stage, formed the basis of a damaging article in the following day's *Scotsman*. Not only did it suggest that the commission had gone soft on defence but also that Owen had been humiliated by the Liberals and deserted by his own supporters on the commission.

When Owen read the article on the way to a party conference at Southport, his fury wasn't simply down to the apparent flaws in the defence policy, an issue about which he knew much and cared deeply. It also related to the underlying strains which had bedevilled his relations with the Gang of Four. In his memoirs, he recalls that from mid-April 1986 he had become increasingly concerned about the commission's attitude to the all-important nuclear question – and two subsequent conversations with Rodgers did nothing to allay his fears. When he eventually saw a draft copy of the report with its omission of an alternative to Polaris, he sensed a challenge to his authority. 'One does not have to believe in conspiracy theories for I know that Bill's formulation was known to Shirley and perhaps to Roy. It was known as well by David Steel.'[6]

Determined to pre-empt the commission's report from becoming Alliance policy, and without consultation, Owen raised the stakes with his speech at Southport. He declared his party's unambiguous commitment to remain a nuclear weapon state and dismissed the commission's conclusion as the sort of 'fudging and smudging' he had left behind in the Labour Party.

Owen's pre-emptory strike on the commission upset his colleagues. The first into combat was Shirley, who had tussled with him the previous year over her desire to become patron of Freeze, the movement to freeze the deployment of cruise missiles. She told him that she understood Social Democratic policy to mean a willingness to abandon British deterrent forces if agreement on nuclear arms reductions led to a much lower level of weapons held by both sides. She reckoned that the wording in the party's White Paper on Defence and Disarmament wasn't consistent with his speech. 'I believe on such sensitive issues we should stick to our stated policy.

If you want changes in that policy I think they should be discussed with your colleagues before they are outlined in a public speech.'[7]

Owen disputed Shirley's interpretation of the lengthy and ambiguous 1985 White Paper. On the contrary, he replied, it was quite clear about its willingness to replace Polaris unless there was a massive reduction in nuclear warheads on the part of the US and USSR. He blamed the whole debacle on the Liberals for briefing the press and placing a misleading slant on events.

Any hopes that the tension would ease were dashed by another equally uncompromising speech by Owen in Bonn on 5 June in which he reiterated the need for the British nuclear deterrent. While Rodgers declared that not only Liberals but also many Social Democrats were 'quite puzzled' by Owen's statements, Shirley, in a speech in Cambridge, distanced herself from Owen. The party leader had every right to express his personal views forcefully on the replacement of Polaris. 'But that commitment is not at present party policy.'[8]

On the eve of the publication of the commission's report on 10 June, she wrote to Owen requesting that he give it credit for what it had achieved, not least in bridging the gap between the two parties on defence, especially on Polaris, while making clear that his own position remained unchanged. 'That would strengthen cooperation between our two parties.' She also urged him not to reject its conclusions, as the alliance between the SDP and Liberals offered the country 'the one sane alternative to the policies of the old parties'.[9]

Rodgers wrote in similar vein. While admitting that there had been some inevitable compromise on the commission, he thought, overall, the final report 'pretty sound'. The Liberals had moved a long way towards the SDP's position.

His logic failed to convince Owen. He countered that as the election drew ever closer they, as an Alliance, would have no alternative but to face up to these types of issues. He felt Rodgers had gone agnostic on nuclear defence. Turning to the SDP's 1985 Defence White Paper, he reminded him that its wording was deliberately

drafted so as not to provoke the Liberals and highlight the fundamental differences that existed between them.

> Nonetheless the meaning of that policy paper was and remains
> quite clear and I am sad that you and Shirley have decided to call
> that into question publicly. You have never once challenged the
> interpretation that I and John Cartwright have put on that policy
> in speeches, both within and outside Parliament since Torquay.
> The first inclination I had that Shirley was wishing to challenge
> it was in a letter that I received about my Southport speech in
> which she appeared to have missed my specific reiteration that
> Polaris would be placed on the negotiating table.[10]

Owen's view was upheld by a clear majority at the National
Committee on 19 June, when Shirley, Jenkins and Rodgers agreed
to abide by his interpretation of the party's defence policy in return
for the right to continue arguing for the commission's 'wait and see'
recommendation over a replacement to Polaris.

The wounds emanating from the altercation over the nuclear
deterrent were still festering at the party's conference at Harrogate
that September. In her presidential speech Shirley publicly
upbraided Owen over defence and urged him to put more emphasis
on disarmament. The conference duly endorsed the commission's
report, but reaffirmed its defence resolution of the previous year by
a large majority.

The sobriety of Harrogate, however, wasn't repeated by the
Liberal assembly at Eastbourne despite successful efforts by Owen
and Steel to improve relations over the course of the summer. While
Steel was busy helping make the commission acceptable to the
SDP, he failed to detect the growing unease within his own party.
Although it overwhelmingly backed the Joint Commission Report,
an amendment which approved European cooperation only on the
proviso that its defence capacity was non-nuclear, was unexpectedly
carried after passionate speeches from three of its MPs. The vote,
a close one, was as much about chastening David Owen as it was

about embracing unilateralism, but besides causing further fissures within the Alliance, it attracted the most unflattering of headlines and a major slide in the polls.

The New Year started on an upbeat note with a rousing Alliance rally at the Barbican at which its new policy document, 'The Time has Come', was unveiled. Joint spokesmen had recently been appointed, which gave Shirley and Rodgers a higher profile in the run-up to the election. In Greenwich a by-election was pending at the end of February following the death of the Labour MP, Guy Barnett. The Alliance's four by-election victories during the 1983–87 Parliament had all been in Conservative seats to date. Now, confronted by a far-left Labour candidate as its main opponent, it sensed an opening, and thanks to an ingenious campaign orchestrated by Alec McGivan, the SDP's national organiser, Rosie Barnes swept to a storming victory.

The Alliance momentum continued with favourable opinion polls and encouraging local election results, so that when the election was called for 11 June 1987, it felt better equipped for battle than in 1983, but despite all the preparation, the campaign never caught fire. The manifesto was uninspiring, the early broadcasts unprofessional and their electioneering defensive as the Conservatives probed ruthlessly at their stance on defence. What's more, its overall message appeared confused as Owen turned his fire on Labour and its unfitness to govern while Steel targeted the Conservatives as the main enemy. With Labour proving surprisingly resilient as it campaigned with panache, not least with a highly acclaimed video about its leader, Neil Kinnock, it pulled ahead of the Alliance in the polls, consigning the third party to the periphery.

When the Alliance campaigning committee met on 31 May it gave serious consideration to a memo prepared by Shirley. It made for sombre reading. The campaign hadn't been positive enough, she concluded. Instead of constantly attacking the other parties the Alliance needed to inject more passion and develop a clear message. The advice was heeded, but unlike 1983, the polls barely moved, so that by the time of the actual election many feared the worst.

Throughout much of 1985 Shirley had been locked in negotiations with Alliance officials in Cambridge with a view to becoming
their candidate at the next election. Ever since its establishment as
a single constituency in 1885, Cambridge had traditionally been a
Conservative seat, although a Liberal victory in 1906 and Labour
ones in 1945 and 1966 meant it couldn't be taken for granted. Given
the Thatcher government's fractious relationship with academia
over cuts in the higher education budget, the brooding presence of Cambridge University at the heart of the constituency
offered fertile recruitment for the opposition parties, making it a
genuine three-horse race. Owing to the government's mid-term
unpopularity, its majority of 5,000 in Cambridge looked vulnerable, encouraging Alliance strategists to make it one of their prime
target seats.

With its intellectual ambience, proactive local party and close
proximity to her Hertfordshire home, Cambridge was just the
kind of seat to appeal to Shirley. Knowing that she was interested,
the Liberals extracted joint selection as the price of their support.
The prospect of her becoming the Alliance candidate seemed to
unnerve Robert Rhodes James, the sitting Conservative MP. He
expressed absolute confidence that he would beat his old friend
and advised her to go elsewhere. She didn't. Joint selection was
agreed to and when it took place in January 1986 she easily beat
Chris Bradford, a Liberal councillor, by 355 to 50. She greeted her
victory by confidently predicting an Alliance gain in Cambridge.
Its success in wresting control of Cambridge City Council from
Labour in May 1987 was an encouraging omen, an election that saw
the defeat of Chris Howard, the leader of the council and Labour's
parliamentary candidate.

With the fight for Cambridge attracting much attention from
the media, there was no shortage of activity, especially on the
Alliance side, where, under the conscientious gaze of Andrew Duff,
one of its leading local councillors, enthusiastic volunteers took to
the streets in large numbers. The Corn Exchange was full to capacity for an 'Ask the Alliance' rally featuring its two leaders, and Roy

Jenkins, Bill Rodgers and Richard Attenborough were among those luminaries who spoke on Shirley's behalf.

Rhodes James's campaign, in contrast, was an understated affair, as befitted a diffident personality who studiously avoided populist gestures and gimmicks. Yet appearances were deceptive. His reputation as an outstanding local MP who had opposed his own government over university cuts, along with the emphasis he placed on tax cuts and independent education, seemed to strike a chord with the electorate, a fact confirmed by Duff, who recalls his surprise at how the grammar schools returned to haunt Shirley. Although she warned him before the declaration to prepare for bad news, she was clearly disappointed and surprised by a Conservative majority of just over 5,000, a result remarkably similar to 1983. Her one consolation was holding on to second place, her 16,564 narrowly exceeding Labour's 15,319. Afterwards, at a wake at Duff's house, she flung off her shoes and accepted a glass of scotch and a cigarette, explaining that she only ever smoked after an election defeat; this, her third in succession, effectively marked the end of her parliamentary career.

Shirley's personal setback mirrored that of the Alliance at large. On a night when the Conservatives were comfortably returned to power with a majority of 101 and a modest Labour revival had consolidated its position as the leading party of the centre-left, the Alliance lost seats overall, including Jenkins in Hillhead, with the SDP reduced to just five MPs.

The disappointment, not least the apparent absurdity of two leaders uncomfortable in each other's company and holding different priorities, convinced many that the case for merger was now cast-iron. Not only was this the view of Steel and the overwhelming majority of his party, it was also the view of many SDP members, especially those who had worked closely with their Liberal counterparts. Such converts, however, didn't include Owen. If anything, the divisions over defence and the difficulties of the campaign had enhanced his disdain of the Liberals and reinforced his separatist tendencies.

In his determination to strike first, he called a press conference at his Plymouth hotel the afternoon after the election to make it abundantly clear that he remained resolutely opposed to merger, declaring that the two parties represented different strands of British politics, liberalism and social democracy.

His early strike caught Steel off guard, but, determined to brook no further delay to his historic vision of realignment, he was ready with a swift riposte. He telephoned Owen on Sunday to inform him that he was writing a paper for his party on merger, a copy of which would be available for him that evening, before inviting the media to his home to provide widespread coverage for his proposals.

Steel's call for merger mirrored similar ones from Shirley, Jenkins and Rodgers post-election. Despite the suspicion of the Owenites that all three were involved in a pro-merger conspiracy, there is no evidence to support this. Jenkins, it is true, had come to the conclusion after the 1983 election that merger was the most appropriate way forward, but it remained more a personal conviction than a public call to arms. Shirley and Rodgers were much more agnostic, Shirley telling Steel in April 1984 that a merger then would be divisive for both parties and would absorb a lot of energy needed for other things. She shared Rodgers's desire, however, for closer cooperation, a conviction strengthened by their standing in joint-selection constituencies and campaigning with the Liberals at the grass roots. In March 1987 she went much further on Tyne Tees Television's *Face the Press*, for, while ruling out merger before the election, she accepted that thereafter her party, regardless of the views of its leadership, would have to 'face head on the question of whether or not we want to merge'. Now, given the disappointment of the election, her endorsement of a merger, along with that of Jenkins and Rodgers, came as little surprise.

Rodgers told Owen that his real challenge as leader was to try and mould a newly merged party in the image of the SDP. He shared many of his reservations about the Liberals, yet whatever their limitations he felt them capable of being led. His rationale was essentially sound, but in his growing contempt for Owen, he, along with Shirley and Jenkins, underestimated the residue of loyalty he commanded from many within the party, especially those to whom the SDP was refreshingly new. To abandon their party would be a bitter pill to swallow. Thus, when Owen announced his intention to resist merger he could count on a sizeable number willing to follow him into the bunker. Such reckless audacity helped account for a venomous six months in which all the fine words accompanying the party's birth were brutally cast aside in this fight to the finish. It was a fight from which few would emerge unscathed.

On the Saturday after the election Owen had discussed with Shirley the way that they would handle Monday's meeting of the National Committee. They didn't touch on their respective views about merger but agreed that it would be for the party membership to decide after a debate at the party conference at Portsmouth. By Monday Owen, having read all the pro-merger moves, was having second thoughts. Later at that meeting Shirley declared that the question of merger now confronted them and proposed they debate it at their party conference before it was put to a vote of all members. Her initiative, however, fell foul of the anti-merger majority in the National Committee who felt that the immediate aftermath of the election was an inappropriate time to consider such matters.

After the meeting was adjourned to 29 June, Shirley wrote to Owen in high dudgeon, telling him that she thought it had been appalling.

> If you disagreed with my paper, as you have every right to do, you should have said so on Sunday. I played it by the book – spoke to no-one and canvassed no-one. I then found your closest colleagues rounding on the paper without seriously advancing a single constructive proposal on how to deal with the post-election situation – and proposals for merger won't just go away. On an issue of such fundamental importance, obviously our members cannot and should not be by-passed.[11]

She now sought a meeting between Owen, the party vice-presidents and herself to seek a basis on which they could find a common way forward, but her proposal was rebuffed. Furthermore, she had no advance warning of the counter proposals that soon appeared from those opposed to a merger.

On 17 June, Owen was unanimously re-elected leader of the SDP by his MPs before proceeding to astound them with his future vision for the party. Knowing that he couldn't withstand the combined pressure of Shirley, Jenkins, Rodgers and Steel for merger, he chose to make the best of a bad hand. In a secret memorandum to his MPs he proposed an amicable divorce for their party whereby those who wished to join with the Liberals were free to do so, while the rest would be encouraged to stay. His plan was comprehensively rejected, since even his staunchest followers couldn't stomach the idea of a formalised split. Believing that he was being too fatalistic, they urged compromise. Consequently, Bob Maclennan was commissioned with the task of drafting an alternative option to full merger for the National Committee to consider. His proposals were outlined at a press conference on 24 June presided over by him and John Cartwright. Members were to be given two choices. One advocated the preservation of the SDP – to be presented as though it were a strengthening of the Alliance; the other supported merger – presented as though it were a takeover by the Liberals. Its publication and Owen's desire for an immediate ballot, his assumption being that the party conference at the end of August would give the pro-mergerites a majority, so alarmed Shirley that she wrote to Maclennan requesting him to reconsider the wording of the two options. More important, she told him that unless he allowed the supporters of merger to have their position expressed in their own words to the membership of the party, he would be responsible for a bitter and irreconcilable split within the SDP's own ranks.

As the struggle for the soul of the SDP intensified, the language became ever more extreme, with Shirley talking about a 'fight to the death' and Owen vowing never to join a merged party even as leader. Their relationship, already fragile, deteriorated even further when he refused to see her or return her phone calls. On one notorious occasion she went round to his office only to be told that he wasn't there despite seeing his silhouette along the curtain, an experience which left her with an abiding sense of bitterness. When confronted by this bitterness many years later, Owen accepted the charge but explained that it was prompted much more by indecision than spite. In the immediate aftermath of the election, when he was physically and emotionally exhausted, he wasn't sure at that stage whether he wanted to stay and fight merger or retire from politics. Had he seen Shirley he feared that she would have discerned his vacillation and made political capital out of it.

As the meeting of the National Committee drew near, Shirley, angry at her rebuff and at what she deemed a crude attempt to manipulate the wording of the ballot, implying that the SDP would be destroyed if a merger went ahead, was quick to retaliate. Fearful that the Committee's Owenite majority might not honestly represent the opinions of the members, she spent a day ringing around as many chairmen and party officers as possible to ascertain their views, faithfully recording their comments. Most were in favour of merger and against the wording on the ballot. At the meeting on 29 June, she conceded the case for an early ballot, but proposed to alter the wording of the two options to reflect more accurately the views of the membership. When she ran into a wall of resistance she responded by revealing the results of her party survey and the names of eighty-two party officers who were in agreement with her. Only then did the Owenites relent and Maclennan remove the more offensive phrase, 'the abolition of the SDP'.

Once there was agreement over the two options and the neutrality of party officers in the campaign, the meeting discussed which option to recommend to the membership. Shirley said that those who opposed merger failed to take into account the 'very considerable determination' of the Liberal leadership for constitutional change. 'I believe that when they see what emerges from the negotiations, they will change.'[12] Her words were in vain as by eighteen to thirteen the National Committee chose to recommend support for negotiations for closer cooperation – Option One – as opposed to negotiated merger – Option Two – but the Owenites suffered a surprising setback when Charles Kennedy, the young, up-and-coming MP for Ross, Cromarty & Skye, a constituency which supported merger, changed sides.

With the ballot due to be sent out on 18 July and returned by 5 August both sides, 'Yes for Unity' and 'Vote for the SDP', issued a statement to all members with the ballot paper. The campaign opened on 2 July and soon degenerated into bitterness, not least with complaints from both sides about electoral irregularities. The Electoral Reform Society, the neutral body charged with overseeing the poll, upheld a complaint from 'Yes to Unity' concerning its opponents' printing of the National Committee's recommendation against merger on the same sheet of paper as the ballot form. At the same time, Shirley was asked by John Cartwright, a leading figure in the anti-merger camp, to investigate the allegation that 'Yes to Unity' had obtained a copy of the national membership list. It transpired it hadn't, but an illegal mass mailing of 30,000 members had been sent out – from information gleaned from local parties.

Launching the 'Yes to Unity' campaign, Jenkins and Rodgers poured scorn on Owen's support for Option One, closer cooperation with the Liberals, which, they argued, would merely foment strife within the Alliance. The real choice, declared Jenkins, was between union or separation ... and separation meant impotence. Steel waded in on private grief by accusing Owen of petty apartheid, and a Liberal Party broadcast called for wedding bells after a six-year engagement.

Owen countered by branding merger defeatist, symptomatic of a lack of nerve emanating from the liberal-minded people in the country, whose nerve always failed. His invective greatly upset Shirley, who assumed it was directed primarily at her, but days later the boot was on the other foot when, at a meeting of SDP local councillors in Nottingham, she said Owen's opposition to merger amounted to 'a pointless act of vivisection'. Her comments brought her a stiff reprimand from Owen when he addressed that same gathering. He warned her that using such emotive language merely exacerbated current divisions and placed barriers on the road to reconciliation. Thereafter tempers cooled, but the gulf between the two sides remained vast.

During the fortnight or so in which the ballot was held many of the leading participants had gone off on holiday. Shirley was climbing in Wyoming but even the majestic splendour of the Rockies couldn't restore her spirits. 'A feeling of apprehension fills me about the SDP vote,' she wrote in her diary before the ballot was due to be announced – and with good reason.[13] While the result itself, a win for the 'Yes to Unity' side by 57.4 per cent to 42 per cent, was broadly in line with expectation, few had anticipated Owen's immediate resignation within an hour of the verdict becoming public. In a short statement he accepted the right of the members to merge, but reiterated his intention to play no part in merger negotiations and hinted that he might make trouble. In a subsequent phone call to Shirley he told her that a new leader would need to be elected forthwith since the party's constitution stipulated that when a leader retired or resigned during the parliamentary recess, the nomination for a successor had to be received within three weeks. With Kennedy immune to her persuasion on the grounds that he was too young, Shirley now set her sights on Bob Maclennan, her junior minister at the DPCP. She proposed to Jenkins that they invite him to serve on the negotiating body for the constitution of the new party, a suggestion which met with his approval on a day when little seemed to go right. 'I feel depressed, overcome with the complexities of my life,' she reflected that evening.[14]

The next day she phoned Maclennan, who was on holiday at his wife's family home in New Hampshire, to sound him out. She found him utterly depressed. 'Says he needs the holiday, sees no point in going on, believes David is going to mount a major campaign backed by the Trustees, and that all is wrecked.' Shirley countered by saying he was needed on the negotiating body and he agreed to think about it. 'He perks up when I mention the leadership,' she observed. 'I suspect that he's not uninterested.'[15]

A charming, intelligent and honourable man with conciliatory tendencies, Maclennan was in many ways the man for the hour. A committed supporter of Owen, he was the author of the defeated ballot option, but, accepting the will of the majority, he was now prepared to work for merger provided the new party contained many of the SDP genes. Yet there was some doubt as to whether he possessed the steely self-confidence and strength of character for the hard road ahead.

Once based at Cape Cod, Shirley arranged to meet Maclennan and his wife Helen to discuss the leadership. Any diffidence he displayed, not least about the Liberals, gradually evaporated in the face of her argument that he, as the author of the original constitution, couldn't allow the vote for merger to be endangered by the lack of a leader. Having persuaded him that he was officer material, Shirley and Maclennan reconvened the following week to consider the nuts and bolts of merger negotiations. Matters of policy would need to be included as well as the new party's constitution.

Maclennan's perceived perfidy was greeted with consternation by SDP MPs. When they met at Westminster on 27 August they subjected him to an uncomfortable grilling as they tried to dissuade him from becoming leader, but with Maclennan resolved on filling the vacancy their words fell on stony ground. Two days later his party elected him unopposed.

On her return from the US, Shirley wrote to Owen to tell him how much she regretted his decision to resign. At the same time she reminded him that OMOV was the fundamental democratic principle that underpinned the party and one which he had strongly supported. 'It means that it is incumbent upon the Party's officers to seek to carry out the wishes of our members. If in all good conscience one cannot do so, then the only alternative is to resign, but not to frustrate their decision in other ways.'[16]

On 30 August, at the SDP conference at Portsmouth, she used her opening presidential remarks to claim that she came to praise Caesar not to bury him. Yet amidst the accolades, there were some stinging barbs about his abrupt departure before the negotiations between the two parties had taken place. Her comments drew heckling from the back of the hall and a public exit of some of Owen's supporters from the platform, convinced that she had abused her presidential position in an unduly partisan way.

Having given a dignified valedictory speech which appealed for an amicable parting of the ways, Owen then proceeded to use a crowded fringe meeting of his supporters to set up the Campaign for Social Democracy (CSD). This act of defiance was met with a mixture of obloquy and ridicule from his former colleagues, especially the idea that a fourth party could hold its own under the British electoral system. The resolution calling for the creation of a new merged party, eloquently introduced by Charles Kennedy, passed comfortably by 228 to 151 and a further boost came with the performance of the new leader. After Shirley had introduced him in glowing terms, Maclennan responded with a forceful speech in which he promised to remain true to the spirit of the SDP during merger negotiations. Winding up the conference Shirley admitted that it had been the most troubled and contentious the party had yet experienced, but, quoting D. H. Lawrence, declared, 'Look, we have come through.'

Her optimism was partly for show as the raising of the rebel standard at Portsmouth told of trouble ahead. At the next meeting of the National Committee on 21 September, later referred to by Rodgers as one of the most unpleasant he had ever encountered, the Owenites returned to the attack over their previous contention that 'Yes to Unity' had indulged in electoral irregularities. They alluded to the confidential report of the Electoral Reform Society, which confirmed that 30,000 members had been canvassed illegally and demanded a copy of the national membership list for themselves, which would help them set up their own party.

When Shirley blocked Mike Thomas's motion on the membership list, claiming that it would breach the Data Protection Act, and challenged him to move her out of the chair, he did precisely that. The vote was fourteen each and she escaped only by using her casting vote, raising further questions as to whether the president should be acting in such a partisan manner. 'Shirley's position was difficult,' wrote Rodgers.

She was President of the whole, divided party and, as ever, she was anxious to reconcile rather than take a hard line. But given the outcome of the ballot, it was her duty to guide the party to merger as smoothly as possible. She was incensed by what she saw as the outrageous behaviour of the Owenites and showed great toughness in seeing the whole process through to a conclusion. It was not her fault that it took so long.'[17]

On 30 September she wrote to Owen to inquire why, after the conclusion of the ballot, his organisation was still in existence. 'On the face of it, it appears that at the very least it is preparing the ground for the campaign against any proposal for the union of the SDP with the Liberal Party which may follow the conclusion of the negotiations.'[18] By setting up the organisation now, she continued, he appeared to be prejudging the outcome of the negotiations to which the party was committed as a result of the members' ballot and the vote at Portsmouth.

She kept up the pressure at the next meeting of the National Committee, when she challenged Owen to resign unless CSD ceased its activities. If his supporters continued to oppose the ballot she couldn't rule out his possible expulsion from the party, a step too far for Maclennan. He did, however, compare CSD with Militant Tendency and joined forces with Shirley afterwards to ask Owen to desist from organising a party within a party.

Amidst all the turmoil of the SDP, Shirley found respite in her private life. Ever since she and Tony King had parted there had been no one permanent to sustain her during her political trials and tribulations. Mark Bostridge, who worked for her briefly during the mid-1980s, recalls this as an unhappy period in her life when, after the glamour of the SDP had worn off, she would go home to an empty flat. That is the way it might have remained had fate not intervened in the form of her good friend Dick Neustadt, eleven years her senior, whom she had first met back in 1969 when visiting Boston on government business.

Richard Elliott Neustadt was one of the US's foremost political scientists and adviser to several of its presidents. Born in Philadelphia into a Jewish family, he had served in the US Navy during the Second World War and the Budget Bureau of the Executive Office of the President afterwards before becoming an adviser to President Truman. When the Republicans returned to the White House in 1953, Dick, a sworn Democrat, swapped public service for academia, but remained in frequent contact with Washington as presidents, senators and congressional committees sought his counsel.

In 1965 Dick returned to his Alma Mater Harvard as the founder of the Kennedy School of Government and the first director of the Institute of Politics, created as a memorial to John F. Kennedy and his vision of engaging educated young people in public service. As an imaginative and devoted teacher who brought the world of high politics into the lecture hall, Dick was idolised by his students. As a man his natural warmth, humour and integrity won him friends wherever he went. It was during a sabbatical at Nuffield College, Oxford, in 1961–62 that he had formed a deep bond with Tony King and when the latter became close to Shirley they used to stay with the Neustadts at their summer home at Wellfleet, Cape Cod.

Although good friends with Dick, Shirley was particularly close to Bertha (Bert), his loyal and devoted wife, so that even after she and Tony separated, she kept closely in touch, not least during her Harvard semester in 1979. By now Bert was suffering from multiple sclerosis and as her condition deteriorated Shirley became one of the few people she was willing to see. On one occasion, as she lay dying, she told Dick that Shirley would make the perfect wife for him.

Bert's death in 1984 cast a deep shadow over Dick. He had nursed her with loving tenderness throughout her illness and now that she had gone life seemed to have lost its meaning. He retreated from public view whenever possible and resisted entreaties from family and friends to socialise. When eventually he gradually emerged from his dark cell he found his salvation in Shirley, and the reason to go on living. Aside from his deep reverence for elected politicians, especially British ones, it was her warmth and understanding that enabled him to rediscover his spark. When he confided to his son Rick that he was thinking of asking Shirley to marry him, Rick replied, 'Oh go on, Dad. It will be such fun.'

Having met up with her at Cambridge during the 1987 election, Dick invited her to Cape Cod. There, one summer day, on the steps of his low wooden house, overlooking a freshwater lake, he proposed. Totally unaware of what was in store, Shirley was flabbergasted. She hesitated, knowing from experience that her manifold commitments and idiosyncratic lifestyle weren't conducive to a transatlantic marriage, especially to someone so used to a conventional wife. There had also been a change in family circumstances caused by the untimely death of her brother.

While Shirley's career reached its apogee with her elevation to the Cabinet, John's had faltered badly following the collapse of his property business during the recession of the early 1970s. Unemployed after 1973, he applied for countless jobs, but nothing had come his way and he was forced to survive on supplementary benefit. If that wasn't enough he lost his second wife, Elaine, to cancer, aged twenty-nine. Committed to bringing up his two young children, Larissa and Alexander, he moved to a spartan farmhouse in the Kent Weald (and later to a flat in Broome Park, near Canterbury), and proved a model parent, winning their undying love in return. In time he married Barbara Blee, a Pole, and moved back to London, finding fulfilment as a sympathetic magistrate in the Inner London Juvenile Court.

Although Shirley had tried to find him a job and help him financially, their relationship remained a distant one, but she was deeply upset when she heard that he had suffered a massive cerebral haemorrhage one day late in March 1987. Heading straight to the hospital she found him unconscious. As she surveyed this distressing sight and recalled the lost innocence of childhood, when the two of them had formed such a close bond, she 'choked with grief for the sensitive, protective, beautiful little boy who had been my brother'.[19]

With John's children, Larissa, nineteen, and Alexander, fifteen, now parentless, and very close to one another, Shirley felt it incumbent upon her to give them a home, an impediment to any future marriage. At the same time she was devoted to Dick, admired his work and enjoyed a lifestyle that combined the intellectual stimulation of Harvard with the beauty of Cape Cod.

By the time she returned to Cape Cod in August her doubts had more or less been assuaged and, as the thought of marriage to Dick began to sink in, surprise gave way to delight. When she conveyed her news to Barbara and Peter Metcalfe (the official announcement was postponed 'til November), Barbara noted how young and pretty she looked.

On Saturday 19 December the small church of St Edmund's in Old Hall Green near Ware was packed to witness the intriguing spectacle of a devout Roman Catholic marrying an agnostic Jew presided over by Father John Feighery, a Roman Catholic missionary priest, aided by Trevor Howard, an Anglican vicar. After a simple, moving service, the couple emerged to the prying lenses of the paparazzi, but even their unauthorised presence didn't spoil the happiness of the occasion. A large marquee in Shirley's garden provided the backdrop for the reception. Despite the political tensions of that time over merger, she was gracious enough to invite some of her most steadfast opponents to the wedding. Although the atmosphere was reasonably civil on the day, the warring factions kept their distance at separate tables.

The task of framing a constitution for the new party dragged on interminably throughout the autumn and beyond its Christmas deadline. Eventually, a constitution emerged which broadly conformed to Social Democrat expectations, though it needed a long, acrimonious meeting between the two sides on 12 January to prepare the finishing touches. There now remained the matter of the policy document demanded by Maclennan to give the new party its own particular identity. In order to avoid undue delay, the two leaders had assigned this responsibility to themselves and their advisers. With Steel happy for Maclennan to take the initiative, the latter drew up a highly controversial document containing unpopular proposals such as the retention of Trident, the extension of VAT to food and the abolition of universal child benefit to help pay for their anti-poverty programme. As early as 10 December, Shirley told Dick Newby, the SDP's national secretary, of her unhappiness with the preamble, which made little reference to the issues about which she cared passionately. If there were no change, she told him, she would make her dissatisfaction known and would disown the document at the party's special conference at Sheffield.

A week later, on the eve of her wedding, the policy document continued to concern her enough to interrupt her preparations to ring the offices of both leaders. She even spent some of the reception broaching the subject with Rodgers and Jenkins before departing confident that she had helped fix the roof. It was nearly a month later, on a flight home from honeymoon in Morocco, that she discovered from a fellow passenger's newspaper that not only had the roof not been fixed but the whole house had caved in.

The failure of the two leaders to keep a close eye on the policy negotiations during the closing stages had blinded them to the storm fast gathering. It was only when the Liberal Policy Committee met less than a day before the deadline of 13 January 1988 that serious doubts began to surface. When extracts from that draft appeared in the press the next day, the explosive headlines made grim reading for many a Liberal MP and, sensing political catastrophe, they conveyed their reservations to their leader in the starkest of terms.

Confronted with such a dangerous mutiny, Steel told a devastated Maclennan that he could no longer be party to the document and emphasised the need to replace it with something more acceptable. On his initiative they began again with a fresh team of negotiators and within a week they had come up with a redrafted version shorn of the most contentious features, which they felt able to put to their respective membership.

On 23 January in Blackpool, the Liberals, in a mood of benign tolerance, voted by a massive majority to accept merger and the following weekend the SDP special conference met in Sheffield. Here the atmosphere was much less harmonious, the presence of CSD hanging over proceedings as a row erupted over its right to use the conference hall for a major rally. Having lost out to CSD over the hall, Shirley was in a discordant mood when she opened the debate, but her message that merger was the only sensible way forward for third-party politics reflected the mood of the majority. With most Owenites abstaining in the vote for the new constitution, the result was never in doubt. That in turn made the vote of the wider membership more or less a formality. While the Liberals voted by an overwhelming majority for merger, the SDP, on a very low turn-out, voted 18,722 in favour compared to 9,929 against.

The determination of the Owenite faction to continue as the SDP did nothing to help the new party, the Social and Liberal Democrats, soon to be the Liberal Democrats, in its infant stage as its support dropped quite dramatically compared to anything achieved by the Alliance. At the same time the days of the SDP were numbered given its declining membership, diminishing resources and abject by-election results. After a disastrous performance at the Bootle by-election in May 1990, it realised the game was up and disappeared from view, its demise likened by Jenkins to the grounding of a loose cannon crashing around the deck of a warship. 'I do not, however, state the facts without a sense of dismay at how badly we all handled things in 1987 and how much was wantonly thrown away.'[20] In retrospect he acknowledged that he, Shirley and Rodgers should have been more sensitive to the concerns of a significant minority of the SDP, an admission echoed by Maclennan. He felt that, whatever the merits of the case, Shirley leapt into merger without realising how divisive it would be to her party. (He did also acknowledge her prescience over the SDP–Liberal Party negotiations and their potential to come unstuck.)

For all its ultimate failure to break the mould, few associated with the SDP regretted their part in its birth and development. It certainly helped in time to create a stronger radical centre. Yet whatever its achievements it is a bittersweet irony that a party conceived in the dawn of hope should collapse amidst such acrimony. Many of the ruptured relationships never healed, but in a spirit of reconciliation David and Debbie Owen hosted a party in January 2006 to celebrate the twenty-fifth anniversary of the SDP's birth. Later that year they invited Shirley on holiday to Greece. She willingly assented, but once there found that the ghosts of times past came back to haunt her. Sensitive to the barriers that still existed, Debbie Owen suggested that Shirley and David went on a long walk to clear the air. They did and in a conversation of extreme candour they revisited the terrain of many of their former battles, letting out all the hurt that had stored up. Gradually, through discussion, explanation and contrition, they put the past behind them and began the long road back. In that context Greece proved a cathartic experience for which Shirley was truly grateful. She later told Debbie Owen that it was one of the best holidays she had ever had.

## Endnotes

1  *Guardian*, 30 August 1983
2  SW to David Steel, 25 April 1984, David Owen Papers
3  SW to David Owen, 25 April 1984, David Owen Papers
4  Roy Jenkins, *A Life at the Centre*, p.585
5  Roy Jenkins, *A Life at the Centre*, p.586
6  David Owen, *Time to Declare*, p.642
7  SW to David Owen, 20 May 1986, David Owen Papers
8  *Guardian*, 7 June 1986
9  SW to David Owen, 9 June 1986, David Owen Papers
10  David Owen to Bill Rodgers, 9 June 1986, David Owen Papers
11  SW to David Owen, 16 June 1987, David Owen Papers
12  *Social Democrat*, 17 July 1987
13  SW diary, 5 August 1987, SW Papers (private collection)
14  SW diary, 6 August 1987, SW Papers (private collection)
15  SW diary, 7 August 1987, SW Papers (private collection)
16  SW to David Owen, 25 August 1987, David Owen Papers
17  Bill Rodgers, *Fourth Among Equals*, p.262
18  SW to David Owen, 30 September 1987, David Owen Papers
19  *Climbing the Bookshelves*, p.328
20  *Observer*, 10 June 1990

# TRANSATLANTIC EMISSARY

One evening in June 1988 Shirley was swimming at Gull Pond, Wellfleet, with Dick's friend Graham Allison, Dean of Harvard's Kennedy School of Government, when he asked her whether she would like to be proposed as a professor there. Ever since her stint as a Fellow of the Institute of Politics (IOP) back in 1979, Allison had been attempting to lure her back, figuring that her status as a prominent female politician from overseas would expand the School's horizons.

Harvard, founded in 1636, was the oldest, richest and most prestigious university in the US. Its Kennedy School had evolved into one of the most renowned graduate schools in public affairs, with distinguished alumni worldwide. To be part of such a stimulating intellectual environment was in many ways Shirley's ideal scenario, especially now that she was married to Dick and free of party obligations. She accepted without hesitation and began work there that September as Public Service Professor of Electoral Politics, combining her academic duties with vigorous campaigning on the side. This included her work assisting the emerging democracies in Eastern/Central Europe, her humanitarian mission in Bosnia and her membership of the House of Lords from January 1993.

Four months into her new role she was invited to become the acting director of the IOP following the appointment of Dick Thornburgh, its director, as Attorney General by Ronald Reagan the previous August and his reappointment by George H. W. Bush in November. Ever since its foundation in 1966, the IOP's prime mission had been to foster ideals of civic engagement and political participation among its students. One means to accomplishing this was its Public Forum, which regularly hosted world leaders in government, business and the media.

With a well-appointed set of offices, a dedicated staff and an enthusiastic team of student volunteers, with whom she worked particularly closely, Shirley set out to give the IOP a more international outlook. Having witnessed the success of a Harvard-inspired conference on Latin American debt in September 1988, attended by representatives of Latin American governments and international financial institutions, Shirley, with the help of her colleague Kathy Eckroad, an expert on Latin America, masterminded a second one the following May. It followed in the wake of the US administration's Brady Plan, which assisted debtor nations to find a way back to solvency. The conference, by encouraging a free exchange of ideas on the Plan, helped clarify some of the main problems in its implementation.

This wasn't the only important conference over which Shirley presided. Aside from the traditional induction for newly elected congressmen, there were the first ever conferences for incumbent congresswomen and for women seeking state or federal office. There was also a greater diversity of speakers at the Forum and plans to include more Fellows from Europe and the emerging democracies. 'The range of this year's activities and visitors attest to the remarkable energy and skill of Shirley Williams,' noted Anne Doyle, the editor of *Proceedings*, the IOP's annual journal.[1] She marvelled at how she had managed to combine all that with her other teaching and speaking commitments. There was even talk of her becoming permanent director, but her status as a non-American told against her. Any disappointment she felt, however, was short-lived as she now turned her attention to wider matters.

The fall of the Berlin Wall and the collapse of Communism in Eastern/Central Europe at the end of 1989 were the cause of great celebration in the West, but Shirley's joy wasn't unconfined. She worried that the transition to the free market wouldn't be the primrose path its supporters claimed, especially with no obvious model to follow. For aside from Poland, Eastern/Central Europe lacked the tradition of a civic society from whose roots democratic shoots could sprout.

It was in this context that she decided to launch Project Liberty as a multilateral, non-party initiative to strengthen these new democratic institutions. Drawing on the expertise of the Kennedy School's public administration tradition and a number of its professors as lecturers, along with senior European politicians, she aimed to offer the leaders and officials of Eastern/Central Europe a way through the transition. It was a tall order, but Shirley didn't allow much to get in her way, persuading many a colleague to help out. Her office, busy at the best of times, was even busier when she was away, with the phone constantly ringing. If Edward Flood, her engaging personal assistant, called some renowned organisation on her behalf, the requests were invariably answered.

Using her many contacts on both sides of the Atlantic, Shirley managed to assemble a generous team of donors such as the European Bank for Reconstruction and Development, the Rockefeller Brothers Foundation and the Pew Foundation. By the spring of 1991, with Poland about to embark upon a programme of privatisation, mirroring similar initiatives elsewhere, the time seemed ripe to organise a workshop on the subject. Held in Gdansk in April, it stressed the relationship between privatisation and democracy and social provision. It proved to be an instructive experience, offering a model for the whole region, as did subsequent workshops on creating a professional independent civil service.

Concerned about the marginalisation of women in the new democracies, especially as rising unemployment took its toll, Project Liberty now turned its attention to raising their profile. For some years previous Shirley had addressed conferences of the all-party 300 Group in Britain, which encouraged greater female participation in both local and national politics. Impressed by what she had seen, she appointed its founder, Lesley Abdela, as consultant to Project Liberty. Her choice proved a shrewd one as Abdela was a passionate and articulate advocate for the cause, while she in turn found Shirley an inspiration to work with, not least for her gifts as a communicator.

The 'Women in Leadership' programme began with a workshop in

Vienna in November 1992 attended by over sixty participants from seventeen different countries. Its purpose was to encourage women in the emerging democracies to enter public life and determine in what ways Project Liberty could best support them. Further consultations with women's organisations in the Czech Republic, Slovakia and Hungary revealed this to be training in career development, political campaigning and media awareness. As a result, a series of workshops featuring local women trainers, as well as outsiders, were held in six countries. In 1994 and 1995 Shirley accompanied Abdela to Bulgaria and Romania, discovering in the former a thriving civic society in which women played an active part, not least in their Parliament. One of their hosts was a Roma woman who took them to a Roma restaurant for a festive evening of singing in which Shirley with her fine voice fully participated. Throughout her time in Bulgaria she kept on remarking how beautifully the young women were dressed, suggesting to Abdela that she *did* care what she looked like.

Romania, in contrast, was more backward, its women more marginalised and oppressed – the legacy of the Ceausescu tyranny – but after laying the foundations of substantial training activity during their initial visit, the following year proved more productive. They started the 222 movement, based on the 300 group, much to the pleasure of many young women keen to participate.

By 1995 Project Liberty was beginning to wind down as Shirley became more absorbed with her commitments elsewhere and the funding began to run dry from American charities. Increasingly, its remaining activities advancing the number of women in public life in the emerging democracies became absorbed into Project Parity, a non-profit organisation founded by Lesley Abdela and Tim Symonds in 1996, with Shirley as its president. She later admitted in the Lords that the sums invested by Project Liberty in Eastern/ Central Europe were relatively meagre, but that isn't to underestimate her contribution towards the new Europe. According to Kathy Eckroad, Project Liberty's assistant director, it could not have happened without her as she was the one with the vision, the drive and the contacts to make it possible.

For all her multifarious activities, Shirley remained resolutely committed to her teaching at Harvard. While commanding the aura of a successful politician it was her natural warmth that principally commended her to her students, most of whom were in their late twenties, very bright and destined for illustrious careers in public service, high finance or academia. Conforming to the Kennedy School's Socratic method of teaching where students interact with their teachers through debate or the re-enactment and analysis of past cases, Shirley liked to draw lessons and challenge previously held assumptions. Not surprisingly one of her many case studies involved abortion, a highly controversial issue in the US then and now. Most students supported the woman's right to choose, so there appeared little scope for discussion. Yet when she deployed the counterarguments, opinion wasn't quite as uniform as before.

She could be fiercely combative in debate but never set out to demean anyone. Her sense of fairness extended to everything she covered. She rarely criticised her fellow politicians, never gossiped about them and, unlike some of her fellow lecturers, refrained from talking about herself.

Drawing up her own courses Shirley concentrated on two areas that previously had hardly featured on the Harvard radar: electoral politics, which included a course on women and politics, and the European Union (as it was now called). The former was especially welcome since it had concerned Dick and Graham Allison that very few of their students opted for elected public office. Because her course was so popular Shirley asked the applicants to write an essay from which she chose the fortunate thirty who would be accepted. According to Samuel Passow, one of her students of the 1994–95 vintage, she was very insistent that politics was about getting elected. An abiding dictum of hers was to never leave a room without asking for someone's support or vote. Politics was also about give and take, not backstabbing, lobbying or finance. The fact that she hadn't raised money for her election campaigns, and didn't charge for public speeches, was a concept quite unfamiliar to her students, especially given the increasing prominence of money in American politics.

What also struck Passow was Shirley's foresight in identifying the role the internet would play in US politics and talking about it in terms of empowerment, giving any local group information, a platform and a capacity for fundraising. He found himself walking out of her classes with the same sense of having listened to John Kennedy. 'There was something elevating about it just at a time when American politics was tainted, inducing a sense of despair. The best people went to Wall Street rather than into politics.' When Polly Trottenberg, later to become assistant secretary for US Transportation Policy under Obama, first entered the Kennedy School she wasn't anticipating a political career, but that all changed after taking Shirley's 'magical' course on Electoral Politics. 'At the time, she was spending a lot of time in Eastern Europe, working on emerging democracies. I thought she had brilliant insight and it got me thinking about a life in politics.'[2]

Aside from her teaching, Shirley was frequently on show at the Forum (this was partly due to the shortage of women candidates), her presence invariably swelling the attendance. With her capacity to formulate her thoughts and articulate them concisely she was essential listening. When Dorothy Zinberg, a lecturer in Public Policy, congratulated her after one accomplished performance, she replied, 'We were brought up like that.'

Very much at home in the stimulating Harvard atmosphere, Shirley nevertheless helped open windows to the world outside. According to Edith Stokey, the former secretary of the Kennedy School, she was a very popular and influential colleague, very persuasive on anything except abortion, something she didn't push. Her year in charge of the IOP helped galvanise it into much-needed change, making it a more vibrant place. Her friend Stanley Hoffmann, the founder of Harvard's Centre for European Studies, considered her contributions at the Forum to be passionate, lucid and eloquent. Whether it was in public or private he found her to be a wonderful conversationalist and an independent thinker who took issue with American claims to the moral leadership of the world. 'One could spend hours in her company without realising she was a politician.'

Shirley's elevation to the Lords in January 1993 raised a dilemma about serving two masters. In 1995 she went part-time at Harvard and effectively left at the end of 1996. She was appointed Professor Emeritus and encouraged to return whenever possible, an offer she has been happy enough to accept. In the opinion of Stanley Hoffmann she could have been a great academic had she so desired, while to Michael Sandel, the renowned American political philosopher, she was a galvanising figure who tried to push Harvard out into the world. Aside from her impact as a female politician, and one from overseas, who shed much light on British and European politics, he considered her the most intellectually dazzling politician that Harvard students had ever encountered. To Graham Allison, she had significantly advanced Dick Neustadt's ideal of linking the worlds of academia and public service, such was the encouragement she had given to her students. 'All in all, she was a great speaker, a great teacher and great colleague, a truly wonderful person.'

It was while Shirley was at Harvard that the crisis in Bosnia erupted, causing her much anger and heartache over the next few years as she failed to persuade Western governments to give it the priority she felt it merited. The multi-ethnic state of Yugoslavia was kept together for many years by the charismatic leadership of President Tito, but his death in 1980 and the fall of the Soviet Union in 1991 unleashed separatist forces as ancient hatreds once again surfaced. The secession of Croatia and Slovenia from Yugoslavia formed the backdrop to the new multi-ethnic state of Bosnia-Herzegovina declaring independence in April 1992. The decision was bitterly opposed by President Milošević, the Serbian leader of Yugoslavia, and the Bosnian Serbs responded by overrunning large parts of Bosnia, laying siege to the capital Sarajevo, and creating mayhem wherever they went.

As Bosnia descended into barbarism, the shocking footage of Serbian-run concentration camps caused outrage in the West but also procrastination as governments feared getting sucked into a potential Balkan bloodbath, especially when few national interests appeared at stake.

With winter fast approaching and the plight of the Muslim refugees ever more desperate, Shirley championed their cause, appealing to the Major government to accept safe havens for them. She twice visited Douglas Hurd at the Foreign Office but the government's continued caution in its desire to protect humanitarian convoys and its troops on the ground drove her to exasperation.

At Harvard she met Lynn Martin, the Secretary of Labor in the outgoing George H. W. Bush administration, and made common cause with her over their mutual concern for Bosnia, not least the appalling atrocities committed against Bosnian Muslim women. In April 1993 they flew to Zagreb, and on a tour of Croatian refugee camps they heard many harrowing tales of the suffering these women had endured. They also listened to the downbeat assessment of the officials in the UN High Commission for Refugees as their mission became ever more fraught, a British soldier remarking: 'Any drunken kid with a Kalashnikov can turn back the whole convoy of food.'

They then donned helmets and flak jackets to accompany members of the French Foreign Legion on the perilous UN forces flight to Sarajevo. On arrival, Shirley found that it had a 'ghostly beauty, once dark muffles the wounds of its buildings ... The old, civilised Hapsburg town has become "a stage-set for hell".'[3] Having witnessed the dangers lurking around every corner, including children dodging snipers in a desperate search of food, she publicly implored the West to strengthen the UN presence in the Bosnian safe havens so they could defend civilians, if necessary by force. Should the Bosnian Serbs fail to respect that demand, the UN should authorise air strikes against the artillery surrounding the enclaves.

She continued to press the British government for stronger action to defend those remaining enclaves, as they became increasingly vulnerable to Bosnian Serb attack, and those humanitarian aid convoys delivering supplies. Her idea had the support of Douglas Hurd, but only if adequate guarantees of safe passage from the warring factions in the area could be ensured.

On 5 February 1994 a lethal mortar attack on the marketplace in Sarajevo, killing seventy, brought an impassioned plea from Shirley to Hurd. She called him a man of humanity and moderation. 'Today's events, however, compel me to repeat the question: how long can the carnage go on? … How many more children must die before the UN Security Council acts on the pledges made at the NATO summit last month?'[4]

The answer was many more. It needed the Serbian capture of Srebrenica in July 1995 and the massacre of some 8,000 Muslims to finally stir the US from its torpor. The American air strikes that followed against Bosnian Serb mortar positions, combined with the growing success of the Croat Muslim Federation and Russian pressure on Milošević to relent, eventually brought the Serbs to the negotiating table. The Dayton Accords that November created an independent Bosnia-Herzegovina with protection for the Serbs there within an independent enclave, signalling a peace of sorts, but not the end of Serbian militant nationalism.

When Shirley was appointed to the House of Lords she took the title of Baroness Williams of Crosby. Although happily ensconced at Harvard, she missed being out of the national spotlight and was most grateful to Paddy Ashdown for helping to secure her a peerage. Once free of all her Harvard commitments she became an assiduous member of the Lords, finding the more stately tone of its debates a considerable improvement on the partisanship of the Commons.

Her absence at Harvard had sheltered her from the painful birth pangs of the Liberal Democrats, but under Ashdown's astute leadership they had nearly recovered by the 1992 election, which gave the Conservatives, under John Major, an unprecedented fourth consecutive term. Kinnock quickly made way for John Smith, while Ashdown revived Jo Grimond's vision of a non-socialist alternative to the Conservatives.

By the end of 1992 the Major government was in freefall following Britain's ignominious exit from the European exchange rate mechanism that September. As it staggered from one crisis to another, Labour and the Liberal Democrats benefited accordingly until the former was rocked by the sudden death of John Smith in May 1994. His successor, Tony Blair, transformed the whole course of British politics by turning his back on past loyalties and reaching out to millions of new converts.

While Shirley had been shunned by Blair at a weekend conference organised by *The Guardian* and the Fabian Society in June (he still had an election for the Labour leadership to win), she saw him as the man able to revive the fortunes of the centre-left. Her enthusiasm was shared by Roy Jenkins, who praised Blair to the hilt in *The Times*, and Bill Rodgers, who admitted that at best Liberal Democrats would be junior partners in any future Labour-led coalition government.

With Ashdown and Blair at one in their commitment to a realignment of the centre-left, negotiations proceeded warily as many Liberal Democrats, fiercely protective of their independence, expressed deep reservations. At their 1995 conference Shirley told a fringe meeting that Ashdown was 'absolutely right' to open the way to cooperation with Labour, but although delegates gave him a mandate to end equidistance from the two main parties it needed all his dexterity to keep his party in step. Even those in his inner circle were enraged by Blair's proposal in May 1996 for a referendum on the powers of a Scottish Parliament, contrary to a previous agreement, especially since it revived the spectre of the 1979 referendum that had postponed devolution by at least two decades.

Even before this volte-face that Shirley informed Ashdown of her growing scepticism of Blair.

My concern is simply this, ministers, even Cabinet Ministers, outside the top four or five posts, have very limited influence on policy. I am no longer as confident as I was that Tony Blair's policy aims coincide with ours, though obviously in some areas they are close. I worry a little about his extreme reluctance to make any commitments on anything, and I worry too about the very conservative nature of some of his senior colleagues, not least the putative Lord Chancellor. As seen through the (admittedly cloudy) prism of the Lords, New Labour seems to lack much conviction on anything.

I hope I'm proved wrong. But if I'm only partly right, we will need to strike a tough bargain. In my view, Tony Blair will not need us very much at the beginning of his administration and consequently we will not get very much from him.[5]

It was a theme to which she returned at the Liberal Democrat conference in 1996, having especially flown across the Atlantic to sound the tocsin. Any cooperation with Labour would depend on its genuine conversion to Liberal Democrat principles. 'We are about policies and ideas; we must not sacrifice these for a few seats in Cabinet,' she said, to thunderous applause.[6]

Her reservations concerned Ashdown enough that he felt obliged to ring her the next day. She reiterated her belief that her previous high opinion of Blair had evaporated as she had become convinced that he lacked a clear set of principles. When Ashdown assured her that he held no burning desire to be in the Cabinet she replied that his position was immeasurably stronger if that was the case.

Despite a pre-election agreement with Labour on constitutional reform, Shirley remained critical of its record on civil liberties. Relishing the opportunity to be given a prominent position in her party's campaign team (unlike in 1992, when she had been deemed a spent force by Des Wilson, the Liberal Democrat campaign manager), she travelled to all parts of the country in a display of stamina that astounded her younger colleagues. With the Conservatives mired in allegations of sleaze and in divisions over Europe, Blair won a massive majority of 179, enough to shelve any ideas he had of inviting the Liberal Democrats, now with forty-six seats, into a coalition. He did, however, keep the language of partnership alive as his government embarked upon an ambitious programme of constitutional reform. On top of that, the Joint Cabinet Consultative Committee was set up, with leading Liberal Democrats participating, and a commission on electoral reform under Roy Jenkins's chairmanship, but this wasn't enough for Ashdown. He continued to hanker after a place at the top table, audacity that brought with it substantial risks, as Shirley made clear to him in a memorandum that October.

By March 1998 the chasm between leader and party grew ever wider as the latter feared for its independence. At its spring conference at Southport, Ashdown was forced to concede that any coalition would need the support of 75 per cent of both Liberal Democrat MPs and the Federal Executive, the party's ruling body. That and the failure of Blair to yield on PR at Westminster helped convince Ashdown it was time to relinquish the leadership. He resigned in August 1999 and was succeeded by Charles Kennedy, a friend of Shirley's and somebody she highly rated.

❧

In January 1998 Shirley had become the Liberal Democrat foreign affairs spokesman in the Lords, and its deputy leader, when Bill Rodgers replaced Roy Jenkins as leader there. It was a portfolio to which she was ideally suited given her lifelong interest in foreign affairs and her wealth of international contacts. She argued for entry into the euro, more aid to the developing world and a more generous reception to asylum seekers as the Blair government vowed to get tough.

Much of her time was devoted to the growing crises in Kosovo and Iraq. Kosovo was a semi-autonomous province of Serbia long regarded as the holy grail of Serbian nationalism following an epic battle there against the Ottoman Empire in 1389, but home to a Muslim Albanian majority. During the previous two decades the Milošević government had gradually curtailed the rights of this majority, which led in time to the formation of the Kosovo Liberation Army (KLA), an ethnic Albanian insurgent force committed to Kosovan independence. Its attacks on Serb targets met with savage reprisals from the Milošević government.

Following a lead from the international community and the US envoy, Richard Holbrooke, a ceasefire was brokered in the autumn of 1998 which was to be overseen by unarmed international monitors. Sceptical that the ceasefire would work, Paddy Ashdown, a doyen of Balkan affairs, returned there that December with Shirley in attendance. After flying to the Macedonian capital of Skopje, where the UN-appointed monitors were based, they travelled to Pristina, the capital of Kosovo, for discussions with the leaders of both sides.

They also accompanied staff of the UN High Commission for Refugees on a tour of threatened Albanian communities, the beauty of the countryside standing in stark contrast to all the devastation in its midst. As they surveyed the desolation of those largely abandoned villages, Shirley noted that all their contacts were men. She thus peeled off from the assembled company and went in search of women with whom she could talk. She was led to rooms hidden at the back of farms, most of them ruined, which harboured up to fifty women and children out of sight of the Serb authorities. There, speaking through a female interpreter, she discovered that many of them had been systematically raped by the Serbs and were very reluctant to talk about it except to another woman. Many hadn't even told their husbands.

With no sign of Shirley at point of departure, Ashdown recalls a worried search that eventually found her sitting on the floor in the gloom of a darkened room with the remaining women and children of the village gathered around her. 'She had seen something I had never seen on all my previous visits. In the Balkans, male-dominated society that it is, conversation with visitors was always conducted by men, while the women were hustled out of the way. But Shirley had managed to cut through all that.'[7] Enticing Shirley away, they left with a sense of foreboding that this village could fall prey to the next Serb attack. Sadly their premonitions were amply vindicated, as the room in which Shirley had spoken to the women was torched shortly afterwards.

Fully acquainted with the simmering hatred on both sides and the weakness of the international monitors in the face of impossible odds, they returned convinced that peace rested on the flimsiest of foundations. Their fears were given added substance by the appalling massacre at Račak the following month when forty-five Kosovo Albanian farmers were butchered by the Serbian army and paramilitary police. The world's outrage was such that peace negotiations at Rambouillet, presided over by the Americans, decreed that both sides should disarm.

The refusal of the Milošević government to comply resulted in NATO airstrikes being unleashed upon Serbian strategic targets in March, but with only limited effect. Indeed, the attacks merely served to rally Serb support behind Milošević as his army ran riot in Kosovo. Amidst the carnage the exodus of refugees grew ever greater until it reached crisis proportions with nearly 1 million having fled across the border.

While NATO dithered as to whether to send in ground troops, Shirley, recalling the fate of Bosnia, pleaded for greater intervention and greater financial support to the governments of Macedonia and Albania to cope with the massive influx of refugees within their borders.

She found a ready ally in Blair, who increasingly became convinced of the need for armed intervention. When the Americans finally agreed to his repeated demands for ground troops and the Russians withdrew their support for Milošević, the Serbs capitulated in early June 1999. Their forces withdrew from Kosovo, leaving the province to a period of painful reconstruction under NATO protection before it formally gained its independence in 2008.

Throughout the summer of 2001 Shirley deputised for Bill Rodgers in the Lords while he recovered from a stroke, and when he decided to retire as leader that October, she fully intended to succeed him. She explained to her friend and rival Tom McNally, Jim Callaghan's former political adviser, that after years of being the perpetual bridesmaid she wanted the chance to prove herself in charge. Her support was by no means universal. A number of those who had worked closely with her in the past doubted her capacity for leadership, especially her administrative deficiencies, but such reservations were swept aside by Roy Jenkins. She was the only person of real stature, he opined. After both candidates had appeared before their fellow peers at a hustings Shirley prevailed by thirty-nine votes to twenty-three.

Her accession to the leadership came at a pivotal time in the evolution of the Lords. The Blair government's ejection of the vast majority of hereditary peers in 1999 and its creation of many new Labour ones had transformed its political balance. From having been overwhelmingly a Conservative House it now became one of no overall control, the approximate parity of the two main parties leaving the Liberal Democrats and the crossbenchers holding the balance of power.

Never a master of parliamentary procedure, Shirley's unmethodical style didn't make for consistency in decision making. There was, for instance, her tendency to fall prey to the guile of her fellow leaders in the Lords: Lord Strathclyde, the leader of the Conservatives, would stop her in the corridor and seek her agreement to another crossbencher on a Lords' committee instead of a Liberal Democrat, knowing that if it sounded sensible she would agree. His tactics worked wonders but would create near despair in the Liberal Democrats whips' office, especially for the Chief Whip, John Roper, whose ability and efficiency failed to mask a fastidious nature. His strengths were Shirley's weaknesses and vice versa, which accounted for their chilly relationship, especially over party discipline. Although the Liberal Democrats had become a more cohesive unit since 1997, their dissenting tradition still lived on. Peers such as Andrew Phillips, Conrad Russell and Tony Greaves had minds of their own and weren't averse to expressing them. Phillips, a good friend of Shirley's, recalls taking a contrary line to her over the euro, which left her distinctly unamused, but she recoiled from bowing to the whips' insistence for disciplinary action, accepting that his deviance from the party line, as with others, was born of deeply held principles.

Her forte, as ever, was the public arena. If she had to make a speech at the last minute or respond to a leader's statement, the whips never worried. They knew she would be brilliant, especially given her feel for the House. To see her leaning diagonally forward towards the government benches in full flow was, according to Andrew Phillips, a compelling sight. Her tributes to Lord Hailsham and Lord Longford were models of their kind, while over Iraq and civil liberties she deployed her righteous indignation to devastating effect.

On 11 September 2001 Shirley and Dick arrived at the University of Notre Dame in South Bend, Indiana, where she was about to give the first of four lectures on 'Christians and Public Life'. On the day after the terrorist attacks on the US, she attended a Requiem Mass for the dead and marvelled at the mood of dignified restraint that permeated the open faculty meeting as they discussed the morally appropriate response to the atrocities.

Contrary to the Conservatives, the Liberal Democrats were more guarded in supporting the government unconditionally post-9/11, so while they backed action against the Taliban in Afghanistan, they were much more sceptical about its counter-terror legislation. They were also adamantly opposed to compelling regime change in Iraq as the British government accused its brutal leader, Saddam Hussein, of possessing illegal weapons of mass destruction.

As pressure on Saddam mounted during the autumn of 2002, Shirley welcomed the unanimity of UN Resolution 1441 calling on Iraq to make full disclosure of its weapons programme. The inspectors must, however, be seen to undertake their work in an honest, impartial manner without unacceptable external interference. Aware that some neo-conservatives in Washington were spoiling for a fight, she pronounced herself profoundly troubled by the repercussions of a war against Iraq. Aside from the stark loss of life,

'There is always the danger that, far from suppressing terrorism, we will encourage a new wave of terrorism, unless – I repeat – our actions are seen to be absolutely fair.'[8]

In the face of Saddam's refusal to offer the inspectorate full disclosure, Shirley continued to counsel caution. The British government, like that of the US, ran the risk of pre-empting the interim report from the arms inspectors, which had found no evidence so far of proscribed activities. She questioned whether the Blair government's primary objective was the disarmament of Iraq's nuclear weapons, a position she fully supported, or regime change, an objective not supported by the UN or international law.

With the Liberal Democrats of one mind in both Houses, all fifty-three Liberal Democrat MPs (and 139 Labour MPs) voted against the war on 18 March 2003. On the same day in the Lords, Lord Strathclyde warned Shirley that her party couldn't campaign as the anti-war party on the doorstep and then back the war in the television studio. She replied that it was perfectly possible to distinguish between support for the armed forces and support for the war they were being ordered to fight. It wasn't enough to blame France for the failure to get a second resolution, without which 'the legitimacy of our actions will continue to be disputed'. She took issue with President Bush's motives for attacking Iraq – American justice didn't equate to a just war – and warned that the destruction of its infrastructure would create 'a human catastrophe on a scale that we cannot imagine'.[9]

Once Saddam had been overthrown she called for a central role for the UN in rebuilding Iraq, and following the failure to uncover weapons of mass destruction she questioned the unaccountable way in which the government had taken the country to war. As she surveyed a country increasingly ravaged by civilian insurgency and material deprivation, she observed that al-Qaeda, no threat in Iraq two years earlier, had become one now. 'On every criterion of success, whether that be security, economic recovery or the grounding of democracy in Iraq, we cannot claim success. The evidence points to failure.'[10]

This was her swansong as leader of the Liberal Democrat peers because, in keeping with a promise she had made to Tom McNally on her election that her term in office wouldn't exceed four years, she announced her retirement from October. She was given a rousing send-off at the Liberal Democrat conference and Lord Strathclyde, on behalf of the Conservative peers, called her a living national treasure. In private some of the tributes were less complimentary, not least from the Liberal Democrat whips. They doubted her capacity to lead given her relative dislike of Parliament and reluctance to take unpopular decisions, something that Bill Rodgers acknowledged. While accepting that she was brilliant in the chamber and liked across all parties, he felt that she wasn't temperamentally suited to the role.

> As Leader of a small party, it is necessary to fight your corner against the big parties in internal committees and to manage the Lib Dem teams. The Leader has to promote and sack the frontbenchers. It is quite exacting for three or four days a week and it is essential to be about the place. But Shirley is not – nor has she ever been – collegiate and that is a shortcoming in a Parliamentary Leader.[11]

Throughout Shirley's leadership there were family complications to contend with as Dick, Bernard and her son-in-law Christopher Honey all suffered serious illness.

From the outset her marriage to Dick had given them both a second spring as they rediscovered true joy in their lives – all the more telling for it being so unexpected. It helped, of course, that each had an abiding respect for the other's work, but more than that both had rare qualities by which to invigorate the other. Dorothy Zinberg recalls a dinner at their apartment in Cambridge, Massachusetts, with a journalist who had come to interview Shirley. On their return in the car afterwards the journalist confessed to bemusement as to why Dick was smiling when discussing some tragedy. Dorothy responded that he was in love. 'She liberated him.'

Semi-retired from 1989, Dick was happy adapting to her frenetic lifestyle, appreciating that there was plenty of wind left in her sails. While involved in some of her work he slipped easily into the role of consort, acting as her minder and her greatest supporter in the manner of Denis Thatcher. When Tom McNally thanked him for all his efforts on behalf of the Liberal Democrats, he replied, 'Tom, I do it gladly. I've completed my CV.'

In 1998 when Shirley returned to British politics in a full-time capacity it naturally followed that their time in the US was now confined to the occasional week lecturing and their two-month summer break at Cape Cod, where they would entertain friends at outdoor barbecues. As a staunch Anglophile who loved London, the House of Lords and the English countryside, Dick integrated easily enough, his graceful demeanour making him popular wherever he went. He became a member of the Reform Club, wrote illuminating articles for the Catholic journal *The Tablet* (of which Shirley was a trustee, as well as an occasional contributor) and lectured part-time at Essex University. Above all, he revelled in his responsibilities as a family man, becoming ever closer to his daughter Beth and granddaughter Rachel after the tragic loss of his son Rick in a white-water rafting accident in California in 1995, a blow he bore with great stoicism. He was also like a second father to Rebecca and her husband, Christopher, as well as being an honorary grandfather to their two children, Sam and Nathaniel, and an honorary uncle to John's children, Larissa and Alexander, his wisdom matched by his great sense of fun.

Although supposedly retired, Dick was by no means idle, writing and lecturing on both sides of the Atlantic. In June 2002 he was struck low by a particularly virulent kind of illness called streptococcal pneumonia, but two weeks of recuperation in the Cape with a new canoe proved thoroughly therapeutic.

He and Shirley began 2003 with a memorable holiday in South Africa, marred only by the death of Roy Jenkins when close to completing a monograph of Dick's great hero, FDR, a task that now appropriately fell to him. In June he was invited to Brazil to advise the staff of the newly elected President Lula da Silva on how best to implement social change, a trip he found immensely stimulating. It was in stark contrast to family matters elsewhere.

Back in 1999, the same year as he was knighted, Bernard Williams was diagnosed with multiple myeloma, a form of bone cancer, but battled on courageously, sustained by the devoted support of his family. In June 2003, having received the medical all-clear to travel, he and his wife Patricia went on holiday with Rebecca, Christopher and the boys to Italy. It proved a traumatic experience. First, Christopher was rushed to intensive care in Siena with serious heart trouble, the result of ongoing problems with blood poisoning and pleurisy; then, after Rebecca and the boys had returned home, Bernard died in Rome of a heart attack. The *Daily Telegraph* called him 'one of the most influential British philosophers of the 20th century, best known for his work on moral philosophy',[12] and his passing left a great void in his two families.

Dick remained full of zest that summer at his beloved Cape Cod, looking after Rachel when work commitments obliged Beth to return to London and instructing his grandson Sam in the basics of canoeing. 'Anyone seeing Dick vigorously paddling across Gull Pond in the silver rose evening,' Shirley later wrote, 'could not have anticipated that five months later he would be dead.'[13]

At the beginning of September he accompanied Shirley to a seminar in Moscow, before briefly returning to the US to discuss a book about his life and work. Once back in Britain, he travelled to Northumberland to welcome Larissa and Roger Speirs's new baby into the world before attending Bernard's memorial service in Cambridge. It was while rearranging boxes of books at home in Hertfordshire the next day that Dick fell off a ladder, severely damaging his right leg. Unable to move and in great pain, he was assisted to bed and died a few days later of a heart attack. His funeral was held in the crypt of Westminster Cathedral and his ashes were later interred in the cemetery at Wellfleet.

Amidst the many tributes that poured in from both sides of the Atlantic, Tony King's obituary in *The Independent* best captured the essence of his life: 'Seldom can a man with strong opinions have had so few enemies. Indeed, there is no reason to suppose he had any enemies at all ... Although he would have been appalled and embarrassed to hear anyone say so, there was always more than a whiff of saintliness about him.'[14]

Numbed by her loss, Shirley buried herself in work, which in addition to an exceptionally busy period in the Lords, comprised sorting out Dick's complex estate and arranging four memorial services, the last of which was at Harvard in April 2004.

Having sold Allum Green, the family home in the New Forest, she gave over her Hertfordshire home to Rebecca and her family in January 2005. It was while moving to a pleasant flat nearby that she tripped on a builders' sheet and fell down some stairs, badly breaking her lower foot. As ever she made light work of it, even driving down to the New Forest the next day, and only consented to visiting hospital when the pain in her leg changing gear convinced her that something serious was wrong. Although confined to crutches for several months, she holidayed in South Africa with the Metcalfes before returning to a busy schedule, opposing control orders and other facets of the government's anti-terror legislation.

She remained one of her party's most precious assets, her national profile and extraordinary popularity ever timeless. At Conference her fringe meetings were always full to capacity and her aura on these occasions won her plaudits from the younger generation of MPs. According to Andrew Duff, her charisma was a rarity in the party, but that aside she gave it an intellectual discipline by forcing it to lift its gaze to the higher peaks, away from the parochialism of the foothills. Although capable of currying popularity by playing to the gallery at Conference, she was equally prepared to speak her mind in private, and sometimes in public, in a manner that discomfited the leadership. A mere glance at Ashdown's diaries reveals his concern whenever Shirley expressed her reservations about getting too close to Blair, while her small part in the downfall of his two successors ruptured her friendship with both of them.

When Ashdown had resigned as leader, Shirley had willingly

endorsed Charles Kennedy as his successor, fully admiring his gifts
as a communicator and his stance over civil liberties and Europe.
For much of his leadership she had no reason to doubt her judgement as the party continued its upward curve and Kennedy showed
real courage over Iraq, but beneath his placid surface fierce currents
were raging as his problems with alcohol became ever more
acute. His refusal to admit to anything more untoward than mere
social drinking kept the story on hold in the lead-up to the 2005
general election.

With Labour tainted over Iraq and the Conservatives under
Michael Howard deemed unelectable, the Liberal Democrats felt
optimistic about their prospects, with Shirley predicting another
thirty seats. A disastrous launch to their campaign featuring
Kennedy's stumbling explanation of the party's flagship policy on
local income tax badly undermined them, and although he later
recovered his poise, the damage had been done. Eleven further
seats were gained, giving them sixty-two overall, the best Liberal
Democrat performance yet, but to most observers it should have
been more.

The feeling of a missed opportunity contributed to the general
disillusion that engulfed the parliamentary party when it regrouped
at Westminster as Kennedy's leadership went into abeyance. After
a discordant party conference in September, further allegations
about the leader's alcoholism brought the crisis to a head as senior
figures felt compelled to act. During the 2005 campaign Shirley had
expressed her concerns to Menzies Campbell, the party's respected
deputy leader, when staying at his home in Edinburgh, and urged
him to wield the dagger. 'You and I are the same,' she told him.
'We are not brutal enough.' Campbell counselled caution, not least
because the evidence wasn't clear cut. Later, along with several other
colleagues, Shirley urged Kennedy to seek help and take a sabbatical
if necessary, but found him in a state of denial, a feeling buttressed
by the clannish loyalty of his inner circle which saw conspiracies
everywhere. In truth the opposite had been the case. The willingness of senior Liberal Democrats to give Kennedy the benefit of

the doubt for all too long had only prolonged the agony to a point where the party had descended into turmoil. It took a threatened mass resignation from his front bench to finally bring him to his knees. Following his dignified parting statement on 7 January 2006, Shirley commended Kennedy for making the right decision for his family and his party and wished him a speedy recovery.

Meanwhile, as the focus switched to the succession, Shirley supported Menzies Campbell, calling him the most authentic voice on a wide range of issues. He was duly elected, but soon found himself floundering, especially at Prime Minister's Questions, where he seemed consumed by nerves. In no time the media turned on him, depicting him as too old and out of touch.

With some specialised coaching Campbell's performances began to improve, but the respite proved relatively short-lived as his position was undermined by forces beyond his control, beginning with Blair's retirement as Prime Minister in June 2007. Keen to revitalise the government's sagging image with some new blood, Gordon Brown, the Prime Minister-elect, sounded out Campbell about the possibility of him, Brown, appointing Shirley and two fellow Liberal Democrats, Julia Neuberger and Anthony Lester, as special advisers. Campbell raised no objection provided that the appointments weren't mere tokenism, that they remained fully independent and that any proposals they made contained a fair chance of being implemented. Brown accepted all those conditions before raising the more audacious proposition that a leading Liberal Democrat such as Paddy Ashdown should become a minister. Campbell replied that that was something that he would have to go and think about. When he and his advisers did they rejected it, but before Campbell could convey his message to Brown, *The Guardian* got wind of the talks, causing much unease within Liberal Democrat ranks.

A week later that unease was again palpable after Brown had lobbed another grenade into their camp on his first day as Prime Minister by inviting Shirley to become an adviser to his government on nuclear proliferation. As word leaked out about the meeting she issued a press release confirming the offer and that she was mulling it

over. Given her overt desire to accept, Campbell felt honour-bound
to agree provided his three conditions were met, and two days later
Brown announced her appointment and that of Neuberger (voluntary action) and Lester (civil liberties), as government advisers.

The reaction within the party was lukewarm. *The Liberator*, the
voice of radical liberalism, opined that Shirley should have refused
Brown's offer and speculation about Campbell's leadership resurfaced, not least from party workers at the Ealing Southall by-election.
At least this was the opinion of Navnit Dholakia, the party's deputy
leader in the Lords, and when he discussed this with Shirley they
agreed that it was a boil that had to be lanced. At a private dinner
between senior Liberal Democrat peers and Campbell's entourage
to strengthen party links between the two Houses on 24 July, five
days before the by-election, Shirley, Dholakia and Bob Maclennan
all told Campbell he should resign. Reeling from this unexpected
assault, a shocked Campbell fought back and landed some telling
blows himself by reminding them of the burden he had inherited.
He departed irritated by the ambush, but any hopes of a second
wind were dashed by the failure of Brown to call an autumn election.
With no election now likely before 2009 at the earliest and with the
Conservatives apparently revitalised under David Cameron's youthful leadership, Campbell's age and performance once again became
an all-consuming media passion. After more negative headlines over
the weekend of 13–14 October and some unhelpful comments from
some of his senior colleagues, Campbell decided to resign immediately, his dignity very much intact. He was succeeded by Nick Clegg,
the home affairs spokesman who was very much on the right of the
party. He and Shirley weren't close, but she liked and respected him,
not least for his coolness under fire.

Shirley's appointment as special adviser to the Brown government
on nuclear proliferation, whatever the political motives that might
have prompted it, was logical enough. Since 2002 she had been

on the Board of Directors of the Nuclear Threat Initiative (NTI), based in Washington, a non-governmental organisation dedicated to deactivating nuclear weapons of mass destruction. She had also been a highly regarded member of other influential American think tanks such as the Council on Foreign Relations and was well acquainted with strategic developments in Russia, chiefly through her work for the Moscow School of Political Studies. What with the general disintegration of arms control systems led by George W. Bush's administration's reneging on the Anti-Ballistic Treaty, and the massive expansion of civilian nuclear power, not least by states sympathetic to international terrorism, she began to fear for the future of the planet unless action was taken fast.

A ray of hope emerged in January 2007 when four elder American statesmen – Henry Kissinger and George Schultz, both former Secretaries of State, William Perry, a former Secretary of Defense, and Sam Nunn, a former chairman of the Senate Armed Services Committee – wrote an open letter in the *Wall Street Journal* calling for the abolition of nuclear weapons. Their initiative galvanised the Blair government into action, with Margaret Beckett, the outgoing Foreign Secretary, adding her support for a nuclear-free world in a speech in New York in June 2007. With the Brown government similarly resolved to make a difference, Shirley embarked on her new role with passionate commitment. Although not an expert on the technical complexities of nuclear weapons, she was fully aware of the hard choices that confronted leading states and was able to express the case for disarmament in simple, forceful language.

In July 2008, following a joint initiative of the Australian and Japanese governments, the fully independent International Commission on Nuclear Non-Proliferation and Disarmament (ICNND) was established to undertake preparatory work for the five-year review of the Nuclear Non-Proliferation Treaty (NPT), a landmark international treaty that aimed to prevent the spread of nuclear weapons. It was partly because of her advisory role for the British government and partly her past association with Gareth Evans, the former Australian foreign minister and co-chairman of the ICNND, through their membership of the International Crisis Group, that Shirley was appointed one of its thirteen commissioners. Once again she proved her worth, participating more fully than many of her colleagues and displaying erudition on every conceivable topic.

In 2008 she gave a presentation to the preparatory committee of the NPT in Geneva along with Lord Malloch-Brown, the Minister of State at the Foreign Office, and Charles Curtis, director of the NTI, and visited Dr Mohamed ElBaradei, the director general of the International Atomic Energy Agency (IAEA). The following year she was present at ICNND plenary meetings in Moscow and Hiroshima, visiting the latter's Peace Memorial Museum and hearing testimony from the remaining survivors of the atomic bomb. When the ICNND report was published in December 2009 it advocated twenty practical steps towards a nuclear-free world, including deep cuts in strategic weapons, improved verification and a ban on all nuclear-weapon testing. Its proposals were welcomed the world over and during a Lords debate on nuclear disarmament the following month Shirley's work on the ICNND won her many an accolade from her fellow peers.

By the time the NPT Review Conference was signed at the UN in New York in May 2010, the change of government at home had brought Shirley's advisory role to an end. With Brown increasingly absorbed by the global financial crisis, the opportunity for direct contact with him was limited. While she applauded his government's proposal to reduce the Trident nuclear-armed submarines from four to three, she would have gone further by decommissioning Trident altogether. (Not only did she know nuclear weapons to be very expensive, she considered them less effective against terrorists than both conventional weapons and, above all, effective intelligence operations.)

The future of Trident divided the Liberal Democrats from the two main parties at the 2010 election, but a coalition agreement to postpone any decision about its future until 2015, political convenience aside, was indicative of a growing consensus within the

British political–military elite towards multilateral disarmament. In February 2009 the Top Level Group, an all-party group of senior parliamentarians and members of the military promoting multi-lateral nuclear disarmament and non-proliferation, was formed under the leadership of Des Browne, the former Labour Defence Secretary. With the US and Russia agreeing the following year to a new Strategic Arms Reduction treaty (START) which proposed substantial reductions in the number of nuclear warheads on either side, the Top Level Group was active in lobbying Republican Senators to ratify the treaty.

The passing of the START treaty gave Shirley some cause for hope at a time when the road towards a safer world remains beset with political obstacles, not least the danger of a nuclear stand-off between India and Pakistan over Kashmir and the ongoing crisis in the Middle East. With these threats in mind, she continues to warn against complacency and play her part in the quest for permanent peace.

### Endnotes

1   Proceedings of the Institute of Politics, 1988–89, p.7
2   Harvard Kennedy School Insight, 17 August 2001
3   *Observer*, 16 May 1993
4   SW to Douglas Hurd, 5 May 1994, SW Papers (private collection)
5   SW to Paddy Ashdown, 15 May 1995, SW Papers (private collection)
6   *The Times*, 27 September 1996
7   Paddy Ashdown, *Diaries*, Vol. 2, Allen Lane, 2001, p.370
8   Hansard, House of Lords, 28 November 2002
9   Hansard, House of Lords, 18 March 2003
10  Hansard, House of Lords, 7 September 2004
11  Bill Rodgers to Mark Peel, 17 November 2010
12  *Daily Telegraph*, 14 June 2003
13  SW, Christmas letter, December 2003
14  *Independent*, 6 November 2003

# 17

# RESTLESS PILGRIM

When Shirley's autobiography was published several critics regretted the lack of space she gave to her religion. The omission wasn't entirely surprising for she has rarely flaunted her faith (none of the men she loved was Catholic) or ever claimed to be the political voice of Roman Catholicism. Equally, the roots of her faith run deep and have influenced her views about marriage, the family, charitable giving and public service. 'One of the absolutely crucial things about being a politician, or a public servant', she told the Catholics in Public Life national conference in 1999, 'is that deep inside yourself you have to be able to say, as your constituents come, "And you too are divine." You have to learn to love the citizens and serve.'[1]

Wherever she is in the world she goes to Mass on a Sunday (or on Saturday evening), and she is a frequent communicant at both Westminster Cathedral and the tiny Chapel of the Annunciation in Furneux Pelham, which she has helped keep open. In private she can be passionate about her faith – and, on occasions, in public. 'I had not prepared for quite how much God would enter my conversation with Baroness Williams of Crosby,' commented Joanna Coles when she interviewed Shirley for *The Guardian* in 1996. 'Ann Widdecombe notwithstanding, it's unusual for a politician – especially an ex-Labour Cabinet minister – to invoke the Lord quite as often as Williams does.'[2]

Following in the footsteps of her father, Shirley's distinct brand of liberal Catholicism became conspicuously clear following her election to Parliament. Although spared the kind of religious fanaticism that so bedevilled American politics from the mid-1970s onwards, the onset of the permissive society and the legislation arising out of it posed an awkward dilemma for Britain's churches. Did they go with the flow and risk becoming rootless, or did they oppose secular forces and appear irrelevant? For Shirley the way forward was Cardinal Newman's middle way, so that while remaining orthodox on 'life' issues she sided with the progressives on those relating to social justice.

Over perhaps the most controversial issue of all, abortion, she has resolutely opposed it (except where the life of the mother is in danger), not only because it denies the sanctity of life, but also because it exacerbates the problem of birth control by placing all the emphasis on the woman. Creating a foetus, she argued, was a dual responsibility. Having voted against the 1967 Bill at every stage she has remained an unswerving opponent as the number of abortions have multiplied. 'Abortion should not be legal,' she told the *Daily Mail* in 2007.

> It has got shockingly out of control. Everyone in this country has ready access to contraception. Yet people are looking at abortion as an alternative to the Pill, which is terrible. Not only may it effect [*sic*] women for ever in terms of guilt, but abortion is now regarded as a lifestyle choice, like going to a different supermarket. What we are seeing is a completely blunted response to the idea of taking a baby's life. At 23 weeks, a baby is a viable human being. It is quite appalling to kill it. We wouldn't do it to an animal.[3]

She opposed the Divorce Reform Act of 1969 on the premise that couples broke up marriages far too easily, particularly when children were involved. She also worried that the feminist desire to free women from their dependence on men would lead to many of them, especially those left with children, becoming destitute without adequate maintenance support.

She follows the Catholic doctrine in opposing euthanasia and gay adoption, rejecting the 2007 Equality Act that compelled Catholic and fostering agencies to provide their services to same-sex couples. While stressing her consistent support for the legalisation of homosexual relations between adults and the creation of civil partnerships, Shirley viewed marriage as something different. For most Christians, marriage was a sacred bond between man and woman not a legal status.

> The trouble with society today is that we never think of the child. A child is not a right or a service, like a meal in a restaurant. It is far better that a child is adopted into a heterosexual family. Such a family is more likely to last, and the child is more likely to fit into a society that remains fundamentally heterosexual.[4]

When an unsuccessful amendment was proposed to defeat the Bill, she joined fellow Catholics from other parties in support, the only Liberal Democrat peer to do so.

She returned to the attack in March 2010 against a new Equality Bill, which attempted to simplify and clarify all previous anti-discriminatory legislation, by proposing an amendment that permitted Catholic adoption agencies to restrict their services to married couples, but it was rejected on procedural grounds.

And yet for all Shirley's attachment to her Church she feels its authorities constantly undervalue women, so that every time she is supposed to recite the words 'for us men and our salvation' in the Nicene creed, she omits the first part. This undervaluation, so contrary to the attitude of Jesus towards women, was particularly marked in her youth, pre-Vatican II. In *God and Caesar*, a series of lectures in which she examines the influence of her faith on her political career, Shirley recalls the occasion when, as a young graduate, she participated in a conference of young Christians from all over Europe who were engaged in politics.

> We were invited one evening to an abbey near Bruges in Belgium for dinner. During the meal, a lively discussion broke out about the role of Christian democracy in the construction of the new European Community, a discussion in which I, the only woman in the group, took a vigorous part. The abbot surveyed with growing disapproval. Finally, down the long polished refectory

table, he sent skidding a full bottle of red wine. 'Those who try to speak like men,' he thundered, 'must learn to drink like men.'[5]

As a long-standing member of St Joan's Social and Political Alliance, a Catholic feminist organisation which supports the ordination of women, she welcomed the life-enhancing papacy of John XXIII (1958–63). His legacy, the Second Vatican Council, with its commitment to greater lay participation and collegiality, excited great hopes of reform, but ultimately fell short of expectation as the conservative Curia reasserted itself under John's successor, Paul VI, and even more so under John Paul II and Benedict XVI. In particular, the formal rejection of contraception for married couples, proposed by the majority of a commission set up by John XXIII, tested the loyalty of even the most devout Catholics. Whereas the hierarchy viewed it as a licence for immorality, Shirley saw it as freeing women from the yoke of unwanted births, and an end to the misery of abortion as the one way to cope with unwanted pregnancies.

> My personal belief is that the Church's opposition to contraception, which of course does not involve the destruction of potential human life, severely undermined its crusade against abortion. As a young MP, I opposed David Steel's private bill to legalize abortion … But I was convinced that the bill's opponents had little chance of stopping the bill from becoming law if they also opposed birth control. That was a view shared by many Anglicans too.[6]

The Vatican's refusal to give ground over contraception showed similar conservatism to its stance over clerical celibacy. Shirley wasn't against the latter, regarding it as a form of dedication and self-sacrifice among religious people, but she didn't believe it should be obligatory for all, especially given the growing shortage of priests. With loneliness a constant companion of chastity, the temptation to succumb to sexual deviance and paedophilia became ever greater in her eyes, the latter made all the worse by the evasion of some parts of the worldwide Catholic hierarchy in admitting to clerical paedophilia abuses. As one notorious case after another came to light, Shirley warned her church authorities that unless they faced honestly the modern world they risked sinking into irrelevance, a theme she pursued with Cormac Murphy O'Connor, the Cardinal Archbishop of Westminster, in *The Tablet* in April 2005. The Cardinal denied that clerical paedophilia was the outcome of either celibacy or loneliness and that the ban on contraception was responsible for the rising demand for abortions, countering that contraception had promoted greater promiscuity. He was, however, sympathetic to her demand for a more active role for women, but counselled restraint as negotiations were at a delicate stage, to which Shirley replied, 'Several centuries is not rushing.'

Five years later, on the eve of Pope Benedict's visit to Britain in September 2010, she urged him to adopt a more inclusive approach to his church.

> Treating the ordination of women as among the most serious of sins, alongside paedophilia within the Church, as in the recent directive by the Congregation of the Doctrine of the Faith, could hardly be more offensive to women, especially among the thousands of religious women who have given their lives to the Church.

She went on to warn that such attitudes were likely to offend the Archbishop of Canterbury, who as a spiritual leader of the Anglican Communion, had sought to reach out to the very people neglected by the Roman Catholic Church. 'It has not been easy, but he has tried to address the society in which we live. I hope the Catholic Church will not seek to exploit the difficulties of the Church of England ... Christianity needs us all to work together, and ultimately, we hope, to become one.'[7]

Shirley has also taken the male leaders of her church to task for their lack of international outreach following the suppression of liberation theology in the developing world by Pope John Paul II, aided by President Reagan, during the 1980s. Although well aware of its limitations, most notably its Marxist connotations, she admired its legacy of hope for the poor of Latin America as their lot improved from the 1970s onwards. Her sympathies were enhanced through her friendship with John Feighery, an Irish missionary priest who spent fourteen years in Brazil tending to the poor and dispossessed. A man of deep erudition and enlightened sentiments, very much on the radical wing of his church, Feighery had always been a great admirer of Shirley and had cause to write to her when in Brazil. His insightful letters made such an impression that she answered at length, thereby instigating a protracted correspondence that continues to this day. The more they communicated the closer they became, so that in time Feighery became one of her most trusted counsellors and unofficial chaplain to her family.

In 1984, while on a visit to Brazil to give a lecture on international relations, Shirley had the opportunity to stay with Father Feighery in Belo Horizonte, a sprawling industrial town where many of the citizens were consigned to a life of poverty, and witness the reality of a faith that gave these people dignity. She was particularly impressed by the vibrant communal worship and mutual giving, especially the cooperative established by Sister Teresa, a Brazilian nun, and she returned resolved to redouble her efforts on behalf of the developing world. She became an influential member of the highly respected Catholic Overseas Development Agency (CAFOD) and advocated additional aid linked to improved education and public health programmes, not least against AIDS, the virulent disease that has destroyed millions the world over.

It was a message she has kept pressing. In her Pope Paul VI Memorial Lecture in November 2009, she argued it was time for the Catholic Church to become less preoccupied with sexual morality and redirect its gaze towards its obligations to the poor. Unhappy about the meagre aid given by the richest countries of the world towards the poorer ones, she called for a Tobin tax, a tax on international financial transactions, as well as a greater awareness of climate change.

With political leaders more inclined to talk about their faith (or non-faith) these days, Shirley's Catholicism has attracted a certain amount of attention throughout her career. It isn't something which she has particularly encouraged and it hasn't always played to her advantage. 'Her Catholicism doesn't make her friends,' opined Dick Taverne, an atheist, and it is true that many of her immediate circle find her religious convictions disconcerting.

She has also upset more traditional voices within her church's hierarchy with her periodic dissent from the pews, but she doesn't travel alone in her spiritual pilgrimage. According to Clifford Longley, the author and broadcaster, her intelligent Catholicism is both loyal and progressive, and quintessentially English, while to John Feighery she is a very articulate public voice devoid of undue piety.

A different perspective is offered by the historian and broadcaster Owen Dudley Edwards, who admires Shirley's Catholicism for her willingness to think through each issue as it emerges. 'She is in fact Catholic in the sense of speaking from and for universal perspective: English Roman Catholics are sensitive to charges of unEnglishness, but there are no chauvinist restrictions to Shirley Williams's theological voice.'[8]

It is this enlighted Christianity which helps explain the respect which she commands from the bishops in the House of Lords, one of whom, Richard Harries, the former Bishop of Oxford, now a crossbencher, is a close friend. There are also those of other faiths who discern in her a person who stands for all the best in the Christian tradition. Her faith has imposed great demands on her, not least in her personal life, but the ethical foundations which have underpinned her political career, not least in her commitment to the disadvantaged, and the spiritual strength which has enabled her to overcome the darker moments have richly compensated.

### Endnotes

1   *Briefing*, 11 August 1999
2   *Guardian*, 29 June 1996
3   *Daily Mail*, 15 November 2007
4   *Daily Mail*, 15 November 2007
5   Shirley Williams, *God and Caesar*, Continuum, 2003, p.16
6   Shirley Williams, *God and Caesar*, p.58
7   *Tablet*, 21 August 2010
8   Owen Dudley Edwards to Mark Peel, 3 June 2013

# 18

# POACHER TURNED GAMEKEEPER

The May 2010 election took place against the background of the 2008 world financial crisis and the 2009 parliamentary expenses scandal which left the electorate in a sullen mood, as Shirley discovered when campaigning across the country. With Labour tarnished by the burgeoning deficit and the Conservatives' campaign lacking clarity, the Liberal Democrats, buoyed by Nick Clegg's confident performance during the televised leadership debates, seemed destined to make spectacular gains. In the event they peaked too early and lost four seats as the Conservatives ended nineteen seats short of an overall majority. With the spiralling deficit requiring immediate attention and the financial markets in a turbulent mood, the priority was to get a new government as quickly as possible, preferably one with a strong mandate.

As the parties engaged in intense negotiations over the weekend after the election, Shirley's preference was for a Liberal Democrat–Labour coalition, but the parliamentary arithmetic failed to add up. Clegg, in any case, was better disposed towards Cameron than Brown, and with less aversion to the free market than his predecessors he was prepared to consider a coalition with the Conservatives, especially now they were the largest party. That possibility became a reality once the Conservatives accepted Liberal Democrat demands for a reformed House of Lords and a referendum on the electoral system, a fact Shirley acknowledged in *The Guardian*:

> So now we embark on a new politics. The generation I belong to, steeped in ideology and partisan commitment, is passing away. My own vision was one of equality and social justice advanced by

state action. The new politics is pragmatic, innovative, suspicious
of state power, and holds to values rather than dogma.[1]

She expressed doubts about whether the coalition would work but
accepted they had an obligation to try. With Cameron and Clegg
establishing a good personal rapport, the new government began in
fine fettle, a harmony that ironically helped undermine its controversial attempts to reform the much-revered NHS, since dissident
Liberal Democratic voices remained silent in the cause of coalition
solidarity. Had they spoken out earlier, much of the later flak could
have been avoided.

Ever since their internal market reforms of the 1980s and 1990s,
the Conservatives had been mistrusted over the NHS and it was to
Cameron's credit that he had managed to overturn that perception
with promises of additional funding, cuts in bureaucracy and no
further top-down reorganisations. These promises, similar to ones
made by the other parties, kept the issue dormant during the 2010
election. Yet buried in the small print of the Conservative manifesto
were proposals by its shadow Health Secretary, Andrew Lansley, to
give GPs control of much of the annual NHS budget and introduce
more competition into providing services, with a view to reducing
ever-rising costs. This radical agenda hadn't suddenly appeared; it
had been carefully compiled over the previous five years but was
shrouded in enough vagueness and ambiguity to deflect suspicion.

Although the NHS wasn't one of the priorities during the coalition deliberations, the agreement for government contained a
renewed pledge to prevent any top-down reorganisation, a pledge
that didn't impress Lansley. He now decreed that all GPs would be
involved in commissioning and that primary care trusts, responsible
for commissioning and funding patients' treatment, and strategic
health authorities, which oversaw commissioning and NHS
trusts, would be abolished. Confronted with the enormity of these
changes, civil servants at the Department of Health warned him
of the rumpus this would cause, but Lansley wouldn't budge. He
wanted a new system that couldn't be undone by a future Secretary

of State and, with little critical oversight emanating from either No. 10 or the Treasury, he was able to get his way. Determined to proceed with haste, he published his White Paper, 'Liberating the NHS', on 12 July, presenting it as a far-reaching change endorsed by the electorate, a claim seemingly at variance with his leader's previous reassurance there would be no further restructuring.

Lansley's White Paper was met with profound scepticism, the unfavourable reaction fuelled by his failure to explain the reasons behind the reforms. Labour complained that public accountability was giving way to unchecked privatisation. The influential King's Fund health think tank warned that the sheer scale of the changes would breed potential disruption and the chief executives of leading hospitals questioned the suitability of GPs buying services. It was against this hostile background that Cameron asked Oliver Letwin, the Cabinet Office minister, and Danny Alexander, the Chief Secretary of the Treasury and Clegg's right-hand man, to review the Bill before its publication. Neither of them were health experts and both succumbed to Lansley's assurances that everything was in good working order.

The publication of the Health and Social Care Bill in January 2011 and its sheer size gave ample opportunity to every interest group opposed to its provisions to mount the barricades. In these circumstances it is perhaps surprising that Liberal Democrat MPs voted for the Bill at second reading, especially given the mood of their activists. Their disquiet had intensified following the vitriol heaped upon the party for its official support of the exorbitant rise in university tuition fees, contrary to its manifesto commitment to abolish them. A group of Liberal Democrats led by Dr Evan Harris, a former MP and now the vice-chairman of the party's ruling federal policy committee, planned to oppose the pro-government health motion tabled at their party's spring conference.

From the moment she read the White Paper the previous July, Shirley sensed trouble. In an interview with *The Guardian* to mark her eightieth birthday, she called the restructuring of the NHS 'as unnecessary as it is dangerous'.[2] In a further article for the paper the following month she argued that the additional resources injected by the Blair and Brown governments had made the NHS as efficient as any health system in Europe and vastly superior to the largely private American system. While fully accepting the need for modest changes to combat rising costs and demographic trends, she set herself firmly against a wholesale transformation. That would destroy the NHS as a public service and split the coalition.

She raised her concerns with Nick Clegg that autumn and began talking to medical and nursing organisations, but it was when reading the Bill itself during the February 2011 recess that her opposition grew ever more pronounced. Never had she come across one so detailed, so complex and so incomprehensible. She told *The Times* that it would dismember 'this remarkably successful public service for an untried and disruptive reorganisation' and she felt she had a moral duty to challenge the Bill, especially as it wasn't part of the coalition agreement.[3]

It was a message she delivered to the Liberal Democrat spring conference at Sheffield in a speech punctuated with rapturous applause. She branded the accountability structures lousy, warned of private hospitals cherry-picking patients and urged delegates to stand up and be counted. By doing so they would strengthen the identity of the party for which they had campaigned so long.

Facing certain defeat, the leadership accepted the two rebel amendments limiting the role of the private sector in the NHS, and Clegg, appreciating the need to fight his party's corner more vigorously in government, promised to relay the concerns back to Downing Street.

Confronted with this Liberal Democrat backlash, the growing professional and public hostility to the Bill, and a potentially hazardous passage for it through the independent-minded Lords, Cameron took fright. On 3 April he promised to pause and hold a listening exercise. An NHS Forum was established under Professor Steve Field, the former chairman of the Royal College of General Practitioners, to review government plans. Calling them unworkable and destabilising, Field's report recommended a number of significant changes: the 2013 deadline for GPs to take over was no longer mandatory, commissioning bodies were to have more lay members and meet in public, and Monitor, the independent foundation trust regulator, wouldn't just be a competition regulator, it would promote integration as well. What's more, MPs would have the chance to examine the revised Bill in committee.

Though she had been sceptical about the listening exercise, Shirley wrote in *The Times* that she strongly supported the Future Forum's recommendations. Yet for all the improvements, her satisfaction stretched only so far. She told the NHS Confederation conference in July that the amended Bill was 'confusing, obscure and ambiguous' and that the Secretary of State's responsibilities had to be made much clearer. It was a theme she returned to in an article in *The Observer* in early September, days before the Bill passed its second reading in the Commons. Warning that she still had 'huge concerns', she declared that the central issue now was whether there would be any legal duty on the Secretary of State to secure a comprehensive NHS free at point of need. At present that duty had been delegated to primary care trusts and strategic health authorities. But in the new Bill section three of the 2006 Act had been repealed. Those responsibilities were no longer delegated. The Secretary of State could set objectives and even intervene in the case of significant failure by a commissioning body but was no longer constitutionally or legally accountable. Taxpayers were entitled to expect the government, the minister and Parliament to be accountable for the quality of the services for which they paid. 'Mr Lansley is right to want greater freedom for doctors to work with their patients and to restrain political interference in the NHS. But to throw out accountability in order to tackle petty interference is to undermine democracy itself.'[4]

The conflicting interpretations of the Secretary of State's responsibilities had been exacerbated by an amendment to the Bill, added after the recommissioning exercise: the 'hands off clause', which required him to respect the autonomy of the commissioning bodies. The minister would have to show that any intervention by him was essential, an exacting test to meet. He could be liable to a legal challenge if he failed to meet that test, making 'hands off' a prudent path to follow. That was a provision that should be dropped, just as the Secretary's duty to secure provision of a comprehensive health service should be reinstated.

At the Liberal Democrat conference at Birmingham an attempt by opponents of the NHS Bill to vote on it failed, but both in the main hall and on the fringe Shirley remained her party's ageless talisman, her stark defiance reflecting the prevailing mood. Irritated that the Commons had only been permitted three days to debate the Bill, she promised there would be no such easy passage in the Lords, where the whips were much less powerful and the government had no automatic majority. There would have to be major concessions before her colleagues passed it. This was no idle threat. There were deep misgivings in the Lords about the Bill, not least from two former Conservative health secretaries and a number of crossbenchers, especially those with legal and medical backgrounds. These misgivings might not be enough to destroy the Bill, but by constant bombardment they could hole it beneath the water line, a fact recognised by Lord Howe, the Conservative health spokesman in the Lords.

Possessing all the charm of manner and clarity of exposition that so eluded Lansley, Howe's diplomatic finesse proved critical throughout the winter of 2011–12 as he deftly piloted the Bill through many a minefield, giving ground where necessary. It was this willingness to compromise that helped Shirley and fellow Liberal Democrat dissidents keep their powder dry when Parliament resumed in the autumn. Under pressure from Clegg to toe the line now that significant concessions had been obtained, they rallied to the government's aid at second reading, defeating the Owen–Hennessy amendment sending the Bill to a three-month select committee, and a Labour one abandoning it entirely. Believing the opposition to be guilty of rank opportunism given that Lansley's Bill built on Blairite foundations, Shirley and other senior Liberal Democrats urged fellow peers, especially Labour ones, to stop playing political games with the NHS. In a letter to *The Guardian* they declared that rigorous scrutiny rather than outright opposition was now the priority and in this spirit Shirley moved amendments that restored the Secretary of State's accountability for the NHS back into the Bill.

Faced with potential defeat, Howe requested that all these amendments be withdrawn in return for further deliberations on what needed to be done, a request with which Shirley was happy to comply. These deliberations began with a constructive meeting with Howe, at which she, Glenys Thornton (leader of the Labour peers), and others agreed a way ahead. Particularly significant would be the role of the House of Lords Constitutional Committee under Margaret Jay, a former Labour health minister. Having previously raised concerns about the Secretary of State's diminishing responsibility for a comprehensive NHS, its report in December recommended no dilution in the Secretary of State's ministerial responsibility to Parliament or legal accountability for the health service.

Working closely with Margaret Jay and Shirley, Howe introduced amendments to this effect when the Lords began its report stage in February 2012. With the Lords unconvinced by the reforms and opposition to the Bill reaching new heights on the internet, especially from medical pressure groups and 38 Degrees, the online citizen campaigning group, the disarray in Conservative ranks mounted as they feared another poll tax debacle. 'In a sign of the fiasco at the heart of the Government,' reported Matt Chorley in the *Independent on Sunday*, 'it is now the Liberal Democrats who speak most warmly about the legislation, having rewritten large passages in a coup led by Baroness Williams.'[5]

Gratified by concessions gained over the powers of the Secretary of State, Shirley now turned her guns on the competition clause, urging Lansley to drop the most contentious part of the Bill. Thanks to the expertise of Tim Clement-Jones, a leading corporate lawyer and former Liberal Democrat health spokesman, and his colleague Jonathan Marks, a brilliant QC, a series of amendments were tabled limiting competition. Without these concessions, Shirley warned Clegg, the Lords and Liberal Democrat spring conference wouldn't support the Bill. Accepting her contention that further concessions were possible, Clegg co-signed a letter with her on 27 February that was sent to all Liberal Democrat MPs and peers to support amendments tabled by Liberal Democrats intended to rule out any US-style market in the NHS.

The next day Lansley confirmed that the government supported the changes outlined in the letter. One of the changes put in place additional safeguards to the private income cap to ensure foundation hospitals couldn't put private profit before NHS patients. Traditionally there had been no cap on private-patient work in NHS trust hospitals and it was only with the advent of foundation hospitals in 2003 that it was felt necessary to impose one. (Two to three per cent on average.) Lifting the cap was a priority for the Conservatives and free market Liberal Democrats, but as the Lansley reforms raised concerns about the fragmentation of the NHS, Clement-Jones managed to persuade the Department of Health to accept a 49 per cent cap on private earnings. This was still too much for Andy Burnham, a former Labour Health Secretary and soon to become Lansley's shadow, who raised the spectre of a US-style health system replacing the NHS, a charge that the Shirley–Clegg letter tried to counter with a clause requiring foundation trust governors to agree to any increase of non-NHS income above 5 per cent a year. During a Lords debate on 6 March, Shirley complained that the legitimate role of competition in the health service – its innovative treatments had helped stroke and heart victims – had been forgotten, and expressed her anger at reading endless pieces on social network sites, especially Twitter, accusing the Liberal Democrats of supporting the commercialisation of the health service.

Her protestations won little sympathy from the *Guardian* columnist Polly Toynbee, who wrote of her 'buckling on the NHS Bill. What did she expect when she marched her people out to rebel – and then turned tail?' Calling Shirley and her colleague Vince Cable, the Business Secretary, among the most amiable of politicians, Toynbee found it 'sad and surprising' they should humiliate themselves by voting for extreme Tory policies. 'Their party grasps at crumbs Cameron and Osborne let fall from the Tory table, while Liberal Democrats give them respectable cover for things that two years ago they would have thought abominable.'[6]

Toynbee's words appear to have drawn blood, for Shirley let fly at the Liberal Democrat spring conference at Gateshead the following day, her raw anger impressing Patrick Wintour, the political editor of *The Guardian*. 'A mixture of decency, lucidity and ferocity, she is at 81 a remarkable life force. She can be the personification of charm, but she is also schooled in years of 1980s infighting, and knows how to wage political war.'[7]

With the Health Bill dominating proceedings it was always going to be a difficult weekend and the procedural chicanery over the choice of motion to be debated did nothing to lighten the mood. At a fringe meeting Shirley described how she felt she was 'fighting an uphill battle for the truth' against opponents of the Bill. Having fired another broadside over Twitter, she reserved her greatest ire for Andy Burnham for opposing policies Labour had introduced and damning those same policies in the name of the Liberal Democrats. As for Polly Toynbee, she accused her of 'putting tribalism before truth'.

There was to be further controversy when a motion endorsing changes to the Bill was chosen over one calling for it to be scrapped. Dubbed the Shirley Williams motion, despite Shirley having no part in its drafting, the attempt by Clegg to use her as his human shield backfired during the brief, passionate debate the next day. Andrew George, one of the Liberal Democrat MPs most hostile to the reforms, spoke for many when he admitted that he didn't relish the prospect of crossing swords with a deity, but the Bill hadn't greatly changed. Its plans were still destructive.

By the time Shirley came to speak it was clear that the momentum was with her opponents. She drew applause for rejecting the idea that the debate was about her. It was absurd to make it about one person. She urged her colleagues not to underestimate what they had achieved and she assured them she would not have stuck with the Bill if she thought it would undermine the NHS.

For once her words failed to resonate as Conference refused by 314 to 270 to endorse the Bill, a blow to the leadership. And yet despite the whiff of mutiny from within the ranks the fight was all but over. A week later, to the relief of many, the Bill passed both Houses comfortably, with only one Liberal Democrat peer voting with Labour against it in the Lords. It had been a gruelling and acrimonious struggle in which few of the leading players emerged with credit. Shirley had certainly been one of the most articulate critics of the Bill, gaining concessions for her pains and winning the *Spectator* Parliamentarian of the Year for 2011. How substantial these concessions were remained a source of bitter debate between her and her critics. Polly Toynbee continued to insist that they didn't add up to anything much as she pronounced the end of the NHS as a national service, while Peter Hennessy was more charitable, recognising Shirley's efforts in committee and the difficulty of securing major concessions. Whatever the truth, the controversies behind the Bill had hardly enhanced the fortunes of the Liberal Democrats as once again they suffered a drubbing in the 2012 local elections. With Clegg's personal ratings even worse than those of his party his future as leader became a matter of speculation, but the idea that Shirley might play Lady Macbeth to his Duncan was one she promptly dismissed. She was critical of Clegg's leadership over the doomed AV campaign in 2011 and his maladroit attempt to reform the House of Lords in 2012, but admired his composure under fire and she looked forward to the day when the Liberal Democrats finally emerged from the chrysalis of protest to leave a permanent mark on government.

When Dick married Shirley, he predicted that the hurricane within her would blow itself out within several years, but over two decades later it has shown no sign of abating. The hair may be greyer and her gait a touch more halting, but otherwise there have been few concessions to advancing years. Physical exercise has always been an invigorating outlet for her enormous energy. She swims regularly during the week in London and at weekends she likes to cycle and walk with friends.

Holidays remain one of her chief pleasures, not least for the opportunity they afford for relaxation, exercise and discovery. An intrepid traveller, there are few parts of the globe that she hasn't visited, but for all the thrill of savouring the unknown, she is also a creature of habit; Cape Cod in the summer with her family. The arrival of her two grandchildren, Sam and Nathaniel, has been a particular joy to her and while not sharing their love of football, she has been instrumental in teaching them how to cycle and canoe.

With her years of service behind her she could be forgiven for scaling down her commitments to enjoy more time at home, but that has never been her way. Always someone who likes being at the hub of events, she feels she still has a part to play. Part of her secret has been her willingness to embrace modernity and fight for the changes she so passionately believes in. Thus amidst all her parliamentary activity and media appearances (she recently became the most frequent panellist on BBC's *Question Time*) there have been additional responsibilities such as her chairmanship of the judges of the National Teaching Awards, a scheme to identify and honour outstanding teachers in the maintained sector.

In September 2008, Shirley was laid low by a hip that required an operation. William Wallace, the Liberal Democrat peer, recalls meeting her in Westminster Underground station with a hefty overnight bag which she couldn't lift. Having carried it up the steps (the lift was out of action) his inquiries about what arrangements she had made for her recuperation were met with a frosty response. She would be fine, she assured him. Her physical strength has always been very important to her and her touchiness reflected an understandable apprehension about growing battle fatigue, but following surgery and convalescence she returned little the worse for wear, her appetite for life undiminished.

Shirley's temporary incapacity had at least given her more time to focus on her autobiography, *Climbing the Bookshelves*, as it neared completion after a decade of intermittent work. For someone not given to personal introspection or confessionals, it wasn't natural territory, but Dick had insisted she do it and with his encouragement she began to delve back into her past.

The book, eventually published in September 2009, gained favourable reviews for its generosity and candour, especially her admission that as a woman she lacked the self-esteem to scale the highest political peaks. The public liked it too, judging by its prolific sales, although a figure of 17,000 in hardback left Shirley rather deflated. Her mother had sold 1 million copies, she remarked.

2010 saw Shirley's eightieth birthday celebrated in style with a dinner in her honour at the Savile Club attended by colleagues and friends. Charles Kennedy spoke warmly of her telling contribution to the Liberal Democrats and Peter Hennessy eloquently touched on her uniqueness as a politician, not least her immense cross-party appeal. 'If you give up what you care about,' Shirley told *The Guardian* weeks earlier, 'you start dying', and as she remains in robust health there is every reason to believe she will continue to offer help and encouragement to many in duress for some years to come.[8]

### Endnotes

1   *Guardian*, 13 May 2010
2   *Guardian*, 14 August 2010
3   *The Times*, 28 February 2011
4   *Observer*, 4 September 2011
5   *Independent on Sunday*, 12 February 2012
6   *Guardian*, 9 March 2012
7   *Guardian*, 12 March 2012
8   *Guardian*, 14 August 2010

# SHIRLEY WILLIAMS

Ever since she first stood for Parliament in 1954, Shirley Williams has been a familiar landmark on the political landscape, a tender sapling that in time grew into a hardened oak well able to withstand the stormy blasts that have come her way. It is a tribute to her enduring appeal that she has remained so active in the public eye, her critical faculties in no way impaired by age. According to Jon Snow of *Channel 4 News*, she is an exceptional performer, 'one of the very few women in politics who can play what remains, to our collective shame, a man's game. My spirits rise if Shirley is to be part of any debate.'[1]

With the influence of highly principled parents to act as her conscience, Shirley's politics were primarily about overcoming injustice and it was this moral conviction, along with her other qualities, that propelled her into the sunlight. As she climbed the lower rungs of the government ladder she seemed destined to reach the very top, only to be beaten by a woman many thought to be her inferior. This book has tried to explain that while this may have had much to do with her being in the wrong party at the wrong time, it also had much to do with a certain indecisiveness of character and feisty independence that refused to kowtow to any institution, group or cause.

Even her ambition was qualified, so that while she enjoyed the public stage and the opportunity to make a difference in government, it wasn't ambition at all costs, especially if that meant stooping to underhand tactics. 'Few if any of her contemporaries matched her appeal although many outstripped her in ruthlessness, organisation and guile,' commented Phillip Whitehead, the former Labour MP.[2]

Always something of a loner at Westminster, as many women

were, Shirley did little to advance her claims by aligning herself with any of the big beasts in the Labour jungle, neither building alliances in Cabinet nor currying favour on the back benches. Such diffidence was manifest in her half-hearted attempt to win the deputy leadership of the Labour Party in 1976, and later in her refusal to challenge Roy Jenkins for the leadership of the SDP in 1982. Had she gone all out to win, the evidence suggests she could have done it and quite possibly become the heir to Callaghan. 'In a very narrow sense Shirley was a bad politician,' remarked David Marquand, 'because she didn't know how strong she was.' Extraordinarily effective when impassioned, such as her tirade against the far left at the Labour conference of 1980, her undoing, he concluded, lay in her failure to gamble. His analysis was shared by David Alton, who felt that she lacked that killer instinct. 'She is a remarkable politician, but such qualities don't make for a street fighter in the British system. We get something different from Shirley Williams.'

Another barrier to her reaching the summit was her record as a departmental minister. Had she held one of the great offices of state her position would inevitably have been strengthened, but for all Wilson and Callaghan's affection for her, this never happened. Their reluctance to promote her may have had something to do with the sexism then still prevalent in British politics, but was more probably due to their conviction that she hadn't quite earned her spurs. In the opinion of David Owen she wasn't at ease with responsibility and decision making, a trait that hadn't bothered either Barbara Castle or Margaret Thatcher, and she never quite lived down Tony Crosland's doubts about her effectiveness in government. 'She was a brilliant performer – as she still is', opined Bill Rodgers, 'but taking charge and managing a team and taking a risk and being unpopular was another matter.'[3]

At Education Shirley had, according to Jim Callaghan, a chance to leave a monument to her work by overseeing a dramatic overhaul of the faltering educational system. It was a tall order at the best of times, especially given the limited powers at her disposal and a profession blind to its own failings. Her Green Paper was in response to this, but for all the talk about raising standards, little concrete had emerged by the time the government fell. 'Had the Labour Government demonstrated the will necessary to implement the Ruskin proposals,' wrote Bernard Donoughue , 'I believe they would have made teaching and schooling ... a more satisfying experience for teachers and children alike, without the battles and demoralisation which resulted from the later Tory tactics of confrontation in the field of education.'[4]

One area where Shirley left her footprints was secondary reorganisation. Although some 60 per cent of schools had already gone comprehensive by the time she became Education Secretary, it was a policy she strongly supported and had helped implement as a junior minister. Once in command she set out to eradicate selection completely in the maintained sector, only to be foiled by the recalcitrance of a few Tory authorities. It was a small consolation to the grammar school lobby, which saw their number reduced to a few hundred. Nothing in Shirley's career, aside from leaving the Labour Party, and the later battle over the NHS, generated controversy quite like her stance over comprehensive education and the passions still stir on all sides of the educational divide. (Easily the most unflattering review of her autobiography came from Sean O'Grady, an ex-grammar school boy, in *The Independent*.)

The debate was given an added twist when the Blair government, in a departure from the previous Labour script, opted for city academies, privately sponsored state-financed schools, signalling, in Alastair Campbell's phrase, 'the end of the bog-standard comprehensive'. Then, in 2010, Shirley's good friend Robert Skidelsky cast a critical gaze over her time as Education Secretary, especially the decision to close the grammar schools. By using the educational system to create a more egalitarian society, he argued, she failed to understand the damaging effect that abolition of selection would have on academic standards, especially on those at the top and the bottom of the ability range. One rather unintentional consequence of the demise of the grammar schools, he declared, was the boost it had given to the independent sector at a time when many of its schools were struggling. As they flourished in the more benign climate of the 1980s, social divisions were exacerbated because of the limited opportunities now available for bright working-class children, with the ability to pay becoming the main determinant to getting on.

Faced with these attacks, Shirley remains unapologetic about comprehensives. She considers them her greatest achievement, not least the way they have opened up untold avenues of opportunity for many children unimaginable under the old system. The fact that many failing schools still exist she wouldn't dispute, but she would attribute much of this failure to them competing on an unequal playing field with the private sector. It is a fair point, though it by no means constitutes the whole story.

Shirley's other main legacy was her part in the formation of the SDP. When assessing its impact, claim and counterclaim vie with each other. To Labour loyalists such as Roy Hattersley it was the great betrayal conceived in opportunism and responsible for giving Margaret Thatcher a full decade in power; to others it proved the salvation of the Labour Party by forcing it to return to its democratic roots. The truth, as so often the case, lies somewhere in between.

It would be hard to deny that the Labour Party had been Shirley's stepping stone to success and political eminence. She owed it much, as did the others, but equally had given back much in return. For years she had fought the blight of extremism on the NEC with ever diminishing returns until there had come a time when she, Owen and Rodgers felt they had reached the end of the road. Whether they were right to leave the party remains an open question – after all, Labour did eventually recover – but to suggest their departure was motivated by self-interest seems wide of the mark. (Admittedly this might have applied to some backbenchers faced with deselection.) For despite all the heady rhetoric that accompanied some of their early by-election triumphs, few of them had any illusions about the perils that lay ahead. One doesn't have to be very astute to know that third parties have rarely flourished in the British two-party system, a point that Denis Healey was forever making to the three of them as he tried to prevent them leaving.

In their magisterial study of the SDP, the authors Ivor Crewe and Tony King refute the argument that the Alliance's most lasting legacy was to delay Labour's recovery for nearly ten years: 'The truth is that the existence of the SDP did not materially affect the outcome of either election. In its unreformed, divided, antediluvian state, the Labour party was doomed to defeat in both 1983 and 1987, no matter what the SDP or anyone else said or did.'[5]

Equally, the claim that the SDP was the midwife of New Labour doesn't stand up to close examination. For when the mould was eventually broken it was Margaret Thatcher and the free market that emerged triumphant, something recognised by Tony Blair as he moved Labour further to the right than Shirley had ever been, either in the Labour Party or in the SDP–Liberal Democrats. In his attempt, and that of Gordon Brown, to put some distance between New Labour and the Conservatives, he embraced many of the policies of Bill Clinton's New Democrats in the US, which combined fiscal prudence and individual opportunity with communal help for the needy.

By conventional standards Shirley Williams's legacy seems rather modest for someone of her ability, but success can be measured in different ways and hers is as an exemplar which appeals to the better angels in our nature. As one of the leading female politicians of the twentieth century her success in overcoming archaic custom and prejudice helped inspire future generations of women to follow in her footsteps. That said, the great leap forward in the number of women MPs cannot disguise the fact that none of them have come close to emulating Shirley in either ability or popular appeal (Mo Mowlam, the Labour Northern Ireland Secretary in the late 1990s, would probably be the closest).

As a young girl growing up in the US, Shirley Williams became captivated by the life and work of Abraham Lincoln, the greatest of all American presidents. Whether she was influenced by the noble sentiments of his second inaugural address, 'With malice towards none, with charity for all', is unclear, but they certainly encapsulate the spirit in which she has lived her life, and that is no mean epitaph.

**Endnotes**

1   Jon Snow to Mark Peel, 31 July 2010
2   Phillip Whitehead, *The Writing on the Wall: Britain in the Seventies*, Channel 4 in association with Michael Joseph, 1985, p.619
3   Bill Rodgers to Mark Peel, 17 November 2010
4   Bernard Donoughue, *Heat of the Kitchen*, p.282
5   Ivor Crewe and Anthony King, *SDP: The Birth, Life and Death of the Social Democratic Party*, Oxford University Press, 1995, p.467

# PERMISSIONS

Extracts from *Against the Tide: Diaries 1973–77* and *Conflicts of Interest: Diaries 1977–80* by Tony Benn, ed. by Ruth Winstone, reprinted by permission of Ruth Winstone

Extracts from the *Dictionary of Liberal Biography*, ed. by Duncan Brack, reprinted by permission of Methuen

Quotations from Vera Brittain included by permission of Mark Bostridge and T. J. Brittain-Catlin, literary executors for the Estate of Vera Brittain 1970

Extracts from *The Diaries of a Cabinet Minister* by Richard Crossman reprinted by permission of Virginia Crossman

Extracts from *Downing Street Diary, Volume Two: With James Callaghan in No. 10* by Bernard Donoughue, published by Jonathan Cape, reprinted by permission of The Random House Group Limited

Extracts from *Downing Street in Perspective* by Marcia Falkender reprinted by permission of Orion

Extracts from *Hammer of the Left* by John Golding reprinted by permission of Methuen

Extracts from *Time to Declare* by David Owen reprinted by permission of David Owen

Extracts from *Fourth among Equals* by Bill Rodgers reprinted by permission of Methuen

Extracts from *Climbing the Bookshelves* by Shirley Williams reprinted by permission of Virago, an imprint of Little, Brown Book Group

Extracts from *God and Caesar* by Shirley Williams © Shirley Williams, 2001, reprinted by permission of Continuum, an imprint of Bloomsbury Publishing Plc

Crown copyright material in the Public Records Office reproduced by permission of the Controller of Her Majesty's Stationery Office

Thanks are due to Baroness Jay for permission to quote extracts from the letters of Lord Callaghan; to Lord Healey for an extract from a letter to Shirley Williams; to Lord Rodgers for extracts from letters to the author; to the Local Studies Collection, Hull History Centre for extracts from the letters of Winifred Holtby; to Special Collections, the Albert Sloman Library, the University of Essex, for letters in the Bill Rodgers papers; to Special Collections and Archives, the University of Liverpool, for letters in the David Owen papers; to Mike Thomas for an extract from a letter to Shirley Williams; to Peter Metcalfe for letters in his papers; to Shirley Williams for letters in her papers; and to Jon Snow and Carol Bracken (now Carol Savage) for permission to quote from emails to the author.

# BIBLIOGRAPHY

**Books**

Abdela, Lesley, *Woman with X Appeal: Women Politicians in Britain Today* (Macdonald, 1989)

Adams, Pauline, *Somerville for Women* (Oxford University Press, 1996)

Adonis, Andrew and Thomas, Keith (eds), *Roy Jenkins: A Retrospective* (Oxford University Press, 2004)

Ashdown, Paddy, *Diaries Vol. 1* (Allen Lane, 2000)

— —, *Diaries Vol. 2* (Allen Lane, 2001)

Bailes, Howard, *Once a Paulina: A History of St Paul's Girls' School* (James and James, 2000)

Baker, Kenneth, *The Turbulent Years: My Life in Politics* (Faber & Faber, 1993)

Balchin, Jack, *First New Town: An Autobiography of the Stevenage Development Corporation* (Stevenage Development Corporation, 1980)

Ball, Stephen J., *Politics and Policy-Making in Education* (Routledge, 1990)

Barnett, Joel, *Inside the Treasury* (Deutsch, 1982)

Bartram, Peter, *David Steel: His Life and Time in Politics* (Star, 1981)

Beckett, Andy, *When the Lights Went Out: Britain in the Seventies* (Faber & Faber, 2009)

Bell, Geoffrey, *Troublesome Business: The Labour Party and the Irish Question* (Pluto Press, 1982)

Benn, Tony, (ed. Ruth Winstone), *Years of Hope: Diaries, Papers and Letters 1940–1962* (Hutchinson, 1994)

— —, *Out of the Wilderness: Diaries 1963–1967* (Hutchinson, 1987)

— —, *Office without Power: Diaries 1968–1972* (Hutchinson, 1988)

— —, *Against the Tide: Diaries 1973–1976* (Hutchinson, 1989)

— —, *Conflicts of Interest: Diaries 1977–1980* (Hutchinson, 1990)

— —, *The End of an Era: Diaries 1980–1990* (Hutchinson, 1990)

Benton, Jill, *Naomi Mitchison: A Biography* (Pandora Press, 1990)

Berry, Paul, and Bostridge, Mark, *Vera Brittain: A Life* (Chatto & Windus, 1995; Virago, 2001)

Bosanquet, Nick, and Townsend, Peter, *A Fabian Study of Labour in Power, 1974–1979* (Heinemann, 1980)

Brack, Duncan et al. (eds), *Dictionary of Liberal Biography* (Politico's, 1998)

Bradley, Ian, *Breaking the Mould? The Birth and Prospects of the Social Democratic Party* (Martin Robertson, 1981)

Brittain, Vera, *Testament of Youth: An Autobiographical Study of the Years 1900–1925* (Gollancz, 1933; Virago, 1978; Fontana, 1979)

— —, *Testament of Friendship: The Story of Winifred Holtby* (Macmillan, 1940; Virago, 1980; Fontana, 1981)

— —, *England's Hour: An Autobiography 1939–1941* (Macmillan, 1941; Futura, 1981)

— —, *Testament of Experience: An Autobiographical Story of the Years 1925–1950* (Gollancz, 1957; Virago, 1979; Fontana, 1980)

— —, (eds Vera Brittain and Geoffrey Handley Taylor), *Selected Letters of Winifred Holtby and Vera Brittain 1920–1951* (A. Brown & Sons, 1960)

— —, *The Women at Oxford: A Fragment of History* (Harrap, 1960)

— —, (eds Alan Bishop with Terry Smart), *Chronicle of Youth: War Diary 1913–1917* (Gollancz, 1981; Fontana, 1982)

— —, (ed. Alan Bishop), *Chronicle of Friendship: Diary of the Thirties 1932–1939* (Gollancz, 1986)

— —, (eds Alan Bishop and Y. Aleksandra Bennett), *Wartime Chronicle: Diary 1939–1945* (Gollancz, 1989)

— —, *One Voice: Pacifist Writings from the Second World War* (Continuum, 2005)

Brivati, Brian, *Hugh Gaitskell* (Richard Cohen, 1996)

Brivati, Brian and Heffernan, Richard (eds), *The Labour Party: A Centenary History* (Macmillan, 2000)

Broad, Roger, *Labour's European Dilemmas: From Bevin to Blair* (Palgrave, 2001)

Butler, David and Kitzinger, Uwe, *The 1975 Referendum* (Macmillan, 1996)

Callaghan, Daniel, *Conservative Party Education Policies 1976–1997* (Sussex Academic, 2006)

Callaghan, James, *Time and Chance* (Fontana, 1987)

Campbell, John, *Edward Heath* (Jonathan Cape, 1993)

— —, *Margaret Thatcher, Vol.1: The Grocer's Daughter* (Jonathan Cape, 2000)

— —, *Roy Jenkins: A Biography* (Weidenfeld & Nicolson, 1983)

Campbell, Menzies, *My Autobiography* (Hodder & Stoughton, 2008)

Carpenter, Humphrey, *OUDS: A Centenary History of the Oxford University Dramatics Society 1885–1985* (Oxford University Press, 1985)

Castle, Barbara, *Fighting All the Way* (Macmillan, 1993)

— —, *The Castle Diaries 1964–1970* (Weidenfeld & Nicolson, 1984)

— —, *The Castle Diaries 1974–1976* (Weidenfeld & Nicolson, 1980)

Catlin, George, *For God's Sake Go!* (Colin Smythe, 1972)

Catlin, John, *Family Quartet* (Hamish Hamilton, 1987)

Chapple, Frank, *Sparks Fly! A Trade Union Life* (Michael Joseph, 1984)

Chitty, Clyde, *Towards a New Education System: Victory of the New Right?* (The Falmer Press, 1989)

Clarke, Peter, *Liberals and Social Democrats* (Cambridge University Press, 1978)

Cole, John, *As It Seemed To Me: Political Memoirs* (Weidenfeld & Nicolson, 1995)

Crewe, Ivor and King, Anthony, *SDP: The Birth, Life and Death of the Social Democratic Party* (Oxford University Press, 1995)

Crick, Michael, *The March of Militant* (Faber & Faber, 1986)

Cronin, James E., *New Labour's Pasts: The Labour Party and its Discontents* (Pearson/Longman, 2004)

Crosland, Susan, *Tony Crosland* (Jonathan Cape, 1982)

Crossman, Richard, (ed. Janet Morgan), *The Diaries of a Cabinet Minister, Vol. 1: Minister of Housing, 1964–1966* (Hamish Hamilton and Jonathan Cape, 1975)

— —, (ed. Janet Morgan), *The Diaries of a Cabinet Minister, Vol. 2, 1966–1968* (Hamish Hamilton and Jonathan Cape, 1976)

— —, (ed. Janet Morgan), *The Diaries of a Cabinet Minister, Vol. 3:*

*Secretary of State for Social Service, 1968–1970* (Hamish Hamilton and Jonathan Cape, 1977)

Crouch, Colin, *The Politics of Industrial Relations* (Fontana, 1979)

Dale, Iain (ed.), *The Politico's Book of the Dead* (Politico's, 2003)

Dawson, John A. and Moir, Christopher (eds), *Competition and Markets: Essays in Honour of Margaret Hall* (Macmillan, 1990)

Day, Robin, *Grand Inquisitor: Memoirs* (Weidenfeld & Nicolson, 1989)

Dell, Edmund, *A Hard Pounding: Politics and Economic Crisis 1974–1976* (Oxford University Press, 1991)

— —, *A Strange Eventful History: Democratic Socialism in Britain* (HarperCollins, 2000)

Desai, Radhika, *Intellectuals and Socialism: 'Social Democrats' and the Labour Party* (Lawrence and Wishart, 1994)

Dickinson, Matthew J. and Neustadt, Elizabeth A. (eds), *Guardian of the Presidency, The Legacy of Richard E. Neustadt* (Brookings Institution Press, 2007)

Donoughue, Bernard, *Downing Street Diary: With Harold Wilson in No. 10* (Jonathan Cape, 2005)

— —, *Downing Street Diary Volume 2: With James Callaghan in No. 10* (Jonathan Cape, 2008)

— —, *Prime Minister: The Conduct of Policy under Harold Wilson and James Callaghan* (Jonathan Cape, 1987)

— —, *The Heat of the Kitchen: An Autobiography* (Politico's, 2003)

Dromey, Jack and Taylor, Graham, *Grunwick: The Workers' Story* (Lawrence and Wishart, 1978)

Duff, Andrew (ed.), *Making the Difference: Essays in Honour of Shirley Williams* (Biteback, 2010)

Dutton, David, *A History of the Liberal Party in the Twentieth Century* (Palgrave, 2004)

Falkender, Marcia, *Downing Street in Perspective* (Weidenfeld & Nicolson, 1983)

Fethney, Michael, *The Absurd and The Brave* (The Book Guild, 1990)

Gaskill, William, *A Sense of Direction* (Faber & Faber, 1988)

Gerard, Jasper, *The Clegg Coup: Britain's First Coalition Government since Lloyd George* (Gibson Square, 2011)

Golding, John, *Hammer of the Left* (Politico's, 2003)

Goodman, Geoffrey, *From Bevan to Blair: Fifty Years Reporting from the Political Front Line* (Pluto Press, 2003)

Gordon, Peter, Aldrich, Richard and Dean, Denis (eds), *Education and Policy in England in the Twentieth Century* (Woburn Press, 1991)

Gorham, Deborah, *Vera Brittain: A Feminist Life* (Blackwell, 1996)

Graff, Ilan (ed.), *40 Years of Inspiration: The Institute of Politics 1966–2006* (The Institute of Politics, Harvard University, 2006)

Graham, Ysenda M., *The Real Mrs Miniver: Jan Struther's Story* (John Murray, 2001)

Harrison, Brian (ed.), *The History of the University of Oxford Vol. VIII: The Twentieth Century* (Clarendon Press, 1994)

Harmon, Mark. D., *The British Labour Government and the 1976 IMF Crisis* (Macmillan, 1997)

Hatfield, Michael, *The House the Left Built: Inside Labour Policy-Making, 1970–1975* (Gollancz, 1978)

Hattersley, Roy, *Fifty Years On: A Prejudiced History of Britain since the War* (Little, Brown, 1997)

— —, *Who Goes Home? Scenes from a Political Life* (Little, Brown, 1995)

Hayter, Dianne, *Fightback! Labour's Traditional Right in the 1970s and 80s* (Manchester University Press, 2005)

Healey, Denis, *The Time of My Life* (Michael Joseph, 1989)

Hencke, David, *Colleges in Crisis: The Reorganization of Teacher Training* (Penguin, 1978)

Hennessy, Peter, *Whitehall* (Secker and Warburg, 1989)

— —, *Having it so Good: Britain in the Fifties* (Penguin, 2007)

Heppell, Timothy and Seawright, David (eds), *Cameron and the Conservatives: The Transition to Coalition Government* (Palgrave Macmillan, 2012)

Hirschfield, M. G. (ed.), *St Paul's Girls' School 1904–1954* (The Favil Press, 1954)

Holden, Andrew, *Makers and Manners: Politics and Morality in Post-War Britain* (Politico's, 2004)

Holmes, Martin, *The Labour Government 1974–1979: Political Aims and Economic Reality* (Macmillan, 1985)

Humphrey, Derek and Ward, Michael, *Passports and Politics* (Penguin, 1974)

Hurst, Greg, *Charles Kennedy: A Tragic Flaw* (Politico's, 2006)

Jefferys, Kevin, *Anthony Crosland: A New Biography* (Richard Cohen, 1999)

Jenkins, Roy, *European Diary, 1977–1981* (Collins, 1989)

— —, *A Life at the Centre* (Macmillan, 1991)

Johnson, Frank, *Out of Order* (Robson, 1982)

Jones, Ken, *Education in Britain: 1944 to the Present* (Polity, 2003)

Jones, Mervyn, *Michael Foot* (Gollancz, 1994)

Josephs, Jeremy, *Inside the Alliance* (John Martin, 1983)

Joyce, Peter, *Realignment of the Left* (Macmillan, 1999)

Kellner, Peter and Hitchens, Christopher, *Callaghan: The Road to Number Ten* (Cassell, 1976)

Knight, Christopher, *The Making of Tory Education Policy in Post-War Britain 1950–1986* (The Falmer Press, 1990)

Kogan, David and Kogan, Maurice, *The Attack on Higher Education* (Kogan Page, 1983)

— —, *The Battle for the Labour Party* (Kogan Page, 1983)

Kynaston, David, *The Financial Times: A Centenary History* (Viking, 1988)

Lawrence, Ian, *Power and Politics at the Department of Education and Science* (Cassell, 1992)

Lawton, Denis, *Education and Labour Party Ideologies 1900–2001 and Beyond* (The Falmer Press, 2005)

Laybourn, Keith, *A Century of Labour: A History of the Labour Party 1900–2000* (Sutton Publishing, 2000)

Lester, Anthony P. and Bindman, Geoffrey, *Race and Law* (Longman, 1972)

MacIver, Don (ed.), *The Liberal Democrats* (Prentice Hall, 1996)

McIntosh, Ronald, *Challenge to Democracy: Politics, Trade Union Power and Economic Failure in the 1970s* (Politico's, 2006)

Maddox, Brenda, *Maggie: The First Lady* (Hodder & Stoughton, 2003)

Mann, William J., *Edge of Midnight: The Life of John Schlesinger* (Hutchinson, 2004)

Marr, Andrew, *A History of Modern Britain* (Pan Macmillan, 2007)

Martineau, Lisa, *Politics and Power: Barbara Castle: a Biography* (Andre Deutsch, 2000)

Maudling, Reginald, *Memoirs* (Sidgwick & Jackson, 1978)

Meredith, Stephen, *Labours Old and New* (Manchester University Press, 2008)

Michie, Alistair and Hoggart, Simon, *The Pact* (Quartet, 1978)

Minkin, Lewis, *The Contentious Alliance: Trade Unions and the Labour Party* (Edinburgh University Press, 1991)

Mitchell, Austin, *Four Years in the Death of the Labour Party* (Methuen, 1983)

Morgan, Kenneth O., *Callaghan: A Life* (Oxford University Press, 1997)

— —, *Michael Foot: A Life* (HarperPress, 2007)

Morris, Max and Griggs, Clive (eds), *Education: The Wasted Years? 1973–1986* (The Falmer Press, 1988)

Mullan, Bob, *Stevenage Ltd: Aspects of the Planning and Politics of Stevenage New Town 1945–1978* (Routledge and Kegan Paul, 1980)

Norris, Pippa, *British By-elections: The Volatile Electorate* (Clarendon Press, 1990)

Owen, David, *Face the Future* (Jonathan Cape, 1981)

— —, *Time to Declare* (Penguin, 1991)

Parker, Peter, *For Starters: The Business of Life* (Jonathan Cape, 1989)

Pearce, Edward, *Denis Healey: A Life in our Times* (Little, Brown, 2002)

Pelling, Henry, *A Short History of the Labour Party* (Macmillan, 1982)

Perkins, Anne, *Red Queen: The Authorised Biography of Barbara Castle* (Macmillan, 2003)

Phillips, Melanie, *The Divided House: Women at Westminster* (Sidgwick & Jackson, 1980)

Pimlott, Ben, *Harold Wilson* (HarperCollins, 1992)

Plaskow, Maurice (ed.), *Life and Death of the Schools Council* (The Falmer Press, 1985)

Pugh, Patricia, *Educate, Agitate, Organize: 100 Years of Fabian Socialism* (Methuen, 1985)

Radice, Giles, *Friends and Rivals: Crosland, Jenkins and Healey* (Little, Brown, 2002)

— —, *Diaries 1980–2001* (Weidenfeld & Nicolson, 2004)

Richardson, Tony, *Long-Distance Runner: A Memoir* (Faber & Faber, 1993)

Risjord, Norman K., *A Popular History of Minnesota* (Minnesota Historical Society Press, 2005)

Robins, L. J., *The Reluctant Party: Labour and the European Economic Community 1961–1975* (G. W. and A. Hesketh, 1979)

Robinson, Robert, *Skip All That: Memoirs* (Century, 1996)

Rodgers, Bill, *Fourth Among Equals* (Politico's, 2000)

Rogaly, Joe, *Grunwick* (Penguin, 1977)

Rosen, Greg (ed.), *Dictionary of Labour Biography* (Politico's, 2001)

Rubinstein, David, *The Labour Party and British Society 1880–2005* (Sussex Academic Press, 2006)

Sampson, Anthony, *The Changing Anatomy of Britain* (Hodder & Stoughton, 1982)

Seldon, Anthony, *Blair* (The Free Press, 2004)

Seldon, Anthony and Hickson, Kevin (eds), *New Labour, Old Labour: The Wilson and Callaghan Governments, 1974–1979* (Routledge, 2004)

Seyd, Patrick, *The Rise and Fall of the Labour Left* (Macmillan, 1987)

Shaw, Eric, *Discipline and Discord in the Labour Party: The Politics of Managerial Control in the Labour Party 1951–1987* (Manchester University Press, 1988)

Short, Edward, *Whip to Wilson* (Macdonald, 1989)

Simon, Brian, *Education and the Social Order 1940–1990* (Lawrence and Wishart, 1999)

Sked, Alan and Cook, Chris, *Post-War Britain: A Political History 1945–1992* (Penguin, 1993)

Sopel, Jon, *Tony Blair: The Moderniser* (Michael Joseph, 1995)

Steel, David, *Against Goliath: David Steel's Story* (Weidenfeld & Nicolson, 1989)

Stephenson, Hugh, *Claret and Chips: The Rise of the SDP* (Michael Joseph, 1982)

Stephen, Andrew, *The Kicking, Squealing Birth-pangs of the SDP* (*Sunday Times Magazine*, 27 September 1981)

Stevens, Robert, *University to Uni: The Politics of Higher Education in England since 1944* (Politico's, 2004)

Stewart, W. A. C., *Higher Education in Post-war Britain* (Macmillan, 1989)

Stuart, Mark, *John Smith: A Life* (Politico's, 2005)

Sykes, Patricia Lee, *Losing from the Inside: The Cost of the Conflict in the British Social Democratic Party* (Transaction Books, 1988)

Taylor, Robert, *The Trade Union Question and British Politics: Government and Unions Since 1945* (Blackwell, 1993)

Thorpe, Andrew, *A History of the British Labour Party* (Macmillan, 1997)

Timmins, Nicholas, *Never Again? The Story of the Health and Social Care Act 2012* (The Institute for Government and the King's Fund, 2012)

Tracy, Noel, *The Origins of the Social Democratic Party* (Croom Helm, 1983)

Vallance, Elizabeth, *Women in the House* (The Athlone Press, 1979)

Walter, David, *The Strange Rebirth of Liberal England* (Politico's, 2003)

— —, *The Oxford Union: Playground of Power* (Macdonald, 1984)

Whitehead, Phillip, *The Writing on the Wall: Britain in the Seventies* (Michael Joseph, 1985)

Wickham-Jones, Mark, *Economic Strategy and the Labour Party: Politics and Policy-Making 1970–83* (Macmillan, 1996)

Williams, Shirley, *Politics is for People* (Penguin, 1981)

— —, *God and Caesar: Personal Reflections on Politics and Religion* (Continuum, 2003)

— —, *Climbing the Bookshelves: The Autobiography* (Virago, 2009)

Young, Hugo, *One of Us: A Biography of Margaret Thatcher* (Macmillan, 1989)

— —, (ed. Ion Trewin), *The Hugo Young Papers: Thirty Years of British Politics* (Allen Lane, 2008)

— —, *This Blessed Plot: Britain and Europe from Churchill to Blair* (Macmillan, 1998)

Ziegler, Wilson: *The Authorised Life* (Weidenfeld & Nicolson, 1993)

## Manuscript Sources

National Archives, Kew

CAB 129 (Cabinet papers)

CAB 134 (Cabinet committees)

PREM 13 (Prime Minister's Office 1966–70)

PREM 16 (Prime Minister's Office 1974–79)

## Private Papers

Paul Berry (Somerville College, Oxford)
Vera Brittain (McMaster University, Hamilton, Ontario)
Lord Callaghan (Bodleian Library, Oxford)
George Catlin (McMaster University, Hamilton, Ontario)
Anthony Crosland (British Library of Political and Economic Science, London)
Victor Gollancz (Modern Records Centre, Warwick)
Winifred Holtby (Hull Central Library)
Peter Metcalfe (private possession)
Lord Owen (Special Collections and Archives, University of Liverpool)
Lord Rodgers (Special Collections, Albert Sloman Library, University of Essex)
Shirley Williams (private possession)
Lord Wilson (Bodleian Library, Oxford)

## Papers of Other Institutions

Fabian Society, British Library of Political and Economic Science, and Nuffield College, Oxford
Hansard: House of Commons and House of Lords debates
Labour Party Annual Conference Reports, NEC minutes and shadow Cabinet minutes, all housed at the Labour Museum of History, Manchester

## Newspapers

*Boston Sunday Globe*
*Cambridge Evening News*
*Chicago Daily News*
*Crosby Herald*
*Daily Express*
*Daily Herald*
*Daily Mail*
*Daily Mirror*
*Daily Sketch*

*Daily Telegraph*
*Daily Worker*
*East Essex Gazette*
*Essex Chronicle*
*Essex County Standard*
*Financial Times*
*Glasgow Herald*
*Guardian*
*Harwich and Dovercourt Standard*
*Hertfordshire Express*
*Hertfordshire Mercury*
*Hitchin Pictorial*
*Independent*
*Independent on Sunday*
*Ipswich Evening Star*
*Letchworth Citizen*
*Liverpool Daily Post*
*Liverpool Echo*
*Luton Evening Post*
*Manchester Guardian*
*Morning Star*
*News Chronicle*
*Observer*
*Oxford Mail*
*Shropshire Star*
*Southern Evening Echo*
*Stevenage Gazette*
*Sun*
*Sunday Express*
*Sunday Telegraph*
*Sunday Times*
*The Times*
*Westminster and Pimlico News*
*Yorkshire Post*

## Periodicals

*Briefings*
*Clarion*
*Economist*
*Encounter*
*Fabian*
*Isis*
*Labour Weekly*
*Liberal Democrat News*
*Liberator*
*New Statesman*
*Paulina*
*Political Quarterly*
*Proceedings*
*Project Liberty Newsletter*
*Prospect*
*Social Democrat*
*Socialist Commentary*
*Spectator*
*Tablet*
*Teacher*
*Times Educational Supplement*
*Tribune*

# INDEX

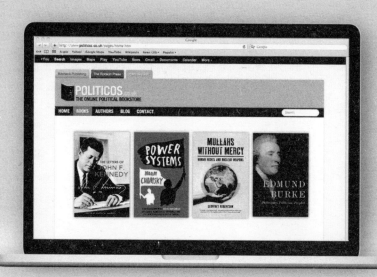